Parmelee & Co. Philad.a

CAPITOL AT WASHINGTON.

Engraved expressly for this work

OUR RULERS AND OUR RIGHTS:

OR,

OUTLINES

OF THE

UNITED STATES GOVERNMENT,

ITS

ORIGIN, BRANCHES, DEPARTMENTS, INSTITUTIONS, OFFICERS, AND MODES OF OPERATION.

BY

ANSON WILLIS.

ILLUSTRATED.

PHILADELPHIA:
PARMELEE & Co., 738 SANSOM STREET.
1869.

Electrotyped and Printed by
HADDOCK & SON, PRS. 108 SO. THIRD.

INTRODUCTION.

THERE is no sentiment that ever gained more universal acceptance among the people of this country, than that contained in the following words: "If our form of government can be preserved, it must be done by the intelligence and virtue of the people."

Few, if any, have ever gainsaid this proposition, or doubted its truth, yet many have doubted the permanence of our institutions: and these doubts arise from their lack of confidence in the intelligence and rectitude of a majority of the people.

These fears are not entirely groundless, in view of the common rule of judging the future by the past; for every observer of the political actions of our people, knows that many things have been done by parties and individuals, that demonstrate the lamentable destitution of one, if not both these elements of safety. Some have intelligence, but very little virtue—others have virtue, but very little intelligence: and some have neither. Now when either of these classes, or all of them combined, bear rule, mischief must follow, and a complete overthrow may be the result.

A general knowledge of the principles and operations of our government, is a part—but by no means all—of that intelligence which is so universally admitted to be necessary to the preservation of it.

But it is no easy task for a young man to gain such an understanding of these things as will qualify him to act his part well, when he arrives at the age which allows him to enter upon his duties as a citizen of the republic, to hold—it may be—official positions in it, or at least to vote understandingly for those who shall administer its affairs.

And it is matter of some surprise that no one has taken it in hand, long before this, to write something of the nature of a text book, in which these things may be found arranged and explained, in so simple and plain a form, as to give the reader a general and comprehensive idea of the structure, institutions and plan of operating the government under which he lives. In no country is such knowledge of so great importance as in ours, where every citizen may make his influence felt in the administration of public affairs, and where that influence always tells for good or evil. Our education is very deficient if it does not embrace a knowledge of the scheme of government; and it seems to us that it is as proper a subject for the instruction of the school-room as many others which are taught there. But if this is neglected, certainly the young man ought not to be left to pick up this knowledge, here a little and there a little, in detached portions, as he may chance to find it scattered through books, newspapers, public speeches and casual conversations; yet these are the only sources from which nine-tenths of the people have gained all they know of the political affairs of their own country; and what is thus gained is rarely acquired till middle life, and in a majority of cases not until a later period.

By these reasons we have been prompted to write the book before you, in order to place these matters, in compact and méthodical form, within the reach of every one who desires to understand them. We have aimed throughout at plainness and perspicuity; not avoiding repetition whenever the subject treated of could be made plainer by its use. Statements will be found in one connection, and again in another, whenever the fact stated appeared to be especially applicable to the subject under consideration.

We think that an attentive perusal of these chapters will give the reader a correct idea of the organization and mode of operating the United States Government, together with an insight into the machinery by which it is done. When this is acquired, it becomes an easy task to understand the government of the thirty-seven

States which compose one great Confederated Union, and to comprehend the fact that every person in the United States lives under two separate and distinct governments, and is amenable to two different codes of laws; first, that of the State in which he resides, and second, that of the United States, commonly termed the General Government. Much in both is analagous, especially the legislative and judicial proceedings. The wisdom of the framers of our Constitution adjusted these IMPERII IN IMPERIO—governments within a government, so that all work harmoniously, and with very little friction, or conflict of authority.

We have not treated of the State governments, nor could we have done so without going far beyond the limits assigned to this work. Each State is noticed, however, in some remarks, as to the time of its entrance into the Union, its size, population, circuits and districts, as prescribed by the laws of Congress. But this is to show their relations to the entire Union, and the relative influence and power they have as various parts of one great whole.

CONTENTS.

CHAPTER I.

The United States.

On the fourth day of July, 1776, a number of delegates from thirteen British Colonies in North America, assembled together in Philadelphia, and after some deliberation upon the oppression and wrongs which the mother country had for many years inflicted, drew up and signed a paper, in which they enumerated the various acts of the King of England, George the Third, by which he and his ministers had deprived the people of these Colonies of their just rights, and oppressed them by acts of tryanny and injustice. They declared that these acts had been continued for several years, that they had become intolerable, and that the King and his ministers would neither hear their just complaints, listen to their remonstrances, nor regard their petitions for redress; and that all their acts combined constituted a just cause for the Colonies to rebel against the authority of England, and to maintain their rights by force of arms, as they found it impossible to obtain them in any other way. They also declared that a Sovereign who would so rule and govern his subjects was utterly unworthy to rule over them, and that they had the right to throw off his authority and to establish a government for themselves. These declarations they printed, and sent forth to the world on the day before named, in justification of the accompanying DECLARA-

TION OF INDEPENDENCE; after this they positively refused any further obedience to him or to the laws of England. The 4th of July, 1776, has for this reason been styled the birth-day of our nation, and has since been celebrated as such on every annual return of it. For seven years after this event, the people underwent a hard and bloody struggle to maintain the position they had taken; nor was it until the year 1783, that our independence was acknowledged by England, or that we were recognized by other governments as one among the family of nations. Not until 1789, did the people of these Colonies, [now States,] organize a government, and take rank among the other governments of the world, with all the attributes, powers and rights of a distinct political power.

Here are three events:—First, the Declaration of Independence;—Second, the close of the Revolutionary war; and Third, the Inauguration of the United States government.

It is now but ninety years since the first, eighty-three since the second, and seventy-seven since the third. The longest period is less than a century, and is but as an hour in the world's history.

And now, without tracing the successive steps by which this nation has advanced from thirteen feeble Colonies to thirty-seven States, [some of which have more wealth, population, and power, than the whole thirteen had in 1776,] and from less than four, to thirty-five millions of people, with equally rapid strides in the arts, sciences, education, inventions and general progress, no thoughtful mind can refrain from looking into the causes of such unprecedented advancement. A few feeble Colonial subjects, in less than a century, becoming one of the great powers of the world, with the prospect of attaining the highest place among the nations, in much less time than it has taken them to gain their present position.

That we have a very extensive territory is true; that we have a diversified climate, a productive soil, with many long and navigable rivers on which to float our productions to market, and that we have inexhaustible mines of coal and minerals of almost every kind, including gold and silver, is true. But we might have all these, and still remain an insignificant people among the families of the earth, for all these have been possessed by nations who have retrograded instead of advanced.

In our case, a wise, just and liberal government has been the principal cause of our progress, and our present and prospective greatness.

No human government is perfect, neither can exact and equal justice be done in every case by human laws. But the scope and design of our legislation and jurisprudence is to dispense justice to all, to place all on an equality before the laws, and to give the same rights to the rich and to the poor. No privileged class is known to our laws, and the lowest may aspire to the highest places of distinction and honor; many have done so, and have reached the most exalted positions. The fullest religious liberty is granted to all; every man may worship as he pleases, when and where he pleases, without molestation or fear. He is not as in many other countries taxed to support a church established by law. He may pay for religious purposes as much or as little as he pleases, and to any church he prefers, or he may pay nothing, and no one can call him to account or use any compulsion whatever in this matter.

Every citizen has a vote for the choice of his rulers, and through his representatives a voice in making the laws by which he is governed.

As to his business or calling, he may do that which best suits his interests or his tastes. He may go when or where he desires, he may stay in the country or leave it without restraint or hindrance; in short, he may do whatsoever seemeth good to him, provided he does not infringe on the rights of others.

To this liberty, to these equal rights, privileges and advantages do we attribute our rapid growth and power. The advantages and benefits of so wise, so liberal and so beneficient a government are not unknown to the people of other countries where they do not enjoy so much freedom; and this accounts for the wonderful immigration to the United States from nearly every country in Europe. This flow has continued for more than three quarters of a century, and is still unabated. It has added many millions to the natural increase of our population, while very few of our own people ever leave their own country with the hope of bettering their condition, or of finding a government under which they can enjoy more liberty or better protection. To gain a clearer conception of the intimate connection between a good government and the prosperity of the country, let us, for example, place Mexico in contrast with the United States. Mexico was settled long before the United States, and in climate and mineral wealth has the advantage of us; yet the ever unsettled condition of its government, together with intolerance of any but the Catholic religion, has prevented any increase of population or any advancement in any thing which gives a nation respectability, greatness or power.

Let us draw another contrast by considering Ireland. An oppressive government has diminished the population, prevented any advancement, and impoverished the country. We might draw many such contrasts between the United States and other countries in Europe, Asia, Africa and South America, which would convince any one who has the power to trace causes to effects, and effects to causes, that a just and liberal government is an essential condition upon which the prosperity of any country depends.

But after all the good we find inhering in our Republican institutions, we have to admit that some things are wrong; that like all other human institutions, errors and imperfections are found in them. Yet what friend to humanity would raise an impious hand to overthrow that in which so much good is found? Let him rather labor to preserve the good, and to correct the remaining evil. Neither our Constitution nor our laws are like the laws of the Medes and Persians, which change not; but may be altered whenever a majority of the people desire it.

And if our people grow in intelligence, wisdom and patriotism, is it not to be hoped that they will preserve what is good, correct what is wrong, and thus perfect and perpetuate our government until it shall become a model worthy of imitation by the people and nations of the whole earth?

in the village, but in battle it is still. None of my young men strike the tomahawk deeper into the war-post—none of them so lightly on the Yengeese. The enemy know the shape of your back, but they have never seen the colour of your eyes. Three times have they called on you to come, and as often did you forget to answer. Your name will never be mentioned, again, in your tribe—it is already forgotten."

As the chief slowly uttered these words, pausing impressively between each sentence, the culprit raised his face, in deference to the other's rank and years. Shame, horror, and pride, struggled fearfully in its speaking lineaments. His eye, which was contracted with inward anguish, gleamed around on the persons of those whose breath was his fame, and the latter emotion, for an instant predominated. He arose to his feet, and baring his bosom, looked steadily on the keen, glittering knife, that was already upheld by his inexorable judge. As the weapon passed slowly into his heart, he even smiled, as if in joy, at having found death less dreadful than he had anticipated, and fell heavily on his face, at the feet of the rigid and unyielding form of Uncas.

The squaw gave a loud and plaintive yell, dashed the torch to the earth, and buried every thing in darkness. The whole shuddering groupe of spectators glided from the lodge, like troubled sprites; and Duncan thought that he and the yet throbbing body of the victim of an Indian judgment, had now become its only tenants.

CHAPTER XXIV.

"Thus spoke the sage: the kings without delay
Dissolve the council, and their chief obey."——*Pope's Iliad.*

A SINGLE moment, however, served to convince the youth that he was mistaken. A hand was laid, with a powerful pressure, on his arm, and then the low voice of Uncas muttered in his ears—

"The Hurons are dogs! The sight of a coward's blood can never make a warrior tremble. The 'gray head' and the Sagamore are safe, and the rifle of Hawk-eye is not asleep. Go—Uncas and the 'open hand' are now strangers. It is enough."

Heyward would gladly have heard more, but a timely effort from his friend, urged him toward the door, and admonished him of the danger that might attend the discovery of their intercourse. Slowly and reluctantly yielding to the necessity, he quitted the place, and mingled with the throng that hovered nigh. The dying fires in the clearing, cast a dim and uncertain light on the dusky figures, that were silently stalking to and fro; and, occasionally, a brighter gleam than common glanced into the darkness of the lodge, and exhibited the figure of Uncas, still maintaining its upright attitude above the dead body of the Huron.

A knot of warriors soon entered the place again, and re-issuing, they bore the senseless remains into the adjacent woods. After this solemn termination of the scene, Duncan wandered among the lodges, unquestioned and unnoticed, endeavouring to find some trace of her, in whose behalf he incurred the risk he ran. In the present temper of the tribe, it would have been easy to have fled and rejoined his companions, had such a wish

CHAPTER II.

The Constitution.

After the Seven Years' war, spoken of in the foregoing chapter, (generally known by the name of the Revolutionary war,) was over and peace restored, the people found themselves without any government, or if the Confederation under which the Colonies had managed to act together during the war, might be called a government, it was certainly inadequate to the wants of a people who had just become independent; and who needed a stronger bond of union than that which had held them together during the struggle for liberty, when a common danger and a common enemy served as a bond during their perilous condition. To supply this want a convention from all the States was called together to draw up a Constitution, which should form such a union, and at the same time be a basis which would support a well organized government. This convention met and performed the task assigned. It framed the Constitution of the United States, about which we subjoin the following remarks.

1. The Constitution of the United States was finished and signed on the 17th day of September, 1787. It was framed by a convention of the greatest and wisest men in the nation at that time, or perhaps at any time. They were chosen for that express purpose, and represented each of the thirteen States excepting Rhode

Island, which had no representation in the convention, and sat several months deliberating on the great work before them. George Washington was the president of the convention; and in the Constitution a clause was inserted declaring that the ratification of it by nine States should be sufficient to establish its authority over all, for although made by the men chosen for that purpose, it was not considered binding upon the people, until it had been sanctioned by three-fourths of the States. This was subsequently done, and the work of the convention became the charter of our liberties, and the great foundation stone of one of the most magnificent structures ever erected by the genius and wisdom of man.

2. The ratification of the Constitution by the several States necessarily required time. Hence the government established by its provisions did not go into operation till March, 1789. In the mean time General Washington had been chosen the first President of the United States, and a Congress had been elected in conformity with the provisions of the new and as yet untried Constitution. The President was inaugurated, the first Congress assembled in the city of New York, and the government of the United States was put into operation.

3. But before the first session of Congress closed, it was thought by a majority of the body that the Constitution in the shape in which the convention had left it, was defective, and that there should be several additions or amendments made to it. In conformity with this opinion ten amendments were proposed and passed

in the manner provided in the instrument itself; to wit, by a vote of two-thirds of both houses. These ten amendments were subsequently ratified by the requisite number of States (three-fourths,) and became a part of the Constitution. In the same manner the eleventh amendment was proposed, passed and adopted in 1794, and the 12th in 1803. From this last date the Constitution remained unchanged until January 31, 1865, when the House passed a resolution in favor of another amendment; the Senate passed the same resolution during the previous session.

4. In order to show more fully how the Constitution is amended, and what proceedings are taken in order to do it, we here insert the resolution, and the subsequent doings of all the parties who must act upon it to consummate the proposed amendments. This example will show how all the amendments have been made, and how others may hereafter be made.

THE RESOLUTION.

5. Resolved by the Senate and House of Representatives of the United States of America in Congress assembled, two-thirds of both Houses concurring, that the following articles be proposed to the Legislatures of the several States as an amendment to the Constitution of the United States, which, when ratified by three-fourths of said Legislatures, shall be valid to all intents and purposes as a part of said Constitution, viz.:

Article 13. First, neither slavery nor involuntary servitude, except as a punishment for crime whereof the party shall have been duly convicted, shall exist within the United States, or any place subject to their jurisdiction.

Second. Congress shall have power to enforce this article by appropriate legislation.

This, as numbered, made the thirteenth article of the amendments, twelve having been made as before stated. [See the Constitution and amendments as inserted in the latter part of the book.]

6. After this resolution had passed both Houses of Congress, and after the proposed amendment had been ratified by the requisite number of States, the Secretary of State, as the laws direct him to do, caused the resolution and the amendments to be published in all the States and Territories, and declared it to be valid as a part of the Constitution of the United States.

This thirteenth article of the amendments to the Constitution as it now stands, is one which has probably received more public attention, and caused more discussion than any other article in the whole document: because by it slavery in all the dominions of the United States has been constitutionally abolished.

7. We will make one other remark in relation to this thirteenth article, to wit: it grew out of the result of the war between the North and South. President Lincoln had, on Jan. 1, 1863, by virtue of his authority as Commander in Chief of the Army and Navy of the United States, issued his proclamation, declaring slavery to be abolished in all the States which had seceded from the Union, but this did not touch slavery in the slave States which had not seceded, viz.: Kentucky, Maryland, Missouri, Delaware, and West Virginia. Moreover there were doubts as to the constitutionality of Mr. Lincoln's act in this respect. But this amendment superseded that question, and made a clean sweep of the whole matter, both in the seceded and in the loyal States.

8. The framers of the Constitution undoubtedly borrowed many ideas incorporated therein from the laws of England, under which they had formerly lived; they constituted Congress with two Houses, the same as the English Parliament, the House of Lords answering to our Senate, and the House of Commons to our House of Representatives. Many other analogies between the two governments can be traced.

9. But while this is true, they as studiously avoided every thing in the English laws which they deemed inconsistent with the principles of a free Republican government.

In article 3, section 3, we find the following:—

"No attainder of treason shall work corruption of blood or forfeiture, except during the life of the person attainted."

This is precisely the opposite of the English law in relation to treason; for when a man is there guilty of treason, his children cannot inherit the father's titles or property. The parent being corrupted by treason, his children are considered corrupted also; this is what is meant by "corruption of blood" in the language of the Constitution. It then declared that no such thing should be allowed in the United States: in other words, it follows the law of God, which expressly declares, "The son shall not bear the iniquity of the father, neither shall the father bear the iniquity of the son." Which do you like best, the English or the American law?

The Constitution of the United States has served in some respects as a model for the State Constitutions;

and no State would be admitted into the Union, whose Constitution contained any thing contrary to that of the United States.. It extends its authority over every State and Territory, restraining them from making a Constitution or enacting any laws inconsistent with any of its provisions. It is the supreme law of the land. It binds the Executive, the Legislative and the Judicial branches of the government as much as the humblest individual. It should be carefully read and understood by every one who lives under it, especially by every one who exercises the elective franchise. It teaches us our rights, our exalted privileges and our duties as citizens of the Republic.

10. Throughout our work we have so often alluded to it and its provisions, that we have thought it advisable to append the whole document to this work that the reader may at any time turn to its pages, and consult its provisions on any point upon which he may desire information.

Read, learn and digest its meaning—keeping in mind that it is the supreme law of the land. Its provisions are binding upon every officer and every citizen ; upon Congress, upon every State Legislature, and upon every court, from the Supreme Court of the United States down to the lowest State tribunal. All are bound to act, legislate, and adjudicate in conformity with the principles of the Constitution.

CHAPTER III.

Congress.

1. THE Legislative branch of our government is styled Congress; in that of England it is denominated Parliament; and in that of France, the Corps Legislatif. Our Constitution places the power of enacting laws in Congress; no other branch of the government can do it. It is emphatically a representative body. Its members represent the people, and are supposed to do just what the entire mass of the people would do if it were practicable for them to assemble in one great body, and there to discuss, and then pass the laws by which they are willing to be governed.

2. It consists of two parts, or Houses, as these parts are called; the Senate and House of Representatives.* Both assemble at the same time, in Washington, on the first Monday of December in each year, for the transaction of business. The meeting at this time is called the regular session—regular, to distinguish it from extra sessions, which the President may call if he deems it necessary. This division of the National Legislature into two branches, was undoubtedly borrowed from the English government; for the law-

* The Legislatures of all the States and Territories are formed after the model of Congress; that is, all have a Senate and a lower House, called in some States by one name, and in others by another, but all meaning the lower branch of the legislative body.

making power in England is divided into two branches; the House of Lords, answering to our Senate, and the House of Commons, quite analagous to our House of Representatives. Indeed it was quite natural for the framers of our government to imitate that of England.

Anterior to the Revolution which separated us from England, our fathers had lived under its institutions and laws, many of which were good, and were subsequently incorporated with the new fabric. Whatever was incompatible with a Republican form of government, and that equality of rights which they determined to bestow upon every citizen, was rejected.

THE SENATE.

3. This branch of the National Legislature is constituted very differently from the House of Representatives. It is composed of two members from each State, without regard to the size or population thereof. New York, now the most populous State in the Union, has but two Senators in Congress, while the least populous State has the same number. They are not elected like the members of the lower House, by the people, but by the Legislatures of the respective States which they represent. They are also elected for a longer term than the members of the House of Representatives; a Senator is chosen for six years, while a Representative in the other House is elected for only two.

4. The word Senate is derived from the Latin word *senatus*, which signifies old; and older men are generally selected for the Senate than for the House of Representatives. Indeed the Constitution declares that a Senator shall be thirty years of age at the time of his

election, and that he must have been a citizen of the United States for nine years; whereas a member of the House is eligible at the age of twenty-five, if he has been a citizen seven years.

5. The Senate, like the House of Lords in England, is often styled the upper House; while the House of Representatives, for the sake of brevity, is generally styled "the House." The Senate is considered the higher and more dignified of the two, because men of age, talent, wisdom and experience are generally selected for this exalted position. Again, the Senate has powers which the House does not possess. When acting in their legislative capacity, both have equal powers, but the Senate, in connection with the President, has the power to ratify treaties. It alone confirms or rejects the President's nominations to offices, and also acts as a high court to try cases of impeachment. These important duties and prerogatives belong exclusively to the Senate without the concurrence of the House. All bills, (the draft of all laws when presented to a legislative body for its approval or disapproval, are called bills, excepting those for raising revenue,) may originate either in the Senate or the House; yet much the larger number of bills do originate in the House, because it has about three times the number of members which the Senate has, and because the members of the House are more immediate representatives of the people than the Senators. A greater number of the people know them, and usually send their petitions and make their wants known to them—and from these wants of the people, laws originate.

6. When the Senate convenes for the purpose of considering the nominations made by the President for the various offices to which he has the right of appointment by and with their consent, it is called an executive session. A vote of approval by a majority, gives the consent of this body; not so, however, when they vote upon the ratification of a treaty; for in this case the Constitution requires an affirmative vote of two-thirds of all present. A two-thirds vote is also necessary to give a judgment in case of the impeachment of any officer of the government who may be arraigned before them for trial.

The Vice President is the President of the Senate; but in case of a vacancy in this office, it then chooses a President from its own members. We next come to the

HOUSE OF REPRESENTATIVES.

7. This is often styled "the lower House." It has equal power with the Senate in the enactment of all laws; for no bill can become a law unless it receives a majority of the votes of both Houses, and in one particular it has a power which the Senate does not possess: it has the sole power of impeachment. We have stated that the Senate has the power to *try* impeachments, but this it never does until the House has first impeached some officer of the government for an alleged crime, after which the Senate resolving itself into a court, tries the accused party, and determines his guilt or innocence. The part which the House takes in cases of impeachment is very analagous to the action of a grand jury, which does not try the accused party, but only says after examining the charges, upon what evidence

it has, that he or she ought to be tried in a court of law—so with the House. It declares that the accused party should have a trial before the Senate. This decision of the House is denominated an impeachment.

8. The members of the Senate, as above stated, are elected by the Legislatures of the respective States which they represent; but the members of the House are elected by the people, by popular vote, as it is commonly said—for any body in any State may vote for a member of the House of Representatives who has the right to vote at all. In the two chapters on Congressmen and Congressional Districts, more may be seen on the subject of electing members to the lower House. After a bill has passed one House, it must be sent to the other, where it is referred to a committee, reported, debated, and finally voted upon exactly as in the other House.

9. But bills for the purpose of raising revenue must originate in the House of Representatives, never in the Senate, although these bills, like all others, go to the Senate for its concurrence, where they may be amended by adding to or striking out such parts as are not approved. No money can be drawn out of the Treasury of the United States for any purpose whatever, unless authorized and appropriated by an act of Congress.

10. This is the order, and these the forms through which every bill must pass before it becomes a law, and they show the care taken to prevent bad laws from being enacted, and the wisdom of the framers of the Constitution, in dividing the legislative power of the government into two branches, to check any hasty and

inconsiderate legislation which might be pushed through one branch, by the cooler and more deliberate action of the other.

11. The House of Representatives has no President like the Senate. Its presiding officer is called "The Speaker." He is chosen by the votes of the members, at the beginning of each Congress, which lasts two years. Consequently he holds his office two years. The Clerk of the House is also elected by its members, as are all its minor officers.

12. Correctly speaking, both the members of the Senate and of the House, are members of Congress, but by custom, Representatives only are called Members of Congress, (abbreviated into M. C.,) and the members of the Senate, Senators.

As there are 37 States now, the Senate has 74 members, and by a law of 1863, the number of Representatives was fixed at 241; but if a new State comes into the Union after an apportionment, her member or members may be added to the 241, and so continue until the next apportionment.

COMPENSATION.

13. Senators and members of the House of Representatives receive the same compensation, the amount of which has been increased three times. It had always been eight dollars per day, down to 1856, when it was increased to three thousand dollars per session. Then in 1866 it was again raised to five thousand dollars per session; and as there are always two sessions to every Congress, each member receives ten thousand dollars during his full term.

14. Mileage is an additional compensation. Until 1865 this was forty cents per mile, reckoned from the residence of the member to Washington by the usual roads or routes between the two places. In 1865 the law was modified, and the sum fixed at twenty cents per mile. "The laborer is worthy of his hire," is a maxim from the highest authority, and is so manifestly just that nobody questions its truth. But giving Members of Congress twenty cents per mile for traveling expenses, when it does not cost them four, (in these days) is as manifestly unjust as the maxim is true. It is robbery by law; and how the majority of thirty-nine Congresses have consented to let this swindle go on, and still continue, is a matter of astonishment to every one who believes that "righteousness exalteth a nation, but sin is a reproach to any people."

The monstrous inequality this law makes in the compensation of members, adds to the wonder that it has existed so long. Those who live near Washington do not receive a hundred dollars for mileage, while those living at the greatest distance pocket twelve thousand dollars of the people's money for what costs them five hundred.

15. During the Revolutionary war, and up to the time that the Constitution went into operation, (April 30, 1789,) the thirteen colonies sent delegates, who met whenever the exigencies of the times required their action, and whenever their safety and convenience dictated. These delegates, without much power or authority, did such things as seemed necessary to be done to carry on the war and to keep things in order.

Their acts generally met with the approval of the people; for in times of such common danger, they were little inclined to question the authority of those who they believed were acting for the general good; and as to their constitutional powers to do any thing, we have only to say, there was no Constitution then but the wishes of the people.

This body of men, denominated the "CONTINENTAL CONGRESS," ceased to exist after the adoption of our present Constitution, which made provision for a constitutional Congress, whose election, power, authority and duties are all clearly defined in the instrument itself.

16. The first Congress after the adoption of the Constitution met in New York, where two sessions were held. It then removed to Philadelphia, where it remained till 1800, when in conformity with an act of Congress, it removed to Washington, where it has remained to this day.

As a Congress continues two years, if at any time we wish to know how many Congresses there have been, or will be up to the time required, reckon the number of years from 1789—the beginning of the first—to the year in question; then divide the sum of the years by two, and the quotient will give the exact number.

CHAPTER IV.

The President.

1. "THE Executive powers of the government shall be vested in a President of the United States of America." Thus reads the first line of the first section of the second article of the Constitution. This article is devoted exclusively to the highest officer in the government. The Executive and the President are in the Constitution synonymous terms. He is likewise denominated "the chief magistrate of the nation." He is himself one of the co-ordinate branches of the government. These are three in number; first, the Legislative [Congress]; second, the Executive [the President]; third, the Judiciary [the Judges of the United States Courts.] These constitute the whole civil power of the nation. Congress enacts the laws, and the President must see that they are faithfully executed; which he does through the various Executive departments, and the different courts. He and the Senate appoint the heads of these departments, and the judges of the courts, and they execute the laws. The heads of departments act under the general direction of the President.

2. The Presidents are elected for four years, and are eligible to re-election. Several times they have been re-elected, and have consequently held the office eight years. The term always commences on the fourth day of March, and terminates on the same day of the

Parmelee & C° Philad.   Engraved expressly for this work.

PRESIDENTS HOUSE.

month. The Presidential elections, the most important and exciting of all elections, occur every four years, and now take place in all the States on the same day, early in November. It is said the President is chosen by the people, and yet they do not directly vote for him at all.

The people elect Electors, and these elect the President and Vice-President. Turn to the third section of the second article of the Constitution, and then to the twelfth article of the amendments of it, where you will find the whole process properly described. He must be thirty-five years of age when elected. And in case of his death, removal, resignation, or any disability to discharge the duties of the Office, the Vice-President then becomes President.

He receives a salary of $25,000 a year for his services besides the use of the presidential mansion, (commonly called the White House,) and the furniture in it, and is debarred from the receipt of any other emolument.

4. Before entering upon the duties of his office, he must take the following oath or affirmation:

"I do solemnly swear (or affirm) that I will faithfully execute the office of President of the United States, and will, to the best of my ability, preserve, protect and defend the Constitution of the United States."

In adition to his civil power, he is Commander-in-Chief both of the Army and Navy, and may grant reprieves and pardons, except in case of impeachment.

He—by and with the advice and consent of two-thirds of the Senate—may make treaties with foreign powers. He has the power, and it is his duty to nominate, and by the advice and consent of the Senate, to appoint ambassadors and other public ministers, consuls, judges, and in short all other officers of the government, whose appointments are not otherwise provided for.

5. It is also made his duty from time to time, to lay before Congress information respecting the state of the country, and to recommend to their notice such measures as he may deem proper and beneficial to the interests of the nation. His principal and most important communication, however, is that made to Congress at the commencement of each session. This is called the "President's Message," and is always looked for with much interest, both at home and abroad; for it, more than any other public document, shows the condition of the government and the country, both in their domestic affairs and foreign relations. At other times the President sends messages to Congress upon some special matter, which he considers it important for that body to know, or which he is requested to lay before it for information.

He may call extra sessions of Congress on extraordinary occasions. And when it passes any bill which he does not approve, and he refuses to sign it, it cannot become a law unless it goes back to Congress, and is again passed by two-thirds of both Houses. This is called his "veto power."

6. He, with all civil officers of the United States, may be impeached, and removed from office, for treason, bribery, and other high crimes.

The foregoing powers and duties are confered upon the President by the Constitution ; but Congress has, at every session it has ever held, increased these powers and duties until he is overwhelmed with them; and we cannot but think that he now possesses more power than the framers of the Constitution ever designed to trust in any one man's hand.

The following are the names of all the Presidents, from Washington, the first, down to the present incumbent:

George Washington, Va., 30th April, 1789, to 4th March, 1797—8 years.

John Adams, Mass., 4th March, 1797, to 4th March, 1801—4 years.

Thomas Jefferson, Va., 4th March, 1801 to 4th March, 1809—8 years.

James Madison, Va., 4th March, 1809 to 4th March, 1817—8 years.

James Monroe, Va., 4th March, 1817, to 4th March, 1825—8 years.

John Quincy Adams, Mass, 4th March, 1825, to 4th March, 1829---4 years.

Andrew Jackson, Tenn., 4th March, 1829, to 4th March, 1837---8 years.

Martin Van Buren, N. Y., 4th March, 1837, to 4th March, 1841---4 years.

William H. Harrison, O., 4th March, 1841, to 4th April, 1841---1 month.

John Tyler, Va., 4th April, 1841, to 4th March, 1845, ---3 years and eleven months.

James K. Polk, Tenn., 4th March, 1845, to 4th March, 1849---4 years.

Zachary Taylor, La., 4th March, 1849, to 9th July, 1850---1 year, 4 months, and 5 days.

Millard Fillmore, N. Y., 9th July, 1850, to 4th March, 1853---2 years, 7 months, and 26 days.

Franklin Pierce, N. H., 4th March, 1853, to 4th March, 1857---4 years.

James Buchanan, Pa., 4th March, 1857, to 4th March, 1861---4 years.

Abraham Lincoln, Ill., 4th March, 1861, to April, 1865--4 years, 1 month, and 8 days.

Andrew Johnson, Tenn., April, 1865, to—

Of these, William H. Harrison died 4th April, 1841, just one month after his inauguration. On the death of Harrison, Tyler, the Vice-President, became acting President. Taylor died July 9, 1850, and Fillmore, Vice-President, became acting President. Lincoln was assassinated on the 12th April, 1865, one month and eight days after he was inaugurated upon his second term ; and Andrew Johnson, the Vice-President, became acting President; this being the third time that such an event has occurred since the government went into operation.

CHAPTER V.

The Vice President.

1. The high sounding title of this officer would lead one who is but little acquainted with our government to think that he stands next to the President himself in dignity and power; that on his shoulders rested a large amount of the duties and responsibilities of administration. Such, however, is not the case. He is, in fact, nearer a cipher than any of the high officers of State. He is merely the presiding officer of the Senate, with not even the power to vote, except in case of a tie vote in that body, when he may give the casting vote. It is only in case of the death, resignation, impeachment, or disability of the President to discharge his duties, that the Vice President becomes an officer of much power or dignity. He is something like an heir-apparent to a throne. The Constitution provides that he shall take the President's place in case any of the foregoing contingencies occur; and up to this date this has happened three times.

2. He is elected at the same time and in the same manner as the President, and for the same term, and must possess the same qualifications; that is, he must be a native citizen of the United States, and of the age of 35 years.

The following is a list of the names of all who have filled this office, from John Adams, the first, down to

Andrew Johnson, the last, with the dates of entrance upon their duties:

John Adams, Mass., 30th April, 1789, to 4th March, 1797—eight years.
Thomas Jefferson, Va., 4th March, 1797, to 4th March, 1801—four years.
Aaron Burr, N. Y., 4th March, 1801, to 4th March, 1805—four years.
George Clinton, N. Y., 4th March, 1805, to 20th April, 1812—seven years, one month, sixteen days.
Elbridge Gerry, Mass., 4th March, 1813, to 23d Nov., 1814—one year, seven months, nineteen days.
Daniel D. Tompkins, N. Y., 4th March, 1817, to 4th March, 1825—eight years.
John C. Calhoun, S. C., 4th March, 1825, to 4th March, 1833—eight years.
Martin Van Buren, N. Y., 4th March, 1833, to 4th March, 1837—four years.
Richard M. Johnson, Ky., 4th March, 1837, to 4th March, 1841—four years.
John Tyler, Va., 4th March, 1841, to 4th April, 1841—one month.
George M. Dallas, Pa., 4th March, 1845, to 4th March, 1849—four years.
Millard Fillmore, N. Y., 4th March, 1849, to 9th July, 1850—one year, four months.
William R. King, Ala.
John C. Breckinridge, Ky., 4th March, 1857, to 4th March, 1861—four years.
Hannibal Hamlin, Me., 4th March, 1861. to 4th March, 1865—four years.
Andrew Johnson, Tenn., 4th March, 1865, to 15th April, 1865—one month, eleven days.

Of these, Clinton died April 20, 1812; from which time till 4th March, 1813, the Vice-Presidency was vacant.

Gerry died Nov. 23, 1814; from which time till 4th March, 1817, the Vice Presidency was vacant.

Tyler became acting President upon the death of President Harrison; and until March 4th, 1845, the Vice Presidency was vacant.

Fillmore became acting President upon the death of President Taylor, 9th July, 1850; and until March 4th, 1853, the Vice Presidency was vacant.

King was elected with President Pierce, in 1852; but died 18th April, 1853. He never took his seat, and the Vice Presidency was vacant till 4th March, 1857.

Johnson became acting President upon the death of President Lincoln, 15th April, 1865; and the Vice Presidency again became vacant, and must remain so till 4th March, 1869.

CHAPTER VI.

State Department, and Secretary of State.

1. The Constitution makes no mention of this department of the government, or of any such officer as Secretary of State, or indeed, of any other of the Executive Departments, or of their official heads. They were all created by acts of Congress; and when it first met, the Constitution was the only guide it had for its action—but that clothed it with all the legislative power of the government. Consequently, at its very first session it passed such acts as were necessary to put the new government into operation. Several departments were created, and the officers for their management appointed. This was the first of all the Executive departments created by Congress. In the outset it was found necessary to correspond and negotiate with foreign governments, and to have some duly authorized official to conduct such correspondence. Hence, this department of the government was established, and at first denominated "the Department of Foreign Affairs;" and the principal officer at its head was denominated "the Secretary for the Department of Foreign Affairs." But before the close of this session of Congress, for some reason it was determined to change the denomination of it from that of "Department of Foreign Affairs," to that of "Department of State;" and that of the Secretary, to "Secretary of

State;" and by these names they have ever since been known.

2. The Secretary of State in our government, is the highest officer after the President. He is what in other governments is called the Prime Minister. In monarchical governments all the high officers of State are called Ministers; but in ours they are known by the modest name of Secretaries.

By a law passed in 1853, the office of Assistant Secretary of State was created. The incumbent acts under the direction of the Secretary. Previous to this act, the principal inferior officer in the State Department was the Chief Clerk, who is appointed by the Secretary.

3. The great seal of the United States is in the custody of the Secretary of State, and it is his duty to affix it to all civil commissions to officers of the United States who are appointed by the President and Senate, or by the President alone.

4. Under the direction and instruction of the President, the law makes it his duty to hold correspondence and give instructions to our Foreign Ministers and Consuls, and also to hold correspondence with public Ministers from foreign governments, and to do all other things relating to foreign matters which the President shall direct him to perforn.

5. It is also made his duty to keep in his office the original copies of all acts, resolutions and orders of Congress. He must also deliver to each Senator and Representative in Congress, and to the Governor of each State, a printed copy of the same; and during

the session of each Congress he must publish the acts and resolutions passed by it in one newspaper in the District of Columbia, and in not more than two in each State and Territory of the United States. He must *also* publish in like manner all amendments of the Constitution, and all public treaties made and ratified between the United States and any foreign State, Prince or Power, or with any of the Indian tribes.

6. And at the close of each session of Congress he must cause to be published 11,000 copies in book form of all the laws, &c., as before stated; and to distribute the same as directed by law to the President and Vice President, and to every ex-President; to all the members of the Senate and House of Representatives; to all the heads of the various departments and bureaus; to all the Judges of the United States Courts, their Clerks and Marshals; to all our Foreign Ministers, Consuls and Public Agents; in short, to all the important officers of the government at home and abroad; in order that all who are in government employ may know what the laws are, and what changes have been made in acts formerly existing. The remaining copies are distributed to the States and Territories according to the number of Representatives in Congress from each of them.

7. It is also made the duty of the Secretary of State to give passports to our own citizens who wish to travel in foreign countries; to cause passports to be issued by such Diplomatic or Consular officers of the United States as the President shall direct; to give such information to our people through the newspapers as he

may from time to time receive from our Diplomatic and Consular agents abroad, as he may deem important to the nation, respecting our commercial interests in foreign countries, and to prepare a form of passport for American ships and vessels of the United States.

8. In the execution of extradition treaties between us and foreign governments, it is lawful for the Secretary of State, under his hand and seal of office, to issue an order for the rendition of any person who has been found guilty of crime in a foreign country, to any properly authorized person; that such criminal may be taken out of the United States to the country where the crime was committed.

9. We have thus sketched the principal duties of this high officer of State, and can readily see that they are arduous. Those which relate to foreign affairs are exceedingly responsible; for peace or war may often depend on the skill and wisdom with which he manages our affairs with foreign governments.

In addition to the foregoing duties, he is a member of the Cabinet, and hence is one of the President's advisers and counselors; and in relation to foreign matters, he has more influence than any other member of that body. He is appointed by the President, by and with the advice and consent of the Senate. He is appointed for four years; that is, during a Presidential term; but may be removed by the President at any time. This, however, is rarely done. He receives a salary of $8,000 per annum.

10. As a matter of historical reference, we append the names of all the statesmen who have filled this

high office, commencing with the first, and placing them in the order of the dates of their appointments, together with the States from which they came:

SECRETARIES OF STATE.

Thomas Jefferson, Va., Sept. 26, 1789.
Edmund Randolph, Va., Jan. 2, 1794.
Timothy Pickering, Mass., Dec. 10, 1795.
John Marshall, Va., May 13, 1800.
James Madison, Va., March 5, 1801.
Robert Smith, Md., March 6, 1809.
James Monroe, Va., April 2, 1811.
John Quincy Adams, Mass., March 4, 1817.
Henry Clay, Ky., March 7, 1825.
Martin Van Buren, N. Y., March 6, 1829.
Edward P. Livingston, La., May 24, 1831.
Louis McLean, Del., May 29, 1833.
John Forsyth, Ga., June 27, 1834.
Daniel Webster, Mass., March 5, 1841.
H. S. Legaré, S. C., May 9, 1843.
A. P. Upsher, Va., June 24, 1843.
John Nelson, Md., Feb. 29, 1844.
John C. Calhoun, S. C., March 6, 1844.
James Buchanan, Pa., March 5, 1845.
John M. Clayton, Del., March 7, 1849.
Daniel Webster, Mass., July 20, 1850.
Edward Everett, Mass., Dec. 9, 1851.
William L. Marcy, N. Y., March 5, 1853.
Lewis Cass, Mich., March 6, 1857.
Jeremiah S. Black, Pa., Dec. 14, 1860.
William H. Seward, N. Y., March 5, 1861.

CHAPTER VII.

Secretary of the Treasury.

1. If any department of the government should ever be abolished, it certainly will not be this; for without it, or some institution very similar in its plan, the government itself would crumble into its original elements,—individual persons. Without money, no government could be sustained. The Treasury is the place into which the money flows, and from which it flows.

2. The United States Treasury is the receptacle of all the funds, (or an account of them,) collected from whatever source, for carrying on the various operations of the government. It was established by a law of Congress in 1789; and with such modifications of the law as experience has proved to be necessary, it remains to this day. We embrace in our account of the Treasury Department, its head, the Secretary of the Treasury, and his duties; for it would be difficult to describe one without the other. This office was created at the same time with the department itself. It is one of great responsibility, and the incumbent should be thoroughly skilled in the science and management of finances; for no man in the United States has such vast sums to provide for, receive, and disburse, as the Secretary of the Treasury. During the late civil war they amounted to hundreds of millions a year.

3. He is appointed like all other heads of depart-

ments, by the President and Senate; holds his office for four years, unless sooner removed; is a member of the Cabinet; and receives $8,000 a year as salary. Connected with him, as aids in the discharge of his duties, are an Assistant Secretary, a Comptroller, and Second Comptroller, five Auditors, Treasurer, and his assistant, a Register and his assistant, a Commissioner of Customs, a Comptroller of the Currency, and a deputy and a Solicitor of the Treasury; all these officials are appointed by the President and Senate.

4. These, with several hundred clerks, constitute the officials and machinery by which this great department of the Government is operated. It would be quite too tedious, and of doubtful utility, to describe the particular duties of each of these officials. Suffice it, therefore, to say, that each one has his specific duties to perform, without any interference with others; and perhaps the world could not show another establishment, where such a vast amount of business is transacted with more order, skill and accuracy than at this office.

5. Here the accounts of all receivers and disbursers of government money, are presented and settled; after having been examined and approved by several of the above named officials, who are charged with this duty.

6. The Commissioner of Customs attends to the accounts of Collectors of duties imposed on imported goods. The First Comptroller must collect debts due to the United States, and superintend the adjustment and preservation of the public accounts.

The First Auditor receives all accounts coming into

the department; the Second, Third, Fourth and Fifth Auditors each examine the accounts of such department as is assigned to them respectively.

It is not necessary to go further in detailing the particular duties of the officers of this department. We have only noticed a few of them, merely as examples of the system of conducting the business of this great branch of the Government.

7. Let it not be understood that all the monies collected and disbursed by the United States are received and paid out at the Treasury building at Washington, which is only the principal office at the seat of Government,—for in addition to this there are Sub-Treasuries in several of the large cities, where the public monies are received and disbursed. The head officers of these Sub-Treasuries, are termed Assistant Treasurers.

The law also makes the Treasurer of the Mint at Philadelphia, and the Treasurers of some of the branch mints, Assistant Treasurers, for they have public monies in their keeping, and if so ordered by the Treasury Department at Washington, they disburse it as directed. The same orders are sometimes given to collectors, post-masters, receiver of the land offices, &c., and they disburse as well as receive government funds; but the accounts of all these must be sent to, and settled in the office of the Secretary of the Treasury.

8. Any one would readily suppose that men intrusted with the receipt and disbursement of such large sums of the people's money, should give security for their fidelity to their trusts. This the law requires,

and this they must do before they enter upon their respective duties. But in spite of all precautions, dishonest men get into those places; and public defaulters are not rare specimens of humanity, among office holders.

9. The following are the names of all who have been Secretaries of the Treasury, from 1789 down to the present time, with the date of their appointment, and the States in which they lived:

SECRETARIES OF THE TREASURY.

Alexander Hamilton, N. Y., Sept. 12, 1789.
Oliver Wolcott, Ct., Feb. 4, 1795.
Samuel Dexter, Mass., Dec. 31, 1800.
Albert Gallatin, Pa., May 14, 1801.
George W. Campbell, Tenn., Feb. 9, 1814.
Alexander J. Dallas, Pa., Oct. 6, 1814.
William H. Crawford, Ga., Oct. 22, 1816.
Richard Rush, Pa., Mar. 7, 1825.
Samuel D. Ingham, Pa., Mar. 6, 1829.
Louis McLane, Del., Aug. 8, 1831.
William A. Duane, Pa., May 29, 1833.
Roger B. Taney, Md., Sept. 23, 1833.
Levi Woodbury, N. H., June 27, 1834.
Thomas Ewing, O., Mar. 5, 1841.
Walter Forward, Pa., Sept. 13, 1841.
John C. Spencer, N. Y., Mar. 3, 1843.
George M. Bibb, Ky., June 15, 1844.
Robert J. Walker, Miss., Mar. 5, 1845.
W. M. Meredith, Pa., Mar. 7, 1849.
Thomas Corwin, O., June 20, 1850.
James Guthrie, Ky., Mar. 5, 1853.
Howell Cobb, Ga., Mar. 6, 1857.
Philip F. Thomas, Md., Dec. 10, 1860.
John A. Dix, N. Y., 1861.
Salmon P. Chase, O., Mar. 5, 1861.
William P. Fessenden, Me., July, 1864.
Hugh Mc Culloch, Ind., the present incumbent.

CHAPTER VIII.

The War Department, and Secretary of War.

1. The name of this department sufficiently indicates the design and object of its creation, and the kind of public business committed to its care and management. The Secretary of War is the head of it, its principal officer. He is one of the great officers of State and a member of the Cabinet. He, like all the heads of departments, is appointed by the President and Senate. Four years is the time for which he is appointed, but, with the consent of the Senate, he may be sooner removed by the President, if he sees fit to do so. He receives $8,000 per annum as his salary. In military authority he ranks next to the President.

2. As stated in another place, the Constitution makes no specific provision for this or any other of the departments into which the government is divided. They are all the creations of Congress, and exist by enactments of law. The War Department, with several others, was created at the first session of the first Congress, which met after the Government went into operation under the Constitution, in 1789.

3. We can convey no better idea of the object of establishing this department and the officer at its head, than by quoting the first section of the act by which they were created: "There shall be an Executive Department, to be denominated the Department of War;

and there shall be a principal officer therein, to be called the Secretary for the Department of War, who shall perform and execute such duties as shall from time to time be enjoined on or entrusted to him by the President of the United States, agreeably to the Constitution, relative to military commissions or to the land forces, ships, or warlike stores of the United States; or to such other matters respecting military affairs as the President of the United States shall assign to the said department; and furthermore, the said principal officer shall conduct the business of the said department in such manner as the President of the United States shall from time to time order or instruct."

4. According to the act by which this department was established, a Chief Clerk, appointed by the Secretary, was the second officer in authority in it, and acted in his stead in case of vacancy in the Secretaryship. But in 1861 Congress passed an act authorizing the President to appoint an Assistant Secretary of War; and in 1862 another act was passed, authorizing the appointment of two additional Assistants. This, however, was intended as a temporary arrangement, to last only during the existence of the lamentable civil war which was at that time in progress, and which necessarily greatly increased the business of the department.

5. The Secretary of War has in his keeping all books, records, and papers, relating to military affairs. Here are to be found the names of all officers and men whether in the regular army or in the volunteer service. Connected with the War Department, are a number of sub-

departments, or bureaus, as these sub-departments are commonly called; among which are the Commissary, the Quatermaster's and Ordnance Departments. These are all under the general supervision and direction of the Secretary.

6. In time of peace the War Department attracts no particular public notice. But in time of war it draws around it more attention than any other branch of the government; for on its good or bad management the weal or woe of the nation depends.

Hence the Secretary of War should be a man well acquainted with military affairs, of sound judgment, and of undoubted integrity. In this department all accounts relating to military matters are kept and adjusted.

In addition to the Assistant Secretaries, the President and Senate were authorized, in 1863, to appoint a Solicitor in the War Department. These, with a large clerical force, transact the business of this important branch of the government.

The following is a list of the names of all who have filled the office of Secretary of War, from the first down to the present incumbent, with the dates of their appointment, and the States in which they lived:

SECRETARIES OF WAR.

Henry Knox, Mass., Sept.12, 1789.
Timothy Pickering, Pa., Jan. 2, 1795.
James McHenry, Md., Jan. 27, 1796.
James Marshall, Va., May 7, 1800.
Samuel Dexter, Mass., May 13, 1800.
Roger Griswold, Ct., Feb. 3, 1801.

Henry Dearborn, Mass., March 5, 1801.
William Eustis, Mass., March 7, 1809.
John Armstrong, N. Y., Jan. 13, 1813.
James Monroe, Va., Sept. 27, 1814.
Willlam H. Crawford, Ga., March 2, 1815.
Isaac Shelby, Ky., March 5, 1817.
G. Graham, Va., April 7, 1817.
John C. Calhoun, S. C., Oct. 8, 1817.
James Barbour, Va., March 7, 1825.
Peter B. Porter, N. Y., May 26, 1828.
J. H. Eaton, Tenn., March 9, 1829.
Lewis Cass, Mich., Aug. 1, 1831.
Benjamin F. Butler, N. Y., March 3, 1837.
Joel R. Poinsett, S. C., March 7, 1837.
John Bell, Tenn., March 5, 1841.
John McLean, O., Sept. 13, 1841.
John C. Spencer, N. Y., Oct. 12, 1841.
James W. Porter, Pa., March 8, 1843.
William Wilkins, Pa., Feb. 15, 1844.
William L. Marcy, N. Y., March 5, 1845.
George W. Crawford, Ga., March 6, 1849.
Charles M. Conrad, La., Aug. 8, 1850.
Jefferson Davis, Miss., March 5, 1853.
John B. Floyd, Va., March 6, 1857.
Joseph Holt, Ky., Dec. 30, 1860.
Simon Cameron, Pa., March 5, 1861.
Edwin M. Stanton, Pa., Jan. 13, 1861.
Ulysses S. Grant, Ill., 1868.
J. M. Schofield, 1868.

CHAPTER IX.

Navy Department, and Secretary of the Navy.

1. The Navy and the Army are the two strong arms of the nation. By these we preserve order at home and protect ourselves against wrongs abroad, or invasion of our rights by any foreign power, whether at home or elsewhere. They may be termed the belligerent parts of the government; and if we institute a comparison between them, it is not easy to determine which is the strongest arm, or which is the most efficient agent of national defence.

2. The Navy Department, like the War Department, was established at an early period after the adoption of the Constitution. The office of Secretary of the Navy was created at the same time that the department itself was. He is appointed by the President and Senate, is one of the highest officers of the Government, one of the seven members of the Cabinet, and receives a salary of $8,000 per annum.

As the President is Commander-in-Chief as well of the Navy as of the Army, the Secretary of course acts under his direction. It is made his duty to execute the President's orders relative to the procurement of naval stores and materials, and the construction, armament, equipment and employment of vessels of war, and all other matters connected with the naval establishment.

3. As in the War Department, a head clerk was formerly second in rank and authority in this; but in the year 1861, by an act of Congress, the office of Assistant Secretary of the Navy was created. Its incumbent fills the second place, and acts as Secretary in the absence of that officer.

Formerly there were five bureaus in this department, but in 1862, three more were added, making eight, as follows:

1. A Bureau of Yards and Docks.
2. A Bureau of Equipment and Recruiting.
3. A Bureau of Navigation.
4. A Bureau of Ordnance.
5. A Bureau of Construction and Repairs.
6. A Bureau of Steam Engineering.
7. A Bureau of Provisions and Clothing.
8. A Bureau of Medicine and Surgery.

The President and Senate appoint all the heads of these bureaus, and select them principally from officers of high rank in the navy. They are all appointed for four years, and each receives a salary of $3,500 per annum.

4. The Secretary appoints all the clerks in each of these bureaus, and distributes such duties to each as he thinks proper. They all act under his direction. He must annually report to Congress the state and condition of his department, and the expenditures of the same, specifying the amounts expended for the items of building, repairing, wages of mechanics, laborers, equipping vessels of the navy, &c., &c.

SECRETARIES OF THE NAVY.

The following list embraces the names of all the Secretaries of the Navy, from George Cabot, the first, to Gideon Welles, the present incumbent:

George Cabot, Mass., May 3, 1798.
Benjamin Stoddard, Mass., May 21, 1798.
Robert Smith, Md., July 15, 1801.
J. Crowningshield, Mass., May 3, 1805.
Paul Hamilton, S. C., March 7, 1809.
William Jones, Pa., Jan. 12, 1813.
B. W. Crowningshield, Mass., Dec. 17, 1814.
Smith Thompson, N. Y., Nov. 9, 1818.
John Rogers, Mass., Sept. 1, 1823.
S. L. Southard, N. J., Sept. 16, 1823.
John Branch, N. C., March 9, 1829.
Levi Woodbury, N. H., May 23, 1831.
Mahlon Dickerson, N. J., June 30, 1834.
J. R. Paulding, N. Y., June 20, 1830.
G. P. Badger, N. C., March 5, 1841.
Abel P. Upsher, Va., Sept. 13, 1841.
David Henshaw, Mass., July 24, 1843.
T. W. Gilmer, Va., Feb. 12, 1844.
John Y. Mason, Va., March 14, 1844.
George Bancroft, Mass., March 10, 1845.
John Y. Mason, Va., Sept. 9, 1846.
William B. Preston, Va., March 7, 1849.
Wiliam A. Graham, N. C., July 20, 1850.
J. P. Kennedy, Md., July 22, 1850.
J. C. Dobbin, N. C., March 5, 1853.
Isaac Toucey, Ct., March 6, 1857.
Gideon Welles, Ct., March 5, 1861.

CHAPTER X.

Interior Department, and Secretary of the Interior.

1. A LITTLE reflection will enable any one to understand that there must necessarily be a constantly increasing amount of business to be done by a government whose territory and population have increased as rapidly as they have done in the United States. In every department there has been an accumulation of work to be done and of duties to be performed.

2. In consequence of this state of things, Congress, in 1849, passed an act creating a new Executive department, called "the Department of the Interior," which act also provided for the appointment of a head to this new branch of government, called the Secretary of the Interior. He is appointed like all the other Secretaries, is one of the high officers of the government, is a member of the Cabinet, and in compensation and dignity ranks with the Secretaries or heads of the other departments.

3. In this act it was provided that the Secretary of the Interior should perform all the duties heretofore devolving on the Secretary of State in relation to the office of Commissioner of Patents; in other words, the Bureau of the Patent Office was transferred from the Department of State to that of the Interior.

In the same manner the General Land Office was transferred from the Treasury Department to this.

The supervisory power theretofore exercised by the Secretary of the Treasury over the accounts of the marshals, clerks, and other officers of all the courts of the United States, was thereby placed in the hands of the new Secretary. The office of the Commissioner of Indian Affairs, heretofore attached to the War Department, was also transferred to this; and the powers and duties of the Secretary of War, in relation to Indian affairs, were devolved on the Secretary of the Interior.

4. The Secretaries of War and of the Navy were by the same act relieved of their duties in regard to the Commissioner of Pensions, and those duties were thereafter to be performed by the Secretary of the new department.

The Census Bureau, heretofore attached to the State Department, and the duties of the Secretary of State in relation thereto, were also transferred to this department.

To the Secretary was also given the supervisory power over the lead and other mines belonging to the United States, heretofore executed by the Secretary of the Treasury.

The powers of the President over the Commissioners of Public Buildings were also transferred to him.

5. He was also charged with the control over the Board of Inspectors and Warden of the Penitentiary of the District of Columbia.

The Secretary of the Interior has the same power in appointing and removing clerks and other subordinates in his department, that the Secretaries of the other departments had over these several bureaus before they were transferred to this department.

This office has a seal, which must be affixed to the commissions of all its subordinate officers.

The President and Senate appoint the Assistant Secretaries.

From the foregoing it is easy to understand what branches of the public service are conducted in this office, and what are the duties of its Secretary.

SECRETARIES OF THE INTERIOR.

6. The following is a list of all who have filled the office of Secretary of the Interior since the establishment of the department:

Thomas H. Ewing, Ohio, March 7, 1849.
Alexander H. H. Stuart, Va., Sept. 12, 1850.
Robert McClelland, Mich., March 5, 1853.
Jacob Thompson, Miss., March 6, 1857.
Caleb B. Smith, Ind., March 5, 1861.
John P. Usher, Ind., Jan. 7, 1863.
James Harlan, Iowa, 1865.
Orville H. Browning, Ill., 1866.

CHAPTER XI.

Post-office Department, and Postmaster General.

1. THE Post-office Department is one of the most important in the government; and one with which the people have more intercourse, and with which they are better acquainted than any other. A post-office establishment is an institution by which the government undertakes to transmit letters and other mailable matter to the places where directed, for the people, instead of leaving them to do this business for themselves, in the best way they can. It is by no means peculiar to our government, but is found in every civilized country, and dates from ancient times.

2. To find the basis of our own establishment, we have to look at the Constitution. There, in Art. 1, Sec. 8, we shall find the words, "Congress shall have the power to establish post-offices, and post roads." These few words are the foundation of all our laws relating to post-offices, post-masters, post roads, transportation of the mail and everything else appertaining to the subject.

3. Post-offices existed in this country before our government did; for while we were in a colonial state under the English government, it had established them at all important points, and also a tolerable mail system for that day and age. These were continued dur-

ing the Revolution, which resulted in the separation of this country from England. After our present government became established, it enacted laws and made provisions for a Post-Office Department; and this, with such alterations and amendments as experience and the growth of the country required, has remained and is in operation at the present day.

4. By law a Postmaster General is placed at the head of this department, who is appointed for four years by the President and Senate; his office is in the General Post Office at Washington; his salary is $8,000 a year; he is a member of the Cabinet, and ranks as one of the high officers of State. He has three assistants, who are appointed in the same manner as himself. He has a seal of his office, an impression from which must be affixed to the commission of every postmaster in the United States; and also to all transcripts of papers and documents which may be wanted from his office. The seal establishes their authenticity, and makes them proof of the same degree as the original papers. He must give bonds for the faithful performance of his duties, and take the usual official oath before he can enter upon those duties.

HIS DUTIES.

5. The laws of the department make it his duty to appoint all other postmasters (who are styled in law, deputy postmasters, but in common language, simply postmasters), whose compensation is less than $1,000 per annum. All others are appointed by the President and Senate, or as he is himself. It is also his duty to

establish post-offices wherever he may deem it necessary; to provide for the transportation of the mail on all the post-roads in the United States, and to foreign countries by sea. He must give all deputies their instructions respecting their duties, and receive from them their accounts of the receipts and expenditures of their respective offices; pay all expenses for the transmission of the mails, and all others which relate to the management of his department; and once in three months render a quarterly account of all receipts and expenditures of the Post Office Department; and finally must superintend, control, and direct all deputy postmasters, agents, mail contractors, and employees in the mail service.

THE MINOR POST-OFFICES.

6. The centre of this great machine is at Washington, the capital of the nation; but its branches extend, like the veins and nerves of the human body, in every direction and to every part. Post-offices, for the accommodation of the people, are found in every city, village, town and neighborhood throughout the length and breadth of the land.

During the late civil war a great many of them were discontinued in the Southern States; some of which have been re-established since the close of the war. For this reason we are not able to state the exact number of post-offices in the United States at the present time; but from the number known before the war, we judge there are not far from thirty thousand. Each has its postmaster, and when necessary, its assistants and clerks. This affords some idea of the vastness of this great government institution for the diffusion of intelligence among the people. It not only reaches out its arms to the remotest boundaries of our own country, but, by the agency of ships, stretches over the seas, and extends to every part of the habitable earth.

POST-ROADS.

7. It is the business of Congress to say what roads shall be post-roads and post-routes, and whether the mails shall be carried by land or by water. In the exercise of this power it has declared that all railroads shall be post-roads. Post-routes are also established between this country and foreign countries, by ships. The Postmaster General is empowered to contract with the owners of ships going to foreign countries, to carry the mails to and from the places of their departure and destination. Thus the ocean is made into numerous mail routes.

RATES OF POSTAGE.

8. Cheap postage is of recent date. England first tried the experiment by making one penny the uniform rate of postage on single letters to all parts of that kingdom. This was very acceptable to the people, and worked so well that the United States followed her example. Here it has proved equally satisfactory to the people, and a perfect success.

In establishing the present rates of postage, two objects were aimed at; first, to diminish the cost of sending letters, and second, to make the rates uniform to all parts of the country, irrespective of distance. Formerly the rates were much higher, and were made to depend on two circumstances; *first*, the distance over which the letter was to be sent, and the rate varied from six to twenty-five cents; *second*, the number of pieces on which the letter was written, counting every piece of paper as a letter.

But by recent laws this has all been changed; any distance within the United States makes no difference in the rate or charge for carrying; and instead of counting the pieces of paper used, *weight* is made the basis of charge. Half an ounce is reckoned a single letter, and every half ounce more, or a fraction of it, is counted as another. Three cents is the rate of a single letter, and an addition of three cents more for every additional half ounce or fraction of it. The uniformity consists in disregarding distance in the computation of the rate charged for transportation. The charges for carrying newspapers and other printed matter, were also greatly reduced from former rates. Formerly, under the old system, postage might be pre-paid, or paid upon delivery of the letter, and the government lost the postage on all letters never called for. But under the present system, all mailable matter, except newspapers and regular periodical publications sent to subscribers, must be pre-paid by postage stamps.

FRANKING PRIVILEGE.

9. This means the right to send letters, documents, &c., through the post office free, or without paying postage therefor. This privilege was so abused that the law was changed, and restricted to a certain class of officers of the government when sending or receiving official communications which relate to the busi-

ness of their respective offices, and to the President, Vice President, Members of Congress, and chiefs of the several Executive departments. Petitions to Congress may also be franked.

DEAD LETTERS.

10. Dead letters are those which are never called for at the respective offices where sent. The law directs that they shall be advertised three weeks in some newspaper in or near the post office where the letter is; and if not called for in three months thereafter, they must be sent to the General Post Office at Washington, as *dead letters.* There they are opened, and if they contain money or valuable papers, they are returned to the writers, and the money and papers are kept at the General Post Office, where an account of them is kept, and will be returned to the owners whenever they call for them.

As in the other departments, we append at the end of this chapter, a list of all the heads of this department, from the first down to the present time.

Without wearying the reader with a detailed statement of the condition of the department for every year since its establishment, we give the number of offices, and the number of miles of post-roads as they were every tenth year. This will be found sufficient to show the wonderful increase of business in this branch of the public service since 1790, the first year after the government was put into operation.

In	1790 there were but	75 post offices, and	1,875 m. of post-roads.	
1800	"	903	"	20,817	"
1810	"	2,300	"	36,400	"
1820	"	4,500	"	72,492	"
1830	"	8,450	"	115,176	"
1840	"	13,463	"	155,739	"
1850	"	18,417	"	178,672	"
1860	"	28,498	"	240,594	"

POSTMASTERS GENERAL.

Samuel Osgood, Mass., Sept. 26, 1789.
Timothy Pickering, Mass., Aug. 12, 1791.
Joseph Habersham, Ga., Feb. 25, 1795.
Gideon Granger, Ct., Nov. 28, 1801.
Reuben J. Meigs, O., March 17, 1814.
John McLean, O., June 25, 1823.
William J. Barry, Ky., March 9, 1829.
Amos Kendall, Ky., March 1, 1835.
John M. Niles, Ct., May 18, 1840.
Francis Granger, N. Y., March 6, 1841.
Charles A. Wickliff, Ky., Sept. 13, 1841.
Cave Johnson, Tenn., March 5, 1845.
Jacob Collamer, Vt., March 7, 1849.
Nathan K. Hall, N. Y., July 20, 1850.
S. D. Hubbard, Ct., Aug. 31, 1852.
James Campbell, Pa., March 5, 1853.
Aaron V. Brown, Tenn., March 6, 1857.
Joseph Holt, Ky., March 14, 1859.
Horatio King, Jan. 1, 1861.
Montgomery Blair, Md., March 7, 1861.
William Dennison, O., Oct. 1, 1864.
Alexander W. Randall, Wis., July 15, 1866.

CHAPTER XII.

Attorney General.

The Attorney General of the United States is one of the high officers of the government, and is a very responsible one. The law by which the office of Attorney General was created we find in an act passed as far back as 1789, at the first session ever held by Congress; in which his duties are thus defined: "Whose duty it shall be to prosecute and conduct all suits in the Supreme Court, in which the United States shall be concerned; and to give his advice and opinion upon questions of law, when required by the President of the United States; or when requested by the heads of departments, touching any matters that may concern their departments.'

By an act passed in 1861, he is charged with the general superintendence of all the Attorneys and Marshals in all the Judicial Districts in the United States and Territories, as to the manner of discharging their duties.

He is appointed by the President and Senate, and holds his office at the pleasure of the President.

He is a member of the Cabinet, and now receives a salary of eight thousand dollars per year. He has an assistant, and clerks to aid him in the discharge of his duties.

His office is in Washington.

This, with the preceding six chapters, contains a brief account of what are properly called Executive Departments of the government; sub-departments are properly termed Bureaus, while the three great divisions into which the Constitution divides the governmental powers, viz.: the Legislative, Executive, and Judicial, should be denominated branches.

ATTORNEYS-GENERAL.

Edmund Randolph, Va., Sept. 26, 1789.
William Bradford, Pa., June 27, 1794.
Charles Lee, Va., Dec. 10, 1795.
T. Parsons, Mass., Feb. 20, 1800.
Levi Lincoln, Mass., March 5, 1801.
Robert Smith, Md., March 2, 1805.
John Breckenridge, Ky., Dec. 1806.
Cæsar A. Rodney, Del., Jan. 20, 1807.
William Pinckney, Md., Dec. 11, 1811.
Richard Rush, Pa., Feb. 10, 1814.
William Wirt, Md., Dec. 16, 1817.
John McPherson Berrian, Ga., Mar. 9, 1829.
Roger B. Taney, Md., July 20, 1831.
Benjamin F. Butler, N. Y., Nov. 15, 1833.
Felix Grundy, Tenn., July 7, 1838.
Henry D. Griffin, Pa., Jan. 11, 1840.
John J. Crittenden, Ky., Mar. 5, 1841.
Hugh S. Legare, S. C., Sept. 13, 1841.
John Nelson, Md., July 1, 1843.
John Y. Mason, Va., Mar 5, 1845.
Nathan Clifford, Me., Oct. 16, 1846.
Isaac Toucey, Ct., Jan. 21, 1848.
Reverdy Johnson, Md., Mar. 7, 1849.
John J. Crittenden, Ky., July 20, 1850.
Caleb Cushing, Mass., Mar. 5, 1853.
Jeremiah S. Black, Pa., Mar. 6, 1857.
Edwin M. Stanton, Pa., Dec. 14, 1860.
Edward Bates, Mo., Mar. 5, 1861.
James Speed, Ky., Dec., 1864.
Henry Stanberry, O., July, 1866.
William M. Evarts, N. Y., 1868.

CHAPTER XIII.

The Cabinet.

1. THE Cabinet is composed of the Secretaries of State, War, Navy, Treasury, and Interior, together with the Postmaster General and the Attorney General, seven in all. They are *ex-officio* members of the Cabinet, and the President's advisers. All of them are nominated to their respective offices, as Secretaries, &c., by him; but cannot act unless by the consent of the Senate. In this respect they are like all other officers appointed by the President and Senate, although in common parlance it is often said the President chooses his own Cabinet. This might seem to mean that he, and he alone chooses them, without advice or consultation with any body.

2. The Senate rarely, if ever, refuses consent to the nominations of the President for these appointments; for it is conceded that without some extraordinary objection, such as notorious bad character or unfitness for the position, the President should have the selection of his own advisers.

3. When they meet with the President to consult with him on the affairs and admnistration of the government, it is called "a Cabinet meeting." Our foreign affairs and relations with other governments form the subjects of much of their deliberations; in England, and in most of the countries in Europe, the men who

fill these positions in those governments, are called Ministers. In England they also hold seats in Parliament, and debate and vote like other members; but in the United States government the members of the Cabinet neither have seats in Congress, nor take any part in its proceedings. As Secretaries, and heads of their respective departments, they annually report to Congress, what has been done in, and what is the state and condition of their departments. They also suggest or recommend to Congress such legislation as in their judgment is required for that branch of the government under their supervision.

4. It is therefore easily understood that the Cabinet is not a body of officials chosen as the advisers of the President; and that that is their only duty. Not so; their membership in the Cabinet only grows out of the offices or places they hold in the government. The moment any one ceases to hold that office, that moment he ceases to be a member of the Cabinet.

5. To the foregoing we will add a little of the history of the Cabinet. Under Washington's administration it consisted of but three members, viz.: the Secretary of State, the Secretary of the Treasury, and the Secretary of War. There was no Secretary of the Navy during his administration. The department of the Navy was not established until 1798, when John Adams was President. Under his administration it consisted of four members, for the Secretary of the Navy was added, and so it continued down to Jackson's administration (1829—1837,) when the Postmaster General was made a member; so that it consisted of five mem-

bers. It stood at that number until John Tyler became the acting President, from the death of President Harrison, 1841—1845, when the Attorney General was made a member; and in 1849, on the third of March, the last day of Mr. Polk's administration, the Department of the Interior was established, and the office of "Secretary of the Interior" was created, and he also was made a member of the Cabinet. Under President Taylor's administration, which commenced on the fourth of March, 1849, and since, the number of Cabinet officers has been seven. Whether it has reached its maximum or not, depends on what Congress may do hereafter in creating other great departments of government. If they do so, their heads, or Secretaries will probably be added to the Cabinet.

6. As a piece of historical information, and for the convenience of ready reference, we here insert the names of those who have been members of the Cabinet, under all the administrations, from Washington's (the first), down to the present year (1869); and for the purpose of showing who was the Vice President with each President, we insert his name also, although he is never a member of the Cabinet. By this it will be seen that several persons occupied the same positions under the same administrations; and that upon every change of the heads of departments, the Cabinet was changed.

FIRST ADMINISTRATION, FROM 1789 TO 1797—8 YEARS.

George Washington, Va., President.
John Adams, Mass., Vice President.

CABINET.

Thomas Jefferson, Va., Secretary of State.
Edmund Randolph, Va., " "
Timothy Pickering, Mass., " "
Alexander Hamilton, N. Y., Secretary of the Treasury.
Oliver Wolcott, Conn. " " "
Timothy Pickering, Mass., Secretary of War.
James McHenry, Md., " " "
Henry Knox, Mass., " " "

SECOND ADMINISTRATION, 1797 TO 1801—4 YEARS.

John Adams, Mass., President.
Thomas Jefferson, Va., Vice President.

CABINET.

Timothy Pickering, Mass., Secretary of State.
John Marshall, Va., " " "
Oliver Wolcott, Ct., Secretary of the Treasury.
Samuel Dexter, Mass., " " "
James McHenry, Md., Secretary of War.
Samuel Dexter, Mass., " "
Roger Griswold, " "
George Cabot, Mass., Secretary of the Navy.
Benjamin Stoddert, Md., " "

THIRD ADMINISTRATION, 1801 TO 1809—8 YEARS.

Thomas Jefferson, Va., President.
Aaron Burr, N. Y., Vice President.
George Clinton, N. Y., "

CABINET.

James Madison, Va., Secretary of State.
Samuel Dexter, Mass., Secretary of the Treasury.
Albert Gallatin, Pa., " " "

Henry Dearborn, Mass., Secretary of War.
Benjamin Stoddert, Md., Secretary of the Navy.
Robert Smith, Md., " " "

FOURTH ADMINISTRATION, 1809 TO 1817—8 YEARS.

James Madison, Va., President.
George Clinton, N. Y., Vice President.
Elbridge Gerry, Mass., "

CABINET.

Robert Smith, Md., Secretary of State.
James Monroe, Va., " "
Albert Gallatin, Pa., Secretary of the Treasury.
George W. Campbell, Tenn., " "
Alexander J. Dallas, Pa., " "
William Eustis, Mass., Secretary of War.
John Armstrong, N. Y., " "
James Monroe, Va., " "
William H. Crawford, Ga. " "
Paul Hamilton, S. C., Secretary of the Navy.
William Jones, Pa., " " "
B. W. Crowningshield, Mass., " "

FIFTH ADMINISTRATION, 1817 TO 1825—8 YEARS.

James Monroe, Va., President.
Daniel D. Tompkins, N. Y., Vice President.

CABINET.

John Q. Adams, Mass., Secretary of State.
William H. Crawford, Ga., Secretary of the Treasury.
Isaac Shelby, Ky., Secretary of War.
John C. Calhoun, S. C., " "
B. W. Crowningshield, Mass., Secretary of the Navy.
Smith Thompson, N. Y., " "
Samuel L. Southard, N. J., " "

SIXTH ADMINISTRATION, 1825 TO 1829—4 YEARS.

John Q. Adams, Mass., President.
John C. Calhoun, S. C., Vice President.

CABINET.

Henry Clay, Ky., Secretary of State.
Richard Rush, Pa., Secretary of the Treasury.
James Barbour, Va., Secretary of War.
Peter B. Porter, N. Y., " "
Samuel L. Southard, N. J., Secretary of the Navy.

SEVENTH ADMINISTRATION, 1829 TO 1837—8 YEARS.

Andrew Jackson, Tenn., President.
John C. Calhoun, S. C., Vice President.
Martin Van Buren, N. Y., "

CABINET.

Martin Van Buren, N. Y., Secretary of State.
Edward Livingston, La., " "
Louis McLane, Del., " "
John Forsyth, Geo. " "
Samuel D. Ingham, Pa., Secretary of the Treasury.
Louis McLane, Del., " " "
William J. Duane, Pa., " " "
Roger B. Taney, Md. " " "
Levi Woodbury, N. H. " " "
John H. Eaton, Tenn., Secretary of War.
Lewis Cass, Mich. " "
Benjamin F. Butler, N. Y., " "
John Branch, N. C., Secretary of the Navy.
Levi Woodbury, N. H., " " "
Mahlon Dickerson, N. J., " " "

Postmasters General, and for the first time considered members of the Cabinet.

John McLean, O.
William F. Barry, Ky.
Amos Kendall, Ky.

EIGHTH ADMINISTRATION, 1837 TO 1841—4 YEARS.

Martin Van Buren, N. Y., President.
Richard M. Johnson, Ky., Vice President.

CABINET.

John Forsyth, Geo., Secretary of State.
Levi Woodbury, N. H., Secretary of the Treasury.
Joel R. Poinsett, S. C., Secretary of War.
Mahlon Dickerson, N. J., Secretary of the Navy.
James K. Paulding, N. Y., " " "
Amos Kendall, Ky., Postmaster General.
John M. Niles, Ct., " "

NINTH ADMINISTRATION, MARCH 4, 1841, TO APRIL 4, 1841.

William Henry Harrison, O., President.
John Tyler, Va., Vice President.

Daniel Webster, Mass., Secretary of State.
Thomas Ewing, O., Secretary of the Treasury.
John Bell, Tenn., Secretary of War.
George E. Badger, N. C., Secretary of the Navy.
Gideon Granger, N. Y., Postmaster General.

TENTH ADMINISTRATION, APRIL 6, 1841, TO MARCH 4, 1845.

John Tyler, Va., (acting) President by death of Harrison.

CABINET.

Daniel Webster, Mass., Secretary of State.
Abel P. Upsher, Va., " "
John C. Calhoun, S. C., " "
Thomas Ewing, O., Secretary of the Treasury.
Walter Seward, Pa., " " "
John C. Spencer, N. Y., " " "
George M. Bibb, Ky., " "
John Bell, Tenn., Secretary of War.
John C. Spencer, N. Y., " "
James M. Porter, Pa., " "
William Wilkins. Pa., " "

George E. Badger, N. C., Secretary of the Navy.
Abel P. Upsher, Va., " " "
David Henshaw, Mass., " " "
G. W. Gilmer, Va., " " "
John Y. Mason, Va., " " "
Hugh S. Legare, S. C., Attorney-General.
John Nelson, Md., " "
Francis G. Granger, N. Y., Postmaster General.
Charles A. Wickliffe, Ky., " "

ELEVENTH ADMINISTRATION—MARCH 4, 1845, TO MARCH 4, 1849—4 YEARS.

James K. Polk, Tenn., President.
George M. Dallas, Pa., Vice President.

CABINET.

James Buchanan, Pa., Secretary of State.
Robert J. Walker, Miss., Secretary of the Treasury.
William L. Marcy, N. Y., Secretary of War.
George Bancroft, Mass., Secretary of the Navy.
John Y. Mason, Va., " " "
Cave Johnson, Tenn., Postmaster General.
John Y. Mason, Va., Attorney General.
Nathan Clifford, Me., " "
Isaac Toucey, Ct., " "

TWELFTH ADMINISTRATION—MARCH 4, 1849, TO JULY 10, 1850—1 YEAR AND 4 MONTHS.

Zachary Taylor, La., President.
Millard Fillmore, N. Y., Vice President.

CABINET.

John M. Clayton, Del., Secretary of State.
George W. Crawford, Geo., Secretary of War.
William M. Meredith, Pa., Sec. of the Treasury.
William B. Preston, Va., Secretary of the Navy.
Thomas Ewing, Ohio, Secretary of the Interior.
Jacob Collamer, Vt., Postmaster General.
Reverdy Johnson, Md., Attorney General.

THIRTEENTH ADMINISTRATION, JULY 10, 1850, TO MARCH 4, 1853—2 YEARS AND 8 MONTHS.

Millard Fillmore, (acting) President, by death of Taylor—no Vice President.

CABINET.

Daniel Webster, Mass., Secretary of State.
Thomas Corwin, Ohio, Secretary of the Treasury.
Charles M. Conrad, La., Secretary of War.
Wm. A. Graham, N. C., Secretary of the Navy.
Alex. H. H. Stuart, Va. Secretary of the Interior.
Nathan K. Hall, N. Y., Postmaster General.
John J. Crittenden, Ky., Attorney General.

FOURTEENTH ADMINISTRATION, MARCH 4, 1853, TO MARCH 4, 1857.

Franklin Pierce, N. H., President.

Wm. R. King, of Ala., who was elected Vice President with Mr. Pierce, but died before he took his seat; and there was no Vice President during Pierce's administration.

CABINET.

William L. Marcy, N. Y., Secretary of State.
James Guthrie, Ky., Secretary of the Treasury.
Jefferson Davis, Miss., Secretary of War.
J. C. Dobbin, N. C., Secretary of the Navy.
Robert McClelland, Mich., Secretary of the Interior.
James Campbell, Pa., Postmaster General.
Caleb Cushing, Mass., Attorney General.

FIFTEENTH ADMINISTRATION—MARCH 4, 1857, TO MARCH 4, 1861.

James Buchanan, Pa., President.
John C. Breckenridge, Vice President.

CABINET.

Lewis Cass, Mich., and Jeremiah S. Black, Pa., Secretaries of State.

Howell Cobb, Ga., Philip F. Thomas, and John A. Dix, N. Y., Secretaries of the Treasury.

John B. Floyd, Va., and Joseph Holt, Ky., Secretaries of War.

Isaac Toucey, Ct., Secretary of the Navy.

Jacob Thompson, Miss., Secretary of the Interior,

Aaron V. Brown, Tenn., Joseph Holt, Ky., and Horatio King, Postmasters General.

Jeremiah S. Black, Pa., and Edwin M. Stanton, Pa., Attorneys General.

SIXTEENTH ADMINISTRATION, MARCH 4, 1861, TO APRIL 12, 1865—4 YEARS, 1 MONTH, AND 8 DAYS.

Abraham Lincoln, Ill., President.

Hannibal Hamlin, Me., Vice-President, first term, and Andrew Johnson, Tenn., Vice-President, second term.

CABINET.

William H. Seward, N. Y., Secretary of State.

Salmon P. Chase, Ohio, Wm. P. Fessenden, Me., Hugh McCulloch, Ind., Secretaries of the Treasury.

Simon Cameron, Pa., Edwin M. Stanton, Pa., Secretaries of War.

Gideon Welles, Conn., Secretary of the Navy.

John P. Upsher, Ind., Secretary of the Interior.

Montgomery Blair, Md., William Dennison, O., Postmasters General.

Edward Bates, Mo., James Speed, Ky., Attorneys General.

SEVENTEENTH ADMINISTRATION, APRIL 15, 1865, TO MARCH 4, 1869.

Andrew Johnson, acting President.
No Vice President.

CABINET.

William H. Seward, N. Y., Secretary of State.
Hugh McCulloch, Ind., Secretary of the Treasury.
Edwin M. Stanton, Pa., Ulysses S. Grant, Ill., and J. M. Schofield, Secretaries of War.
Gideon Wells, Conn., Secretary of the Navy.
James Harlan, Iowa, Orville H. Browning, Ill., Secretaries of the Interior.
James Speed, Ky., Henry Stanberry, Ohio, Wm. M. Evarts, N. Y., Attorneys General.
William Dennision, Ohio, Alexander W. Randall, Wis., Postmasters General.

EIGHTEENTH ADMINISTRATION, MARCH 4, 1869.

Ulysses S. Grant, Ill., President.
Schuyler Colfax, Ind., Vice-President.

CABINET.

*Elihu B. Washburne, Ill., Secretary of State.
Hamilton Fish N. Y., " " "
†Alexander T. Stewart, N. Y., Secretary of Treasury.
George S. Boutwell, Mass., " " "
John A. Rawlins, Secretary of War.
Adolph E. Borie, Penna., Secretary of the Navy.
Jacob D. Cox, Ohio, Secretary of the Interior.
J. A. J. Cresswell, Md., Postmaster General.
Eben Rockwood Hoar, Mass., Attorney General.

---

* Resigned a few days after his appointment.
† Disqualified on account of his mercantile pursuits. A law of 1792 forbids a merchant from accepting the position.

CHAPTER XIV.

United States Courts.

1. UNDER this caption we need make but a few general remarks; for, under the appropriate titles of the different kinds of courts, we have treated of each, with considerable detail. The legal tribunals created by acts of Congress, and consequently called United States Courts, are known by the names of the United States Supreme Court, the Circuit Courts, the District Courts, and the Court of Claims. To these must be added the local courts in the District of Columbia, and the Territorial Courts. The former are permanent institutions, as much so as the Circuit or District Courts. But the latter are temporary; designed to last only during the time the Territorial government lasts; for when the Territory is admitted as a State, its former government ceases to exist; and as the courts are a part of the government, they also pass away; and State courts are created in their places.

2. These brief remarks are merely introductory to the four following chapters, in which the reader will find a fuller account of the United States courts ; and we hope a better understanding of that branch of the government denominated the Judiciary.

CHAPTER XV.

Supreme Court of the United States.

1. We have before stated that the government of the United States was divided into three branches or great departments, the Legislative, the Executive and the Judiciary. The two former we have already described. We come now to the third, which although the last, is by no means the least part of the great machine by which the people are governed, and their rights protected. When our government is spoken of, in a figurative sense, as an "arch," the Judicial Department is very appropriately styled, "the key stone of the arch;" for as the arch would fall without the key stone, so would our form of government fall without the Judicial branch; for in all cases of dispute or disagreement as to what the Constitution means, or how the laws should be construed and interpreted, we look to the Judicial decisions for the settlement of all such questions.

2. And especially do we look to the decisions of the Supreme Court of the United States; for it is the highest tribunal in the nation. Its decisions are final, for there is no superior tribunal to which questions or causes can be taken; and when it has, in due form, declared how the Constitution must be understood, or how the laws should be interpreted and applied, this decision settles the matter and becomes the law of the land, as to the questions involved in the decision.

3. This court at the present time has one Chief Justice and nine Associate Justices; all appointed by the President, by and with the advice and consent of the Senate. They are appointed for life, or during good behavior; they may, however, be impeached for bribery or other high crimes, and then removed from office. They may also resign; for there is no power which can compel any man to hold office; but if they conduct themselves properly and choose to retain their offices, there is no power by which they can be removed, except the power of death. The Constitution itself makes this povision, in order that the judges may be removed as far as possible from the influence of party politics. They have nothing to fear from the success or defeat of any political party. It is therefore expected that their decisions will not be biased by party or political considerations; and it may not be amiss to say that the provision for keeping the judges of the United States Courts in office for life, meets with almost universal approbation; and has caused many to hope that the States would alter their Constitutions and adopt the same plan; believing it to be the surest way of preserving a pure and independent Judiciary, on which depend the rights and liberties of every citizen of the commonwealth.

4. This court holds but one term in a year, which commences on the first Monday of December, and sits until it has disposed of the business before it. Its sessions are always held at Washington, the capital of the nation; there it has access to the Congressional and Law Libraries, and to all the departments and records of the government when necessary.

There is a class of causes which may be commenced in this court. In these cases it has original jurisdiction. They are such as affect ambassadors, other public ministers, and consuls; and those in which a State shall be a party. In other cases it has only appellate jurisdiction. The greater part of its business is to hear and determine appeals from inferior courts, mainly from the United States Circuit Courts; and in some instances from the highest State courts.

5. It has not only original, but exclusive jurisdiction in causes where a State is a party, and when proceedings or suits against ambassadors, or other public ministers or their servants, are instituted. Its power to try appeals from lower courts, called its *appellate* jurisdiction, gives it the position of the highest court in the nation.

It has power also to restrain or to prohibit proceedings in the United States District Courts, when acting as courts of Admiralty; or in cases of maritime jurisdiction. The judges of this court hold the Circuit Courts, and allot themselves among the judicial circuits. The Chief Justice receives $6,500 per year salary, and the Associate Justices each $6,000.

The practice and rules of procedure in this court are very similar to those of the Courts of Chancery and King's Bench, in England. Issues of fact are tried by jury, the same as in other courts.

OFFICERS OF THE COURT.

6. The officers of this tribunal are the Judges, the Attorney General, a clerk, a crier, and a reporter. The three last named are appointed by the court. It is the

duty of the Marshal of the District of Columbia to attend this court, and to serve process issuing from it.

An Attorney or Counselor-at-Law, to be admitted to practice in this court, must have been a practitioner in the Supreme Court of the State where he lives.

7. The following are the names of all the Chief Justices of the Supreme Court of the United States, from its establishment to the present time; with the dates of their appointments, and the States from which they were appointed:

John Jay, N. Y., Sept. 26, 1789.
John Rutledge, S. C., July 1, 1795.
William Cushing, Mass., Jan. 27, 1796.
Oliver Ellsworth, Ct., March 4, 1796.
John Jay, N. Y., Dec. 19, 1800.
John Marshall, Va., Jan. 27, 1801.
Roger B. Taney, Md., Dec. 28, 1835.
Salmon P. Chase, O.

8. The following are the names of the Associate Justices, with the dates of their appointments and the States from which they were appointed:

John Rutledge, S. C., 1789.
William Cushing, Mass., 1789.
Robert H. Harrison, Md., 1789.
James Wilson, Pa., 1789.
John Blair, Va., 1789.
James Iredell, N. C., 1790.
Thomas Johnson, Md., 1791.
William Patterson, N. Y., 1793.
Samuel Chase, Md., 1796.
Bushrod Washington, Va., 1798.
William Johnson, S. C., 1804.
Brockholst Livingston, N. Y., 1807.
Thomas Todd, Va., 1807.

Levi Lincoln,* Mass., 1811.
John Q. Adams,* Mass., 1811.
Gabriel Duvall, Md., 1811.
Joseph Story, Mass., 1811.
Smith Thompson, N. Y., 1823.
Robert Trimble, Ky., 1823.
John McLean, O., 1829.
Henry Baldwin, Pa., 1830.
James M. Wayne, Ga., 1835.
Philip Barbour, Va., 1836.
John McKinley, Ala., 1837.
John Catron, Tenn., 1837.
Peter V. Daniel, Va., 1841.
Samuel Nelson, N. Y., 1845.
Levi Woodbury, N. H., 1845.
Robert C. Grier, Va., 1846.
Benjamin R. Curtis, Mass., 1851.
John A. Campbell, Ala., 1853.
Nathan Clifford, Me., 1858.
Noah Swayne, O., 1862.
Samuel Miller, Iowa, 1862.
Stephen J. Field, Cal.

*Declined the appointment.

CHAPTER XVI.

Circuits and Circuit Courts.

1. In the last chapter we gave an account of the United States Supreme Court. We now come to the United States Circuit Courts, the next in dignity, power, and jurisdiction. Unlike the Supreme Court, which, as stated, is always held in Washington, the Circuit Courts are held in every State, at such times and places as Congress by law directs. It would add some interest and utility to our work if they were inserted here, so as to show when and where these courts are held. But we omit this, because they are so often changed, that what is now correct might not remain so after another session of Congress. These changes are made to accommodate the people in the State, or the judges of the court. As now arranged, the whole of the States are divided into nine circuits, each circuit comprising several States; some more and some less, according to the size and population of the States comprised in a circuit. Then the court is held in each State in the circuit. This arrangement is made in order to bring these courts within convenient reach of all the people in every part of the country.

2. The Circuit Courts are held by the Judges of the Supreme Court, who allot the circuits among themselves, and then travel each through his own circuit, until he has visited and held a session in every State which lies within it. A Judge of the Supreme Court

is the presiding and supreme magistrate in every Circuit Court, but the Judge of the District Court of the district in which the Circuit is held, sits with the Judge of the Supreme Court, as Associate Justice.

JURISDICTION.

3. These Courts have both original and appellate jurisdiction. Causes may be appealed from the District Courts to the Circuit. They also have concurrent jurisdiction with the State courts, where the matter in dispute exceeds the sum of $500, and the United States are plaintiffs; or where an alien is a party, or where the suit is between citizens of different States. They have exclusive jurisdiction in all cases of crimes against the laws of the United States, except where the law especially confers the power on other courts. It extends to all cases under the revenue laws of the United States.

4. There is also a certain class of cases, (too tedious to be described here in detail), which may be removed from State and from District Courts, into these courts, and be tried and determined in the same manner as if they had been commenced here.

The officers of Circuit Courts are, first, the Judges; second, the District Attorney of the district in which the court is held; third, the Marshal of the district; and fourth, a Clerk, who is appointed by the court.

5. It may be interesting, and perhaps useful to know how the different circuits are formed, and what States lie in each. They have been from time to time increased in number, as the number of the States increased. In some cases States have been at first placed in one circuit, and afterwards detached and placed in another.

6. By the Acts of 1862 and 1863, the circuits were arranged as follows:—

First Circuit—Rhode Island, Massachusetts, Maine and New Hampshire, (by Act of 1820.)

Second Circuit—Vermont, Connecticut, New York, (Act of 1837.)

Third Circuit—New Jersey and Pennsylvania.

Fourth Circuit—Maryland, Virginia, Delaware and North Carolina.

Fifth Circuit—South Carolina, Georgia, Alabama, Mississippi and Florida.

Sixth Circuit—Louisiana, Texas, Arkansas, Kentucky and Tennessee.

Seventh Circuit—Ohio and Indiana.

Eighth Circuit—Michigan and Illinois.

Ninth Circuit—Wisconsin, Missouri, Kansas and Minnesota.

Tenth Circuit—California and Oregon.

But in 1866 this arrangement of the circuits was again changed; and this was done, we suppose, to make the circuits approximate nearer to the number of Associate Justices, as reduced from nine to six by the same act; for, it was then enacted that hereafter there should be no more Associate Justices of the Supreme Court appointed, until they were reduced (by death or resignation), to six.

7. The circuits by this last act were reduced to nine, and were arranged as follows:

First and Second Circuits to remain as before.

The Third was made up of the States of Pennsylvania, New Jersey and Delaware.

The Fourth, of Maryland, Virginia, West Virginia, North Carolina and South Carolina.

The Fifth, of Georgia, Florida, Alabama, Mississippi, Louisiana and Texas.

The Sixth, of Ohio, Michigan, Kentucky and Tennessee.

The Seventh, of Indiana, Illinois and Wisconsin.

The Eighth, of Minnesota, Iowa, Missouri, Kansas and Arkansas.

The Ninth, of California, Oregon and Nevada.

We have inserted both of these circuit arrangements, because one new State (Nebraska), has been admitted since the act passed. Others will soon come in, and very probably the old number of circuits and judges will be restored.

CHAPTER XVII.

Judicial Districts, and District Courts.

1. WE come now to the lowest grade of United States courts, excepting the local courts in the District of Columbia, and the Territorial Courts. A United States District Court is held by a District Judge in every district. Every State constitutes at least one district, several of the larger States are divided into two, and some into three. There are at the present time fifty-nine Judicial Districts, and consequently the same number of District Judges, District Attorneys, District Clerks and Marshals. The Judges, Attorneys and Marshals are all appointed by the President and Senate; the Clerks by the respective courts.

TERMS.

2. By the law of 1789 every District Judge was required to hold four sessions a year, at such times and in such places as Congress directed. This is done to this day in a great majority of the States; but by later laws, in some of the districts only two or three sessions a year are required.

JURISDICTION.

3. These courts have exclusive jurisdiction in all admiralty and maritime causes. These relate to maritime contracts, and to crimes against the laws of the United States, committed on the sea and on navigable

lakes and rivers. It embraces in this country all contracts respecting vessels and navigation; such as chartering, repairing, and fitting them out, seamen's wages, &c. They have in some cases concurrent jurisdiction with the Circuit Courts, in cases of piracy, and exclusive cognizance of cases where seizures are made for a violation of the revenue laws, or laws relating to imposts and navigation; and causes against consuls and vice consuls where the amount claimed does not exceed $100. In short, they have concurrent jurisdiction with the Circuit Courts, of all crimes against the laws of the United States, the punishment of which is not capital. The trial of issues of fact in all causes except civil causes of Admiralty and maritime jurisdiction, must be by jury.

4. Appeals are taken from these courts to the Circuit Courts. The judges are appointed like those of the Supreme Court, for life, or during good behaviour, and receive various amounts as salary, some more and some less, according to the amount of services to be performed in their respective districts.

5. When vessels are captured in time of war, either by the public armed vessels or by private armed ships, the facts and circumstances of the capture must be brought before a United States Circuit or District Court for adjudication; when the vessel and cargo are either condemned as a prize, or restored to their owners. When either of these courts adjudicate such cases, it is called a Prize Court.

6. For the same reason given for showing the composition of the Judicial Circuits in a condensed form,

we will here give the number of Judicial Districts in each State as they now exist, and the total number in all the States. They are as follows:—

Alabama, 3.
Arkansas, 2.
California, 2.
Connecticut, 1.
Delaware, 1.
Florida, 2.
Georgia, 2.
Illinois, 2.
Indiana, 1.
Iowa, 1.
Kansas, 1.
Kentucky, 1.
Louisiana, 2.
Maine, 1.
Maryland, 1.
Massachusetts, 1.
Michigan, 2.
Minnesota, 1.
District of Columbia, 1.

Mississippi, 2.
Missouri, 2.
Nevada, 1.
New Hampshire, 1.
New Jersey, 1.
New York, 3.
North Carolina, 3.
Nebraska, 1.
Ohio, 2.
Oregon, 1.
Pennsylvania, 2.
Rhode Island, 1.
South Carolina, 2.
Tennessee, 3.
Texas, 2.
Vermont, 1.
Virginia, 1.
West Virginia, 1.
Wisconsin, 1.

Total, 59.

CHAPTER XVIII.

Court of Claims.

1. THIS court was established by act of Congress in 1855. A brief extract from the law itself, will best explain the object of its creation, its jurisdiction, powers and duties. The law reads thus: "A court shall be established to be called the Court of Claims, to consist of three judges, to be appointed by the President and Senate, and to hold their offices during good behavior; and the said court shall hear and determine all claims founded upon any law of Congress, or upon any regulation of an Executive department, or upon any contract express or implied, with the government of the United States; which may be suggested to it by a petition filed therein; and also all claims which may be referred to said court by either house of Congress."

2. On the third of March, 1863, the jurisdiction of this court was enlarged, and two additional judges appointed, (making five,) from the whole number of which the President was authorized to appoint one a Chief Justice for said court.

3. The mode of commencing proceeding before this tribunal is by petition; in which the claimant must fully set forth his claim, how it arose, its amount, and the parties interested therein. After the case has been heard and determined, the court reports to Congress what its decision is, and if favorable to the claimant, a bill is passed for his relief.

4. It holds one session a year, in Washington, commencing on the first Monday in October, and continuing as long as business before it requires. It not only tries claims against the government, but by its enlarged jurisdiction, conferred in 1863, it also tries counter claims, and set-offs, which the United States may have against the claimant. Appeals are taken from the Court of Claims to the Supreme Court of the United States, when the amount in controversy exceeds $3,000.

5. Before the establishment of this court, the only remedy persons having claims upon the government had, was by petitioning to Congress for relief; which experience proved to be a long, tedious and expensive mode of obtaining their dues. The petition now goes to this court, where it is heard and adjudicated in the same form, and by the same rules of procedure which are observed in other courts; for Congress has conferred upon it all the powers commonly possessed by other courts of law. It also has a seal.

6. It has greatly facilitated the settlement of claims against the government, and has relieved Congress of a great amount of labor, which was urgently pressed upon it at every session.

7. In addition to the five judges, it has a Solicitor, an Assistant Solicitor, and a Deputy Solicitor, all of whom are appointed by the President and Senate; and are officers of the court, whose duty it is faithfully to defend the United States in all matters and claims before this court.

The Judges receive $4,000 per annum salary. The

Solicitor and Assistant Solicitor receive $3,500 each, and the Deputy Solicitor $2,500 per annum.

A bailiff, a clerk, a crier and messenger, all of whom are appointed by the court, make up the remaining officials.

In order to give the reader a better idea of proceedings in this tribunal, it may be stated that claimants stand in relation of plaintiffs, and the government in that of defendant.

CHAPTER XIX.

District Attorneys.

1. In the twelfth chapter we spoke of the appointment, position and duties of the Attorney General of the United States, and originally intended to place our remarks upon the District Attorneys, next in order; but subsequently changed this plan, and determined to place them immediately after those upon the courts; for next to the judges, they—the District Attorneys—are the higest officers in both the Circuit and District Courts. By reading this and the twelfth chapter consecutively, a better understanding of both these classes of officials may be gained, and a clearer insight into the judicial machinery of the government.

2. In another place we have spoken of the division of the United States (see political divisions), into Judicial Districts, in each of which there is held a District Court, and a District Attorney is appointed for each court, in the same manner that the Attorney General is appointed. He bears the same official relation to these courts, and has similar duties to perform in them, that the Attorney General has in the Supreme Court. It is his duty "to prosecute in such district all delinquents for crimes and offences cognizable under the authority of the United States, and all civil actions in which the United States shall be concerned." They are his clients, and he must enforce their rights, and defend them, in the same

manner that any attorney protects and defends his client in any of the State courts. In case of necessity, he may appoint a substitute to act in his place. All fees over and above what he is allowed as compensation for his services, he must report and pay into the United States Treasury.

3. He must defend collectors of the customs and other revenue officers in his district, when suits are brought against them in their official capacity, and must report to the Solicitor of the Treasury the number of suits determined and pending in his district. And when prize cases have been determined, or are pending in the District Court of his district, he must report the state and condition of each case to the Secretary of the Navy.

District Attorneys are appointed for four years, but may be removed at the pleasure of the President. Their compensation depends on the amount of business to be done in their respective districts. When important ports of entry, such as New York or Boston, lie in their districts, their duties are very numerous, and they receive a corresponding compensation.

CHAPTER XX.

United States Marshals.

1. UNITED States Marshals, commonly called simply Marshals, are the ministerial officers of the United States courts. Their duties and responsibilities are very similar, and nearly identical with the duties and responsibilities of sheriffs in the courts of the several States. They are appointed by the President and Senate, for a term of four years. They appoint their own deputies, and their compensation consists of fees instead of a salary; and depends entirely upon the amount of business they have to transact. There is a Marshal in every Judicial District in the United States, and there are fifty-nine of these districts in all, as stated in another place. Every State forms at least one district, while the larger States are divided into two or three.

2. A District Court is held in every district; and it is the Marshal's duty to attend the sittings of these courts, and also those of the United States Circuit Courts, when they happen to sit in his district. The Marshal for the District of Columbia must also attend the sittings of the Supreme Court, and execute its precepts. We have said that they are the ministerial officers of the United States courts; for it is their duty to serve all writs and precepts emanating from them, whether of a civil or criminal character; and to execute the judgments and decrees of these tribunals; and for this

purpose they are authorized by law, (if necessary), to command such assistance as they may need in the execution of their duties. Before they enter upon the duties of their office, they must be bound to the United States for the faithful performance of them, and must solemnly swear to do them, without malice or partiality; and that they will take only lawful fees. They are also held answerable for the delivery to their successors of all prisoners who may be in their custody at the time of their removal, or at the expiration of their term of office.

3. They also have the custody of all vessels and goods seized by any officer of the revenue. It is their duty also to summons, and to pay jurors and witnesses in behalf of any prisoner to be tried for a capital offence, under the laws of the United States. In the remarks made under the head "Census," we stated that it was made the duty of the Marshals to superintend and direct the enumeration of the people; and to collect such statistical facts as the law requires. This they do through deputies, whom they appoint for that special purpose.

The United States Marshal is also required, on the first day of January and July of each year, to make a return of all the fees and emoluments of his office to the Secretary of the Interior; and if they amount to more than $6,000 per year, he must pay the surplus into the Treasury of the United States.

CHAPTER XXI.

Grand Jury.

1. By turning to the fifth article of the amendments to the Constitution, you will find these words: "No person shall be held to answer for a capital or otherwise infamous crime, unless on a presentment or indictment of a Grand Jury; except in cases arising in the land or naval forces, or in the militia, when in actual service, in time of war or public danger." This constitutional provision makes a Grand Jury a very important agent or instrumentality in the execution of the laws, and also a safegaurd of the liberties and rights of the people. It secures every person from the expense and disgrace of a trial for infamous crimes, unless a Grand Jury of his countrymen shall find upon inquiry and investigation, that there are good reasons for believing that the person so charged has committed the alleged offence.

2. This provision not only protects those who are charged with these crimes against the laws of the United States, but those also who may be charged with such offences against the laws of any State; for no State can arrest and try any person for a capital or infamous crime without these preliminary proceedings of a Grand Jury; and should it do so, the United States Supreme Court would set its laws aside, as contrary to the Constitution of the United States. Here we see that the government is just as careful to protect its

citizens from injustice by hasty judicial proceedings, as it is to punish them after a fair and impartial trial.

3. A Grand Jury, when called to take cognizance of violations of the laws of the United States, to find indictments against those who are charged with them, is summoned by a judge of a United States court in the circuit or district where the alleged crime has been perpetrated; and it must take notice of all crimes against the laws of the United States, which may be brought to its knowledge, within the circuit or district in which it sits. Hence, if ordered by a Circuit Judge, its powers extend over all those States which lie in that circuit. But when ordered by a District Judge, its powers extend only to that district in which it sits, and a district never embraces more than one State, and in many cases a State is divided into two or three districts.

4. This shows us how much more extensive is the jurisdiction of a Grand Jury, when acting under the laws of the United States, than when acting under State laws. In the former it extends generally all over a State, and sometimes over several States. But in the latter it is confined to the county in which it sits.

GRAND AND PETIT JURIES.

It may be interesting and useful to our young readers, to explain here the difference between a Grand and a Petit Jury, as they are commonly denominated. First, a Grand Jury never acts but in criminal cases. A Petit Jury acts in both criminal and civil cases. The finding or conclusion arrived at by a Grand Jury is called a presentment, or an indictment. The finding of a Petit Jury is called its verdict.

5. Second, a Grand Jury sits alone (not in the presence of the court), and deliberates upon such matters of a criminal character as it possesses knowledge of, or which may be brought to its notice by the court or by other persons; and when it finds that great evils exist, and wrongs have been perpetrated, it presents them to the court, and calls the attention of the law officers to them; which is equivalent to a recommendation that judicial proceedings should be commenced to abate the evil, or to punish the wrong doer. This is called a presentment of the Grand Jury.

And when they find, upon such evidence as they have, that a great crime has been perpetrated, or that they have good reason so to believe, and that it has been perpetrated by some person specified, they report their finding or conclusion to the Court. This is called an indictment by the Grand Jury; after which the person so charged is arrested, if at large, and can be found, and is either imprisoned or held to bail for his appearance at court to stand trial.

6. A Grand Jury never tries a case. It only says to the court by its presentment or indictment, that the case presented, or the person indicted, ought to be brought before the court, and tried for the alleged wrong or crime.

A Petit Jury sits with the court, hears the pleadings and arguments of counsel on both sides, listens to the evidence of witnesses; and then hears the charge of the judge, as to the law applicable to the case; after which they withdraw and deliberate alone upon the case, and if they agree in a criminal case, their verdict is "Guilty," or "Not Guilty;" if in a civil suit, they say how much one party is indebted (if any), to the other.

7. The object aimed at in that article of the Constitution which stands at the head of this chapter, is to protect persons from false charges of crime, and hasty adjudication of such charges; for it substantially amounts to a declaration that no person shall be punished for a capital or infamous crime, unless one jury, before trial, shall, upon information and belief, charge him with the offence; and another, after trial, shall find him guilty of the alleged crime.

The above remarks are as applicable to Grand and Petit Juries, acting under State, as those which act under the United States laws.

CHAPTER XXII.

Admiralty and Maritime Jurisdiction.

In ancient times—and long before this government existed—civilized and commercial nations had codes or laws which related especially to transactions upon the sea. Those respecting ships of war and warlike operations at sea, were called the laws of Admiralty; those respecting vessels engaged in commercial affairs were called Maritime laws; and the courts empowered with jurisdiction to hear and try causes, or to take any judicial proceedings in those cases, were styled Courts of Admiralty and Maritime Jurisdiction. These laws, in many respects, differed so materially from the laws relating to affairs on land, that the authority and power to take proceedings in, and adjudicate upon them, was conferred upon a particular class of courts. Hence we see the origin of the names of such tribunals.

In this country, the United States District Courts have been designated by the laws as the courts which shall have original and exclusive authority to adjudicate this class of causes; yet an appeal from the District to the Circuit Courts may be taken.

KIND OF CASES.

The word Maritime designates that which relates to the sea. Yet, in the United States, cases which come within Admiralty and Maritime jurisdiction, are not restricted to the sea, or to transactions relating to business or crimes done on it, but are made to embrace those which occur on navigable lakes and rivers, and include seizures made for the violation of the laws of impost, navigation or trade, suits for the recovery of seamen's wages, contracts for building, repairing or fitting out vessels, and, briefly, all contracts where the subject-matter relates to the navigation of the sea. The District Courts have Admiralty and Maritime jurisdiction in all these cases, without regard to the amount claimed, and in criminal as well as in civil suits.

The foregoing remarks show the workings of our judicial system, as it applies to business done, and crimes committed upon the high seas.

CHAPTER XXIII.

Congressmen.

1. CONGRESSMAN, in the most comprehensive sense in which the term may be used, means any member in either branch of Congress. But there is a more restricted sense in which it is most commonly used, and in this sense it is generally understood; that is, a member of the House of Representatives, the lower of the two Houses. These are elected by the people, in each State, and in the Congressional districts of that State; and they are the only persons either in the Legislative, Executive, or Judiciary branches of the government, for whom the people vote directly. They are elected by single districts, that is, but one member is chosen in one district. They are elected for two years, that is, during the term of a Congress, which lasts two years, and always holds two sessions. The President may call an extra session, if in his judgment the exigencies of the country are such as to require its action before the time of the regular meeting. This has been done on several occasions.

2. The Constitution prescribes the qualifications of members of the House of Representatives (which see). They are also stated in Chapter III, where much other matter relating to this subject may be found. The Constitution is silent as to the number of members of which the House shall be composed, excepting that it specifies how many each State should have, until the first enumeration of the people in 1790; and since then Congress has from time to time fixed the number, which is now 241—to which must be added one for Nevada, and one for Nebraska, which States were admitted since the last apportionment.

CHAPTER XXIV.

Congressional Districts.

WHENEVER the population of a State is so small that it is entitled to only one Representative in Congress, the whole State forms but one Congressional district; but whenever it is entitled to two or more, then it is divided by its Legislature into as many districts as its population entitles it to return members; so that every member of Congress is chosen by single districts. The act thus districting the States was passed in 1862. In large cities, certain sections or wards are constituted a Congressional district. In the country, a county or several counties are formed into a district; but in all cases a district must consist of contiguous territory, not scattered, a piece here and a piece there, in different parts of the State or country.

These districts must be re-arranged every ten years, and as soon as may be after the census is taken (which is every ten years), and the population known and published. The reason for this re-arrangement becomes apparent from the fact that the number of the population is constantly changing. In some States and counties it is rapidly increasing; in others increasing very slowly, or not at all, or indeed may be decreasing. In new Western States it has increased uniformly so rapidly that at the end of every decade they have been entitled to an increase of Representatives; while some of the older States, not increasing so fast, have actually lost, so that what we state as the number of Representatives of each State now, may not be exactly correct after the next census. Hence we see that Congressional Districts are not permanent political divisions, but are liable to frequent changes. If they were permanent, they would probably be laid down in our common maps, as counties sometimes are. They are now generally designated by the ordinal numbers, as 1st, 2d, 3rd, 4th, &c., Congressional districts of such a State.

CHAPTER XXV.

Clerk of the House of Representatives, and Secretary of the Senate.

1. THE name of the first mentioned officer indicates the nature of his duties. He of course must keep a record of the proceedings of the House of which he is Clerk. In addition to the ordinary duties of his position, Congress requires him to give bonds in the sum of twenty thousand dollars, that he will faithfully apply and disburse the contingent funds of the House, which may come into his hands. He, with the Secretary of the Senate, is authorized to advertise for proposals for supplying the Senate and House of Representatives with stationery and printing.

2. He must lay before Congress the names and compensation of all clerks and messengers employed in his office, and a detailed statement of all expenditures from the contingent fund of the House, together with a statement of all appropriations made by Congress during the last session, and all new officers created by it, and their salaries.

3. He is chosen by the members of the House, holds his office two years, and receives a salary of $3,000 a year. He has the use of the Congressional Library, and is entitled to the franking privilege.

SECRETARY OF THE SENATE.

The duties, compensation, mode of election, powers and privileges of this officer, are so much like those of the Clerk of the House, that to describe them would be little more than to reiterate the former part of this chapter.

CHAPTER XXVI.

Speaker of the House of Representatives.

1. THE Speaker of the House of Representatives is the presiding officer thereof. He is chosen by the members of that body, and is selected for this important position in view of his knowledge of parliamentary law and usages. He is elected for the full term of the Congress which chooses him. His compensation, by an act of 1856, was fixed at double the amount received by other members of the House; for his duties are much more arduous than those of an ordinary member.

2. The law provides that in case of the death, resignation, impeachment, or any other disability of both the President and Vice President, the President of the Senate *pro tem.*, must then act as President; but in case there happens to be no President of the Senate, then the Speaker becomes acting President.

3. The Speakership of the House of Representatives has always been regarded as a very respectable and honorable position. The following are the names of all the Speakers of the House, since the establishment of the government, down to 1869.

Frederick A. Muhlenburgh, Penn.,	1789 to 1791
Jonathan Trumbull, Conn.,	1791 " 1793
Frederick A. Muhlenburgh, Penn.,	1793 " 1797
Jonathan Dayton, N. J.,	1797 " 1798
Theodore Sedgwick, Mass.,	1798 " 1801
Nathaniel Macon, N. C.,	1801 " 1807
Joseph B. Varnam, Mass.,	1807 " 1811

Henry Clay, Ky.,	1811 to 1814
Langdon Cheeves, S. C.,	1814 " 1815
Henry Clay, Ky.,	1815 " 1820
John W. Taylor, N. Y.,	1820 " 1821
Philip R. Barbour, Va.,	1821 " 1823
Henry Clay Ky.,	1823 " 1825
John W. Taylor, N. Y.,	1825 " 1827
Andrew Stephenson, Va.,	1827 " 1835
John Bell, Tenn.,	1835 " 1837
James K. Polk, Tenn.,	1837 " 1839
Robert M. T. Hunter, Va.,	1839 " 1841
John White, Ky.,	1841 " 1843
John W. Jones, Va.,	1843 " 1845
John W. Davis, Ind.,	1845 " 1847
Robert C. Winthrop, Mass.,	1847 " 1849
Howell Cobb, Ga.,	1849 " 1851
Lynn Boyd, Ky.,	1851 " 1856
Nathaniel P. Banks, Mass.,	1856 " 1858
James L. Orr, S. C.,	1858 " 1859
William Pennington, N. J.,	1860 " 1861
Galusha A. Grow, Penn.,	1861 " 1863
Schuyler Colfax, Ind.,	1864 " 1869

CHAPTER XXVII.

Acts of Congress.

1. In a comprehensive sense, an act of Congress is any act done by it, whether it is making a law, the passage of a resolution, or any proceedings taken by it. But in a more restricted sense, and what is usually meant by "an act of Congress," is a bill (as a proposed law, when laid before any Legislative body is called), passed by both Houses of Congress into a law, according to the forms and prescribed rules always adhered to in the enactment of laws, and afterwards signed by the President, or passed by the votes of two-thirds of both Houses, when the President refuses to sign it.

2. Hence every law of the United States is an act of Congress, properly introduced, examined, and generally debated, altered and amended if thought best, and then voted for by a majority of the members of the House in which it originated, after which it is sent to the other House, where it goes through the same form, and, if approved by both Houses, it is then sent to the President for his signature, and, when signed by him, the bill becomes a law, "an act of Congress." These laws are then published in some of the newspapers in every State and Territory, also in pamphlet and book form, and distributed to every State and Territory, to the Members of Congress, and to all the principal officers of government at home and abroad, that the

people may know what the laws are by which they are to be governed.

3. Every law passed by Congress is preceded by these words: "Be it enacted by the Senate and House of Representatives of the United States of America, in Congress assembled." This is called the enacting clause.

A resolution, when passed by Congress, although in some instances of the same force as law, is an act of Congress of a very different character from those acts by which laws are enacted, for these must all be done according to established parliamentary usages and forms, such as laying it (the proposed law) before Congress in the form of a bill, printing it, referring it to an appropriate committee, to be afterwards reported by that committee, the placing it in its order upon the records of the House, and the calling it up in its regular order, to be debated and voted upon.

4. But resolutions are offered in writing, and often passed on the spot, though they are sometimes laid over and referred to a committee, then called up at the proper time, and debated, passed or rejected.

Some of the most important work of Congress is done, however, by means of resolutions; for instance, its proceeding relative to an amendment of the Constitution is done by the passage of a resolution through both Houses. Many other matters upon which Congress acts, are disposed of in the same way. Its requirements of the President, the heads of Departments, and other officers of the government, are made by resolutions, and have the binding force of law; for a disregard of these requirements or instructions, when made or given to any of these officers, would be considered the same as a violation of law, and would render the official liable to censure, or perhaps to impeachment, or removal from office.

5. Other resolutions are merely expressive of the sentiments or opinionsof Congress, such as the thanks it frequently votes to officers of the army and navy for brave and gallant conduct in the discharge of their duty in perilous situations. Such a recognition of the merits and good conduct of any man in the public service, is considered highly honorable to him who receives it.

Some resolutions are concurrent—that is, both Houses of Congress must concur in or pass the same before they have any power or validity. The Constitution prohibits either House of Congress from adjourning for more than three days without the concurrence of the other House. A final adjournment, or any other, for more than three days, would require the passage of a concurrent resolution.

6. Other resolutions may pass in only one House, but are equally binding upon the members and officers of that House which passes them; but they do not bind the officers of the other House: such, for example, as relate to adjournments for not more than three days; to the order of business in that House; directions to the officers and employes of that body, &c., &c.

CHAPTER XXVIII.

Ratio of Representation.

1. The ratio of representation simply means the ratio between the whole population of the United States, and the whole number of their Representatives in Congress; and this of course includes the ratio between the people of any individual State, and the Representatives it is entitled to; both being estimated upon the same basis, and determined by the same rule.

2. The distinctive characteristic of our government is, that it is a *popular* government. Its power is vested in the people. They elect their rulers, who are the servants of the people, and these rulers are expected to carry out the people's wishes. Upon such a system, it is a matter of the first importance, to distribute this power equally among all the people, and after having fixed upon the ratio between the whole population and the whole number of Representatives; or, in other words, after having determined how many members shall compose the lower House of Congress, the next step is to apportion these members among all the States in the ratio of their population. If one State has twice the number of inhabitants that another has, it will be entitled to twice the number of Representatives in Congress. If one has ten times the inhabitants that another has, it will be entitled to ten times the number of Representatives, and so on; with this one exception, which is, that by a provision in the Consti-

tution, every State, without regard to its population, is entitled to one Representative in the lower House.

3. The adjustment of this matter is all provided for in the Constitution, that is, in its general features; but it devolves upon Congress in every tenth year to re-adjust and re-apportion the Representatives among the several States, according to the population of each State as shown by the last census, which is taken every tenth year; and when the apportionment is once made, it remains the same for the next ten years, when the census is taken again, and a new apportionment is made.

4. Up to the present time (1869,) this has been done nine times. It was done the first time by the convention which formed the Constitution. That apportionment is found in the Constitution, and is as follows:

To New Hampshire,	3	Pennsylvania,	8
Massachusetts,	8	Delaware,	1
Rhode Island,	1	Maryland,	6
Connecticut,	5	Virginia,	10
New York,	6	North Carolina,	5
New Jersey,	4	South Carolina,	5
		Georgia,	3.

By this it will be seen that the first Congress consisted of but 65 members.

The Constitution also provided that the Representatives should not exceed one to every 30,000 people. The next year after the government went into operation, (1790), the first census was taken, and as soon as the result was known, a new apportionment was made. This was done in 1792, and was made upon the ratio of one Representative to every 33,000 of representative* population.

5. In 1800, the second census was taken; and when Congress made the apportionment, which was done in 1803, it did not change the ratio, but left it at one Representative to every 33,000 of the representative population.

In 1810, the third census was taken, and in 1811 the ratio was fixed at one Representative for every 35,000 of the population.

In 1820, the fourth census was taken, and in 1822 Congress fixed the ratio at one Representative for every 40,000 of the population.

In 1830, the fifth census was taken, and in 1832 the ratio was fixed at one Representative to every 47,000 of the population.

In 1840, the sixth census was taken, and in 1842 Congress again declared that the ratio should be one Representative to every 70,000 of the population.

6. In 1850, the seventh census was taken, and in conformity with the law passed this year, the number of members was for the first time limited; the limit being 233; and the Secretary of the Interior was ordered to take the census returns, and divide the whole representative population by the number 233, and to make the quotient the ratio between the Representatives and the people.

7. We have never seen the result of the Secretary's estimate, but, taking the population of 1850 and di-

* The Representative population includes all free persons, white or black; to which (according to the provisions of the Constitution), three-fifths of all the slaves were to be added. But this proviso, now that slavery is abolished, has become a nullity.

viding it by 233, would produce a quotient of nearly 94,000; and this we take as the ratio, after the time when it was done, in 1852; that is, one Representative to every 94,000 of the population.

8. In 1860, the eighth and last census was taken, and by the foregoing rule one Representative was allowed for every 127,000 of the population.

In 1850 Congress adopted the principle of permanently fixing the number of members of Congress, to save the trouble of doing it as heretofore, every ten years. An act was passed limiting it to 233; but notwithstanding this limitation, it was provided that if any new State came in, it should have its member, which would add to the number. But this increase was to continue no longer than until the next apportionment, when the number was to fall back again to the old figure.

But in 1862 this law was modified so as to make the whole number of members to consist of 241 after the 3d of March, 1863, because it was found that by this number a closer approximation to an equality between the States, on the basis of their population, could be attained than by the number 233. And here it stands now, at 241, with its numbers apportioned among the several States as follows:

Alabama,	6	Mississippi,	5
Arkansas,	3	Missouri,	9
California,	3	New Hampshire,	3
Connecticut,	4	New Jersey,	5
Delaware,	1	New York,	31
Florida,	1	North Carolina,	7
Georgia,	7	Ohio,	19

Illinois,	14	Oregon,	1
Indiana,	11	Pennsylvania,	24
Iowa,	6	Rhode Island,	2
Kansas,	1	South Carolina,	4
Kentucky,	9	Tennessee,	8
Louisiana,	5	Texas,	4
Maine,	5	Vermont,	3
Maryland,	5	Virginia,	8
Massachusetts,	10	West Virginia,	3
Michigan,	6	Wisconsin,	6
Minnesota,	2		

9. Nevada and Nebraska have been admitted as States since this apportionment, with one member each, so that the House at present consists of 243 members; and if other new States should come in before 1870, they also will each bring in one member. But after 1870, according to the present law, the number will be brought back again to 241. But it must be borne in mind that Congress has the power to alter all this, and to enact that Congress shall consist of any other number of members, although it is not probable that this will be done soon.

10. We have taken the pains to make all the foregoing statements, not so much to show how the House of Representatives is *now* organized, as to show the general plan upon which it is constituted, and to show how the several States are constantly changing the number of their Representatives, and consequently their relative power and influence in Congress. This can be readily understood by remembering the fact that new States come into the Union every few years, and that the population increases much more rapidly

in the Western States than in the Eastern, and that, consequently, the West is rapidly gaining power in Congress, while the Atlantic States are losing it.

11. One other remark in regard to the number of members of which the House is composed, may properly be made here; and that is, that in the apportionment no regard is had to the Territories or to their population. In this adjustment, the States and their population only are regarded, and the number of members is all given to the States. Every Representative from a Territory is an addition to that number, but it must be remembered that a Territorial member has no right to vote on any question, but has only the right to debate; and for this reason he is not, in the fullest sense, a member, and is not counted in adjusting the number of which the House is made to consist.

CHAPTER XXIX.

Census.

1. A CENSUS is an enumeration, or counting, of the inhabitants of any country. History informs us that this was done in very ancient times. One of the books in the Old Testament (Numbers) was named from the circumstance that it contains an account of the numbering of the Israelites, by the order of Moses. That numbering was a *census* of the people composing the Jewish nation. It not only gives us the total number of the people, but that of each tribe; much after our own mode of doing the same thing. We take ours by States, and we find the total of the whole nation. In ancient times, a census seems to have been taken more for military than for any other purpose. This is one of the objects in the present day; but in modern times many uses are made of a census. It not only shows the military power of a nation, but when taken with the distinctions of sex, and age, with an account of the births, marriages, and deaths during each year, it throws much light upon a variety of interesting topics; such as the longevity, the rate of mortality, the ratio of increase and the average duration of human life. These and many other important facts are obtained by a census.

2. In the United States the census is the only means by which Congress determines the number of Representatives each State is entitled to have in that body.

Hence the Constitution itself makes provision for the enumeration of the people once in ten years,—called a decade. The first was made in 1790, the next in 1800, and so on every tenth year. If the number of any year ends with a cipher, we know that the United States census was taken, or will be taken in that year, whether we look backward or forward.

3. Up to the present time (1869), according to the provisions made in the Constitution, a census has been taken eight times, and under the head of recapitulation on page 120, we find what it was each time. We also find that from the first (1790), to the last (1860), the population had increased from 3,929,827, to 31,747,514. At the present time it approximates nearly to 40,000,000; indicating a growth unparalleled by any nation in ancient or modern times.

We will next state how this great national work is performed. The Constitution simply declares that it shall be done, but the laws specify *how* it shall be done, and *who* shall do it.

The United States Marshals are the officers designated by the law, as the persons who shall make the enumeration of the people in each State and Territory; in addition to which they are also required to procure other statistical matter, as directed by Congress.

4. In order to accomplish this work, it is necessary to employ a number of assistant marshals, one of whom must visit every house in his district, and ascertain the number of persons belonging to it, together with such statistical information as is required. This

is all returned to the marshal, and by him sent to the Department of the Interior at Washington, where, under the direction of the Secretary of the Interior, it is made into a report, and then laid before Congress, to be used by it in apportioning to the States their quota of Representatives. This apportionment is actually made in the Department of the Interior, and then laid before Congress, for its examination and approval. The marshal appoints and commissions his deputies, who must be sworn to perform the duties assigned to them, to the best of their ability.

5. In the Department of the Interior, there is a board whose duty it is to superintend the work of taking the census. It prepares, prints, and sends to every marshal the blanks to be used by him and his assistants; and when they have made returns of their work, the board arranges them preparatory to laying them before Congress. After this they are published, and make a very valuable work of reference; for they contain a vast amount of statistical information; such as the number of acres of land under cultivation, the number of bushels of grain of every kind produced in the year; the number of horses, cattle, sheep, swine, &c., raised; the number of manufacturing establishments, and the amount of their productions; the number of churches, schools, colleges, &c.; the number of deaf, blind, idiotic and insane persons; together with much other matter, quite too voluminous for insertion here.

6. All this is done by order of Congress, and of course paid for from the United States Treasury.

We annex a tabular statement of the population of each State and Territory, at each time the census has been taken by the United States. It shows the increase at each decade, from 1790 to 1860, together with the increase of the number of States and Territories.

POPULATION AT DIFFERENT PERIODS.

STATES.	1790.	1800.	1810.	1820.	1830.	1840.	1850.	1860.
Alabama	....	....	....	127,901	309,527	590,756	771,623	64,201
Arkansas	....	....	....	14,255	30,388	97,574	209,897	35,450
California	....	....	....	....	....	....	92,597	65,439
Connecticut.	238,141	251,202	262,042	275,102	297,675	309,978	370,792	60,147
Delaware	59,096	64,273	72,674	72,749	76,748	78,085	91,532	112,216
Florida	....	....	....	....	34,730	54.477	87,445	140,425
Georgia	82,548	162,101	252,433	340,983	516,823	691,392	906,185	1,057,286
Illinois	....	....	12,282	55,102	157,445	476,183	857,470	1,711,951
Indiana	....	4,875	24,520	147,178	343,031	685,866	988,416	1,350,428
Iowa	....	....	....	....	....	43,112	192,214	674,913
Kansas	....	....	....	....	....	....	....	107,206
Kentucky	73,077	220,955	406,511	564,135	687,917	779,828	982.405	1,155,684
Louisiana	....	....	76,556	152,923	215,739	352,411	517,762	708,002
Maine	96,540	151,719	228,705	98,269	399.455	501,793	583,169	628,279
Maryland	319,728	341,584	380,546	407.350	447,040	470,019	583,034	687,049
Mass'chus'ts	378,717	423,245	472,040	523,159	610,408	737,699	994,514	1,231,066
Michigan	....	....	4,762	8,765	31,639	212,267	397,654	749,113
Minnesota	....	....	....	....	....	....	6,077	172,123
Mississippi	....	8,850	40,352	75,448	136,621	375,651	606,526	791,303
Missouri	....	....	20,845	66,577	140.455	383,702	682,044	1,182,012
N. H.	141,899	183,762	214,360	244,022	269,328	284,574	317,976	326,073
N. J.	184,139	211,949	245,555	277.426	320,823	373,306	489,555	672,035
New York	340,120	586,756	959,049	1,372,111	1,918,608	2,428,921	3,097,394	3,880,735
N. Carolina	393,751	478,103	555,500	638,829	737,987	753,419	869,039	992,622
Ohio	....	45,365	230,760	581,295	937,903	1,519,467	1,980,329	2,339,511
Oregon	....	....	....	....	....	....	13,294	52,465
Penn.	434,373	602,361	810,091	1,047,507	1,348,233	1,724,033	2,311,786	2,906,115
RhodeIsland	69,110	69,122	77,031	83,015	97,199	108.830	147,545	174,620
S. Carolina	249,073	245,591	415,115	402,741	581,185	594,398	668.507	703,708
Tennessee	35,791	105,602	261,727	22,761	681,904	829,210	1,002.717	1,109,801
Texas	....	....	....	....	....	....	212,592	604,215
Vermont,	85,416	154,465	217,713	235,749	280,652	291,948	314.120	315 098
Virginia	748,308	880,200	974,622	1,065,129	1,211,405	1,239.797	1.421,661	1,596,318
Wisconsin	....	....	....	....	....	30,945	305,391	775,881
Territories.								
Colorado	....	....	....	....	....	....	....	36,538
Dakota	....	....	....	....	....	....	....	2,576
Nebraska	....	....	....	....	....	....	....	28,841
Nevada	....	....	....	....	....	....	....	17,364
New Mexico	....	....	....	....	....	....	61,547	83,009
Utah	....	....	....	....	....	....	11,380	40,699
Washington.	....	....	....	....	....	....	....	11,168
Dist. of Col.	....	14,093	24,023	33,039	39,834	43,712	51,687	75,080

Total Population in 1790........ 3,929,827
" " " 1800........ 5,305,937
" " " 1810........ 7,239,814
" " " 1820........ 9.638,191
" " " 1830........ 12,866.020
" " " 1840........ 17,069,453
" " " 1850........ 23,191,876
" " " 1860........ 31,443,321
To which add Indians and others in Indian territory, not included in Census.. 304.192
Grand Total in 1860........ 31,747,514

CHAPTER XXX.

The United States Flag.

1. The United States flag, "the stars and stripes," is too familiar an object to require much description; for every body has seen it, and almost every one has admired it. And no wonder, for it is the handsomest flag in the world,—Red, White and Blue;—those alternate red and white stripes in beautiful contrast with the blue field bedecked with stars;—as though a piece of the sky had been taken to add more beauty to our national emblem which makes it in truth, "The star-spangled banner."

2. But there is a little history about it, which it is well to know. In 1794, when there were only fifteen States, Congress passed an act declaring that the flag of the United States should consist of fifteen stripes, alternate red and white, and that the union be fifteen stars, white in a blue field. The stars and stripes were by this act to be equal in number. But this act was repealed by another, passed in 1818, which declared that it should consist of only thirteen stripes, alternate red and white; and that the Union be twenty stars; and that upon the admission of every new State into the Union, one star be added to the union of the flag. This has been done, and now there are thirty-seven stars in the blue field. By this arrangement our flag is, and always will be emblematic of two things; the thirteen stripes indicate the thirteen original States, while the stars show, and will always show, the numbet of States in the Federal Union. The stars will continue to increase until the last State shall be added; and when thus completed, will probably form a constellation of fifty or more stars, representing so many States.

CHAPTER XXXI.

The Laws of the United States.

1. A CLEARER and more comprehensive idea of the laws under which we live, may be obtained by a sort of analysis of them, or a division of them into their several kinds. By this process we shall find four different laws, emanating from four different sources or authorities; each having the power to enact, and to demand obedience to its enactments.

The first of these is the Constitution of the United States. This is considered as an enactment of the people themselves; for it was made by their Representatives chosen for that purpose, and afterwards ratified by them through another body of their Representatives, viz., the Legislatures of the several States. In the Constitution itself we find a large body of laws, and those of the most important and essential character; for they not only bind every person in the country, but they bind Congress itself, which is the law making power of the Government.

2. The whole body of the law found in the Constitution is called "Constitutional law." It is of the highest authority, and paramount to all other laws, excepting the laws of God. Statute laws may be changed or repealed at any time by the same power that enacted them, but the Constitution cannot be changed except by a vote of two-thirds of both Houses of Congress, and the approval of three-fourths of all the Legislatures of the States in the Uuion. Thus it takes a long time to change or

amend it, and no one body of men can alter it; but any amendment must have the approval of all the Legislative bodies above named. Then it is deemed to have been sanctioned by three-fourths of the people themselves, for it is done by their immediate Representatives. So much, for one kind of law.

3. The next in order are the laws enacted by Congress. These, like all laws make by legislative bodies are denominated statute laws. These laws, while in force, are as binding as those found in the Constitution. But this distinction must be observed; the statutes as before stated may be amended or wholly repealed at any time when Congress is in session, and may be set aside by the Supreme Court in case they are found to be contrary to any of the provisions of the Constitution. All the laws enacted by Congress, unless they are for some local object, are equally binding in every State and Territory of the United States; and are uniformly applied and executed in all, by the United States courts. The foregoing remark shows us the wide difference between an act of Congress which extends to, and embraces the whole national domain; and an act of a State Legislature, which has no authority or power beyond the limits of the State where it was enacted,

4. The laws contained in the Constitution are few in number in comparison with the statute laws. These are exceedingly numerous, and are made to meet the necessities and wants of the people in all their relations to the government and to each other; to regulate the army, the navy, our diplomatic intercourse with foreign nations, and in short everything which requires legis-

lative interference; while those relate only to the fundamental principles on which the government is based, and may be compared to an outline map, which only shows the boundaries and some of the principal mountains, rivers, cities and other prominent features of the country intended to be delineated.

5. Thus much for Constitutional and statute laws. We will now notice another kind, quite different from either in the mode of enactment, but just as binding on Congress, the Executive, the Judiciary, and on every citizen as any Constitutional provision, or act of Congress. We mean the various treaties made between us and foreign nations, and Indian tribes. Treaties when made and ratified by the respective governments by which they are made, are of the same authority and as binding upon the citizens of both countries, as any Constitutional or statutory law in existence; and any violation of the provisions of a treaty between us and any foreign power is made punishable, as much as the violation of any statute upon the books. This of course applies to individual citizens. If the treaty be violated by either of the national authorities, it then becomes a subject of diplomatic arrangement, or may lead to a war between the governments concerned. We have thus disposed of the third kind of law, according to our mode of division.

6. At the commencement of this chapter we spoke of four kinds of laws to which the citizens of the United States are subject. The three already noticed are by far the most important, whereas the fourth—the laws of nations—are, so far as individuals are con-

cerned, of minor importance, as they relate rather to the duties of governments and their agents, to the duties and obligations of armies, and of naval commanders in times of war. All these, with many other matters, are regulated according to the law of nations, which law is not a series of enactments of any law-making power of any government upon earth, but consists of rules laid down by the great writers upon this subject, as rules or laws which should regulate the conduct of one nation towards another, according to the admitted principles of right and humanity, especially in times of war. These laws and principles have been approved of and sanctioned by almost all civilized nations, and hence have been denominated "the law of nations," and are observed by all governments of civilized countries who wish to sustain an honorable character among the family of nations. The violation of the law of nations exposes the violator to the condemnation of the world, and to the danger of retaliation by war with the injured nation.

7. While on the subject of laws, it will not be irrelevant to say that the United States courts, and especially the Supreme Court, are the expounders of the laws of the country, and of the "law of nations" whenever they apply to matters in which our government or our citizens are concerned. The courts themselves make no laws, but by their decisions in cases adjudicated by them, they declare what is the true meaning and intention of the Constitution and the laws. They declare how these should be understood, construed and applied. Hence the decisions of the courts are

regarded with almost as much deference as the laws themselves, determining, as they do, the interpretation and true meaning of them.

8. In the foregoing remarks we have made no allusion to the laws of the States, which have no authority or power outside of the State by which they are enacted; and shall not do so now, as it would be foreign to the object of our work. We therefore will close the chapter on this subject with the addition of a single remark, that every person in the United States lives under two distinct and separate governments and codes of law, viz.: First, the United States government and its laws; and, second, the government and laws of the State where he resides.

9. But how is a conflict between the laws of the United States and the laws of the States avoided?

Answer—By the following Constitutional provision, found in the sixth article of that instrument, and in these words:

"This Constitution, and *the laws of the United States*, which shall be made in pursuance thereof, and all treaties made or which shall be made under the authority of the United States, *shall be the supreme law of the land*, and the judges in every State shall be bound thereby, anything in the Constitution or laws of any State to the contrary notwithstanding." This answers the question. The Constitution, treaties with foreign nations, and the laws enacted by Congress, are supreme, and override any law passed by any State, if it conflicts with any of these. The United States courts, and the courts of any State, are bound to disregard and set aside any State law in case it is found to be contrary to the United States laws.

CHAPTER XXXII.

Naturalization Laws.

1. By far the greater part of the people in the United States are natives of the country, and are, consequently, citizens by birthright. They have all the rights and privileges which the government affords, without being required to do anything to procure them. A native citizen has the right to vote, the right to buy, hold and sell lands, and the right to protection by his government when in a foreign country or upon the high seas. But an alien does not enjoy these rights. An alien is one who was born in some foreign country, and before he can be a citizen, he must remain in the country at least five years; and then must, in addition to this, do such things as our naturalization laws require of him. After he has done this he becomes a citizen, and has all the rights of a native, with this exception—he never can be President or Vice President of the United States, because the Constitution positively declares that both of these high officers shall be native citizens, and the one exception to this provision has no application now.

2. The United States have always pursued a very liberal policy towards aliens, or foreigners, as they are sometimes called, for they have enacted laws easily complied with, by which any alien may become a citizen, after which he possesses the same rights as a native, with the exception before stated.

WHAT AN ALIEN MUST DO TO BECOME A CITIZEN.

3. The Constitution authorizes Congress to pass such laws as it may judge right and proper on the subject of naturalization. This has been done from time to time. The first act of this kind was passed in 1790, since which various other acts have been passed modifying the first.

An alien, in order to become a citizen, must go before some United States court, or some court of record of some State, at least two years before his admission, and then and there declare under oath that it is his intention to become a citizen of the United States, and must renounce all allegiance and fidelity to any foreign prince, potentate, State or sovereignty whatever, and particularly by name, the prince, potentate, State or sovereignty whereof such alien may, at the time, be a citizen or subject.

4. And at the time he is admitted he must, before some of the courts before named, again swear to the same things, with the addition that he will support the Constitution of the United States. When all this is done, the court before whom the oath is taken, and the renunciation made, makes a record of the proceedings, and gives the person naturalized a certificate that he was made a citizen by the said court at the time and place therein named. This certificate gives him all the rights of citizenship in any State or Territory in the United States. All laws relating to naturalization are made by Congress. No State has the right to pass any law on this subject. Yet Congress confers authority on the State courts to naturalize an alien.

Indeed, State courts naturalize more than the United States courts. But Congress should not allow State courts to naturalize at all, because such monstrous frauds have been perpetrated by them in some of the States.

5. In addition to what we have said on this subject, it should be stated that an alien must, in all cases, have lived in the country five years before he can be admitted to citizenship. But in 1862 an act was passed making an exception to this requirement in favor of any person who was twenty-one years of age, and had enlisted, or who should thereafter enlist in the army, and be honorably discharged therefrom. In such cases, a good moral character, with *one* year's residence, without any previous declaration of intention, was sufficient. Our naturalization laws require good moral character in all cases of those who apply for admission to citizenship. But the courts have been exceedingly remiss in this matter, and almost everybody who makes application is admitted to this exalted privilege without any regard to the character of the applicant.

The law requires that if an alien has borne any title of nobility in the country from whence he came, he must renounce such title before he can be made a citizen of the United States.

6. There is an exception to what is above stated in the definition of an alien; that is, that he is one who was born in some foreign country. A child may be born out of the United States; yet if its parents, at the time of its birth, were citizens, the child is also a citizen by

virtue of its parent's citizenship, and, consequently, never needs naturalization to possess all the rights it would have, had it been born in the United States.

7. In this connection another provision of our naturalization laws should be noticed; and that is, that children born in a foreign country, and of foreign parentage, become citizens of the United States without personal naturalization, upon the following conditions: *First*, that they came into the country before they are twenty-one years of age; and *Second*, that their father became a naturalized citizen before they have reached that age—that is, the naturalization of the father makes all his children citizens who reside in the country, and are under the age of twenty-one at the time of the parent's naturalization. This is a very liberal provision of the law in favor of the minor children of those who become citizens.

CHAPTER XXXIII.

Neutrality Laws.

1. The neutrality laws of the United States, like those of other nations which have enacted them, have the same design and are intended to accomplish the same object; which is, to preserve peace, and to maintain friendly relations with other nations, States or powers. It is the duty, the interest, and should be the policy of all governments, to live in peace with other nations, whenever it can be done without the sacrifice of honor or self-preservation. It is the duty of every government so to control the actions of its own citizens or subjects, as not to allow them to perpetrate such acts towards other governments as would tend to embroil the two countries in a war, or to disturb their friendly relations and intercourse.

The most civilized and enlightened nations have for this purpose enacted neutrality laws, which if obeyed by the citizens of the country that enacts them, do much to prevent wars and unfriendly feelings between nations.

2. A single illustration will, perhaps, place the whole scope, design and nature of neutrality laws in a clearer light, than a verbose recital of, or commentary upon their provisions. Our illustration may be thus put; A, B and C, we suppose to be three different nations. A and B are at war with each other, but both on friendly terms with C. Now C, by her neutrality

laws, prohibits her citizens or subjects within her territory from enlisting or fitting out men, or organizing any expedition by sea or land to aid either of the belligerent nations, A or B; because this would be a hostile act towards the other, and might lead to a war between it and C.

The neutrality laws of the United States, now in force, were enacted in 1818, and are very similar in their provisions to laws of other nations upon the same subject, and are declaratory of the pre-existing laws of nations.

3. These laws, however, do not prohibit the citizens of the United States from leaving their country, and then enlisting or engaging in war upon either side. It does not prohibit a citizen from leaving his country; and after he has left it, the government has no control over him. Hence, in spite of neutrality laws, it is no uncommon thing to find the subjects of governments engaging in a war against a nation with which their own government is at peace. The violation of the law consists in accepting an office, or enlisting, or procuring enlistments or fitting out expeditions by sea or land, while in the United States.

By our law this is declared to be a high misdemeanor, and is punishable by fine and imprisonment. The President of the United States is authorized to employ either the land or naval force of the country to prevent any hostile expedition against any nation, state, colony or people, which are at peace with us.

CHAPTER XXXIV.

Elections.

1. One of the cardinal principles upon which our government is founded, and one to which the people adhere with the greatest tenacity, is that governments derive their just powers from the consent of the governed; and although all the people cannot in person be present to approve or to disapprove of the laws by which they are to be governed, yet under our form of government we approximate as nearly to such a condition of things as is practicable. This is effected by the Representative system. A few are chosen who represent the wishes and sentiments of the many

The men chosen to make and administer our laws, are not so chosen from the personal regard the people have for them; but for the principles they are known to entertain, and which correspond with those of the people who choose them. The Representative is bound to carry out the sentiments of those who elect him, and to do what they would do if they acted for themselves.

2. From this principle it becomes a matter of the first importance to know what the will of the people is in regard to the various questions which arise from time to time, relating to the policy of the government, and the laws to be enacted to carry out that policy. The means used to determine these questions are our elections. These are looked to with great interest,

and sometimes with great excitement, as they furnish the only occasions in which the mass of the people can act upon the government, by electing such men as they want to make and administer their laws. Hence at the close of our elections it is pretty well known what measures are to be pursued, by the principles of the men elected.

3. These remarks, however, apply with greater force to the State governments, and to the election of State officers than to the officers of the United States; for Congressmen are indeed the only officials in the general government for whom the people directly vote. Though it is often said that the President is elected by them, this is not strictly correct. The people do not vote directly for either President or Vice President. They vote for electors, and these electors vote for those officers. This, it is true, is but a circuitous way of reaching the same result; for the electors have always faithfully carried out the wishes of their constituents, and voted for the same candidates for whom the people would have voted if our constitutional forms allowed them to vote directly for these candidates, without the intervening and cumbrous machinery of Presidential electors. We think a great improvement in the *modus operandi* would be effected by such a change in our Constitution as would give the election directly to the people.

4. There is some analogy between the election of the President and the election of the United States Senators. In the first instance the people choose electors, and these elect the President; in the latter,

the people elect the members of their Legislatures, and these elect the Senators. Then, as to the other officers of the general government, they are appointed by their superiors: the most important ones by the President, by and with the advice and consent of the Senate, and the minor ones by the heads of departments, or some one higher in rank than the appointees. Thus we see that, with the exception of the members of the House of Representatives, the people do not vote directly for any of the officials of the United States government. Yet by this kind of proxy vote, about the same result is obtained.

5. Of all our elections none is considered of so much importance as the Presidential. These come, as before said, every four years, because the Constitution provides that the term for which a President is chosen, shall be four years. We have thought it would be quite interesting to some of our readers, and at the same time would help to preserve the political history of our nation, to give a brief account of each Presidential election, together with the names of the candidates and some of the prominent circumstances connected with them. This will be found in the following chapter, and we hope will materially aid those who wish to know something of the men and times gone by. Our elections, both for the general and State governments, are by ballot, instead of *viva voce*, (the living voice), as in some countries.

The ballot is a small piece of paper, with the name of the candidate or candidates printed or written upon it, and then folded in such a manner as to hide them, so that no one but the voter can tell what names are on his ballot. A vote by *viva voce*, is when the voter, in the presence of the inspectors of the election, audibly and clearly calls out the name of the candidate for whom he votes, and thus proclaims in the hearing of all present how he votes. But the ballot enables the voter to vote secretly if he chooses to do so.

6. Our elections for President, for Congressmen, for Governors of the several States and their respective Legislatures, are more exciting than those for other minor officers. Much is said and much is written of a very inflammatory character. The liberty of the press and the liberty of speech are most shamefully perverted, sometimes into abuse and slander. When these vicious practices shall cease, as we hope they will, the government will stand on firmer ground than it now does.

CHAPTER XXXV.

Presidential Elections, with notices of Facts and Circumstances connected with them.

THE convention which formed the Constitution of the United States, fixed upon the first Wednesday of January, 1789, for the election of the first Presidential electors, and the first Wednesday of February of the same year for the election of the first President, and the first Wednesday of March (which was the fourth), for putting the new government into operation. The election of the electors, and of the President by them, were carried out to the letter; but the government did not get into operation until the 30th April, nearly two months after the specified time, for the elected Members of Congress were tardy in convening at New York (the place fixed upon for the first session); and it was not until the 30th of April, that Washington was inaugurated as President. But as the fourth of March was the time which it was intended that it should take place, it was reckoned as the date from which Washington's administration commenced; and the date both of the commencement and termination of every Presidential term since. Hence, the fourth of March of every fourth year is an important epoch in our political history, as it is the time when a new administration comes into power, or the commencement of the second term of an incumbent who has been re-elected.

FIRST ELECTION, 1789.

George Washington was unanimously elected President, and John Adams, Vice President. The Vice Presidency at this and the three succeeding elections, was determined according to the provisions of the Constitution, as it then stood; which were, that the candidate for President who received the highest number of votes should be President; and he who received the next highest should be Vice President. But this provision was changed by the twelfth amendment, proposed in 1803, which went into effect at the next election, 1804. Previous to that we hear nothing of any candidate for Vice President. By the provisions of said amendment, the electors vote one name for President and another for Vice President. But previous to that, the electors voted for two candidates without designating which for President, or which for Vice President, knowing that the one receiving the largest number would have the first place, and the next highest the second. This caused much confusion and uncertainty as to the intentions of the electors. After four elections conducted upon this plan, the Constitution was amended; since which, without change, all the elections have been conducted as directed in this amendment.

In our comments on the first election we may as well notice another great change which has gradually taken place in regard to the mode of choosing the electors. The Constitution says that the Presidential electors shall be appointed, in each State, in such manner as the Legislature thereof shall direct. Now this left the

Legislature with power to appoint them itself, or to order their appointment or election in any other way. The electors for the first Presidential election, we think (though we have seen no historical record of the fact), were all chosen by the State Legislatures; but soon after we find that different methods were used in different States. In some, the Legislatures chose them; in others they were elected by popular vote; and it seems that this plan was the one most approved of, for it finally became almost universal, and was adopted by every State except South Carolina, which never did give this election to the people, (at least not before the Rebellion). For these reasons we cannot give the popular vote of the earlier Presidential elections, as we have done of those in later years; because the people in several of the States did not directly vote for electors. When we have given it, it must be remembered that South Carolina is not included.

But eleven States participated in the first election. North Carolina and Rhode Island had not at this time ratified the Constitution; consequently they could take no part in it. At this time political parties were very indistinctly defined. The only noticable political difference consisted in approval or disapproval of the new Constitution. Its friends were called Federalists, among whom Washington was numbered. Those who had opposed the adoption of the Constitution were called anti-Federalists. At the first election there were but sixty-nine electors.

SECOND ELECTION, 1792.

Washington and Adams were both re-elected to

the same positions for a second term. Washington was again unanimously elected. Vermont and Kentucky had both been admitted into the Union since the last election; which made fifteen States that took part in this. At the second election there were one hundred and thirty-two electors.

THIRD ELECTION, 1796.

There were four candidates in the field at this time for the office of President of the United States, viz.: John Adams, Thomas Jefferson, Aaron Burr and Thomas Pinckney.

Adams	received	71	electoral	votes.
Jefferson	"	69	"	"
Pinckney	"	59	"	"
Burr	"	38	"	"

This result made Adams President, and Jefferson Vice President.

A new State—Tennessee—had been admitted since the last election, which made sixteen in the Union at this time.

FOURTH ELECTION, 1800.

The same four candidates were again in the field at this election; Adams and Pinckney as Federalists, and Jefferson and Burr as anti-Federalists, who about this time took the name of Republicans.

Jefferson and Burr	received 73	of the electoral votes.	
Adams	"	64	"
Pinckney	"	63	"

No one having received a majority, the election, according to the provisions made in the Constitution, went to the House of Representatives, for the first time. The result was that Jefferson was elected President, and Aaron Burr, Vice President. This result was not effected until the thirty-sixth ballot, and occupied seven days. The contest was between Jefferson and Burr, the two candidates who had received the highest vote of the electors.

No new States had been admitted since the last election, so there were but sixteen which participated in this.

The result of this election proved the complete overthrow of the Federal party; and it never regained its power.

FIFTH ELECTION, 1804.

The twelfth amendment of the Constitution having been duly ratified before this election, we now, in accordance with its provisions, for the first time find candidates for the Vice Presidency brought forward.

Mr. Burr having been dropped, Thomas Jefferson and George Clinton were put forth by the Republicans for President and Vice President, and Charles C. Pinckney and Rufus King by the Federalists, for the same positions.

Jefferson and Clinton each received 162 of the electoral votes.

Pinckney and King only received 14 votes.

The admission of Ohio, in 1802, made seventeen States in the Union at this election.

SIXTH ELECTION, 1808.

Mr. Jefferson, after having served two terms, retired; and James Madison was nominated by the

Republican party for President. With this change, candidates were the same on both sides as at the former election.

Madison received 122 electoral votes for President, and Clinton 113 for Vice President.

The latter died April 20, 1812, and consequently did not serve out his full second term.

Pinckney and King each received 47 electoral votes.

No new State had been admitted since the last election; consequently but seventeen States participated in Madison's first election.

SEVENTH ELECTION, 1812.

Mr. Madison was re-elected President and Elbridge Gerry, Vice President. But he died on the twenty-third of November, 1814, leaving the Vice Presidency vacant for the second time during Madison's administration. Mr. Madison's second term was distinguished on account of the second war with England, which continued from 1812 to 1815.

De Witt Clinton and Jared Ingersoll were run in opposition to Madison and Gerry, who received each 128 electoral votes. Clinton 89, and Ingersoll 57.

There were eighteen States at this time. Louisiana had been admitted since the last election.

EIGHTH ELECTION, 1816.

The same party which had twice elected Jefferson, and twice elected Madison, now put James Monroe up as their candidate for President, and Daniel D. Tompkins for Vice President.

A very feeble opposition was made by the Federalists,

who again nominated and ran Rufus King. But he only received 34 votes, while Monroe received 183.

In the early part of this year, Indiana was admitted as a State, making nineteen in the Union at this election.

NINTH ELECTION, 1820.

Monroe and Tompkins were both re-elected without opposition. Their term of office did not expire until the 4th of March, 1825, making twenty-four years in succession during which the Republicans (who about this time denominated themselves Democrats), had held the reins of government in their hands. All three of the Presidents held the office for two terms, and were all Virginians.

Between 1816 and 1820, four new States had been admitted, viz.: Mississippi, Illinois, Alabama, and Maine, making twenty-three which took a part in Mr. Monroe's second election.

TENTH ELECTION, 1824.

At this time there were four candidates for the office of President, viz.:

Andrew Jackson,	who received	99	of the	electoral votes.
John Quincy Adams,	"	84	"	"
William H. Crawford,	"	41	"	"
Henry Clay,	"	31	"	"

Neither of the candidates having received a majority, the election for the second time went to the House, where the vote was taken by States, Adams receiving 13, Jackson 7, and Crawford 4 votes. Mr Adams was elected President.

John C. Calhoun, against whom there had been very

little opposition, had been elected by the electors by a large majority.

Twenty-four States participated in this election, Missouri having been admitted since the last. But only eighteen of them chose their electors by popular vote. Six of them continued to elect them by their Legislatures.

ELEVENTH ELECTION, 1828.

At this election Andrew Jackson succeeded to the Presidency, and John C. Calhoun was re-elected Vice President.

The opposition candidate for President was John Quincy Adams, and for Vice President, Richard Rush.

Jackson received 650,028 of the popular, and 178 of the electoral votes; and Adams received 512,158 of the popular, and 83 of the electoral votes. This was perhaps the most strongly contested and most bitter election that ever transpired in this country.

No new State had been admitted since 1824, so there were but twenty-four States in the Union at this election.

TWELFTH ELECTION, 1832.

Andrew Jackson was re-elected President, and Martin Van Buren Vice President, by the Democratic party.

Henry Clay was the opposing Whig candidate for the Presidency, and John Sergeant, of Pennsylvania, for the Vice Presidency.

Of the popular vote,	Jackson	received	682,502
"	Clay	"	550,189
		Jackson's majority,	132,313

Of the electoral vote, Jackson received 219, and Clay, 49.

There had been no increase of States since the last election, so but twenty-four States voted at this.

THIRTEENTH ELECTION, 1836.

The Democrats nominated their Vice President for the office of President, and Richard M. Johnson, for that of Vice President, at this election.

Gen. William Henry Harrison and several other candidates, without concert of action or unanimity of design, were run in opposition to Van Buren, but he had a majority over all.

The popular vote stood for Van Buren,	762,149
For Harrison and others,	736,736
Van Buren's majority,	25,413

Michigan and Arkansas were admitted early in this year, which made twenty-six States at the period of this election.

FOURTEENTH ELECTION, 1840.

The same candidates were again nominated at this election that ran at the last; with this exception, that the Whigs dropped all others and concentrated on General Harrison.

Hence the opposing ticket stood:

Whig—William Henry Harrison, for President, and John Tyler for Vice President.

Democratic—Martin Van Buren, for President, and Richard M. Johnson, for Vice President.

The popular vote showed this result:

For Harrison,	1,274,783
" Van Buren,	1,128,702
Harrison's majority,	46,081

This was one of the most exciting elections ever known in the United States. The Whigs adopted the practice of singing political songs at their meetings. It was called "The Log-Cabin and Hard-Cider Campaign," because the Whigs built log cabins and held their meetings in them, and drank hard cider, to burlesque the remark of a Democrat, that General Harrison lived in a log cabin and drank hard cider.

He lived only one month and two days after his inauguration; and John Tyler became acting President, in conformity with the provisions of the Constitution, which were now applied for the first time since the government was established.

No new State had been added since 1836, so that the same number acted in this election, as took part in the previous one, viz.: twenty-six.

FIFTEENTH ELECTION, 1844.

The Whig and Democratic parties placed themselves in battle array, with Henry Clay as candidate for President, and Theodore Frelinghuysen for Vice President, on the side of the Whigs; and James K. Polk for President, and George M. Dallas for Vice President, on the Democratic side.

The popular vote at this election showed the following result:

For Polk and Dallas,	1,335,834
" Clay and Frelinghuysen,	1,297,033
Polk's majority,	38,801

The Abolitionists ran Mr. Birney for President, and he received 62,270 votes.

This was the third time Mr. Clay had been a candidate, and the third time he had been defeated, to the great sorrow of a majority of the people of the United States, for many who voted against him on purely party grounds, really desired his election.

The most prominent question at issue between the contending parties at this time was the annexation of Texas, which the Democrats favored, and the Whigs opposed.

Mr. Polk's administration was distinguished by the war between the United States and Mexico, which grew out of the annexation of Texas. Since 1836, there had been no accessions of new States, and hence there were but twenty-six in the Union at this election.

SIXTEENTH ELECTION, 1848.

The political tide turned at this election in favor of the Whigs, or, in the triangular fight, Democrat slaughtered Democrat, and Gen. Taylor won the field. The order of battle was on this wise: the Whigs massed their forces under Gen. Zachary Taylor, while the Democrats divided theirs into two divisions, with as much hostility to each other, as to their old and common enemy the Whigs. Gen. Lewis Cass was at the head of the first and largest division, while Mr.

Van Buren commanded the second and smaller division.

"When Greek meets Greek, then comes the tug of war."
When Democrat meets Democrat, then comes defeat.

But to drop military figures, the respective candidates at this election were: Whig, Zachary Taylor for President, and Millard Fillmore for Vice President; Democrat, Lewis Cass for President, and William O. Butler of Kentucky for Vice President. Free Soil Democrats, Martin Van Buren for President, and Charles F. Adams for Vice President.

After the election, the popular vote showed this result:

Taylor and Fillmore	1,362,024
Cass and Butler	1,222,419
Van Buren and Adams	291,678

Mr. Van Buren opposed the regular Democratic candidate on the ground that he (Van Buren) was opposed to any further extension of slavery, while Mr. Cass and his friends were not.

Gen. Taylor died on the 9th of July, 1850, after administering the government 1 year, 4 months and 4 days, and for the second time since the government was put into operation, the Vice President became the acting President.

Since the year 1844, four new States, viz.: Texas, Florida, Iowa and Wisconsin had been admitted; which made thirty States in the Union at this election.

SEVENTEENTH ELECTION, 1852.

At this election the Democrats regained their lost

power, with Franklin Pierce for their Chief Magistrate, and William R. King* for the second.

The Whigs put General Winfield Scott in nomination for President, and William A. Graham of North Carolina for Vice President.

Pierce and King received	1,590,490	popular votes.
Scott and Graham "	1,378,589	"
Majority for Pierce and King	211,901	

Perhaps no Presidential election ever occurred in the United States, in which there was less interest than in this; for neither party appeared to be very well pleased with their candidates.

This Whig defeat was so disastrous to that party that it disbanded immediately afterwards, and became extinct.

Since 1848, California had been admitted, making thirty-one States at the time of this election.

EIGHTEENTH ELECTION, 1856.

The Presidential campaign of this year was opened with three candidates for the Presidency in the field; as follows:

James Buchanan and John C. Breckenridge, for President and Vice President, on the Democratic side.

As stated in our notice of the election of 1852, the Whig party had become extinct. But a new one had been organized, whose members called themselves Republicans, for the purpose of opposing the further extension of slavery.

*William R. King, of Alabama, died April 18, 1853, and never took his seat.

This party nominated John C. Fremont and William L. Dayton, for President and Vice President.

A fraction of the American party yet remained alive, and they put Millard Fillmore and Andrew J. Donnelson in nomination as their candidates. This party was organized in opposition to the election of foreigners to office.

The popular vote showed this result:

For Buchanan and Breckenridge	1,803,029
" Fremont and Dayton	1,342,164
" Fillmore and Donnelson	874,625

Buchanan was elected, but by a plurality vote. Fremont and Fillmore together had a majority of 413,760 votes; thirty-one States, the same as at the last election, participated in this. Mr. Buchanan's administration is distinguished as the one under which the late rebellion broke out, and which was followed by our civil war. He fell into disgrace by refusing to do anything to suppress the rebellion.

NINETEENTH ELECTION, 1860.

The period for another Presidential election returned in November of this year, and four candidates were put into the field.

Abraham Lincoln, by the Republican party, for President, and Hannibal Hamlin for Vice President.

Stephen A. Douglas, by the Northern Democrats, for President, and Herschel V. Johnson for Vice President.

John C. Breckenridge, by the Southern Democrats, for President, and Joseph Lane for Vice President.

John Bell, by the American party, for President, and Edward Everett for Vice President.

Three candidates against one, so divided the strength of the opposition to Mr. Lincoln, that it insured his election; but by a plurality vote.

The popular vote for	Lincoln and Hamlin was	1,866,452
	Douglas and Johnson	1,375,157
	Breckenridge and Lane	847,953
	Bell and Everett	590,631

The three latter together had a majority of 947,289 votes over Lincoln. The whole vote was much larger than any ever before given at a Presidential election, and amounted to 4,680,193. By the census taken this year, the whole population in the States, including slaves, and excluding the Territories whose population cannot vote for President, was 31,148,048. Two new States, Minnesota and Oregon, had been admitted since the last election, making thirty-three States which voted at this.

The ostensible and prominent questions which divided the supporters of these candidates at this election, were as follows:

Lincoln's opposed the extension of slavery; Breckenridge's favored it.

Douglas's favored the submission of the question to the new States to be admitted; leaving them to decide whether slavery should be allowed in them or not.

Bell's ignored the whole question, and called their platform "The Constitution and the Laws."

TWENTIETH ELECTION, 1864.

The twentieth Presidential election took place this year. Abraham Lincoln was re-nominated by the

Republicans. Mr. Hamlin was dropped for Vice-President, and Andrew Johnson (a Democrat,) was nominated in his place, on account of his loyalty during the rebellion.

Gen. George B. McClellan and George H. Pendleton were nominated by the Democratic party as their candidates for President and Vice President.

The popular vote was as follows:

For Lincoln and Johnson	2,223,035
" McClellan and Pendleton	1,811,754
Total popular vote	4,034,789

This shows more than a half a million less votes than at the election of 1860. The cause of this was that eleven of the Southern States had seceded from the United States in 1860 and 1861, and still continued in that condition; and consequently did not vote at this election. But two new States had been added since the last election, viz.: Kansas and West Virginia. These made 35 States in all, but by deducting the 11 seceded States, only 24 were left to vote at this election.

Mr. Lincoln's administration will long continue to be one of the most distinguished on record, on account of the civil war which raged during the whole period of it.

His assassination, within little more than a month after he had entered upon his second term, filled the nation with sincere mourners, and shocked the moral sense of the world to an extent rarely felt at any previous event.

His death elevated the Vice President to the position of acting President; this being the third instance of the kind in the history of our government.

TWENTY-FIRST ELECTION—1868.

This was the last Presidential election, and will be, until November, 1872.

General Ulysses S. Grant, of Illinois, and Schuyler Colfax, of Indiana, were the Republican candidates for President and Vice President. They were elected by about 300,000 majority of the popular vote.

Horatio Seymour, of New York, and Francis P. Blair, of Missouri, were the Democratic candidates for the same office.

This was the third successive election at which the Republican party succeeded. The two great issues in this contest related to questions affecting the public debt, and the manner of reconstructing the States lately in rebellion.

The Republicans advocated the payment of the public debt in gold—that is, that portion of it which the government had stipulated thus to pay, and the portion, also, which had been generally understood as payable in gold. They also advocated that mode of reconstruction known as the Congressional plan.

Some of the Democrats advocated the payment of the debt in paper money; and as to reconstructing the seceded States, they advocated the plan of Mr. Johnson, the acting President.

The States of Virginia, Mississippi and Texas, took no part in this election, not having complied with the conditions imposed by Congress.

CHAPTER XXXVI.

Electors.

1. An elector, in the broadest sense of the word, means anybody who votes at an election for any person for any office or position, whatever it may be, and who is generally styled a voter. But in a more restricted sense, and that in which it is used here, elector means a person chosen to elect the President and Vice President of the United States. Two different methods have been used to choose these electors, and both were in conformity with the Constitution; for it says that each State shall appoint, in such manner as the Legislature thereof may direct, a number of electors equal to the whole number of Senators and Representatives to which the State may be entitled in Congress. Now this left the Legislatures of the respective States to appoint the electors themselves, or to direct their appointment in any other way. Hence in some States the Legislatures chose them, and in others they passed acts directing their election by the people; and as far down as 1824 in six of the States the Legislatures continued to appoint or elect them themselves; while in all the remaining States their election was given directly to the people, and this method has now become universal in all the States, and is the one which seems to be most approved by the people.

2. These electors, when chosen, must meet in their respective States on the first Wednesday of December —that is, when a Presidential election occurs (which

is every fourth year;) and when assembled, they are denominated the electoral colleges, and vote for one man for President, and another for Vice President; after which these votes are sent to the President of the Senate of the United States by a messenger selected for that express purpose. When this is done, the duties of the electors are completed, and they have nothing more to do in the matter. The college is dissolved, never to meet again. But in four years, at the next Presidential election, a new college will assemble for the same purpose, and to perform the same duty.

3. When these votes reach Washington, the Senate and the House of Representatives assemble together on the second Wednesday in February, and in their presence the votes are opened and counted, and it is then declared who has been elected President and Vice President of the United States for the next four years. Until quite lately the Presidential elections were held in different States on different days; but by an act of Congress, one day for this election is now designated throughout all the States, and that day is the first Tuesday after the first Monday in November. This is the method which the Constitution has declared shall be used in the election of the President; but it is a clumsy and cumbrous piece of machinery—a wheel within a wheel—and we hope it will soon be worn out, and the people will be allowed to vote directly for the candidates they prefer. This would enable them to vote for their choice for Vice President, which they cannot always now do, for the electors are bound to vote for the Vice President who runs on the ticket with the President. Hence if a voter wishes to vote for a certain candidate for President, he must vote for the Vice President who runs on the same ticket, whether he prefers him or not.

CHAPTER XXXVII.

Ambassadors, Foreign Ministers, Charge d'Affaires.

1. FOREIGN Ministers are the representatives of one nation to another, and are the agents used to regulate their political relations and commercial intercourse; to make treaties, and to settle disputes and misunderstandings which may occur between them. The office of a foreign minister is one of great dignity and honor. He ought to have extensive knowlege of national affairs, sound judgment, prudence and wisdom; for by these he may prevent contention, strife and war. This officer is not peculiar to our government, or to our times. Nearly all civilized nations of any standing or importance, both receive and send them, and did so in ancient times.

2. By the laws of nations, ambassadors are exempt from arrest, imprisonment or prosecution; because they are the representatives of the sovereign or nation who sent them. Even their servants are secure from arrest, and their property exempt from seizure for debt. The law of Congress protecting foreign ministers to this country, is but an enactment of what was before known to be the law of nations, all over the civilized world; and a violation of this well recognized law without reparation and satisfaction, would be a cause of war against the offending party.

3. Our own foreign ministers of all grades are ap-

pointed by the President, by and with the advice and consent of the Senate. They are not, however, the representatives of the President, but of the government of the United States. We said of all grades, for there are grades of these officials, different in dignity and power. They are distinguished also by different names which indicate their rank, viz.: Ambassadors, Envoys Extraordinary, and Ministers Plenipotentiary, Ministers Resident, and Chargé d'Affaires.

AMBASSADORS.

4. This title in our country has no very specific meaning. It designates, however, a minister of the highest grade; but does not distinguish between one who goes to reside in the country whither he is sent, and one who is sent for some special purpose; such as that of negotiating a treaty of peace, or some other particular matter with which he is charged, and when that is accomplished returns home. In the latter case he is frequently styled a commissioner, because he was duly authorized, and *commissioned* by his government to act for it; but in both cases the officer is an ambassador, for that word means a person authorized and sent to transact business for his government.

ENVOYS EXTRAORDINARY AND MINISTERS PLENIPOTENTIARY.

5. These titles designate ministers of the highest class; but generally refer to such as go to reside in the country where sent, and with full power to act for their government, in all matters and things of a diplomatic character.

Where negotiations become necessary between the

two nations, permanent ministers of this grade are only sent to great powers—governments of the higher class.

At the present time we have twelve foreign ministers of this class, one in each of the following countries: Austria, Brazil, Chili, China, France, England, Italy, Mexico, Peru, Prussia, Russia, and Spain. Those to England and France, receive in cash $17,500 per year salary, the one to Peru, $10,000, and each of the others $12,000.

MINISTERS RESIDENT.

6. These are not considered so high in rank as those termed envoys extraordinary and ministers plenipotentiary. Yet they are clothed with nearly the same powers, but are sent to countries of less importance, and receive less salaries, viz.: $7,500.

At this time we have twenty of this grade, one in each of the following places: Argentine Confederation, Belgium, Bolivia, Costa Rica, Denmark, Ecuador, Guatemala, Hawaiian Islands, Honduras, Japan, Netherlands, United States of Columbia, Nicaragua, Paraguay, Portugal, Sweden, Norway, Switzerland, Turkey, and Venezuela.

COMMISSIONERS.

7. There are a still lower grade of ministers (if we may call them so), or government agents, who reside abroad. They are sent to look after the interests of our government and its citizens in places of not much importance, and where there is but little to do. They also receive but small pay. We have now but two of them, one in Hayti, and one at Liberia, in Africa.

CHARGE D'AFFAIRES.

8. These officials rank as the lowest grade of ministers or diplomatic officers, and are not clothed with much authority or power, excepting when authorized to act in the room of a minister of higher rank, whose place is for the time being vacant. In this case consuls have been authorized to act in place of ministers; but not unless authorized to do so by the President of the United States.

SECRETARIES OF LEGATION.

9. Secretaries of Legation may with propriety be noticed under the general head of ministers, although they are not ministers of any grade, but are appointed by the same powers that appoint ministers, and accompany them merely as their secretaries. In the absence of a charge d'affaires, they are sometimes authorized to act in his place. The position is not one of great dignity, nor is the compensation large.

CHAPTER XXXVIII.

Consuls.

1. CONSULS are officers not peculiar to our government. They are known and employed by many, if not all of the civilized nations of the world, and are recognized by the law of nations. Their duties and fields of action are always in foreign countries—never at home. Although they are the agents of the government that employs them, yet many of their duties require them to act for and in behalf of the private citizens of their country who may happen to be within their consulate.

2. The Constitution provides that the President and Senate shall appoint all our consuls. The President signs their commissions, which bear the great seal of the United States, and which prove to the government where they are sent that they are duly appointed and authorized to discharge the duties of consuls at the ports or places to which they have been appointed.

3. In order to show the nature of a consul's duties, such as the laws impose upon him, we will state the substance of several acts relating to this subject.

1. Whenever a vessel belonging to a citizen of the United States arrives at the port where he is stationed, it is his duty to receive the ship's papers, and to see if they are all correct.

2. It is his duty to provide for sick, disabled, and destitute American seamen, and to send them home by some vessel going to the United States.

3. He must hear the complaints of seamen, and settle disputes between the captain and men; and for good cause he may discharge the whole ship's crew.

4. It is made his duty to receive and take care of the personal property of any citizen of the United States who has died within his consulate, and to send any balance which may be left after paying his debts and necessary expenses, to the Treasury of the United States, to be held in trust for the legal claimants. He must also give notice to the Secretary of State of the death of such person.

4. For the purpose of carrying out and executing certain treaties made between the United States and China, Japan, Siam and Turkey, consuls to those countries have been empowered with judicial functions. They were allowed to act as judges, and to try and punish citizens of the United States who had committed crimes there. These, however, were extraordinary powers in special cases, and by no means common to the consular office.

5. In the absence of a minister or diplomatic agent of the United States, the President may authorize a consul to perform the duties of such foreign minister; but these powers are rarely conferred on them. Their ordinary duties relate to commercial affairs, and to such as are before stated.

6. A vice consul, or deputy consul, is one appointed to act temporarily in case of sickness or absence of the consul. His powers, while acting, are the same as those of the consul in whose place he acts. Every consul is required to give bonds for the faithful performance of his duties. (6)

7. Our commerce has been extended to almost every part of the globe, and for this reason we need a great number of these officials. Their services are required at all great seaports, and at many smaller ones. Their compensation varies according to the amount of business to be transacted by them, from $7,500 down to $500. Some do not receive any salary, but are allowed the fees they are authorized to charge for their services.

8. A consul is to some extent a representative of his government, and is therefore treated with consideration and respect. An insult to him is looked upon as an insult to his country, for he is a kind of general agent for his government and people. It is his duty to give them all such information as he possesses in relation to the laws and practices of the country to which he is sent, which it would be important for them to know whether at home or abroad; and especially is it his duty to look after the interests and welfare of his countrymen when they are within his consulate, and to see that no wrong or injustice is done to them by the people or government where he resides.

CHAPTER XXXIX.

Treaties.

1. If two individuals enter into a written contract or agreement, in which each agrees with the other, to do, or not to do, certain things therein stated and specified; these individuals or parties to the contract, as they are called, perform an act which is most like a treaty between two nations, States or powers, of anything we can think of as a comparison or illustration, if called to answer the question "what is a treaty."

In one case two individuals make the contract; in the other two nations or governments make it, and it is called a treaty, when governments are the contracting parties.

2. Treaties have often been of great service to the world, both in ancient and modern times. By these negotiations, wars have been prevented, friendly relations maintained, and commercial intercourse kept up, advantageously to both parties. Treaties may be negotiated by any persons properly authorized by their government to do so; and any government may authorize such persons as they see fit, to perform these important acts. In many cases the ordinary ministers who represent their governments to other governments, negotiate ordinary treaties. But in cases where something of an extraordinary character is to be arranged, special ministers or commissioners are sent for this express purpose. This was the case at the treaty of Ghent, (so called from the name of the place where

the commissioners met to arrange it,) in 1814; by which a peace was brought about between England and the United States, after the last war between those powers. Special ministers, or commissioners, as they were denominated, were appointed and sent for this very purpose. A treaty of peace was agreed upon by the commissioners of the respective countries, and hostilities ceased as soon as the news reached the United States.

3. In some cases our government has authorized its commanding generals to make a treaty with the hostile nation. It has also given the same power to the commanders of our national vessels; and also, in a few cases, to our consuls, in countries at a great distance from home, such as China, Japan, Siam and Turkey.

The persons authorized to negotiate a treaty, rarely act without instructions from their government, as to the times and conditions of the proposed treaty. Much, however, must be left to the sound judgment and discretion of the negotiators as to the details.

4. It must be borne in mind that a treaty, although mutually agreed upon by the agents of the nations concerned, is not binding upon either party until properly ratified according to the forms of the respective governments interested. The modes of ratification differ in different governments. In ours the Constitution confers this power upon the President, by and with the advice and consent of two-thirds of the Senate.

In absolute monarchies this power rests in the hands of the King or Emperor alone. As before stated, every government may confer the power to negotiate a treaty upon such agents as it pleases. It also has the power to prescribe such modes of ratifying or confirming it, as it pleases.

5. But when once made and approved, it becomes binding not only upon the respective governments that made it, but upon all the citizens and subjects of that government. It has been held in this country by our greatest lawyers and statesmen, that the provisions of a treaty bind Congress, the President and every citizen as much as any Constitutional provision or act of Congress. And for this reason our treaties are published in the papers in every State and Territory in the Union, in the same manner, and to the same extent, as the laws of Congress.

6. The violation of a treaty by either of the parties thereto, is reprehensible and criminal. It is derogatory to the character of any nation or individual that does it. It destroys the confidence of one nation in the other, leads to unfriendly feelings and acts between the parties, and may bring on a war, if satisfaction is not given. Yet such things have been done, and evil consequences have always followed. "If you make a bargain, stick to it," is a common, trite, and wise saying.

Just here it seems proper to call attention to the fact that the Constitution prohibits any State from making any treaty with any foreign government. The reason for this provision is very obvious, for, if allowed, a State might confer privileges upon foreign powers which would be incompatible with the interests of other

States. Therefore the treaty-making power is kept wholly in the hands of the general government, for in it every State has its representatives, and a voice in every treaty which it makes.

7. So numerous are the treaties which the United States have made with nearly every civilized nation upon earth, that it would require a very large volume to contain them. They are published with the laws, and generally in English and in the language of the nation with whom the treaty is made. They may be found in the United States Statutes at Large. It would require too much space in a work of this kind, to give even their titles.

8. Wars have been stopped; boundry lines between nations have been established; commercial intercourse arranged; the purchase and sale of lands, and a variety of other things have been the subjects of, and formed the matter of treaties. Several of our most important ones relate to the purchase of territory. We accquired the States of Louisiana, Arkansas and Missouri, by a treaty with France in 1803. It was called the Louisiana purchase; for it was nothing more than a purchase and sale of lands. We also acquired Florida of Spain, in 1819, in the same way, and California and New Mexico of Mexico, in 1847.

9. The immense quantities of land purchased of the Indians, were obtained by treaties with them. We are sorry to say that in some cases they have treacherously violated their treaty obligations; but at the same time it should be said by way of extenuating their offence, that our own government agents appoin-

ted for the purpose of taking care of the interests of the poor Indians, have, in connection with the white traders among them, shamefully cheated and wronged them, and provoked them not only to disregard their obligations, but to perpetrate murders, robberies, and thefts upon the whites who live near them. At this time and for several years past, the Indians are very hostile to us, and are prosecuting a war with the whites in their vicinity for the reasons above stated. "Honesty is the best policy."

10. In the early part of the year 1867, a treaty was negotiated by William H. Seward, our Secretary of State, on the part of the United States, and Edward de Stoekl, the Russian Minister to the United States, on the part of Russia, for the cession of the Russian possessions in North America to the United States.

This treaty may be regarded as one of the most important of all our treaties with foreign powers ; for by it the United States acquire between 350,000 and 400,000 square miles of territory, in addition to our already immense possessions ; and places by far the greater part of the northwestern coast of North America under the control of the United States government.

For the purpose of giving a specimen of a treaty, and showing some of the details of this negotiation, we here insert it in full, as agreed upon by the contracting parties. $7,000,000 in gold is the consideration which the United States paid Russia for this territory. This treaty has been ratified by both the United States and the Russian governments and the money ($7,000,000 in gold) has been appropriated for the purpose and paid to the Russian Minister.

THE RUSSIAN TREATY.

The following is the text of the Russian-American treaty:—

The United States of America, and his Majesty, the Emperor of all the Russias, being desirous of strengthening, if possible, the good understanding which exists between them, have for that purpose appointed as their plenipotentiaries, the President of the United States, William H. Seward, Secretary of State, and his Majesty the Emperor of all the Russias, Mr. Edward de Stoeckl, his Envoy Extraordinary and Minister Plenipotentiary to the United States, and the said plenipotentiaries, having exchanged their full powers, which were found to be in due form, have agreed upon and signed the following articles:

ARTICLE I. His Majesty, the Emperor of all the Russias, agrees to cede to the United States, by this convention, immediately upon the exchange of the ratifications thereof, all the territory and dominion now possessed by his said Majesty on the continent of America and in the adjacent islands, the same being contained within the geographical limits herein set forth, to wit: The eastern limit is the line of demarcation between the Russian and British possessions in North America, as established by the convention between Russia and Great Britain, of February 28 (16), 1825, and described in articles third and fourth of said convention in the following terms: Commencing from the southernmost point of the island called Prince of Wales' Island, which point lies in the parallel of 50 deg. 40 min. north latitude, and between the 131st and 133d deg. of west longitude, meridian of Greenwich. The said line shall ascend to the north along the channel called Portland Channel, as far as the point of the continent where it strikes the 56th degree of north longitude. From this last mentioned point the line of demarcation shall follow the summit of the mountains situated parallel to the coast as far as the point of intersection of the 141st degree of west longitude of the same meridian, and finally from the said point of intersection the said meridian line of the 141st degree in its prolongation as far as the Frozen Ocean. With reference to the line of demarcation laid down in the preceding article, it is understood—first, that the island called Prince of Wales' Island shall belong wholly to Russia, and now, by this cession, wholly to the United States; second, that whenever the summit of the mountains which extend in a direction parallel to the coast from the 56th degree of north latitude to the point of intersection of the 141st degree west longitude shall prove to be at the distance of more than ten marine leagues from the ocean, the limit between the British possessions and the line of coast which is to belong to Russia as above mentioned—that is to say, the limit of the possessions ceded by this convention—shall be formed by a line parallel to the winding of the coast, and which shall never exceed the distance of ten marine leagues therefrom. The western limit, within which the territories and dominion conveyed are contained, passes through a point in Behring's Strait on the parallel of 65 deg. 30 min. north latitude, at its intersection by the meridian, which passes midway between the island of Krusenstern, or Ignaalook, and the island of Ratmanog, or Noonerbook, and proceeds due north without limitation into the same Frozen Ocean. The same western limit beginning at the same initial point, proceeds thence in a course nearly north-west through Behring's Strait and Behring's Sea, so as to pass midway between the north-west part of the island of St. Lawrence and the south-east point of Cape Choukottki to the meridian of 172 deg. west longitnde. Thence, from the intersection of that meridian, in a south-westerly direction, so as to pass midway between the island of Attou and the copper island of the Koranddorski couplet or group in the North Pacific Ocean, to the meridian of 193 deg. west longitude, so as to include in the territory conveyed the whole of the Aleutian Islands east of that meridian.

ART. II. In the cession of territory and dominion made by the preceding article, are included the right of property in all public lots and squares, vacant lands, and all public buildings, barracks, and other edifices which are not private, individual property. It is, however, understood and agreed that the churches which have been built in the ceded territory by the Russian government shall remain the property of such members of the Greek Oriental Church resident in the territory as may choose to worship therein. Any government archives, papers, and documents relative to the territory and dominion aforesaid, which may be now existing there, will be left in possession of the agent of the United States; but an authenticated copy of such of them as may be required will be at all times given by the United States to the Russian government, or to such Russian officers or subjects as may apply for them.

ART. III. The inhabitants of the ceded territory, according to their choice, reserving their natural allegiance, may return to Russia within three years; but if they should prefer to remain in the ceded territory, they, with the exception of uncivilized tribes, shall be admitted to the enjoyment of all the rights, advantages and immunities of citizens of the United States, and shall be maintained and protected in the free enjoyment of their liberty, property and religion. The uncivilized tribes will be subject to such laws and regulations as the United States may from time to time adopt in regard to aboriginal tribes of that country.

ART. IV. His Majesty, the Emperor of all the Russias, shall appoint, with convenient dispatch, an agent or agents for the purpose of formally delivering to a similar agent or agents, appointed on behalf of the United States, the territory, dominion, property, dependencies, and appurtenances which are ceded as above, and for doing any other act which may be necessary in regard thereto; but the cession, with the right of immediate possession, is nevertheless to be deemed complete and absolute on the exchange of ratifications, without waiting for such formal delivery.

Art. V. Immediately after the exchange of the ratifications of this convention, any fortifications or military posts which may be in the ceded territory shall be delivered to the agent of the United States, and any Russian troops which may be in the territory shall be withdrawn as soon as may be reasonably and conveniently practicable.

Art. VI. In consideration of the cession aforesaid, the United States agree to pay, at the Treasury in Washington, within months after the exchange of the ratifications of this convention, to the diplomatic representative, or other agent of His Majesty, the Emperor of all Russias, duly authorized to receive the same, million dollars in gold. The cession of territory and dominion herein made is hereby demanded to be free and unincumbered by any reservations, privileges, franchises, grants, or possessions, by any associated companies, whether corporate or incorporate, Russian or any other, or by any parties except merely private individual property holders; and the cession hereby made conveys all the rights, franchises and priviliges now belonging to Russia in the said territory or dominion and appurtenances thereto.

Art. VII. When this convention shall have been duly ratified by the President of the United States, by and with the advice and consent of the Senate, on the one part, and on the other by His Majesty, the Emperor of all the Russias, the ratifications shall be exchanged at Washington within from the date hereof, or sooner, if possible. In faith whereof the respective plenipotentiaries have signed this convention, and thereto affixed the seals of their arms.

CHAPTER XL.

Extradition Treaties.

1. In the preceding chapter we spoke of treaties generally. We now come to a particular kind of them called extradition treaties, which are of so recent date, that they form a new feature in our diplomacy.* Among our treaties with foreign nations, we find nothing upon this subject further back than the year 1842, when a treaty of this kind was made between the United States and England, the necessity for which arose out of the fact that persons frequently committed crimes in England, and then fled to the United States (and *vice versa*), to escape detection and punishment; for they could not be punished in the country to which they fled, inasmuch as it had no jurisdiction of a crime committed in a foreign country. To check this evil, a treaty was made between the two powers, in which they mutually agreed to deliver up, each to the other, any criminal who had perpetrated crimes of a certain kind (which were named in the treaty), in his own country, and afterwards fled to the other. This worked well. Its tendency was to check crime, and at the same time to multiply the chances of detection and punishment.

2. Subsequently, treaties of the same kind were

*Diplomacy, the art, science and skill of conducting and managing negotiations, treaties and international affairs. It also relates to the customs, usages and privileges of foreign ministers. All the foreign ministers to any government, are called the diplomatic body.

made between the United States and the following countries:

France,	in	1843
Prussia, and 17 other German States	"	1852
Switzerland,	"	1855
Baden	"	1857
Sweden,	"	1860
Venezuela, South America,	"	1861

The time is probably not distant, when treaties of this sort will be made between us and all the civilized nations of the world; for the intercourse between us and foreign nations is greater than ever before.

The effect of these international arrangements is to render the perpetration of crime more dangerous than it would be if they did not exist. Flight from the country where the crime was committed, was formerly one of the most effectual methods of escaping the penalty. But extradition treaties, Atlantic cables, and land telegraphs, have nearly spoiled this game.

3. An extradition treaty, then, is a mutual agreement between two nations to deliver up, each to the other, upon demand and proper proof of criminality, such persons as have committed crimes in one country and then fled to the other, that they may be taken back, tried and punished where the offence was committed. But these demands for escaped criminals cannot be sustained if made for any crime whatever. They will only be complied with when the crime is one which is named in the treaty itself. These crimes, upon examination of a number of such treaties, we find to be: 1. Murder, or an assault with an intent to

commit murder. 2. Piracy. 3. Arson. 4. Robbery. 5. Forgery, or the uttering of forged papers, or the making or circulating counterfeit money, either paper or coin. 6. Rape. 7. Embezzlement, and 8. Burglary.

4. It should be observed that a mere demand for an alleged offender is not sufficient. Proof enough to convince the judge before whom the case is brought, must accompany the demand. He must be satisfied that the party demanded has committed the alleged offence; when this is done, the judge reports his finding to the Secretary of State, whose duty then is, under his hand and seal of office, to issue the final writ of extradition; after which the criminal may be taken out of the United States (by force if necessary), and back to the country where he committed the crime, there to be dealt with according to the laws which he violated.

5. In some of our extradition treaties it is expressly stipulated, that neither party (government) shall be bound to surrender its own citizens, or any person for merely a political offence. In others it is agreed that the provisions in the treaty shall not apply to cases where the crime was perpetrated before the treaty was made. This plea, we think, would be held to be a good defence in all cases, whether so stipulated in the treaty or not.

6. The treaties between different nations for the surrender of criminals, are so analagous to one of the provisions contained in our Constitution, that to insert it here will give the reader a clear comprehension of its mean-

ing. If is found in the second section of article 4, and reads thus:—

"A person charged in any State, with treason, felony, or other crime, who shall flee from justice, and be found in another State, shall on demand of the executive authority of the State from which he fled, be delivered up, to be removed to the State having jurisdiction of the crime.

CHAPTER XLI.

Letters of Marque and Reprisal.

1. THE Constitution (Art. 1, Sec. 8), gives Congress power to declare war, and to grant letters of marque and reprisal. This is an act never to be done, but in time of war. Congress itself does not issue the letters, but authorizes the President to do so. An act was passed in 1863, expressly giving him this authority. A letter of marque and reprisal may be thus defined:

2. It is a written commission signed and sealed by a competent authority of our nation, giving to the commander of a private armed vessel, called a privateer, authority to capture the ships and goods belonging to the subjects of another nation, between which nations there is an existing war. This is a general definition. But when such letters are issued by the United States, they are signed by the President, and sealed with the seal of the United States. Without such commission, thus signed and sealed, any capture made by the commander of a private vessel, would be piracy. If a capture is made, it must be made according to the laws of war, as recognized by civilized nations, and according to the instructions given by the President. Any conduct on the part of a privateer, contrary to these rules, would vitiate his proceedings, and he would not be entitled to the property he had captured.

3. The captured vessel is called a prize, and must be taken into some port of the United States, or into some port of a country in amity with the United States,

where legal proceedings are taken before some court of competent jurisdiction ; and the capture and all the the circumstances of it enquired into ; and if all is found to have been done according to the laws of civilized nations, the captured vessel and cargo is condemned as a prize. But if not condemned, the captors lose her. When adjudged to be a lawful prize, the ship and cargo are sold and the money divided between the officers and men, according to rank, and according to the laws of Congress on this subject. These laws give the whole to the captors, when the ship taken is of equal or superior force to the ship making the capture; but if of inferior force, then the United States takes one half.

4. Privateering, as this business is called, was once considered a lawful and honorable mode of warfare. It was generally practiced between belligerent nations; but in later days its propriety and morality have been questioned. It is beginning to be looked upon as a kind of robbery not very distantly related to piracy. That it is robbery no one can deny, and, query, "Can it be justified, on the ground that the robber and the robbed are the subjects of nations at war with each other?"

5. In Europe an effort has been made to do away with this species of warfare. We hope it will yet succeed, and that all nations will agree to abolish this system of plunder. Innocent parties are generally the sufferers, while but small injury is done to the power of the hostile nation.

CHAPTER XLII.

Suffrage.

1. THE right of suffrage, in its political sense means the right to vote for such officers as are elected by the people; including officers of the general government, as well as those of the State government, for when the right of suffrage is conferred upon a man, it gives him the right of voting for every elective officer, from the President of the United States down to the lowest State or municipal officer.

In the Constitution, or laws of Congress, we find but little said on the suffrage question; because Congress has never claimed the right or power to legislate on this subject. It has been conceded that this matter is one which belongs to the States; whatever qualifications the respective States required of their citizens to vote for their own State officers, have been accepted by the general government as the qualifications necessary to authorize them to vote for President, Vice President and Congressmen, the only officers of the United States government for which the people, under the provisions of the Constitution as it now stands, can vote.

2. From this statement we see that persons who, in one State may vote for President, Vice-President and Congressmen, cannot do so in another State; because the qualifications of voters in some States differ from those of voters in others. For example, some States require a residence in the State of one year, before a man can enjoy this franchise, other States but six months. In most of the States, it is required of for-

eigners to become citizens by naturalization before they are allowed to vote. But in some this is not required. In some of the States colored persons can vote. In others this right is not given to them under any circumstances. Although it has long been conceded that the power of conferring the right of suffrage was one which belonged exclusively to the States, and although they have been allowed to do in this matter as it seemed right to them; yet it is a question worthy of serious thought, whether Congress ought not, by law, to establish a uniform qualification of voters, one that is alike in all the States, whenever the elector votes for President, Vice President or Congressmen; for the people in all the States are affected as much by the votes given for those officers, in any one State, as they are by those given in their own.

3. But it has always been a troublesome question to determine in any government where people vote at all, "who ought, and who ought not to vote?" In the United States the elective franchise is extended further than in most other countries. Yet this question here has caused a great amount of political discussion. The Constitutions of several of the States have been changed in the effort to adjust this question on a correct basis. Up to this day, it remains unsettled in some of its features and details. Some contending that it is too much extended, that is, that it is granted to persons who ought not to have it, while to others it is denied.

4. The question of suffrage was never more discussed throughout the country than at the present time; but the discussion turns principally upon the justice and propriety exhibited in extending this right to the colored people, as they are now all free.

CHAPTER XLIII.

Seals.

1. SEALS are of great antiquity. We read of them and of their use as far back as the days of Queen Esther. They were then used as they are now, to give additional proof of the authenticity or genuineness of any document or paper to which they were attached; it being much easier to counterfeit a mere signature than the impression of a seal. They are of various devices, patterns and designs, and generally are emblematic of some historical fact, event or sentiment. They are used on papers and documents emanating from the government, or from some department of it. The law requires them to be attached and affixed to commissions, and many other papers, without which the paper would have no legality or validity. Formerly, the usual mode of sealing a paper, was to place melted wax on the margin, and then press the seal into the wax. This left the impression of the seal, and the work was finished.

2. But this mode of affixing seals was rather a slow process, and required more time than could often be spared for that purpose. In view of which, Congress, in 1854 passed the following law:

"In all cases where a seal is necessary by law to any commission, process, or other instrument provided for by the laws of Congress, it shall be lawful to affix the proper seal by making an impression therewith directly on the paper to which such seal is necessary, which shall be as valid as if made on wax or other adhesive substance."

The United States have a seal, denominated "The Great Seal." This is in the care and custody of the Secretary of State, and it is his duty to affix it to all civil commissions* to officers of the United States, appointed by the President, by and with the advice and consent of the Senate, or by the President alone.

But the law forbids it even to be so affixed to any commission, or other instrument, until the President has first signed it. Without his signature, the instrument has no validity. The seal is then affixed in proof of the genuineness of his signature.

3. The Secretary of State and all the other secretaries of the great departments, each have a seal of office which is affixed to commissions, and to other instruments emanating from their respective offices.

Several of the most important bureaus are required by law to have seals of office; for example, the Land Office and the Patent Office. When the United States gives a patent (title) to land, it must be sealed by the Land Office seal. A patent right must be issued under the seal of the Patent Office.

4. One of the most common and important uses of seals arises from the necessity people are often under to have copies of records, maps, and various other papers, the originals of which are in some of the departments at Washington, to be used as evidence in courts,

---

*The word commission, here means a document or certificate, given to one who has received an office, in proof of his appointment to and his authority to discharge the duties of that office.

where trials and other legal proceedings are pending. In order to provide for this necessity, Congress has enacted that copies of such records, maps and papers belonging to any of the government officers, under the signature of the head of such office, or of its chief clerk, with the seal affixed, shall be as competent evidence in all cases as their original would be.

GREAT SEAL OF THE UNITED STATES.

In chapter XC we have given a number of forms of seals. Over the name of each State we have placed the great seal of that State, or, as it is sometimes called, its coat of arms. These various devices are the mere conceptions of the artist, yet they are emblematic of some political sentiment or of some characteristic of that State.

CHAPTER XLIV.

Bonds.

1. THE vast sums of money annually collected from duties, from the sale of public lands, and from all other sources from which the revenue of the nation is raised; and then the disbursement of the same to the army, to the navy, to the civil officers, and to the various employees of the government, and to the different purposes for which the public money is appropriated, requires a host of officials and agents to transact all this business. Hence the government has collectors of customs, collectors of taxes, postmasters, receivers of money for the sale of public land, and so on; all of whom are receivers of the public money. These pay it into the United States Treasury, from whence it is paid out directly to parties having claims against the government, or to agents who disburse it to those to whom it is due.

By the dishonesty of the officers and agents who receive, hold or disburse these funds, the government would be the loser, and the people would be defrauded of their money. We say the people, because every man who cheats or defrauds the government, cheats and defrauds every man, woman and child in the country. Hence the detestable character of public swindlers and defaulters.

2. But to guard against this as far as possible, the law requires a man when he accepts of one of these offices, to take an oath, or make a solemn affirmation, promising faithfully to perform the duties of the office he enters upon. But even this does not always secure

honesty. Some men will violate their oaths for money. A further remedy is resorted to for further security against dishonesty. For this purpose laws have been made, requiring all officers and agents who receive, hold or disburse the public money, to give bonds with sufficient security for the faithful performance of their trust. These bonds hold the sureties as well as the officer, and are signed by one and sometimes two or three bondsmen of sufficient means to insure the government against loss. It would be too tedious and uninteresting to enumerate all the government officers who have to give bonds before they can enter upon their duties. Therefore we stated before that the law requires all of this class to do so. We are not aware of any exceptions.

These bonds are given for various amounts, which correspond with the amount of money to be received or held by the officers who execute them, and when signed by the office holder or person bound to the government, and by his surety, are held in the Treasury Department as security for the faithful performance of whatever the bounden parties have agreed to do. In case of any failure or defalcation, all the parties signing the bond are held responsible for the amount named in the bond; and may be sued by the government, and made to pay all damages.

But notwithstanding all these precautions, and in spite of oaths and bonds, the government is defrauded of millions of money by the very men it favors with positions of honor and emolument. Reader, should you ever hold a position under your government, let not the sin of perjury blacken your soul, nor the crime of dishonesty tarnish your character. "Honesty is the best policy." "An honest man's the noblest work of God."

CHAPTER XLV.

Oaths.

1. An oath is an appeal to God, by him who makes it, that what he has said, or what he shall say, is the truth. It is the most solemn form under which one can assert or pronounce anything. To utter a falsehood while under oath is perjury, a crime of the darkest hue. One which God has declared he will punish, and one which is made infamous, and punishable by fine and imprisonment by the laws of the land.

2. The Constitution (Art. 6, Sec. 3) requires that Senators and Representatives, and members of the several State Legislatures, and all executive and judicial officers, both of the United States, and of the several States, shall be bound by oath or affirmation to support the Constitution. Then in the second article, section eight, the form of the oath required of the President before he enters upon his duties, is given in these words:—

"I do solemnly swear (or affirm) that I will faithfully execute the office of President of the United States, and will to the best of my ability preserve, protect and defend the Constitution of the United States."

3. This is all the Constitution says about oaths; but it is enough to show that no man (unless he commit perjury) can accept office, either under the United States or any State government, unless he in good faith will support the Constitution.

But in the laws enacted by Congress, we find that not only official oaths are required; but in a great variety of other cases, men who transact business with the government are required to verify their accounts and statements with an oath. This is particularly the case with those who do business with the custom house; such as merchants, shipowners, and masters of vessels. Many oaths must be put in the form of affidavits; that is, the oath must be written and signed by the deponent, that the statements made may be preserved.

4. The form of official oaths varies according to the nature of the duties to be performed by the deponent. The oath must be taken before the officer enters upon his duties. Should he neglect or refuse to do this, his acts will be illegal, and he would make himself liable to punishment.

After the late civil war broke out, Congress for the purpose of preventing those who had voluntarily taken part in the rebellion, from holding thereafter any office under the government, passed an act requiring every one before he could accept any office, either in the civil, military, or naval departments, to take an oath in the following form:—

5. I, A. B., do solemnly swear (or affirm) that I have never voluntarily borne arms against the United States, since I have been a citizen thereof; that I have voluntarily given no aid, countenance, counsel or encouragement to persons engaged in armed hostility thereto; that I have neither sought, nor accepted, nor attempted to exercise the functions of any office whatev-

er, under any authority or pretended authority in hostility to the United States; that I have not yielded a voluntary support to any pretended government, authority, power or Constitution, within the United States, hostile or inimical thereto. And I do further swear (or affirm) that to the best of my knowledge and ability, I will support and defend the Constitution of the United States, against all enemies, foreign and domestic; that I will bear true faith and allegiance to the same; that I take this obligation freely, without any mental reservation or purpose of evasion, and that I will well and faithfully discharge the duties of the office on which I am about to enter. So help me God."

So strong and comprehensive an oath as this was never before required from any officer of the government. It answers the requirements of the Constitution, and substantially comprehends all contained in any other forms heretofore used. It is at once an oath of allegiance, an oath of support of the Constitution, and an oath to discharge faithfully the duties of the office taken. This goes by the name of the TEST oath, and frequently "The Iron-clad Oath."

6. The object of binding all officers of the general and State governments, by oath, is to place them under the most solemn obligation to be faithful and honest in the discharge of their duties. They cannot be otherwise without committing one of the most flagitious crimes. And yet, lamentable to say, men have accepted office under these most solemn obligations, and have afterwards utterly disregarded them, and have been unfaith-

ful in every respect, both in the support of the Constitution, and in the discharge of their official duties. For this cause, although we have an excellent form of government, perhaps the best in the world, yet in its administration a great deal that is wrong and corrupt is found; and fears have been entertained that it would be broken down and destroyed by the corruption of those who administer it. Good men should always be chosen to make and administer the laws in any country, and under any form of government.

CHAPTER XLVI.

Revenue.

1. The revenue of any government is its income, or money raised from any source whatever to defray the expenses incurred in its administration. These expenses are always heavy, are counted by millions, and the subjects or citizens of the government must pay them in some way; either by duties on imported goods, by direct taxation on property, by payments for certain rights and privileges conferred by the government, &c., &c. Different governments resort to different methods to raise their revenue.

2. The United States have always raised the greater part of it by duties on imported goods. These have sometimes been found sufficient to defray all expenses; and at other times insufficient, depending on circumstances of a high or low tariff, or on ordinary or extraordinary expenses of government. In times of war all these resources put together have been insufficient, and it has become necessary to borrow money to sustain it. War expenses have been the source of most of the national debts in all countries.

3. At the close of the civil war between the North and South, the national debt amounted to nearly 3,000,000,000 of dollars; and this in addition to the vast amounts paid during the existence of the war. This created the necessity for increasing the revenue of the country, and the government to resort to direct taxation, in addition to all its ordinary resources, and

to all the money it borrowed to sustain the expenses of the war. And now after it is over, the taxes are continued for the purpose of paying its enormous public debt. This furnishes us with a forcible example of one of the great evils of war.

4. The proceeds of sales of the public lands have been another source of revenue to the United States, which few other governments possess; because their territory is not as extensive as ours, and they have but little if any public lands to dispose of. The empires of Russia and Brazil may be exceptions to this general fact.

5. Duties collected on imported goods, the sale of public lands, the income of the Post Office Department, and direct taxation, (when resorted to) are the principal sources from which the revenues of the United States are raised. There are comparatively small amounts, however, raised from other sources; such as the duties paid upon the tonnage of vessels, forfeitures of goods smuggled or attempted to be smuggled into the country; forfeiture of vessels engaged in the smuggling business, prizes taken in time of war, fees paid for licenses granted, and for services rendered by certain government officials, &c. But all these put together are insignificant in amount compared with the first named.

6. The revenues of any government afford a tolerably correct indication of its wealth, population and power. Small and weak ones have small revenues. Wealthy, populous and strong ones, have large revenues.

CHAPTER XLVII.

Internal Revenue.

1. In our chapter on Revenue, we observed that direct taxation was one of the means to which the government had to resort when the proceeds from import duties and ordinary sources fail to meet its expenses.

The late civil war caused an emergency of this kind. All former wars in which the United States had been engaged did not require one-quarter of the money for their prosecution that this did; and of course the ordinary revenues of the government were entirely insufficient to defray its expenses. This state of things became apparent soon after the war commenced. To meet it, Congress, as early as 1861, (the war broke out in April of this year,) passed an act called "the Internal Revenue Law," by which twenty millions of dollars were to be raised annually by direct taxes upon houses and lands in each of the States and Territories ot the United States.

2. By subsequent acts not only houses and lands were taxed, but almost every sort of property and business. Licenses were required for persons to carry on their profession, trade or business; incomes were taxed; deeds, mortgages, notes, bonds, bank checks, and papers of almost every kind were invalid unless they had a revenue stamp upon them. Manufacturers had to pay such a per-centage on whatever they made. Scarcely any calling, trade, profession, or business or thing escaped it, directly or indirectly.

So thorough a taxation the people never experienced before; and it is to be hoped they never will again. This is one of the fruits of war. But what makes this doubly aggravating, is that this was a civil war. The people have this enormous load of taxation to carry to pay for killing each other. When will men learn war no more? When will men cease to be wicked and foolish?

3. To carry out the objects and provisions of this bill, it became necessary, in the first place, to divide every State and Territory into collection districts, entirely different, however, from the collection districts for the collection of the custom duties. These, as stated in another place, are located along the sea coast, and on the shores of gulfs, bays and sounds, or on the shores of such navigable lakes and rivers as are accessible to vessels from some foreign country; whereas, the collection districts for the collection of internal revenue are necessarily located in every part of each State and Territory, as much inland as along the coast. As far as practicable, they are made, both in number and territory, identical with the Congressional districts.

4. This law also made it necessary to create a host of new officers to execute its provisions. In the first place, an officer is appointed in the Treasury Department, and denominated the commissioner of internal revenue. He is, like all officers of his grade, appointed by the President and Senate, and receives a salary of four thousand dollars per annum. He is charged with the duty (under the direction of the Secretary of the Treasury) of preparing all the instructions, forms,

blanks, stamps and licenses to be used throughout the country, by all officers and agents employed in the collection of these taxes, and to see to the execution of the law relating thereto.

5. Then comes an assessor and a collector, each with a deputy or deputies if need be, for every district. One to assess the value of all the property liable to taxation, and the other to collect and receive the moneys so assessed. The collectors pay the moneys so received into the Treasury at Washington, or into such banks or other places as may be directed by the Secretary of the Treasury.

The money to be thus raised is apportioned to each State and Territory in proportion to their representation in Congress; and a separate account of this tax is kept in the Treasury Department with each State and Territory.

6. Much more might be said about other subordinate officers and agents employed by the government for the purpose of carrying out the provisions of the revenue laws; and much more might be said about many of its details; for it contains an unusual number ot provisions, in no less than three hundred and twenty-nine sections. But many of these have already been changed by subsequent acts; and will probably be modified by every Congress that may meet, until the whole law shall become unnecessary by the paying off of the whole national debt, or such a reduction of it as will enable the government to dispense with this extraordinary means of meeting its obligations. The very frequent modifications of all the tax laws, renders it quite unnecessary to dwell with much minuteness on their provisions in detail.

I hope this outline of the objects of the law, and the account given of the principal officers engaged in carrying it into effect, will satisfy the general reader. (7)

CHAPTER XLVIII.

Custom House and Custom House Officers.

1. CUSTOM houses are government offices, generally located in seaport cities and towns, for the purpose of collecting the duties charged upon imported goods. Nearly all goods brought from foreign countries into the United States, are brought by ships and other vessels by sea. Hence seaports are the popular localities for custom houses. Ports where they are established, are called ports of entry Here vessels from foreign ports are allowed to enter, and here the duties on foreign goods are collected by custom house officers appointed for that purpose.

The principal of these officials is called collector of customs. He is appointed by the President and Senate, and holds his office during the pleasure of the President. This office is one of great responsibility; for the collectors of customs receive and pay over into the United States Treasury by far the greater part of the revenues of the country; that is, under ordinary circumstances. But under the present extraordinary exigencies of the nation, which grew out of the late civil war, the government has been obliged to resort to direct taxation to sustain its expenses; and a larger amount has been raised by this means than by duties on imports.

2. A collector of customs is therefore required to give heavy bonds for the faithful performance of his duties.

He must give his bonds and take his official oath before entering upon his duties, which are numerous and various. He has the power, also, with the approbation of the Secretary of the Treasury, to appoint the subordinate custom house officers, such as weighers, measurers, gaugers, inspectors, watchmen, store keepers, &c. These he nominates, and the Secretary of the Treasury confirms or rejects them.

HIS DUTIES.

3. These duties require him to collect all duties which Congress has imposed on every kind of imported goods brought into the port or ports of which he is the collector. In order to do this he requires a deputy, and in large ports, several of them, whom he appoints, together with as many of the above named subordinates as the business done at the port requires.

He must receive all reports, manifests, and documents to be exhibited on the entry of any ship or vessel, whether domestic or foreign; and all accounts of all the goods they have on board. He must estimate the duties to be paid thereon, receive the moneys paid therefor, and take all bonds for securing the payment thereof, and grant all permits for landing the goods. Once in three months he must transmit all moneys collected by him to the Treasury Department at Washington, together with full and accurate accounts of all his transactions relating to the collection of duties at the port of which he is collector.

4. He must examine the manifests not only of all ships and vessels with their cargoes which arrive within the port or district for which he is collector, but

also those of all vessels which depart from thence to foreign countries. In this way the government obtains a knowledge of the amount and value of the whole exports and imports of the country. He must also give clearances to all vessels when they sail from his port for foreign ports or countries. No vessel can lawfully depart without such clearance.

5. The manifests and clearances of ships and vessels are so often spoken of in the laws relating to commerce, navigation and the revenue, that it may be interesting and useful to those not familiar with these matters, to give the form of an American manifest and clearance. These are among the most important of a ship's papers.

A SHIP'S CLEARANCE.

6. This document is couched in the following terms:

"*District of* *Port of* , *ss.*

"These are to certify, to all whom it may concern, that A. B. master or commander of the ship (brig, barque, schooner), burthen tons or thereabouts, mounted with guns, navigated with men, built, and bound for , having on board , hath here entered and cleared his said vessel according to law.

"Given under our hands and seals, at the custom house of , this day of , one thousand , and in the year of the Independence of the United States of America."

This is signed by the collector and by the naval officer of the port, when the commander is prepared to depart with his vessel to his destined port.

A SHIP'S MANIFEST.

This is a document of a very different character. Its principal object is to show of what her cargo consists, in quantity, kind and value. The form of a manifest is as follows:

"Report and manifest of the cargo laden on board of the , whereof is master, which cargo was taken on board at the port or ports of , burthen tons, built at , in the State of , and owned by , merchants at , and bound for ."

This, together with a particular description of the marks and numbers of every bale, box, case, barrel, bundle or parcel on board of the vessel, is the manifest. It must be given to the collector of whatever port the vessel arrives at; and the master of her must swear that it is in all respects a true and accurate account of all the cargo on board, to the best of his knowledge and belief.

8. The collector of the port can then compute the duties to be paid upon each article, and when these are paid, or secured to be paid, he gives permits to land the cargo, and deliver the goods to their respective owners. Then come in the duties of weighers, gaugers, measurers and inspectors of the customs, after permits are obtained to land the goods. If they are such as require to be weighed, gauged or measured, these officers are sent to do it; and the inspector must allow nothing to leave the ship until he has examined the marks and numbers, to see if they correspond with the permit and the manifest. If he suspects that there is an attempt to defraud the government by false

names and marks, he is authorized to open the package, box, case, cask, or whatever contains the goods, and to examine them. In this way smuggling is prevented, and the revenues arising from duties on imported goods secured.

9. The compensation of collectors of customs varies from a few hundreds to many thousands of dollars per year. It depends upon the amount of business done at the port. At New York, Boston, Philadelphia, New Orleans, Baltimore and San Francisco, the compensation is enormous, and should be reduced; for, in addition to their salaries and fees for services rendered, they receive a part of the forfeitures of goods smuggled or attempted to be smuggled into the country.

SURVEYORS.

10. Next to the collector in rank and authority, among custom house officers, is the surveyor of the port. He aids the collector in collecting the revenue; but his duties are of a different character. He is appointed in the same manner as the collector, and for four years; but may be removed by the President at his pleasure. His compensation, like that of the collector, depends on the amount of business at the port.

HIS DUTIES.

11. He must superintend and direct all inspectors, weighers, measurers and gaugers within his port, and must visit all vessels arriving therein, and report the same to the collector, with a description of each, of her nationality, cargo, &c. It is also his duty to examine all goods entered for the benefit of drawback.

THE NAVAL OFFICER.

12. The naval officer is another of the principal custom house officers employed in the collection of the revenue. He is appointed in the same way as the collector and the surveyor, and is removable in the same manner. His compensation, also, is dependent on the same circumstances. His duties, to some extent, are the same as the collector's, and serve as a check or a sort of re-examination of his work, for the sake of accuracy and correctness. Hence it is his duty to receive copies of all manifests and entries, and to compute the duties on all goods subject to pay duties. He must keep a separate record thereof. He must countersign all permits, clearances, certificates, debentures, and other documents to be granted by the collector. He must also examine the collector's computation of duties, and his receipts, bonds, and expenditures, and certify their correctness, if found right.

COMMISSIONER OF CUSTOMS.

13. In the year 1849 a new bureau was created by act of Congress in the Treasury Department, the head of which is styled "the commissioner of customs." This was done to increase the operative power of the department, and to relieve the first comptroller of the Treasury, whose duties had become too onerous to be efficiently performed by one man. By the act in question, all the duties and powers of the first comptroller of the Treasury, so far as they related to receipts from customs, and to the accounts of collectors and other officers of customs, were transferred

to the new commissioner and bureau under his supervision. Hence it became his duty to examine and adjust all accounts with custom house officers, to prepare forms of all papers to be used in the collection of the revenue from customs, and to direct the form and manner of keeping accounts of the same; to bring suits for the recovery of all debts due from revenue officers, and to report to Congress any default or neglect of duty on their part. This affords another example of the manner in which Congress is made acquainted with the conduct of government officials, and the state of things in every department and bureau. The commissioner of customs is appointed by the President and Senate, holds his office for the same time, and receives the same compensation as the first comptroller of the Treasury.

CHAPTER XLIX.

The Public Lands.

1. THE whole area of land lying within the boundaries of the United States, is, according to published official statements, 3,002,013 square miles, or 1,921,288,-320 acres. Before the establishment of the present government, and during our colonial condition, much of this land had been sold and otherwise disposed of by the English government, and had become the property of individuals. Their possessions were not disturbed by the United States or by any of the State governments after the Revolution, which changed the whole country from the possession of the English to that of the American government; with the exception of that which belonged to those who were enemies to the United States during the Revolution. This was confiscated, and fell back into the possession of the United States, or of the States in which it laid.

2. But all which had not been disposed of became the property of the government, excepting such portions as belonged to the Indians—the original owners of the whole of America. Thus the government became a great land holder from its very outset. From this, and from what follows, it will be seen that it has been one of the greatest land dealers in the world; for in addition to that here spoken of, it has purchased immense tracts, from which many of the present States and Territories were formed.

The Louisiana purchase, as it has always been termed, was made of France in 1803. Out of it the States of Louisiana, Arkansas and Missouri were formed. The sum of $15,000,000 was paid for it. Then in the year 1819, the United States by treaty purchased Florida of Spain. In 1836, Texas seceded from Mexico, and after a war with her gained her independence, and in 1845 asked to be admitted as one of the United States. This proposition was accepted, and she was admitted accordingly. All her public lands came into the possession of our government.

3. Subsequently to this, and after the late war with Mexico, we purchased of her all the northern part of that country, embracing California, New Mexico and other extensive regions. This again added several hundred thousand square miles to our public domain.

To all these must be added the immense tracts bought of the Indians. And to all of which must be added the great purchase made early in the year 1867, from Russia, of all her possessions in North America, for $7,000,000 in gold. This increases our public domain, by between three and four hundred thousand square miles.

4. But the government does not want all this land. It has no use for more than a few acres in certain locations, for the sites of public buildings and of military works.

The object, therefore, is to sell it to those who want it for farms and other purposes, that it may furnish homes for the people, be made productive, and thus add to the wealth of the nation. To accomplish this a

General Land Office was established by act of Congress, in 1812, at Washington. This office was at first attached to, or was a bureau of the Treasury Department, but in 1849 it was attached to the Department of the Interior. The head of this office is called

COMMISSIONER OF THE GENERAL LAND OFFICE.

5. He is appointed by the President and Senate, must take the usual official oath before entering on his duties, and must give the usual official bond. He keeps the seal of his office, and fixes an impression of it upon all papers emanating from the Land Office. He, with his clerks and assistants form the bureau, keep all the records and papers pertaining to the public lands, and perform all duties relating thereto. He receives reports from surveyors and from the district land officers, gives them their instructions, and reports to the President and to Congress when required to do so.

He issues all patents for lands granted by the United States, and sends and receives by mail all papers and documents relating to his official business, under the franking privilege. Every patent for land is issued in the name of the United States, is signed by the President and by the commissioner of the Land Office, and is then recorded in books kept for that purpose.

SURVEYORS GENERAL AND DEPUTY SURVEYORS.

6. When it is deemed necessary and expedient to bring the lands in any particular State or section of the country into market, a surveyor general is appointed for that State or section, and also a sufficient number of deputy or assistant surveyors to perform

the work; which is done under the direction of the surveyor general, who is himself directed by law as to the manner of procedure. He is appointed for four years, taking the usual oath, and gives bonds for the faithful performance of his duties.

MODE OF SURVEYING THE PUBLIC LANDS.

7. The law directs how the lands shall be surveyed and mapped. Where it is practicable, they are laid out into square miles, each of which contains 640 acres, and is called a section.

These sections are then sub-divided into halves, quarters and eighths of sections; that is, into lots of 320, 160 and 80 acres. The boundary lines are all run north and south, and east and west. Thirty-six of these sections, which make a plat of six miles square, are put into a township. These townships are designated by numbers, but when inhabited are named by the inhabitants as their fancy dictates.

SALE OF THE PUBLIC LANDS.

8. After the lands have been surveyed and properly mapped into townships and sections, they are brought into market and offered for sale in such quantities as are wanted by the purchaser; from 40 acres, one sixteenth of a section, up to a whole section; or as many sections as the buyer pleases to take.

DISTRICT LAND OFFICES.

9. District land offices for the sale of lands are established for this purpose at as many places in the State or Territory where the lands are situated, as is deemed necessary for the convenience of purchasers.

Here are kept maps of all the lands lying in the district, and buyers may make their selections both of quantity and location as suits them. Here they will find

A REGISTER OF THE LAND OFFICE AND A RECEIVER OF PUBLIC MONEYS FOR LANDS.

10. The first named officer will register the application made for land in a book kept for that purpose, and the second will receive the money paid for it. These officers are appointed by the President and Senate, and report their proceedings to the General Land Office at Washington. The receiver transmits all moneys received by him to the United States Treasury once in a month or once in three months, as directed.

SCHOOL LANDS.

11. As before stated, the public lands are surveyed into sections of one mile square, and thirty-six of these sections make a township. For the purpose of encouraging education, Congress has enacted that section number 16 in every township, shall not be sold, but reserved for the township, to be applied to the support of common schools in that town. By this measure the government appropriated one thirty-sixth part of its lands to aid the work of educating the children in the new States. And in addition to this it has made other munificent donations of land for the establishment and support of colleges and other institutions of learning.

12. In addition to all this the United States have donated large tracts of land to the several States in which it lay, to aid them in building their State

houses, &c. Large quantities of land have also been given to aid the construction of railroads.

HOMESTEADS.

13. The government has always sold its lands at a very low price, preferring to give the people cheap farms, rather than to raise more revenue from this source.

But in 1862, Congress passed an act called "the Homestead Law," the object of which was to cheapen the public lands to a mere nominal price to heads of families, male or female, or to persons 21 years of age or over, or to persons who had served in the army or navy of the United States, whether 21 years old or not. By the provisions of this act such persons are allowed, for the trifling sum of ten dollars, to enter upon and claim 160 acres of land, provided the claimant swears that the land is applied for his or her own use, and for settlement and cultivation. But no patent (deed) is to be given until the applicant has actually settled upon and cultivated the land for the space of five years. Such applicant must also make affidavit that he has never borne arms against the United States.

By this liberal policy, persons of very limited means may provide themselves with comfortable homes for life; and the unoccupied lands will be settled and occupied faster than if the old price of one dollar and twenty-five cents per acre had been demanded. The revenue from the sale of lands will of course be less, but the wealth of the country will undoubtedly be increased by the measure.

MINERAL LANDS.

14. Exceedingly rich and valuable mines of gold, silver, copper, lead and other minerals have been found upon the public lands. That the benefits of mining them might be extended to the many, instead of being monopolized by a few, a different rule for selling them has been made. After they have been surveyed, mapped and described, they, like other lands, are offered for sale, but in quantities of not more than 40 acres. These are generally sold at auction, but no bid less than five dollars per acre will be received. If not sold at public sale, they are then subject to private sale at that price.

REVENUE FROM LANDS.

15. Any one can easily comprehend what almost boundless wealth there is in these public lands; and although the government has not realized as much revenue from them as it might have done had it held them at higher prices, yet to the purchasers, the people, they are worth ten times more than the government received for them. Yet notwithstanding the low prices, they have yielded and will long continue to yield a considerable part of the revenues of the country.

LEGISLATION RELATIVE TO THE PUBLIC LANDS.

16. This vast estate, which the people of the United States own in their public lands, is constantly changing its character from that of public to that of private property; for the government is disposing of more or less of it every year to individuals. By this process the public dominion is diminishing, but private prop-

erty is as constantly increasing. The land only changes owners, and is converted from an unproductive to a productive state, and this augments the wealth of the nation.

17. It is easy to understand that it has required a great amount of care, labor and legislation to manage and take care of so great an estate. Surveys, maps and records of it, must be made and preserved at Washington; and Congress has found it necessary at almost, if not at every session, to pass acts in relation to it. All the laws enacted relative to the public lands would, if collected into one book, make a ponderous volume.

CHAPTER L.

Bounty Land and Land Warrants.

1. Bounty lands are lands given by the government to the officers and men who have served their country, either in the army or navy. Everybody knows that the pay of soldiers in the army, and seamen in the navy, is small. For this reason our government donated a certain quantity of land to each officer and private, as a further compensation for their services. The quantity given was made to depend on the length of time spent in the service. Those who engaged to serve a year, and actually served nine months, receive 160 acres. Those who engaged to serve six months, and actually served four months, received 80 acres; and those who served one month, received 40 acres. No distinction was made between officers and privates, because officers received higher wages than privates.

2. The United States own such vast quantities of land that they could in this way compensate the soldiers better, with a less burden of taxation upon the people, than other nations. Immense quantities of the public lands have been disposed of in this way, and many a soldier has thus been furnished with a home and with a competence for life. In case of his death in battle, or before he received his land, it was given to his widow or children if he had any.

Every one entitled to land, for military or naval services, receives from the Department of the Interior a certificate, or land warrant, as it is more specifically termed, and this entitles him to go anywhere upon the public lands which have been surveyed and brought into market, and not otherwise disposed of, and select the quantity named in his warrant, which is often denominated a military land warrant. Upon the return of this certificate or warrant to the land office, with proof of the location of the land, the government gives the owner a patent or government deed of it, which is the best title to land that a man can have.

3. Land warrants are often bought and sold like stocks, for whoever lawfully holds the warrant, whether for service or by purchase, is entitled to the land.

So careful has the government been to secure the benefits of this provision to those who have served their country in time of war, that it does not allow land granted for military services to be sold for the debts of the warrantee before he has received his patent.

CHAPTER LI.

Duties and Tariffs.

1. Few if any questions or subjects ever came before the National Legislature, which have required more legislation, caused more debate, or brought out a greater diversity of opinion, than those relating to duties and tariffs.

Duties are the taxes which the government imposes upon goods imported from foreign countries into our own. This is not peculiar to our government, for all others do the same thing.

In ours two different objects have been sought by the imposition of duties, both of which are clearly stated in the preamble to the first act ever passed by Congress (July 4th, 1789), on this subject. They are in these words: "Whereas it is necessary *for the support of the government*, for the discharge of the debts of the United States, *and the encouragement and protection of manufactures*, that duties be laid on goods, wares and merchandise imported."

First, the support of government.

Second, protection to our own manufactures.

2. A government is an expensive institution, and requires a great deal of money to carry it on. This must be had from some source. To raise it by the imposition of taxes or duties on merchandise imported from foreign countries, has been considered the cheapest mode of collecting it, and the least burdensome upon the people. Hence by far the greatest part of the

revenue of the United States has been raised in this way. Then comes the second object; which is to raise the price of imported articles by just as much as the duty on them amounts to, thus enabling our own manufactures to compete with those of foreign countries. It has been thought to be a good policy to make our own goods as far as we can, and thus render ourselves more independent of foreign countries. But on this question there have been two opinions, which have been so strong as to form the principal difference between different political parties; one contending that the tariff (rate of duties) should be so low that only money enough should be raised from duties to support the government; or, in other words, that the duties on imports should be so graduated as to bring the greatest amount into the Treasury of the United States, without regard to the question of protection to home manufactures; or, that the incidental protection a low tariff would give, was sufficient.

3. On the other side it is contended that our best policy is, and that our economical interests would be best promoted by, imposing so high a duty on imported goods as to prevent to some extent their importation, and thus to build up American manufactures. Much has been said and much has been written on both sides of this question, both in and out of Congress, and the policy of the government is unsettled to this day. Hence the great amount of legislation on this subject. Sometimes the high tariff party, having a majority in Congress, would pass an act fixing a high rate of duties; and when the low tariff party

gained the ascendency, they would change the tariff, and fix the duties at a lower rate. For the last thirty years the government has been vibrating between these two systems, very much to the detriment of our prosperity, and the question still remains unsettled, and will probably be submitted to as many changes in the future as it has been in the past.

4. The collection of duties on imports is a very large branch of the business of the government, requiring a great many custom houses and custom house officers. There are probably two hundred of the former in all the States; yet most of the revenue is collected at a few of the largest seaport cities, such as New York, Philadelphia, Boston, Baltimore, New Orleans and San Francisco. Every seaport where vessels from foreign countries are allowed to come in and discharge their cargoes, and pay the duties thereon, is called a port of entry. After the vessel has been reported to the collector of the port, and her duties paid or secured to be paid, and the owner of the goods desire them delivered at some other place where there is no custom house, that privilege is granted, and the place where the goods are finally discharged is called a port of delivery.

5. Among the powers which the Constitution confers upon Congress, is that of laying duties on goods imported. Congress alone has this power. No State can exercise it. It also declares that all duties shall be equal in all the States.

Not only has the tariff (which means the rate of duties charged) been a source of much debate and legislation, but also the mode of imposing these taxes. Two modes have been advocated. Sometimes one and sometimes another has been adopted and practiced. The system of *ad valorem* duties is one, and that of *specific* duties is the other. *Ad valorem duties* are laid upon the cost of the article in the country whence it was brought. Hence when goods were low, the duties would be correspondingly low, and *vice versa* when high. But this plan has been subject to great objections, for importers have been often known to have false invoices made out, wherein their goods were marked much below their real cost, and by this means the government is defrauded and honest dealers injured. To avoid this, the other mode has been resorted to, viz.:

"Specific duties," by which the tax is laid upon the article itself—that is, the duty is so much per pound, yard, gallon, &c., without regard to what was the price originally paid for it.

6. There are a great number of imported articles, upon which there is no duty. These are called free goods. But the laws are so often changed that what are free goods now may be taxed at the next session of Congress; and goods paying duties this year may be put on the free list next.

DRAWBACKS.

7. When the duties on foreign goods have been paid, and they are afterwards exported, the duties which have been paid are refunded to the owner. The money thus paid back is called a drawback. All imported goods are entitled to drawback whenever they are taken out of the United States.

8. In this connection, we see no impropriety in noticing another thing, though of an exactly opposite character to duties; and that is,

BOUNTIES ON EXPORTED GOODS.

These take money out of, instead of putting it in the treasury, yet the government in a few cases has allowed bounties upon exported articles. Fish taken by American vessels, refined sugar and distilled spirits made from imported sugar and molasses, are examples. This was done to encourage domestic industry and enterprise.

CHAPTER LII.

Tonnage.

In the last chapter we treated of duties and tariffs, but only as they related to imported goods. In this we will speak of another kind of duties differing very materially from the first. The first kind is imposed only upon foreign productions, but the latter upon home-made as well as foreign; and this is the duty which the government lays upon the tonnage of ships and other vessels.

Tonnage is the capacity of a ship or any other vessel for carrying weight, which is always reckoned by the ton; and is ascertained by measuring the length, breadth and depth of the vessel. This has been deemed a proper subject of taxation, for the purpose of adding to the revenue of the country.

At a very early period (1790) in our history these duties were imposed, both on our own and on foreign vessels, though heavier duties are laid on foreign than upon American vessels. In the first act passed on this subject, in 1790, this duty on our own was only six cents per ton, while that on foreign bottoms was fifty cents.

Congress alone has the power to impose these duties. No State can do it. In 1862, such were the wants of the treasury, that the tonnage duties both on American and foreign vessels were increased ten cents per ton. This tax is collected only once in a year, by the collector of the port where the vessel happens to be.

CHAPTER LIII.

Revenue Cutters.

1. REVENUE cutters are small sized vessels belonging to the government, and are used for the purpose of aiding revenue officers in the collection of duties on imported goods; or, in other words, to prevent smuggling. These vessels are built and used exclusively for this purpose, and are not reckoned as any part of the navy, though officered and manned much in the same manner. The commissioned officers are appointed by the President and Senate.

The duties assigned to revenue cutters are, to sail along the coast and look after ships and other vessels going into any of the ports of the United States; to board them and examine their papers, that is, if going into an American port, and within four leagues of the coast; to examine the manifest of the cargo and every part of the vessel; to put proper fastenings upon the hatches and other communications with the hold; and to place a man or men on board who must remain with her until her arrival into port, when she is delivered over to the charge of the proper custom house officer.

2. The officers of revenue cutters are deemed officers of the customs, and hence are subject to the orders of the Secretary of the Treasury and the collectors and other revenue officers at the ports where employed. But if so directed by the President, in an emergency they may coöperate with the navy; and in such cases if the officers or men are wounded in the discharge of their duties, their names may be placed on the navy

pension list, and they will be entitled to the same rate of pension as other officers and seamen of the United States navy.

3. Revenue cutters are distinguished from other vessels by the pendant and ensign they carry. These have such marks upon them as the President shall direct; and in case any ship or other vessel liable to seizure shall not bring-to upon request of the commanding officer of the cutter, he is authorized to fire into such vessel, after exhibiting his pendant and ensign, in order to compel her to obey his orders and allow herself to be boarded and examined. This he may do without incurring responsibility for life or property that may be destroyed by the act.

4. One of the objects designed to be accomplished by the use of revenue cutters, and the duties assigned to them, is to prevent vessels from running goods ashore after having neared the coast, and thus to escape payment of the duties. This could be done in the night or in foggy weather without detection but for the vigilance of these vessels, which are well armed and well manned. Formerly they were all sailing vessels, but steamers are now used also.

5. The commander of a revenue cutter must report weekly to the collector of the port where he is stationed, the transactions of the cutter, with the names and description of all the vessels he has boarded; specifying whether they are American or foreign vessels, whether loaded or in ballast, together with all such information as it may be necessary for the revenue officers of the port to possess.

CHAPTER LIV.

The Mint.

1. The United States mint, located at Philadelphia, is one of the most important establishments of the government. An act of Congress, passed in 1792, was the first step towards its creation. Its design was, and its principal business has been, to coin the precious metals into money. It has been for more than eighteen hundred years the usage of civilized governments to coin their own money. Ours, at a very early period of its existence, began to do the same thing, and will probably continue to do it as long as it shall exist. Before the art of coining was known, the precious metals were used as a standard of value, but they passed from one to another by weight. The plan of cutting them into small pieces, and then stamping their value upon them, by which their worth could be known as soon as seen, was an improvement upon the former mode. This process is denominated coining. It has of late been brought so near perfection that our pieces of money are fine specimens of art.

2. This establishment, like all others belonging to the government, is under the direction of officers chosen for that purpose.

They are a director, a treasurer, an assayer, a melter and refiner, a chief coiner, and an engraver.

All of them are appointed by the President and Senate. The director appoints assistants and clerks.

All must give bonds for the faithful performance of their respective duties, upon which they enter under oath. The duties of these different officers may almost be known by the names they bear. The director is the head of the institution, and the others act under his general direction, each having his appropriate duties to perform. In the month of January of each year the director must make a report to the President of the operations of the mint and its branches for the preceding year.

3. Any person may take gold or silver bullion or ores to the mint and receive it back in coin, for a very trifling expense. Before it is coined, after its value has been determined by the assayer, the director will give a certificate for it, which is of the same value as the bullion deposited.

4. We have stated that the principal business at the mint is the conversion of the precious metals into coin or money. But this is not its exclusive business. Another part is to melt and assay these metals, and to run them into ingots or bars either of pure or standard gold and silver, according to the wish of its owner. In our article on the assay office at the city of New York, we have explained this process more fully than we need to do here.

Until 1835 the mint at Philadelphia was the only establishment in the United States for coining money. But in that year a law was passed establishing branch mints at New Orleans, in Louisiana; at Charlotte, in North Carolina; and at Dahlonega, in Georgia. In 1852, another branch was established in California; in

1862, another at Denver, in Colorado Territory; and in 1863, another at Carson City, in Nevada Territory, since made a State; in 1864, another at San Francisco, in California, and another at Dales City, in Oregon. Except the one in California, but little has ever been done at these branches. Political reasons in some cases had more to do with their establishment than any necessity for them. We need not take time to name these officials or to explain their operations. They are all similar to the principal one at Philadelphia; for the laws relating to that are made to apply to these branches.

6. The Constitution gives Congress the exclusive right to coin money, and prohibits all the States from doing it. This Congress does by the laws it passes in relation to the subject, and the various officers and workmen employed to execute the work are only the agents of Congress.

The various coins which Congress has from time to time ordered to be made are of the following names and value:

Gold.	*Value.*	*Silver.*	*Value.*	*Copper.*
Eagle,	$10 00	Dollar,	$1 00	One cent,
Half-Eagle,	5 00	Half-Dollar,	50	Two cents,
Quar. Eag.,	2 50	Quar. Dol.,	25	Three cents, and
Doub. Eag.,	20 00	Dime,	10	formerly 1-2 c.
Three Dols.,	3 00	Half Dime,	5	But these are now
One Dollar,	1 00	Three ct. piece,	3	discontinued.

7. Our coins are not made of pure gold and pure silver, but of standard gold and silver; that is, gold or silver alloyed or mixed with some baser or less valuable metal. By the law of 1837, standard gold and silver were declared to be nine hundred parts of pure

metal, and one hundred parts alloy—equal to one-tenth alloy. Gold coins are alloyed with silver and copper, equal parts of each. Silver coins are alloyed with copper alone. Gold is declared to be worth fifteen times as much as silver by weight.

In addition to our own coins, Congress has from time to time passed laws declaring the value of foreign coins, and making them a legal tender. But these laws were all repealed by the act of 1857, and it was made the duty of the director of the mint to have them assayed, and to determine their weight, fineness and value; for they are still used by banks and merchants, and pass at the value determined by the mint.

The mint, up to 1861, had coined in gold, silver, and copper coin, 800,662,475 pieces, worth $799,923,362.

CHAPTER LV.

Assay Office.

1. In 1853 the Secretary of the Treasury was authorized to establish an office in the city of New York for the receipt, melting, refining and assaying of gold and silver bullion and foreign coin, and for casting the same into bars, ingots or disks. The assistant treasurer of the United States in New York, is treasurer of said assay office, and the Secretary of the Treasury appoints such other clerks, assistants and workmen as shall be necessary for the management of its business.

2. Persons having gold or silver bullion, ores or foreign coin, may deposit them in this office, and here it will be refined and assayed (at no more cost than the actual expenses of doing the work), and its value ascertained, and the owner will be paid therefor in coins of the same value and metal as that deposited. It is not coined in this office, but cast into bars, ingots or disks—either of pure metal or of standard fineness, as the owner may prefer—the true weight and value of which are stamped thereon; and the owner may either take them in payment for his bullion or foreign coin, or it will be coined for him at the United States mint, if he wishes. The bars spoken of are often kept in that form, and are used as coin among banks, brokers and merchants, who receive and pay large amounts of

the precious metals. With them it passes as coin, for, as stated, its exact weight and value are stamped upon it.

3. This establishment was located at New York more for the convenience of the thousands who do business there, than for the necessity of such an institution; for at the mint at Philadelphia there is a department for doing the same work as is done here. But at New York, the great emporium of America, there is a larger amount of foreign coin than in any other place, and it is often advantageous to its owners to have it converted into American coin, that it may be used with greater facility. Although many foreign coins do circulate in this country, but few know their value. Consequently they do not pass so readily; and for this reason they are melted and run into bars of known value, or re-coined into American money.

CHAPTER LVI.

National Banks.

1. THE banking system established by an act of Congress in 1863, has brought a great number of banks into existence, and upon a plan so different from any heretofore in use, that it seems germane to our subject to notice it.

If the "national banks," for so they are called, are not institutions of the government, they are institutions which exist by the authority of the government.

It legalizes their existence, and to some extent controls their actions. By the act referred to, any number of persons not less than five may associate themselves together for the purpose of banking, by compliance with the following conditions:

2. First: They must, under their hands and seals, make a certificate which shall specify,

1. The name assumed by such association.

2. The place where its business is to be conducted.

3. The amount of its capital stock, (which cannot be less than $50,000), and the number of its shares.

4. The names of its shareholders, and the number of shares held by each.

5. The time when such association shall commence business.

6. A declaration that said certificate is made to enable such persons to avail themselves of the advantages of this act.

3. This certificate must be properly acknowledged before some competent person, and must be sent to the comptroller of the currency in the Treasury Department, to be recorded and kept by him. When this, and all other acts which the law requires, has been done by the association, the comptroller of the currency gives them a certificate under his hand and official seal, to that effect, and that they are authorized to commence business. This constitutes the association a corporation. They have the right to make and use a common seal, and have all the rights, and are liable to all the responsibilities of ordinary legalized corporations; and may exist not to exceed twenty years from the passage of this act. Every shareholder is made personally liable for the debts of the association or bank, to the amount of the par value of his stock.

4. In order to secure the holders of bills issued by these banks, they must deposit with the Treasurer of the United States, United States bonds bearing interest to an amount not less than one-third of the capital stock paid in. These bonds are safely kept by the said Treasurer. The comptroller of the currency then issues to the bank an amount of bank notes equal to the amount of bonds thus deposited, less ten per cent. In case the bank should fail to redeem its circulating bills, its bonds are sold, and with the proceeds the comptroller of the currency redeems them, or orders them to be paid at the United States Treasury. The bonds held by the Treasurer as security for the redemption of the bills issued by the association, must be transferred to him in trust; thus giving him entire

control of them in case it becomes necessary to sell them in order to redeem the bills of any association which may have failed to pay them on demand.

5. This act of 1863 has brought a great number of new banks into existence. It allowed banks already existing under State laws, to become banking associations under this act. Most of the existing State banks have done so, organizing themselves under this law. Hence with few exceptions, (which will probably soon disappear), we have a uniform system of banking all over the United States. The bills of these banks pass in any part of the country. The holders of them are more secure, because there is ample security for their redemption (in case the bank fails to pay) deposited in the United States Treasury, where they will be paid on presentation.

6. The bill-holder is also better protected against counterfeits than he was under the old system; for all the bills issued by these associations are engraved by the government, and the plates and dies on which they are printed are kept by the comptroller of the currency in the Treasury Department. The engraving is done in the best possible manner, and it is exceedingly difficult to counterfeit them. Besides this, they all have the imprint of the seal of the Treasury on their face, and are numbered and countersigned by the treasurer and register. With all these guards and precautions, we have the best paper currency ever used since the establishment of the government.

7. This act necessarily threw upon the Treasury Department a great increase of labor, and in order to pro-

vide for it, a separate bureau was created, which is denominated the bureau of currency; the chief officer of which is called the comptroller of currency. He acts under the general direction of the Secretary of the Treasury. This bureau is charged with the execution of this and all other laws that may be passsed by Congress respecting the national currency. The comptroller of the currency is appointed by the President and Senate, has a deputy, receives a salary of $5,000 per year, holds his office five years, has an official seal, gives bonds to the amount of $100,000, and takes and subscribes the oath of office prescribed by the Constitution and the laws. His duties are numerous and very responsible, he having hundreds of millions under his care.

The term national banks, given to these institutions, and national currency to the bills they issue, were given from the fact that they were organized by an act of Congress, and that the security for the redemption of their bills consists exclusively of national bonds; no other securities will be taken.

CHAPTER LVII.

Military Academy.

1. The Military Academy, located on the west bank of the Hudson river, at West Point, in the State of New York, and about 50 miles from the city of New York, is one of the government institutions. It had its origin in an act of Congress passed as early as 1802. Under this act this far-famed military school was commenced, but on a scale, in every respect, very much inferior to what it has since become.

2. Its name explains its character and objects. It was established and has been continued at a great expense, for the purpose of teaching and training up young men in the science and art of war, that in any emergency the country might have a sufficient number of men, educated and skilled in all such arts and sciences as appertain to war. Hence, mathematics, engineering, gunnery, drawing, natural and experimental philosophy and military tactics, are among the principal branches taught. In all of these, able professors give instruction to the cadets, as the pupils are called. Chemistry, geology, and the French language are also taught at this institution. The instruction is thorough, the discipline excellent, and some of the graduates of this celebrated school rank high among the scientific men of the country.

3. Congress controls and regulates this establishment, as it does all other departments, institutions, and

works belonging to the government. It enacts all laws relating to its officers, professors, and cadets, and to the management of the institution.

4. By a law passed in 1843, the number of cadets to be admitted was made to correspond with the number of Senators and Representatives from each State. Every State and Territory is entitled to send as many cadets as it has Senators and Representatives in Congress. This gives each Territory, however, but one; as a Territory has no Senators, and but one Representative. By the same law the District of Columbia is allowed one. To give every part of the country an equal chance, it was enacted that each Congressional district in each State and Territory should be allowed to send one cadet, to be educated at West Point. These are generally nominated for appointment by the Congressmen from their respective districts, and the President appoints. The cadet must be an actual resident of the district for which he is appointed.

5. In addition to these, it is provided by the same act, that ten more cadets may be appointed at large; *i. e.*, without regard to Congressional districts. These provisions would make the number of cadets at the present time (1869), to be three hundred and fifteen. In order to be admitted as a cadet, the candidate must be well versed in reading, writing and arithemetic; must not be under 14 nor over 21 years of age; and must sign articles, agreeing to serve the United States eight years. After he has finished his studies and has graduated, he is considered as a candidate for a commission in the army, according to the duties he may be competent to perform.

6. The Military Academy may be considered a branch of the War Department. Men who have been educated there have rendered the country signal service in times of war, have made able commanders, and have proved themselves thoroughly skilled in military science. Not only in the military service has it been a benefit to the country, but in the civil walks of life. Many of its graduates have distinguished themselves as engineers, astronomers, and in other scientific professions and useful employments.

7. There is an annual examination of the cadets, and of the general affairs of the institution, by a committee appointed by the President, for that purpose.

It is composed of Congressmen and military officers. It is the duty of these examiners to attend the examination, inspect its discipline, and course of instruction, look after its fiscal affiairs, and all other matters relating to the Academy, and report the same to the Secretary of War, for the use of Congress.

CHAPTER LVIII.

Naval Academy.

1. We will place our notice of this institution next to that of the Military Academy, as there is a strong analogy between the two. We remarked on that, that it might be considered a branch of the War Department. So we say of this, it may be considered a branch of the Navy Department. Both are designed to educate and train men for future public service, in different departments.

2. This school is now established at Annapolis, in the State of Maryland, near Washington. Like the Military Academy, it has its superintendent and professors. The pupils are called midshipmen. They are taught navigation and such other branches of science as are necessary to make them good seamen and naval officers. They are selected upon nearly the same plan as cadets. Each Congressional District in every State and Territory, is entitled to send two students to be educated at the Academy. The District of Columbia is also entitled to send two. Besides which, the President is allowed to appoint ten additional ones at large, and three more from the boys enlisted in the navy.

3. After their graduating examination, if they pass, they are commissioned as ensigns in the navy, and rank according to merit. Before admission, they are examined according to the regulations made by the Secretary of the Navy, and must be between the ages of fourteen

and seventeen years, sound, robust, and of good constitution.

4. The course of study in this, as well as in the Military Academy, is adapted to the profession which the students are expected to follow,—the one in the navy, the other in the army. More are educated at these great national schools than the government needs in time of peace. Hence it is that many of the graduates are engaged in civil employment. Thus these institutions have been of great service to the country, outside of the army and navy, for they have added to the number of well educated and scientific men, who may be useful in any of the walks of life. Their graduates elevate the standard of intelligence in the community, especially when they engage in the work of instruction.

Both of these institutions are supported at the expense of the government. The tuition and board of cadets in one, and of the midshipmen in the other, costs them nothing.

CHAPTER LIX.

Armories and Arsenals.

As early as 1794, Congress enacted that three or four arsenals and magazines, with an armory attached to each, should be established for the safe keeping of military stores. An arsenal is a place where arms and military stores are kept. An armory is a place where arms are made or repaired. The armories where arms are manufactured are at Springfield, in Massachusetts, and at Harpers' Ferry, in Virginia. But there are many others where they are repaired.

In 1808, the President was authorized to purchase sites and to erect as many more arsenals and manufactories of arms as he might deem expedient. Each of these establishments was formerly under the direction of a superintendent; but they are now placed under the direction of the Ordnance Department. The office of superintendent of the armories at Springfield and Harpers' Ferry, was also abolished in 1842; and its duties have since been performed by such officers of the ordnance corps as were designated by the President. In each armory there is employed a master armorer, who superintends the workmen. We have not the means of knowing what number of these establishments have been authorized in the United States, but in addition to those already named there are arsenals and armories at Pittsburgh and Bridesburgh, in Pennsylvania; at Washington city; at Watervliet, in New York; Watertown, Mass.; at Columbus, Ohio; at Indianapolis, in Indiana; and at Rock Island, in Illinois. They are parts of the military establishment of the country, and belong to the War Department.

CHAPTER LX.

The Army and Navy.

1. A DETAILED and minute description of the various departments, officials, works and modes of operation in these two great government establishments, would require a larger volume than the present to contain it. We must, therefore, in a work of this kind, be content to speak of them in the most general terms. Indeed it would be quite uninteresting to the general reader to peruse a detailed account of the division of the army into corps, brigades, regiments and companies, with all the grades of officers commanding them; or of all the appendages to an army, such as the commissary department, the quartermaster's department, and many other important attachments to a regular army. And what we say of the army would hold true of the navy.

2. We will then only say that the army and navy are the two great arms of our government, as they are of all others. They are the means of defense against attacks or invasions from other powers; as well as of offense, when circumstances require us to invade foreign countries, or to enforce our rights upon the high seas, though this is especially the duty of the navy, which has rights all over the seas equal with those of any other nation. But to resist foreign aggression, or to defend our rights on the seas, is by no means the only reason for maintaining an army and a navy. Experience has shown that such is the depravity, the law-

lessness, and the wickedness of a part of mankind, that nothing but compulsion will keep them in order; nothing but force will keep them from the violation of the best of laws. This reckless and vicious class of persons are so numerous that laws could never be executed, nor order preserved, if no military or naval power stood behind the civil power to enforce the laws when they are resisted by any considerable body of persons. But for the known fact that the military power stands ready at the call of the executive authority of the government, resistance to every law which was distasteful to the most depraved and vicious, would be made. Thus order at home almost as much requires the military power, as our defense against the wrongs or invasions of foreigners.

3. The navy cannot act in all emergencies as the army can, because it is necessarily restricted in its actions. It can only act on the seas or upon places accessible to it by water; whereas the army can operate any where upon land. It never has been the policy or the practice of the United States to keep a large standing army, for it has been thought inconsistent with a Republican government; first, because it seemed to imply a want of confidence in the intelligence and patriotism of the people, the majority of whom are deemed law-abiding, patriotic, and willing without compulsion to support the authority of the civil power of the government. And another reason is that a large army is a very expensive thing. Indeed the army and the navy are by far the two most expensive departments of the government. Economy, therefore,

is another reason why our standing army has always been small in times of peace. In this connection we will notice another fact which renders it unnecessary for our government to maintain a large army at any other time than when we are at war, and that is our militia system, which was established immediately after the organization of the government. By a law of Congress, it was enacted that every sound and healthy man, with a few exceptions in special cases, between the ages of 18 and 45, should be enrolled and equipped for military duty. Then, by the laws of the States, they are required on certain days in each year to meet in companies, regiments or brigades, for drill and practice in military exercises.

4. By these means military organizations are kept up in every part of the country, together with some knowledge of the military art. These, in time of war or domestic insurrection, may be called out with but a few days' notice; and a large army of citizen soldiers can be raised in a very short time. With such facilities for raising men, it is unnecessary to keep a standing army of much magnitude. A few thousand men to guard our fortifications and military posts are sufficient.

The late civil war between the South and the North gave ample evidence of this; for when it became necessary to raise a million of men, it was done in a short time, and after a little practice they became good soldiers. Until the recent civil war, the navy of the United States was, in comparison with that of several other nations, small and weak. But during the rebellion the necessity of greater force in this arm of our government, very soon brought into existence the most powerful navy in the world; and to-day our navy ranks as one of the best, if not the very best in the world; notwithstanding that it has been greatly diminished since peace was restored.

5. The necessities of the case called for many more vessels than the government had, and a large number were purchased which had been built and used for commercial purposes. Besides these a great number were built, and many English vessels which had run the blockade, or attempted to do so, were taken as prizes, and immediately placed in our navy. Hence perhaps no navy upon earth ever grew from smallness to greatness, and from weakness to power so rapidly as did the American navy from 1861 to 1865, or during the continuance of the rebellion.

Not only was the number of ships, men and guns greatly increased, but the power and efficiency of our guns were augmented beyond anything known before; as was also the power of our ships of war for offense or defense. When we see cannon which will send balls five miles, and do terrible execution, and iron-clad ships so constructed as to be as impervious to cannon balls as a rock is to small shot, we may place our navy on an equality, if not in advance of any other which can be found on earth. In this respect we stand on a proud eminence in contrast with any other nation.

6. We have said already that since the restoration of peace among ourselves, the force of the navy had been greatly reduced and brought down to a peace

standard. Yet it is still of sufficient power to answer any emergency that is likely to occur. From a late report of the Secretary of the Navy, we learn that the present naval power of the country consists of 278 vessels of all descriptions; carrying 2,351 guns, and about 13,600 seamen, which in case of war could easily be doubled.

7. We have in another place spoken of the naval academy, and said that its object was to educate young men for the naval service. The government has also appropriated ships, and established schools on board of them, for the instruction of boys in navigation and naval warfare. These are called apprentices; and for good conduct and proficiency in their studies, they are promoted to the naval academy, and placed in the line of promotion. Thus the government is training up a class of young men for the navy who will not only be well educated, but well drilled in all the arts and sciences which pertain to the naval service. "In time of peace prepare for war," is a proverb on which the government is now acting.

8. For the construction of our vessels of war and for their equipment and repairs, several navy yards have been established along the coast and on some of the navigable rivers. Here the ships are built, armed, equipped, manned and fitted out for their destination. The principal navy yards are at Philadelphia, Pa., Brooklyn N. Y., Norfolk, Va., and Pensacola, Fla.

9. Not half of the vessels belonging to the navy are, however, now (in time of peace) in commission, that is, in active service. The rest are either laid up, or in process of repair. Most of those in commission are

employed in what is called squadron service. The Secretary of the Navy in a late report enumerates seven of these squadrons; viz.: the European, the Asiatic, the North Atlantic, the South Atlantic, the North Pacific, the South Pacific and the Gulf squadrons. The names given to these squadrons indicate their whereabouts, and their cruising grounds. These squadrons consist of six, eight, ten, twelve or fifteen vessels, as the work to be done may require. It is their duty to visit the sea ports of the various countries along the coasts of which they cruise, in order to protect our merchantmen against pirates or enemies of any description, which may molest them or interfere with their rights and privileges ; and also to look after the interests and dignity of the United States.

10. These squadrons are under command of a high naval officer of the rank of commodore or rear admiral, whose ship is called the flag ship of the squadron. Many of our naval officers have distinguished themselves for bravery, skill, and patriotic devotion to their country, and have occupied the highest position of honor, and the most exalted places in the esteem and affection of their countrymen.

In 1862, Congress enacted that there should be nine grades of officers in the navy, and that their corresponding rank with military officers should be as follows:

1. Rear-Admiral,	with	Major-General.
2. Commodores,	"	Brigadier-Generals.
3. Captains,	"	Colonels.
4. Commanders,	"	Lieutenant-Colonel.
5. Lieut.-Commanders,	"	Majors.
6. Lieutenants,	"	Captains.
7. Masters,	"	First Lieutenants.
8. Ensigns,	"	Second Lieutenants.

9. Midshipmen, with no corresponding rank in the army.

CHAPTER LXI.

Articles of War.

1. As a sequel, or as a kind of appendix to what has been said about the army, it seems appropriate to make some remarks upon the "articles of war," as they are commonly called. These are not, as some might suppose them to be, rules made by the highest officer in command, for the government of the officers and soldiers of inferior rank; but they are laws of Congress, acts of that body. Hence they come from the highest authority in the land, and are as binding upon the highest in command as upon the humblest private.

2. They relate, of course, exclusively to the army, and consist of one hundred and one articles, each containing some specific rule or direction for the government of either officers, soldiers, or attachees of the army. They form a complete code of laws for them all while in actual service. The first one of these requires every officer in the army to subscribe these rules and regulations, before he enters upon his duties; thus signifying his approval of them, and tacitly promising to regulate his conduct by them.

3. But to recite the provisions of each article would require more space than we can appropriate to this theme. Let it suffice, then, to enumerate some of the principal subjects embraced in these articles, showing what matters relating to the army Congress has seen fit to regulate by legislation. These are—

1st. Directions to both officers and men to attend public worship, accompanied by penalties prescribed for any improper behavior on such occasions.

4. They prohibit the use of profane oaths and execrations, of contemptuous and disrespectful language against their superiors, the raising of a mutiny among the troops; and the striking, raising any weapon, or offering any violence to a superior officer. They prescribe the oath or affirmation which every officer and private must take upon his entrance into the army, and the penalties for the violation of any of the articles of war, or the omission of any duties incumbent upon them. They contain rules for the enlistment, dismissal, and discharging of men, and for granting them furloughs and leave of absence, with penalties for desertion, or absence without leave.

5. They prohibit duelling or challenging to a duel; make rules for sutlers in the army; prohibit embezzlement of public property, or public money; sleeping while on guard; drunkenness; absence from parade; raising false alarms; cowardice; disclosing watchwords; aiding or corresponding with the enemy. They prescribe the rank and grade of officers; direct how courts martial shall be constituted; how proceedings shall be conducted in them; and how deceased officers' and soldiers' money, effects and arms, shall be disposed of.

6. These are the most important among the provisions of the articles of war, and, with others of less note must be read and published once in every six months to every regiment or troop in the service. In

many instances they prescribe specifically what punishment shall be inflicted for any violation of these rules and regulations; but in other cases they leave the mode and amount of punishment to the discretion of the court martial before which the accused is tried. Penalties for military offences rise in severity, corresponding with the turpitude of the crime, from a small fine or imprisonment, up to death. The sentence of any court martial may, however, always be modified, commuted, or set aside by the President of the United States, who is, as is well known, commander-in-chief both of the army and navy. A general court martial is composed of commissioned officers, not less than five, nor more than thirteen in number.

CHAPTER LXII.

Chaplains.

1. If chaplains are not officers of the government, they are at least employees of it, for they are appointed by its authority, and paid from its treasury. Those in the army receive the same pay and emoluments as a major of infantry; or this was the compensation allowed by act of Congress in 1812. But by an act of 1862, it was fixed at $100 per month, and two rations per day, for those in the army or hospitals. By the act of 1812, one chaplain was allowed to every brigade; but by an act of 1861, (during the civil war,) one for every regiment was allowed.

Navy chaplains, in 1835, received $1,200 per year. But in 1860 this was raised to a lieutenant's pay; and this in 1862 was $1,800 per annum.

Chaplains in Congress receive $750 per annum.

2. The United States also employ a chaplain in the military academy at West Point.

From the foregoing it will be seen that in time of war, with one chaplain for every regiment, and one for every ship of war, and others in hospitals and military posts, quite a large number of clergymen are employed by the government.

This provision for the religious instruction of those who cannot, from their peculiar position, attend the preaching of the Gospel, or other religious services, is certainly an indication that our government respects religion, and looks after the spiritual as well as the temporal interests of its army and navy.

3. In the appointment of chaplains, the government pursues a liberal course. No particular preference is given to any denomination, but they are appointed from almost every religious sect, and allowed to conduct religious services after the forms of the church to which they respectively belong.

Every body knows what the duties of a chaplain are. So we need not explain them here, and will only add that a faithful chaplain in the army in time of war has much to do besides preaching and holding regular services. The wounded, the sick, and the dying, should be the particular objects of his attention. He should not only minister religious instruction and consolation to them, but look after their physical comforts. Many of these clergymen, during the late most unfortunate civil war, distinguished themselves by their exertions to promote the bodily comforts of those unfortunate men, as well as to give them religious instruction, not refusing to nurse the sick and wounded whenever they could relieve their pains or mitigate their sufferings.

CHAPTER LXIII.

The Naval Observatory.

1. THIS institution is located in Washington, and was established by act of Congress in 1842, and put into operation in 1844. Its name indicates the particular object or purpose of its establishment. The "naval observatory" suggests the idea that it has some connexion with the navy, and so it has; for the immediate object in founding it was to determine such astronomical problems as would be of great service to the navy. It is well known that astronomy lies at the foundation of nautical science, and that without the knowledge of the former, but little skill in the latter could ever be acquired.

2. The observatory was built and furnished with various astronomical and philosophical instruments, and a corps of professors were appointed to watch the movements of the heavenly bodies, and to make such observations and experiments as would enable them to determine many unsettled questions which relate to the science of navigation; and incidentally to another great government work, having especial reference to the same subject; that is, the coast survey.

The coast survey has already been ot great service to the interests of navigation—whether national or commercial vessels are regarded—and, when finished, much greater benefits are to be expected. When a sufficient number of observations and experiments shall have been made at the naval observatory, and published to the world, much valuable information will be added to what is already known. And indeed it would be disreputable to a nation having so large a navy and such a vast number of merchant ships upon the ocean, to do nothing for or add nothing to the science of navigation. It would be an unwise policy if economy only were studied, and we would justly deserve the reproach of being penurious, short-sighted, and miserably wanting in disposition to promote the general good of the world.

3. During the first nine years after the government of the United States went into operation, we had no Navy Department. The administration of the affairs of the very small navy which we then had, was placed in the hands of the Secretary of War; and after a Navy Department was established, but little was done by the government to improve nautical science until the naval observatory was built; since that, much attention has been given to this important subject, and it is expected that corresponding results will follow.

4. This institution owes more to that enlightened and truly patriotic President, John Q. Adams, than to any other man. He recommended it as far back as 1823, and again in his first message to Congress. But political opposition to the man prevented his recommendations from being acted upon till nearly 20 years after they were made. This opposition was finally overcome, and we, and posterity after us, will reap the fruits of Mr. Adams' suggestions and labors to pro-

mote the cultivation of that science which is at once a benefit and an honor to our country.

5. The professors are assiduous in their labors, and publish the results of their observations and the facts they have determined. These are not only of use to our own seamen, but to those of all nations who are doing business on the great deep. Here the charts made by the coast survey are deposited, and from hence all our national vessels are furnished with them, and with all the nautical instruments they require.

The charts, instruments and books relating to astronomy and navigation, found here, make it the head quarters and depot of nautical science in the United States.

CHAPTER LXIV.

Coast Survey.

1. THE coast survey, the naval observatory and light houses are all of a similar character—government works in their purposes, and in their utility. The plan of making a survey of the whole coast, and of keeping it lighted, is one founded in a wise and generous policy. It aids commerce and encourages navigation, by making known the hidden dangers of the sea, and by giving directions how to avoid them.

2. This government undertaking has not been as vigorously prosecuted as some other enterprises conducted by it. As early as 1807, Congress passed an act authorizing the President to have this work done. Much of it has been done, yet it is not finished at this day. Our acquisition of Florida, Texas and California has greatly extended our sea coast since the work was commenced, and its accomplishment has cost more time and labor than was anticipated at the beginning, yet we think it ought to have been completed in much less than 60 years.

3. This work, like that relating to light houses, is under the management of a board, consisting of a superintendent, two principal assistants, two naval officers and four officers of the army. These nine constitute the board. Then there are as many officers of the army and navy employed in the execution of the work as are deemed necessary. And the public vessels, by direction of the President, may be used in order to fa-

cilitate the work, for much of it must be done at sea. The survey extends 20 leagues from the shore. The surveyors must make accurate charts (which I will call sea maps), of the whole coast, in which are laid down all the islands, shoals, roads or anchorage grounds within twenty leagues of any part of the shore of the United States. The courses or distances between the principal capes or headlands must be laid down, together with the soundings (depth of water) and every thing else necessary to make a complete and accurate chart of every part of our coasts.

4. An annual report of this work must be made to Congress in December of each year, accompanied with charts, showing the progress of the work, the number of persons employed, the expenses incurred, the amount of work finished, and what is unfinished. These reports and charts are carefully preserved, and copies of them may be had at Washington for the use of our naval and merchant ships, to which they are of great service, as guides whenever they are on or near the coast. This work, in its utility, is not confined to ourselves; but the important information obtained by it is of great use to the navigators of all nations who come into our ports or cruise on our coasts. They derive the same benefits from this work that we derive from theirs of the same kind. It is creditable to any nation to do such things as are beneficial to the world, such acts as contribute to the welfare of humanity. Shipwrecks belong to the list of terrible calamities which often befall those "who go down to the sea in ships, that do business in great waters." Whoever diminishes these is a public benefactor.

CHAPTER LXV.

Light Houses, Buoys and Beacons.

1. THESE are all government establishments, and we must therefore notice them. They are built, lighted, repaired, and taken care of, wholly by the government. Every body knows the object for which they are constructed. Guided by them, the mariner may approach the coast in the night with safety; while without them many noble ships would be wrecked, which now safely arrive in port. Humanity and interest both dictate their construction near the entrance to every sea port; and at the most dangerous and prominent points all along the sea coast. This our government has wisely done, not only on the sea coasts, which stretch for thousands of miles along our borders, but also along the shores of our navigable lakes and rivers.

2. Keepers are appointed by the government to keep them in repair, and to see that they are properly lighted every night. We have no means of knowing the number of these useful establishments, but there must be several hundred of them; for we have more sea coast than any other nation upon the globe, with a still greater length of lake and river shore. They are located at prominent points, and at dangerous places, all along the extensive lines of coast and shores.

3. All this work, like everything else done by the government, must be done according to law. To the end that light houses should be constructed and kept in repair, and that competent men might have the

whole matter in charge, a law of 1852 authorized the President to appoint two officers of the navy of high rank, one officer of the corps of engineers of the army, one officer of the topographical engineers, and two civilians of high scientific attainments, to form a LIGHT HOUSE BOARD for the United States. This board is attached to the Treasury Department, and the Secretary of the Treasury superintends its operations. The board has in charge the building, illumination, and inspection of light houses, light vessels, buoys, beacons, sea marks and their appendages.

4. The Secretary of the Treasury is president of the board, and may convene them whenever he deems it necessary.

The law makes it the duty of the board to divide the whole of the sea, gulf, and lake coasts, into light-house districts; not exceeding 12 in number. An officer of the army or navy is assigned to each district, as a light-house inspector.

We have not in detail enumerated all the duties devolving on this board, and therefore say in general terms that they have the control of everything relating to light houses, light ships, buoys, beacons, or other means of directing vessels in and out of port, or of guiding them while sailing along the coast in the night.

5. As foreign vessels receive the same benefits from our light houses as our own, there is nothing unfair or illiberal in requiring them to contribute something towards the expense of maintaining them. For this purpose Congress has imposed a tax, or laid a duty of 50

cents per ton on all foreign vessels entering any ports of the United States. This is called "LIGHT MONEY," and needs no explanation. It is collected in the same way as tonnage duties are, *i. e.* by the collector of the port where the ship arrives. Light money is not required of vessels owned by citizens of the United States, provided that they are regularly registered as the law directs, or have a sea letter.

7. A sea letter is a document or certificate, given by the collector of a port, to the captain of an American vessel, certifying that she belongs to a citizen or citizens of the United States. Armed with this, the captain can prove to all whom it may concern, anywhere in the world, the ownership and nationality of his vessel. This is a protection to her and her cargo, especially in times of war. It is one of a ship's papers.

CHAPTER LXVI.

The Smithsonian Institution.

1. THIS institution, though differing materially from almost every other government establishment, should be noticed in a work of this kind; although nothing but the official machinery by which it was at first set in motion, and is continued in operation, belongs to the government. The funds with which it was founded, were furnished by an individual, and he a foreigner. The history runs thus: A noble-hearted Englishman, whose name was James Smithson, residing in the city of London, bequeathed all his property to the United States of America, for the purpose of founding in Washington an establishment to be known as the "Smithsonian Institution," for the purpose of increasing and diffusing knowledge among men. The United States accepted the bequest, and in 1846 passed an act for the purpose of carrying out the beneficent design of Mr. Smithson. This act created "an establishment," as it is denominated in the act, by the name before stated. It might have been called a corporation, for it has perpetual succession, and many of the powers incident to a corporation.

2. By this act the President and Vice President of the United States, the Secretary of State, the Secretary of the Treasury, the Secretary of War, the Secretary of the Navy, the Postmaster General, the Attorney General, and Chief Justice, the Commissioner of the Patent Office, and the Mayor of Washington—during

Parmelee & Co. Philad. Engraved expressly for this work.

SMITHSONIAN INSTITUTE

the time they shall hold their respective offices, together with such other persons as they may elect honorary members—were constituted the establishment under the name of the Smithsonian Institution.

3. It is located at Washington, and is managed by a board of regents, composed of the Vice President of the United States, the Chief Justice of the United States, the Mayor of Washington, three members of the Senate, and three members of the House of Representatives; together with six other persons. The board choose their own officers, and report their proceedings to Congress at each session thereof.

4. In order to carry out Mr. Smithson's noble design of founding this institution, rooms have been prepared for the reception of all objects of art, natural history, plants, and geological and mineralogical specimens which now or hereafter may belong to the United States, and such as may hereafter be obtained. These are classified and arranged so as to facilitate their examination and study. A vast collection has already been obtained and deposited in the institution, and it is constantly increasing by donations, by the researches and industry of its professors, and by exchanges made with kindred institutions at home and abroad. These are open to the examination of the public, and offer an opportunity to students and others to extend their scientific knowledge. This, together with the reports of its professors, of experiments and new discoveries, make it indeed an institution "for the increase and diffusion of knowledge among men."

CHAPTER LXVII.

Patent Office, Patent Rights, and the Commissioner of Patents.

1. THE foundation of our patent laws is found in the Constitution of the United States. In the powers it confers on Congress, the following is found: "To promote the progress of science and useful arts, by securing for limited times to authors and inventors the exclusive right to their respective writings and discoveries." On this authority, Congress has passed numerous acts for this purpose. We find one of this kind as early as 1790.

2. A patent right is an exclusive right, granted by an officer denominated the Commissioner of Patents, in conformity to law, to the inventor or discoverer of any new and useful article. The exclusive right is conferred by acts of Congress, on compliance of the inventor with certain conditions which are clearly specified in the law. The evidence that such exclusive right has been conferred on any individual, is contained in a document, called "letters patent," issued at the patent office in Washington; signed by the Secretary of the Interior, (formerly by the Secretary of State), countersigned by the Commissioner of Patents, and sealed with the seal of his office. Thus protected, he alone can make, use and sell the article he has invented, for the term of fourteen years; and upon showing a good reason therefor, the commissioner will extend the term

seven years longer, or Congress will pass a special act for that purpose.

3. This was the law up to 1861; and is still in force as to patents granted anterior to that date. But a new act was then passed, extending the term of an original patent to seventeen, instead of fourteen years, and prohibiting any extension of such patents.

An inventor, before he can obtain a patent, must swear that he believes he is the inventor or discoverer of the art, machine or improvement, for which he solicits a patent. He must also give in writing a clear, minute description of it; and, when necessary, must make and deliver a model of his invention; which in all cases must be something new, unused and unknown before, or his application will be rejected. There is considerable expense attending the procurement of a patent right.

4. But when obtained, no person except the patentee, has any right to make, sell or use the article patented, until the time has expired for which this exclusive right was granted, without the permission of the patentee. Any person doing so is liable to a heavy penalty, and may be prosecuted in the Circuit Court of the United States; this court having original jurisdiction in all cases arising under the patent laws. But a writ of error or an appeal lies to the Supreme Court of the United States.

5. The Patent Office, when first established, was a bureau of the State Department, and the Commissioner of Patents acted under the direction of the Secretary of State. But after the creation of the Department of the

Interior, in 1849, it was transferred to it, became a bureau of the new department, and the commissioner now acts under the general direction of its secretary.

THE COMMISSIONER OF PATENTS

6. Is appointed by the President and Senate. His duties are best explained in the language of the law itself, which, in speaking of the creation and appointment of this official, says that his duties shall be "to superintend, execute and perform all such acts and things touching and respecting the granting and issuing of patents for new and useful discoveries, inventions and improvements, as are herein provided for, or shall hereafter be by law directed to be done and performed."

He has the charge and custody of all books, records, papers, models, machines, and all other things belonging to the patent office; and has the privilege of sending and receiving letters and packages by mail, relating to the business of the office, free of postage. He has the power to appoint his clerks, examiners and subordinates; among whom are patent office agents, who may be appointed in not more than twenty of the principal cities and towns in the United States. It is their duty to forward to the patent office all such models, specimens and manufactures, as shall be intended to be patented.

7. In cases of appeal from the decision of the commissioner, the appeal may be made to the board of examiners, or to the Chief Justice of the District Court of the United States for the District of Columbia.

There is a seal for the patent office, which the commissioner keeps, and which he must affix to patents when granted, and to other papers and records issued from his office, which are wanted as evidence in other places.

He is also authorized to publish a classified and alphabetical list of all patents issued at the patent office. This he frequently does, for the information of the public.

CHAPTER LXVIII.

Copyrights.

1. A COPYRIGHT is an exclusive privilege given to any citizen of the United States to print, publish or sell any book, map, chart, engraving, or musical composition of which he or she is the author. This right is given by the laws of Congress. No State can give it. The object of the law is to encourage authors, and to compensate them for their labors. This compensation they would not receive if everybody might print and publish their productions. A copyright is a kind of property, and may be sold and inherited like other property.

2. A compliance with the laws on this subject is necessary, however, before the right can be secured. First, the author must deposit in the office of the clerk of the United States District Court of the district in which he resides, a printed copy of the title page of such book, map, chart, &c., and this must be recorded in the clerk's office. Second, within three months after the publication of the book or other work, the author must deposit a copy of it in the office of the same clerk. Third, he must also give information to the public, by causing to be inserted on the title page, or on the page immediately following it, the following words, viz.: "Entered according to act of Congress, in the year——, by A. B., in the clerk's office of the district of———." The author or proprietor is also required to deposit a copy of his work in the office of the Secretary of the Interior within three months after its publication.

3. When all these legal provisions are strictly complied with, the author receives from the Department of the Interior his letters—his copyright—which secure to him, his heirs or assigns, the exclusive right to print, publish and sell his work for the term of twenty-eight years. And if, in violation of this right, any person or persons shall print, publish, or sell the work thus secured to the author, he or they may be prosecuted for damages in the Circuit Courts of the United States, which courts have exclusive jurisdiction in these cases, with right of appeal to the Supreme Court.

4. The penalty for printing and publishing any work for which a copyright has been granted within twenty-eight years from the time when the title page was recorded, is a forfeiture of every copy thus printed, and a fine of 50 cents for every sheet found in his possession. One half of this fine is paid to the author, and the other to the United States. But the suit for the recovery of any damage done or penalty incurred for the violation of the copyright laws, must be brought within two years after the cause of action arose.

5. Up to 1849 the department of the Secretary of State was charged with the duty of issuing copyrights, and with all other things pertaining to the duty of government in securing them to authors. But at that time the Department of the Interior was created, and this business was transferred from the Department of State to this department, together with all the books, maps, charts, papers and documents relating to copyrights.

Our government is not peculiar in securing this right to authors. In nearly every civilized country where literature is cultivated, you will find copyright laws.

CHAPTER LXIX.

Pensions, Commissioner of Pensions, Pension Office and Pension Agents.

1. PENSIONS are annual allowances in money, made by the government to those men who have been either in the army or navy of the United States, and who have been wounded or disabled in the service of their country. It amounts really to extra pay, over and above the monthly pay of an officer, soldier or sailor, at the time the wound was received. It has cost the United States millions of dollars to support these pensioners; for there never was a time since the establishment of the government when it had not more or less of these unfortunate men to provide for by money paid from the United States Treasury in the shape of pensions. At first there were the disabled soldiers and sailors of the Revolutionary war to be provided for, immediately after the government was put into operation. But few if any of them remain. Then came the second war with England, called the war of 1812, (from the year in which it commenced,) which greatly increased the number of pensioners. Then the war of 1846-7, with Mexico, added thousands to the pension roll. But all these wars put together never threw so many men on the government for support, or partial support, as the late civil war between the North and South. At no former period was the pension list so large as at present. It will remain so for years to come, requiring an appropriation of many millions annually to aid these unfortunate men who have become wholly or

partially incapable of supporting themselves. These greatly increase the expenses of the government, and afford a forcible comment upon the evils and horrors of war.

2. The pension laws not only provide for officers and men who have been disabled by wounds, but it provides for the widows and orphan children of such as have been killed in battle or died of sickness contracted while in the service of the country. These provisions, it will be readily seen, greatly increase the number of pensioners upon the government. These receive the same in amount as the husband or father would have received had he survived his wounds.

3. It is not intended, in granting a pension to a person, to give him a full support. Pensions are moderate amounts, generally about half the pay which the recipient received at the time he was wounded. Officers' pensions are graduated according to their rank.

4. From what has already been said on this subject, it will be plainly seen that it requires much care, labor, and attention to keep correctly the list of pensioners upon the government, and to detect all the frauds which pension agents and other interested parties may perpetrate upon it.

5. In order to accomplish this benevolent design of the government, a bureau was established in the War Department (since transferred to the Department of the Interior), at the head of which an officer denominated the Commissioner of Pensions, is placed. This bureau is properly the pension office. The commissioner is appointed by the President and Senate, and holds his office during the pleasure of the President. It was his

duty formerly, under the direction of the Secretaries of War and the Navy, but now under the supervision of the Secretary of the Interior, to execute all such duties relating to pensions as the President shall direct. He is charged to carry out all the laws in relation to this matter.

6. The persons entitled to pensions are necessarily scattered all over the States and Territories, and many of them could not bear the fatigue or expense of making their demands at Washington. To render this unnecessary, the Secretary of War is authorized to appoint pension agents in all the States and Territories. These agents receive the money due to pensioners in the district where they reside, and distribute it as directed by the Commissioner of Pensions. In this way most of the pensions are paid—the agents receiving a per centage for their services.

7. It is not the intention of the government to give pensions where they are not necessary for the support of the recipient; and when it is ascertained that pensioners are in good circumstances, and do not need government aid, their names are stricken from the pension roll.

In order that the pensioners shall have and enjoy the full benefits of this government bounty, the law protects the pension, and does not allow it to be taken away from the recipient, by any process of law, for debt, or for any cause whatever.

The preceding provisions are extended not only to those who have been injured in some of the great wars, but also to those who have been disabled in any of the Indian wars, of which we have had many, and which we are still having.

CHAPTER LXX.
Hospitals and Asylums.

1. The hospitals and asylums for the sick, disabled, and insane in any country, are the evidences of the humanity, benevolence and Christian charity of the government of that country; and we know of none, in ancient or modern times, where these benevolent institutions exist in greater number, or with greater efficiency than in the United States. They have been established by the general government and by the several State governments; by charitable societies and by individuals; not only for the sick and infirm, but for the blind, the deaf, the insane and the idiotic. We do not propose to go into any general history or description of these institutions, but only to notice those established by the United States government, and now under its control, in order to show its care for those who have served their country, but are unable to provide for their wants.

2. The hospitals and asylums for sick and disabled soldiers and seamen, are located in different parts of the country; and in such places as are the most accessible and convenient to those who are under the necessity of retiring to these places of refuge.

The United States have established four kinds of these institutions, principally for relief of their soldiers and seamen. The first of these are

THE MARINE HOSPITALS.

3. These are located near important sea ports. At

these places seamen depart for, and arrive from their voyages, and are found in the greatest numbers; and here the funds for support of the marine hospitals are collected, as is the tonnage on ships, viz.: by the collectors of the ports. For this purpose the law authorizes the collectors of customs to demand and receive the sum of twenty cents per month from the wages of every sailor; and every master of a vessel is obliged to render to the collector an accurate account of the number of seamen on board his vessel, and of the time they have been employed by him, since his last entry into any port of the United States. These twenty cents the captain must pay the collector, but he is allowed to deduct it from each seaman's wages. In this manner the funds for the building, furnishing and support of the marine hospitals are raised. The collectors of the ports pay them into the United States Treasury, and the Treasurer disburses them to the directors of the hospitals as they are needed. The directors are appointed by the President. They appropriate the funds, and have the general direction and management of the institutions.

4. These provisions are contained in an act entitled "An act for the relief of sick and disabled seamen," passed in 1798. Seamen, whether in the merchant service or in the naval service of the United States, were indiscriminately taxed for the support of these hospitals; and both have the same rights, privileges and benefits in them. The money thus collected from seamen is called "hospital money," and the fund is denominated "the marine hospital fund." In 1864, there were 24 marine hospitals in the United States.

NAVY HOSPITALS.

5. In 1811, an act was passed to establish navy hospitals, for the exclusive use of such seamen as belonged to the navy. This new institution was at first placed under the management of a board of commissioners known as the commissioners of navy hospitals. This commission consisted of the Secretaries of the Navy, Treasury and War. But in 1832 this was changed; and the Secretary of the Navy was made sole trustee of the navy hospital fund, which was made up of $50, 000 appropriated by Congress for that purpose, together with twenty cents per month collected from seamen belonging to the navy, and the fines imposed on navy officers, seamen and marines.

6. The Commissioners were authorized to purchase or erect suitable buildings for navy hospitals.

We need not go further in our remarks upon these institutions, for in all their objects and purposes, they are so similar to those of the marine hospitals just described, that anything further would be little more than repetition.

MILITARY ASYLUMS.

7. In 1851, Congress passed an act for the establishment of military asylums, for the purpose of making the same provisions for wounded and disabled soldiers as had already been made for that class of seamen. These institutions are located in different sections of the country where deemed most eligible and convenient for those who need such a place of refuge. They are placed under the government of a board

of commissioners, consisting of the general in chief, and eight other military officers of high rank, who submit their acts to the Secretary of War for his approval.

8. The officers of these asylums must be taken from the army, and consist of a governor, a deputy governor and secretary, who is also treasurer. The funds for their support are raised by a tax of twenty-five cents per month on the soldiers, to which are added the fines and penalties adjudged against soldiers by courts martial, with forfeitures for desertion, &c.

Persons receiving pensions from the government may be admitted into these asylums upon condition that they surrender their pensions to the use of the institution while they remain in it.

The commissioners are authorized to buy sites and buildings for these institutions, and to receive donations of them. They also furnish them with whatever is necessary for the comfort of the inmates, and make such laws and regulations for their government as they deem proper.

Deserters, mutineers, and habitual drunkards, are excluded from the benefits of these asylums.

INSANE ASYLUM.

9. Among these benevolent institutions provided by a generous government for the support of those who have faithfully served their country, the insane asylum ought to be noticed. The title of this establishment is "the government hospital for the insane." Its objects are the cure and kind treatment of the insane of the army and navy, and of the District of Columbia. It is

under the control of a board of nine visitors, all of whom must be citizens of the said District. They are appointed by the President, and annually report to the Secretary of the Interior the condition of the asylum and its inmates. They serve without compensation.

10. But the superintendent, who must be a physician, receives $2,000 per annum for his services. There is a farm attached to the asylum, which is under the direction of the superintendent, who receives patients upon the order of the Secretary of War or Navy, and upon the order of the Secretary of the Interior. He may receive indigent insane persons residing in the District of Columbia. If other than indigent persons are admitted, they must pay for the privilege a sum not less than the cost of their support.

11. The foregoing might suffice for what we have to say upon these government establishments, because it includes all which are permanent institutions, designed to be in perpetual operation, and very different from the military hospitals in time of war. These are for temporary purposes, and are established wherever the army happens to be, and especially near where the great battles have been fought, that immediate relief may be given to the sick and wounded. These are established by the commanders of the army, and are under their control. And here let it be recorded to their praise, that since military hospitals were known, never have any been seen which for order, cleanliness and efficiency in administering to the comfort and care of the sick and wounded soldiers, surpassed those of the United States during the late civil war.

CHAPTER LXXI.

Commissioner of Public Buildings.

1. THE buildings at Washington belonging to the United States, are the grandest, the largest and the most expensive in the country. The capitol in which Congress meets, is the largest and most expensive building ever erected on the continent, and is surpassed by few in the world. The Treasury building, the General Post Office, and the Patent office, are all splendid structures, as are also many others devoted to the transaction of public business.

2. These all require repairs, alterations, care and oversight, that they may be preserved and kept in order. The duty of superintendence of these public buildings was formerly placed in the hands of three commissioners and a superintendent of public buildings.

But in 1816, an act was passed by which the offices of superintendent and three commissioners were abolished, and their duties all put into the hands of one man, who is denominated "the commissioner of public buildings." He is appointed by the President and Senate, and can hold no other office under the United States. He must give bonds for the faithful performance of his duties, and must reside near the capitol. In the discharge of his duties he acts under the direction of the President and the presiding officers of the two Houses of Congress.

3. It is made his duty to report to Congress at the commencement of each session, the manner in which all appropriations for the public buildings have been applied, the condition they are in, together with that of the public grounds, and also to report the means necessary for their perservation. It is his duty to take charge of and superintend all the buildings belonging to the United States in Washington, and to perform all such duties as the laws from time to time require of him.

CHAPTER LXXII.

Congressional and Law Libraries.

1. In the capitol there is a large library, consisting of two parts; one part called the Congressional library, the other, the law library. The latter is made a part of the former by an act of Congress. Both are subject to the same laws and rules, and both are supported by appropriations made by Congress. This institution bearing the title of "Congressional library," might lead to the supposition that it was established for the exclusive use of Congress. But this is not so. Its use has been extended to the judges of the Supreme Court; to all the heads of departments, to the Attorney General; to all the members of the diplomatic corps, (foreign ministers); to the secretary of the Senate; to the clerk of the House of Representatives, to the chaplains of Congress, all ex-Presidents and to the solicitor of the Treasury.

2. It has a librarian, appointed by the President and Senate, who is allowed to appoint two assistants. No book or map is allowed to be taken out of the library by any person, except the President, Vice-President, members of the Senate and of the House of Representatives.

3. Here are kept all the laws which have ever been enacted by Congress, together with a record of all its proceedings, the laws of all the different States, with many of those of foreign countries; also a large col-

lection of books on promiscuous subjects, useful to Members of Congress and to those who have to administer the government. No where else can so complete a history of the acts and proceedings of the government be found, as in the Congressional library at Washington.

This institution dates back to the year 1800, when an act was passed making the first appropriation of $5,000 for its establishment. The books purchased with this $5,000, with those belonging to both Houses, were placed together, and thus this library was commenced.

CHAPTER LXXIII.

The Official Register.

1. CONGRESS, in 1816, passed an act authorizing and requiring the Secretary of State, once in two years, to print and publish a book called "the official register," in which he was ordered to register the names of every officer and agent of the government, in the civil, military and naval departments, including cadets and midshipmen, together with the compensation received by each; the names of the State and county where born; and the name of the place where employed, whether at home or abroad.

To the list of persons employed in the Navy Department, the Secretary of the Navy is required to subjoin the names, force and condition of all the ships and vessels belonging to the United States, and when and where built.

This work has been published and distributed, as the law directs, ever since the passage of the act, and is sometimes denominated "the blue book." It is a very convenient and useful publication, as it shows in compact form the whole official force of the government in each department, together with the cost of maintaining it.

So small a number of this work is published, that but few except officials ever see it. It can be found in the Congressional library at Washington, where twenty-five copies of each edition are deposited.

CHAPTER LXXIV.

The Government Printing Office.

1. BUT few people have any adequate idea of the enormous amount of printing done by the government. All the proceedings of both Houses of Congress are printed; all the laws are printed, and hundreds of bills which are never passed into laws, are printed. The President's messages and all the reports of heads of departments and bureaus; the reports and commissions of army and navy officers, of investigating committees, of various superintendents, agents, and government employees, and a multitude of other things quite too tedious to enumerate, are all printed in great numbers, often reaching thousands of copies. It is easily understood that the government printing is a heavy item in its expenses, and everybody knows it is much heavier than it ought to be. The people are taxed to pay for large editions of books and documents that are never read, and in which the public feel little or no interest.

2. Until 1860, the government hired men to do this work, and a printer was employed by each house of Congress. But great complaints were made of the enormous expense to which the country was subjected in this item of its expenditures; and at the date named, Congress passed an act establishing a government printing office, to be under the direction of a superintendent of public printing. The sum of $150,000 was appropriated for the purchase of necessary buildings, machinery, and materials for the purpose. By the pro-

visions of the act it was made the superintendent's duty to overlook all the public printing and binding, not only of Congress, but of all the departments, and of the United States courts; to purchase all necessary materials and to employ all the workmen required. And that Congress may know how the establishment is conducted and at what expense, the superintendent is required to report to Congress at the commencement of every session, the work done, the number of hands employed, and the exact state and condition of the establishment. He is prohibited from paying more for work done in this office than is given for the same services in private printing offices in Washington.

3. The superintendent is also charged with the duty of procuring all blank books, maps, drawings, diagrams, views and charts, which may be ordered by Congress, or by the heads of departments and bureaus. But the superintendent himself is not left to act always as he may think proper, for in many cases he must have the approval of the joint committee on printing of both Houses of Congress.

We have given a brief but comprehensive view of this government establishment. Whether it will answer the purposes of its creation, and prove to be a means of saving to the government, remains to be seen.

4. If it should be successful, the people may congratulate themselves that one change has been made for the better, and that one effort to curtail taxation, and to lessen the public expenses, has been accomplished. Among the causes which may produce the overthrow of our government, few are more danger-

ous than the reckless extravagance with which our rulers appropriate and spend the public moneys, seeming to forget the fact that such extravagance falls with crushing weight upon the laboring classes, who always pay directly or indirectly the greater portion of the expenses of the government. And those who make our laws would do well to consider that nothing is more dangerous to our present form of government, than the enactment of laws that appear burthensome or tyrannical. History teaches us that a free people will endure much before rising against their own form of government. But when once impelled to such a course, all odious laws, and those who make them, must share a common fate.

CHAPTER LXXV.

Prisons.

1. ALTHOUGH Congress has passed laws for the punishment of almost every crime which has ever been punishable by the laws of any civilized nation, and has prescribed various kinds of punishment for different crimes, such as fines, imprisonment, and death by hanging, imprisonment is by far the most common. Yet we find nothing in the laws to show—nor have we ever known—that the United States have ever built a prison or directed one to be built; although thousands have been put in prison for violations of the United States laws. But how is this done when they have no prisons? The answer is that they use the prisons of the States wherever they will allow it. This arrangement between the general and State governments has been made in nearly if not all the States; the United States paying for the support of their prisoners.

2. But in case any State should refuse to make such an agreement, the United States marshal of any district where a prisoner is to be confined, is authorized to procure some building where the prisoners may be safely confined in the district where they have been tried and convicted, or where they have been arrested and are held for trial.

This is a far more economical plan than it would be for the United States to build prisons all over the country, and then to employ keepers of them. It exemplifies the friendly relations existing between the States and the general government.

CHAPTER LXXVI.

Agriculture.

1. In May, 1862, Congress passed an act, the two first sections of which read as follows:

Sec. 1. "There is hereby established at the seat of government of the United States, a department of agriculture; the general designs and duties of which shall be to acquire and diffuse among the people of the United States, useful information on subjects connected with agriculture, in the most general and comprehensive sense of that word, and to procure, propagate and distribute among the people new and valuable seeds and plants."

Sec. 2. "There shall be appointed by the President, by and with the advice and consent of the Senate, a commissioner of agriculture, who shall be the chief executive officer of the department of agriculture; who shall hold his office by a tenure similar to that of other civil officers appointed by the President, and who shall receive for his compensation a salary of three thousand dollars per annum."

2. We have inserted these two sections of this law, because we could not by any language of our own, convey any better idea of the objects and purposes for which this new department was created. In the language of the law it is called a department, but as its head ranks no higher than a commissioner, we think it would be more properly styled a bureau of the Department of the Interior.

3. The duties of the head of this bureau are to acquire and preserve in his department all the information concerning agriculture which he can obtain by means of books, correspondence and experiments. For this latter purpose a propagating garden is provided for his use. He is also to collect as many new seeds and plants as he is able to obtain, to test their value by cultivation, and then to distribute them among agriculturists. He superintends the expenditure of all money appropriated by Congress to the department, and reports the same annually to Congress, together with his acts, experiments, &c.

He has the power to appoint a chief clerk and such other subordinates as Congress may deem necessary. The commissioner and his chief clerk both give bonds for the right appropriation of all moneys received by them, and for the faithful performance of their respective duties.

This bureau is yet in its infancy. Sufficient time has not elapsed for its development, or to show the results of its experiments. It will undoubtedly become an important and useful institution hereafter.

CHAPTER LXXVII.

Indians.

1. EVERY one acquainted with the history of America, knows that when first discovered by Christopher Columbus in 1492, the whole continent, North as well as South, was peopled with Indians. They were the aborigines or first inhabitants of the country; and according to the recognized rules and usages of the world, they were the owners of the soil. This right has been admitted by our government, and hence we have purchased these lands at such prices as were agreed upon by the two parties. The Indians placed a lower value upon them than the whites; for, with the exception of small patches here and there, which they cultivated for corn and tobacco, they made no use of their lands except for hunting grounds; while the whites wanted them for cultivation. In this way the whites have become the possessors of nearly all the land once owned by the Indians, whose possessions now are very small.

2. Their idle habits, their frequent wars among themselves, and the wars with the whites growing out of their murderous propensities, have almost exterminated the whole race. There is now but a small remnant left of what was 200 years ago a mighty host. Many of these tribes have become entirely extinct, others are nearly so; and scarcely one of them is found whose numbers are not greatly diminished. It is melancholy to contemplate the fate of these poor savages.

As nearly as can be ascertained, there are not more than abut 300,000 of them left in the United States. These are mostly to be found west of the Mississippi river, and stretching thence to the shores of the Pacific. A few of them have remained among the whites, and become civilized; but most of them have kept aloof from civilization, perferring their wandering habits, and relying on hunting and fishing for a subsistence.

They do not admit themselves to be citizens of our government, neither do we claim them as such, nor do we exercise any jurisdiction or authority over them, except for the perpetration of crimes. We treat them as foreigners, not as citizens, and hence we make treaties with them as we do with foreign nations.

3. Our treaties with them have related principally to the purchase of lands and to stipulations of amity and frendship between us. But they are sometimes treacherous, and do not act toward us as they have agreed to do. This has led to a number of wars between us and them; the fault of which has not always been on the side of the Indians. The whites have often treated them badly; have often cheated them, and killed them; and this has led to some of the wars we have mentioned.

4. The preceding remarks might have been omitted in a work of this kind, had they not seemed to be appropriate as an introduction to the notice we ought to take of the numerous treaties with the Indians, the officers and agents of the government in making and carrying out those treaties, and of the numerous laws passed by Congress in relation to Indians and Indian affairs.

5. The Indians are unlearned, ignorant and barbarous. It has required a great deal of wisdom and good management on the part of the government, to keep on good terms with them, and to prevent them from murdering the whites, or from stealing their property, where they have settled near them. The United States have also restrained our own citizens from purchasing their lands, from trading with them, and especially from selling them intoxicating liquors, of which they are very fond. If these negotiations were allowed between them and the whites, the Indians would, in numerous instances, be over-reached and cheated by unscrupulous and dishonest white men. This would lead to murders and wars, for an Indian seems to have no idea of redress for a wrong done to him, other than that of killing the wrong-doer. The government, through its agents, buys their lands, and pays them in money or in goods, according to the terms of the treaty. Hence the necessity of government officers appointed to execute the laws relating to Indians and Indian affairs.

6. There is in the War Department a bureau for this express purpose, the head of which is called the

COMMISSIONER OF INDIAN AFFAIRS.

He is appointed by the President and Senate, and performs his duties under the direction of the Secretary of War.

In addition to this officer, there are superintendents of Indian affairs, and Indian agents, over whom the superintendents exercise a directing power. These superintendencies and agencies are not permanent establishments, but are continued as long as any considerable number of Indians remain near the agency. When they have sold their lands and removed farther west, the agency is discontinued, or removed to the place where the Indians have located themselves.

The President may discontinue any Indian agency whenever he thinks it expedient to do so.

7. The bureau of Indian affairs, we have said, was attached to the War Department, but after the establishment of the Department of the Interior, in 1849, it was detached from the War Department and attached to that of the Interior, the Secretary of which exercises supervisory power over it.

8. As before stated, the Indians are not citizens of the United States. They have no Representatives in Congress, and in adjusting the number of Representatives to which any State is entitled from the number of its inhabitants, the Indians (excepting a few who are taxed), are not counted. The government has exercised parental care over them in endeavors to prevent them from warring upon each other, and to induce them to adopt the habits of civilized life; in the payments made for their lands, in the pains it has taken to furnish them with agricultural and mechanical implements; in the employment of mechanics and teachers to reside among them and to instruct them in science and the mechanical arts. It also employs interpreters, for but few of them can speak the English language.

9. The superintendents and agents, if so directed by

the President, make treaties of amity and friendship with them, and for the purchase of their lands. The government does not allow citizens or foreigners to reside among them or to trade with them without a license; and for the purpose of keeping on friendly terms with them, it often makes valuable presents of such articles as they need.

10. Superintendents and agents are appointed for four years; give bonds for the faithful performance of their duties, and report and account to the Department of the Interior for the money and goods paid to and distributed among the Indians.

INDIAN FUNDS AND INDIAN ANNUITIES.

11. In order to prevent them from squandering their money for rum and useless trinkets, and to save them from being cheated by dishonest traders, the United States government has invested the money paid for their lands in sound and safe stocks, and annually pay them the interest, through its superintendents and agents. The disbursement of this interest, called Indian annuities, among the different tribes and individuals to whom it belongs, is an important part of the duties of these government agents.

CHAPTER LXXVIII.

Passports.

1. PASSPORTS are one of the devices or means used by governments to protect their citizens when in foreign countries. They are written documents, issued and signed by an authorized agent of the government which gives them. The design of a passport is, First: to give authentic information to whom it may concern, to what nation the bearer of the passport belongs; and second, to protect him, and secure to him all the rights and privileges which the government has a right to claim for its citizens by virtue of any treaty of amity and friendship existing between it and the country whither its citizens may go.

The passport informs the world that the bearer of it is a citizen of the United States, and that he travels under its protection, and that it would demand and exact satisfaction of any one who wronged or injured him who bears such credentials.

2. In the United States, the Secretary of State is the officer authorized by law to issue passports. He has the authority also to cause them to be issued in foreign countries by our foreign ministers and consuls, under such restrictions and rules as may be designated by the President. This is allowed as a matter of convenience to our citizens who happen to be in foreign countries without them; who need their protection, and who would be subjected to much delay and expense by going or sending home to procure them.

Passports are not granted to any other than citizens of the United States, whether issued by the Secretary or by any diplomatic or consular agent of our government.

3. Besides these passports, which are given only to our own citizens when in foreign countries, or who intend to go there, there is another kind issued to foreigners who wish to go among the Indians in the Indian territory, or on the Indian reservations. Indeed, our own citizens are not allowed to go among them without permission. But foreigners cannot go without a passport from the Secretary of War, which specifies the route over which the bearer must pass, and the length of time he is allowed to remain among them. This is done to prevent unfriendly foreigners from fomenting mischief, or from exciting unkind feelings towards our government or people. Such unfriendly feelings have been created by foreigners, and we have often experienced the bitter fruits of it, especially in times of war.

4. Still another kind of passports is used in this country, and should be noticed under this head. They are passports for American ships or vessels. When they are about to sail for a foreign port, the laws of the United States require each to procure one, under a penalty or fine of two hundred dollars upon the master if he departs from the United States for a foreign country (other than some port in America), without it. The passport is prepared by the Secretary of State and is approved by the President. This is given to the master by the collector of the port from which the vessel sails, and is one of the ship's papers, by which her nationality is known, and her protection shown to be that of the United States.

CHAPTER LXXIX.

Reports.

1. As Congress is the law-making power of the government, and legislates for every department thereof, assigning such business to each as it deems proper, giving directions, and prescribing the duties of all the government officials, agents, commissioners and employees, nothing is more obvious than that it should be kept well informed and advised of what has been done in each department and bureau; and by every head, or principal officer and agent of the government wherever employed. And for this purpose it is enacted that the Secretaries of State, Treasury, War, Navy, Interior, and Postmaster General, together with the commissioners of the different bureaus, and boards attached to these departments, shall annually report to Congress. Heads of departments report directly to Congress. So do many of the commissioners who are at the head of bureaus. Boards report to the heads of departments to which they are attached.

2. In this way Congress is kept advised of whatever is done in every department, bureau, or board, to which any of the public business is entrusted. These reports not only furnish the law-making power with such information as it needs, but serves as a check to any official misconduct. The annual reports of the Secretaries of the Treasury, War, and Navy, together with that of the Postmaster General, are State papers which rank in importance next to the annual message

of the President. To them the people look for a detailed account of the state and condition of those great departments over which these Secretaries preside, and which so materially affect the pecuniary and other great interests of the nation.

3. The foregoing remarks upon reports, may not be considered of sufficient importance to deserve an insertion here, but they throw some light upon the movements of the machinery by which the government is operated, and show how officials are held responsible to the superior power.

In this connection we may notice another kind of reports, which come from another source. After each Congress has convened and organized, the President of the Senate and the Speaker of the House appoint what are denominated the standing committees of each of these bodies.

When bills are presented to be passed into laws, or petitions are sent in, they are always referred to the appropriate committee, which examines them and then reports to the body (of the Senate or House) their conclusions upon the merits or demerits, propriety or impropriety, of granting the petition, or of passing the bill under consideration.

These reports generally govern the action of Congress when they come to vote upon the passage of the law. But that is not always the case; the body of either House may think differently from its committee, and act contrary to its recommendations.

CHAPTER LXXX.

Commissioners.

1. In the history and laws of the United States, the word "commissioner" occurs so frequently, that it may add something to the utility of our work to make a few remarks about them, to show their relations to the government, when acting either in permanently established official positions, or as temporary agents.

In the first place, they act as heads of bureaus in the various departments. These bureaus, with their commissioners at their heads, are permanent sub-departments and officials of the government, established and provided for by law; such are the commissioners of the land office, patent office, pension office, &c.

2. In the second place, they can hardly be considered officers, but rather temporary or special agents. In the multifarious duties devolving upon Congress, the President, and all the departments, it not unfrequently happens that is impracticable for them to do certain things necessary to be done. The business to be transacted may be at a great distance from the capital, even in a foreign country. In these cases commissioners are appointed to do such business. They have been appointed to negotiate a peace, to make treaties of various kinds between us and other powers, and to negotiate with the Indians for the purchase of their lands. The United States courts appoint them to take bail, or to take testimony to be used on trials, and do various other things necessary in trials and proceedings before them.

Congress frequently appoints commissioners to obtain information, or to investigate some matter on which they expect to legislate. In all cases they must report their proceedings, either to Congress, to the President, or to the head of the department under whose instruction they act. Permanent commissioners report once a year, or oftener if required, that Congress may know the condition of affairs in their respective bureaus. Special commissioners, after they have performed the work assigned, make their report; after which their duties cease, and their commission comes to an end.

3. The foregoing may be thought too simple and too well understood to require any description. This is so, as it regards intelligent adults; but it should be borne in mind that these pages are written with special reference to the youth of the country.

It should be added that the lowest grade of diplomatic agents, who represent our government to some of the most inferior powers, are called commissioners. We are thus represented at the present time in the Republics of Hayti and Liberia.

4. By recent acts of Congress, the powers of commissioners in some cases have been enlarged. They now examine persons charged with crimes against the laws of the United States; hold them to bail, discharge them, or commit them to prison; and do other magisterial acts, preliminary to the trial of the accused. When acting in such cases, they are clothed with some of the powers of a court.

CHAPTER LXXXI.

Religion.

1. THE people of the United States glory in the fact that in their country there is no religion established by law, as in England and several other countries. Where this is the case, no other than the one established by law is tolerated; or if tolerated, special favors and benefits are conferred on the national church, at the expense of all others.

We enjoy complete religious freedom, and it is hoped we always shall. The Constitution guarantees this, in the following words: "Congress shall make no law respecting an establishment of religion, or prohibiting the free exercise thereof."

In another place it says, that "no religious test shall ever be required as a qualification to any office or public trust, under the United States."

What power in a few words! These words in our Constitution have been, and will be of inestimable value to our country; for they have greatly increased its population and wealth. This feature of our government has caused thousands to migrate to the United States, where they will neither be persecuted, nor taxed, to support a church in which they do not believe. Everybody is left to worship when and where and as he pleases. This is called religious liberty, and is as it ought to be. True Christianity never required the support of the State, and where it has been given, it has invariably been corrupted. We hope the day is not far off when every government on earth will follow our example in this respect.

CHAPTER LXXXII.

Proclamations.

1. A PROCLAMATION is an official notice given by one high in authority, for the purpose of giving reliable and authoritative information to the people that something has been done, or will soon be done, which is important for them to know, that they may act, or refrain from acting according to the information contained in the proclamation. These proclamations are made known to the country through the most extensive channels of information that can be used for conveying intelligence to everybody in the realm. In our day, and in our country, the newspapers are the best means that can be used for this purpose. But in ancient times, and before the art of printing was known, swift riders or runners were dispatched to every part of the kingdom or country over which the proclamation was to be made known. These messengers carried it with them, and proclaimed it in the ears of all the people.

We have made these general remarks about proclamations for the purpose of introducing the following observations upon those official papers so often issued by the President, and also by the Governors of the respective States. These, as above stated, are for the purpose of giving important information to the people. It is now the custom of the Executive to designate some day selected by him as a day of thanksgiving, recommending the day to be observed in a religious manner, in acknowledgment of God's favor to us as a nation. This is made known to the people by a proclamation of the President. A day of fasting and prayer is designated and proclaimed in the same way. Important changes in the commercial affairs between us and some foreign country are made known by the same method.

2. A memorable proclamation was made by President Lincoln, in 1862, by which he made known to the country, and especially to the Southern States, that if they continued their war against the United States for one hundred days after its issuance, he would then, in virtue of his authority as commander-in-chief of the army and navy, liberate the slaves in all the seceded States. At the expiration of the time, which was on the first of January, 1863, he issued another proclamation, in and by which he did emancipate all the slaves in every State which had rebelled against the United States government.

The blockading of our ports at the commencement of the civil war, and the imposition of an embargo upon our shipping, previous to the last war with England, were both subjects which brought out proclamations from the President who then filled the Executive chair.

4. The above example shows the character of cases which cause proclamations to be issued. In some instances they have the authority of law; in others they are merely recommendations; and in others only communicate important intelligence in regard to our public affairs at home or abroad.

CHAPTER LXXXIII.

Treason.

1. WE do not propose in this work to treat of crimes generally. But treason, which is a great crime, and which aims at the existence or at the peace of the government, may with propriety be briefly noticed in a work of this kind.

The Constitution itself defines treason in these words (see article 3, section 3): "Treason against the United States shall consist only in levying war against them, or in adhering to their enemies, giving them aid and comfort." Then an act of Congress, passed on the 30th of April, 1790, approved and signed by Washington, again defines in nearly the same words, and makes the penalty therefor to be death by hanging.

2. By another act passed 17th July, 1862, it was made discretionary with the court trying the case to put the offender to death, or to imprison him for not less than five years, and to fine him for a sum not less than ten thousand dollars. The penalty for this crime, even in its mildest form is very severe; thus showing how atrocious this offense is considered.

3. None but a person owing allegiance to the United States can commit treason against them. The same acts which would be treason in a citizen would not be treason if perpetrated by a foreigner.

"Misprision of treason" is the concealment of it by a person who knows it has been committed. This also is a grave offense, and is punishable by a seven years' imprisonment, and a fine not exceeding one thousand dollars.

4. Any person tried for treason, must be indicted by a grand jury; and then tried by a petit jury in the Circuit Court of the United States within three years after the crime has been committed; otherwise it is barred by limitation—or, in other words, outlawed.

CHAPTER LXXXIV.

Impeachment.

1. In the second article, section four, of the Constitution, these words are found: "The President, Vice-President, and all civil officers of the United States, shall be removed from office on impeachment for, and conviction of treason, bribery, or other high crimes and misdemeanors."

2. Impeachment is a procedure against office holders only, for the purpose of removing them from office. It inflicts no other punishment; but the guilty party may afterwards be prosecuted for his crime in a court of law, and punished in such a manner as the law directs.

3. The Constitution gives the House of Representatives the sole power of impeachment. Its action, however, is not final. Its proceeding in cases of impeachment are analagous to an indictment by a grand jury.

It simply charges that the official has committed a crime for which he should be tried and removed from office if found guilty.

4. The Senate alone has the power to try the accused party. When trying a case of impeachment it acts as a court, and from its decision there is no appeal. The President cannot pardon a criminal who has been impeached. When the President of the United States is tried, the Chief Justice of the Supreme Court presides, but in no other case. No person can be convicted in a trial of impeachment, unless two-thirds of the Senate concur in finding the accused guilty of the alleged offence.

CHAPTER LXXXV.

Missouri Compromise.

1. We should not devote a chapter to this subject any more than we should to hundreds of other acts of Congress which need not be noticed in a work of this kind, but for the fact that few if any acts passed by that body have caused so many comments or so much political discussion as this. It may therefore be both interesting and useful to state what the Missouri Compromise was, what its objects were, and how it came to be repealed.

2. The act containing what has long been denominated the Missouri Compromise was passed on the 6th day of March, 1820. The object of the act was the admission of the State of Missouri into the Union. The Compromise inserted in one of its sections was proposed by Henry Clay, of Kentucky, and was designed to reconcile a high dispute between the Members of Congress on the question, "Shall Missouri be admitted as a free or a slave State?"

3. It was admitted as a slave State, but upon the condition (proviso) that in none of the Territory of the United States lying north of the line of 36 degrees and 30 minutes, north latitude, should slavery ever be allowed. This proviso was denominated a Compromise; because it was designed to settle the vexed question as to how far northward slavery should be allowed to extend.

4. It was called the "Missouri Compromise," simply because it was incorporated in the act of Congress which admitted that State into the Union. It remained in existence until the year 1854, thirty-four years. During all that period it was looked upon as a permanent settlement of the boundary line between free and slave territory.

The repeal of this act was strongly opposed by those who objected to the extension of slavery. It caused a great deal of political excitement, and was immediately followed by the troubles in Kansas, where the contest between those who wanted the State to come in free, and those who wanted it to be a slave State, ran so high as to cause not only great political commotion, but even bloodshed and civil war between the contestants in that then new Territory. Kansas remained a Territory until January, 1861, when it was admitted as a State.

5. As stated in the commencement of this article, no act of Congress ever caused so much political discussion as this. It was passed to quiet a contest that shook the whole country; and when it was repealed, it created another of still greater magnitude. The Kansas imbroglio followed hard after; and the late disastrous civil war came soon enough to lead many wise men into the opinion that it had much to do in bringing on that terrible calamity.

CHAPTER LXXXVI.

Mason and Dixon's Line.

1. SHOULD any reader say that this is not pertinent to the subject treated of in this work, he would not be far out of the way; for, strictly speaking, it has nothing to do with it. But the phrase "Mason and Dixon's line," has been used in connection with the political sayings and doings of the country so often that it would be very natural for any one to ask, "What is it?" and "What is meant by it?" To answer the question, we reply as follows: Mason and Dixon's line is not a myth nor an imaginary line, with no particular location. It was a real line, and a boundary line, located between Maryland and Pennsylvania; between which two colonies there had been much contention and many hostile acts, amounting at times almost to a civil war. This arose from a dispute respecting the boundary lines between them. Maryland had been granted to Lord Baltimore, and Pennsylvania to William Penn.

2. This was long before the Revolutionary war. But the boundary line was not accurately defined. These disputes caused so much trouble between the contending parties, that commissioners were appointed in England to make an accurate survey, and to determine, from the language used in the charters or grants, as they were called in that day, the exact boundary line between them. Messrs. Mason and Dixon were selected in England to run this line; which they did. These men were eminent mathematicians and astronomers, and had the confidence of all parties. They performed their work so much to the satisfaction of all

parties that the line drawn remains to this day. Thus was ended a long continued quarrel of more than seventy years' standing.

3. But these facts did not give this line its great notoriety. It arose from the circumstance that Pennsylvania and all the States north of it became free States, while Maryland and all the States south of it remained slave States. Mason and Dixon's line, without any intention of making it such, became the boundary between the free and slave States.

The line run by these men went no further west than those States extended, and was a straight line running east and west. But as new States were created and added to the original thirteen, some utterly refused to admit slavery, while others did admit it. Ohio, Illinois and Indiana, on the north side of the Ohio river, refused to admit, while Kentucky eagerly embraced it. Hence the Ohio river became a sort of Mason and Dixon's line; that is, it became the line so far as these States were concerned. The phrase by this time came to mean the boundary line between slavery and freedom, instead of the line run by Mason and Dixon between Pennsylvania and Maryland. Thus, like many other terms in our language, it became far more comprehensive in its significance than in the original meaning. In the latter sense, Mason and Dixon's line ran wherever the boundary lines ran between free and slave States, whether east and west, north and south, or any other points of the compass. But the late civil war sponged out this famous line. It has no existence now excepting that part of it which originally and at present forms the boundary between Pennsylvania and Maryland.

CHAPTER LXXXVII.

Political Divisions.

1. WHEN we wish to understand the geography of our country, we take a map and notice its boundaries, its mountains, lakes, rivers, towns, &c.

And if we wish to understand its government we must notice how it is divided for political purposes; first, into States, and then into a variety of districts. We shall find Congressional districts, judicial districts, collection districts, land districts, and light-house districts. All these have their uses, and are parts of the machinery by which the government is operated. If it were not for the necessity there is of frequently changing the boundaries, numbers and localities of these districts, it would be useful and interesting if the United States were mapped out so as to show all these political divisions at a glance, in the same manner as the States and counties are now shown.

2. The first great division is into States. These have particular reference to the constitution of the Senate and House of Representatives. Each State is entitled to two Senators, regardless of its size or population; and to as many Representatives as its population will admit. Each State is really a Senatorial district in its relations to the general government; and as Congressmen are elected by single districts, each State is sub-divided into as many Congressional districts as it has Representatives in the lower House. But when a State has only one Member of Congress,

as is the case with several, the whole State is comprised in one Congressional district.

JUDICIAL DISTRICTS.

3. We now come to another sort of districts, made for an entirely different purpose. For the convenience of the people the United States courts are held in every State, and at different places in the same State. For this purpose the whole country is first divided into judicial circuits. Several States—3, 4, or 5—are embraced in one circuit. In all these States and at different places in them, a Circuit Court is held.

4. Then comes a lower grade of courts, called the United States District Court. These also are held at different times and places in each State; and for this purpose the whole country is divided into judicial districts, each State forming at least one, but some of the larger ones, two or three. Thus much for divisions for judicial purposes.

COLLECTION DISTRICTS.

5. Another class of districts has been formed, for the purpose of collecting the duties on imported goods. These are called "collection districts." They extend along, and embrace the whole sea coast and the shores of navigable lakes and rivers. In a few instances they are located inland, at points where goods may be brought into the United States by land. Each collection district has a port of entry, and very often several ports of delivery; also a collector of customs, and generally a custom house.

6. Another class of collection districts was formed

during the late civil war. They grew out of the war, and were established for the collection of the tax termed the "internal revenue," which had to be levied to pay the war expenses. These districts differ entirely, both in their objects and in the Territory embraced within them, from those established for the purpose of collecting duties on imports, and correspond as far as practicable with the Congressional districts in each State.

LAND DISTRICTS.

7. Land districts may also be noticed among these divisions. In every State and Territory where there are public lands for sale, after they are surveyed and mapped, they are divided into districts—two, three or four, in each State and Territory—as convenience and economy may dictate. In each district a land office is established for the sale of the lands in said district.

LIGHT HOUSE DISTRICTS.

8. Again, the whole of our sea coasts, both on the Atlantic and Pacific oceans, together with the shores of the navigable lakes and rivers, are divided into twelve light house districts (or their number must not exceed that), for the purpose of building, repairing, illuminating and superintending the light houses on all the coasts and shores wherever located. These are the principal divisions we have to notice. It is important to have a knowledge of them, for with such knowledge we can better understand how government affairs are conducted.

CHAPTER LXXXVIII.

District of Columbia.

1. The District of Columbia, in regard to its size, population, or political power, is one of the most insignificant places in the United States. It is not a State or Territory, but a small district ten miles square, originally cut out of the States of Maryland and Virginia and ceded to the United States as a site for the capitol. Here the capitol or house in which Congress meets is located, together with the Presidential mansion, and other public buildings occupied by the government. Its population has grown to the present size, about 80,000, since the year 1800, when it became the capital of the nation, and when Congress first assembled here, its former sessions having been held at New York and Philadelphia. The city which has grown up around the capitol is named Washington, after the great and good father of his country.

2. The people who live here occupy an anomalous position, for, with the exception of the political rights granted to them by Congress in their own local affairs, they have no political power whatsoever. They cannot vote for President or Vice President; they have no Representative in Congress, nor any voice in the enactment of the laws by which they are governed, further than to make their own municipal regulations as granted to them in the charter which Congress gave to the city; this they do through a mayor and common

council. They are governed by Congress, which is their legislature, although they have no power to send a single member to represent them in it.

3. Besides the courts of justice of the peace, there are four high courts, with their judges, and other law officers; first a Circuit Court, second, a District Court, third, an Orphan's Court, and fourth, a Criminal Court; all these must be recognized as United States courts; because they were established by the laws of Congress, and because their judges are all appointed by the President and Senate, and are paid out of the United States Treasury.

In saying that the District is ten miles square, and that it was ceded to the United States by Virginia and Maryland, we state what was the case up to 1846, when Congress re-ceded to the State of Virginia that part of it which formerly belonged to her. This part lies west of the Potomac river, and is of no use to the United States; as the capitol, with all the other public buildings, and, indeed, the whole city of Washington, stands on the east side of the river, and in the part formerly belonging to Maryland.

The villages of Alexandria and Georgetown were both included in the District; but in 1846, Alexandria, which stands on the west side of the Potomac, was thrown out by the re-cession to Virginia.

The capitol is one of the finest State houses in the world. It has been much enlarged, and has cost nearly $5,000,000.

CHAPTER LXXXIX.

States.

1. As has been said in another place, people who live in the United States, live under two separate and distinct governments; first, that of the United States, and second, that of the particular State in which they reside. This, at first thought, would seem to create confusion, if not a conflict, of authority, and to place the citizen in doubt as to what law he should obey when in his own mind there seems to be an antagonism between the laws of the two governments. This is easily overcome, however, for the Constitution of the United States, which is paramount to all other law, regulates this by its own provisions. Neither Congress, nor the legislature of any State can make any law contrary to it; and if either of these legislative bodies should do so, there is a power which has the authority to set any such law aside; and that is, the United States Supreme Court. Its decision in regard to any question which may arise as to the rightful authority of Congress, or any State legislature, is final; there being no appeals from its decisions.

This court is the regulating power and the final resort. To use a mechanical figure, it keeps all the small wheels (the State governments), revolving within one great wheel (the general government), with but little friction, and without any serious collisions.

2. In the preceding pages we have treated only of

the United States government, without any intention of explaining the State governments. We shall not now depart from that plan, but shall mention them only in general terms, as parts of the great whole, to shcw what political power they possess, what they relinquished to the general government, to what extent they are sovereign powers, and how they fall short of being complete sovereignties.

3. The Constitution of the United States expressly declares that Congress shall have and exercise certain powers, and also that no State shall possess or exercise them.

Congress has the exclusive power to lay duties on imported goods, to regulate commerce with foreign nations and with Indian tribes; to pass naturalization laws, to coin money, to establish post offices and post roads; to grant patents and copyrights; to declare war, and to do many other things which the States are prohibited from doing, for if invested with such powers there would be an immediate conflict of laws, and unavoidable collision between the United States and the State governments.

4. Now, when the several original States adopted the Constitution, they agreed to be governed by its provisions, and therefore conceded to Congress all the rights and powers therein specified; thus relinquishing all authority to exercise them themselves. And as the new States came into the Union, they did the same thing. Hence all the States voluntarily surrendered a part of the powers which belong to a sovereign State. Sovereignty implies full power to do any thing without

the control of another. The United States government is a complete sovereignty. The States are not, because they agreed, for the general good of all, to surrender certain powers to the general government.

5. In everything except these surrendered rights or powers, the States are sovereign. In all matters pertaining to their own domestic affairs, they enjoy full power to enact such laws as they please, taking care that no law, however, shall conflict with the Constitution of the United States, or with any law which Congress has the exclusive right to enact.

6. The States are the first, most important, and most permanent of all the political divisions of the country. They are now, in size, location, and territorial limits, just what they were when first formed; with one exception, and that is Virginia. When that State seceded with most of the other Southern States, before the late civil war, the people in that part of the State lying west of the Alleghany mountains (nearly one half of it,) refused to leave the old Union, seceded from the old State and organized themselves into a new one, styling it West Virginia. This they could not do, however, without the consent of Congress; but this was readily given, the division was consummated and a new State was carved out of an old one. This is the first, and thus far, the only instance in which this has been done.

In the following chapter we give the several States in alphabetical order, making it easy to turn to them, and to find any desired information contained in the brief summary of facts relating to each.

CHAPTER XC.

Individual States.

ALABAMA.

Alabama, (so called from the Indian name of the principal river, which means "here-we-rest,") was admitted into the Union of States, December 14, 1819, and made the twenty-second State.

It has an area of 50,722 square miles, equal to 32,462,080 acres, and had a population in 1860 of 964,201, by which she was entitled to six Representatives.

It forms a part of the fifth judicial circuit, and is divided into three judicial districts, viz.: Northern, Middle and Southern districts of Alabama.

It has one port of entry, (Mobile,) and two ports of delivery, viz.: Tuscumbia and Selma.

The capital of the State is Montgomery.

The State election is held on the 1st Monday in August. The Legislature meets on the second Monday in November, but meets only once in two years.

The enacting clause of its laws is as follows: "Be it enacted by the Senate and House of Representatives of the State of Alabama, in General Assembly convened."

UNITED STATES SENATORS.

Under this caption, after the general remarks upon each State, we shall give the names of all the men who have represented that State in the United States Senate, from the commencement of the government (1789) down to the end of the year 1867, in chronological order, together with their terms of service. This affords a convenient means of reference to the prominent statesmen in each State, in days gone by.

Those from Alabama were—

William R. King,	from	1819 to 1844. 1846 " 1852.
John W. Walker,	"	1819 " 1822.
Henry Chambers,	"	1825 " 1826.
Israel Pickens,	"	1826. Superseded

the same year by—

John McKinley,	"	1826 " 1831. 1837 " 1841.
Gabriel Moore,	"	1831 " 1837.
Clement C. Clay,	"	1837 " 1841.
Arthur P. Bagby,	"	1841 " 1849.
Dixon H. Lewis,	"	1844 " 1847.
Benjamin Fitzpatrick,	"	1852 " 1861.
Jeremiah Clemens,	"	1849 " 1853.
Clement C. Clay, Jr.,	"	1853 " 1861.

Alabama seceded from the Union in 1861, and consequently was not represented in the United States Senate from that time until 1868.

ARKANSAS.

Arkansas was admitted into the Union, January 15, 1836, (Michigan admitted the same day,) making the twenty-sixth State.

She has an area of 52,198 square miles, equal to 33,406,720 acres.

Her population in 1860 was 435,450, which entitles her to three Representatives in Congress.

Arkansas lies in the 8th judicial circuit, and forms two districts, Eastern and Western.

She has no ports of entry or delivery.

This State was a part of the Louisiana purchase, made of France in 1803.

The capital of the State is Little Rock.

She holds her State election on the first Monday in August.

The Legislature meets on the first Monday in November, but only once in two years.

The enacting clause of the laws is: "Be it enacted by the General Assembly of the State of Arkansas."

UNITED STATES SENATORS.

William S. Fulton,	from	1836	to	1844.
Ambrose H. Sevier,	"	1836	"	1848.
Chester Ashley,	"	1844	"	1847.
William K. Sebastian,	"	1848	"	1861.
Solon Borland,	"	1848	"	1853.
Robert W. Johnson,	"	1853	"	1861.
Charles B. Mitchell,	"	1861	"	1861.

Arkansas was one of the seceding States, and the remarks made at the end of the list of Senators from Alabama, are equally applicable to this State.

CALIFORNIA.

California was admitted in 1850, making the thirty-first State. It has an area of 188,982 square miles, equal to 120,948,480 acres. The population for 1860 was put down at 370,994; but this estimate was not regarded as reliable. Congress, by special act, allowed her three Representatives in Congress.

By act of 1866, this State, with Oregon and Nevada, constitutes the ninth judicial circuit, and forms two judicial districts. California has seven ports of entry, viz.: San Francisco, Monterey, San Diego, Sacramento, Sonoma, San Joaquin and San Pedro; also, one port of delivery, Santa Barbara. This State, as seen by its area, is very large, and will probably in some future day be divided into two. California was obtained from Mexico by treaty, in 1848.

The capital is Sacramento. She holds her State election on the first Wednesday in September. Her Legislature meets on the first Monday in December, but meets only once in two years.

The enacting clause of her laws is: "The people of the State of California, represented in Senate and Assembly, do enact as follows."

UNITED STATES SENATORS.

John C. Fremont,	from	1850	to	1851.
William M. Gwin,	"	1850	"	1861.
John B. Weller,	"	1851	"	1857.
H. P. Haun,	"	1859	"	1862.
David C. Broderick,	"	1856	"	1859.
Milton S. Latham,	"	1860	"	1866.
John Conness,	"	1863	"	1869.
Cornelius Cole,	"	1867	"	1873.
J. A. McDougall,	"	1861	"	1867.

CONNECTICUT.

Connecticut is one of the original thirteen States. Her area is only 4,674 square miles, equal to 2,991,360 acres. The population in 1860 was 460,147; this gives her four Representatives in Congress.

Connecticut is part of the second judicial circuit, and forms one judicial district. She has five collection districts, and consequently five ports of entry—New London, New Haven, Fairfield, Middletown and Stonington; also twenty-two ports of delivery.

This State has two capitals, Hartford and New Ha ven, and holds her State election on the first Monday in April. The Legislature meets on the first Wednesday in May.

The enacting clause of her laws is: "Be it enacted by the Senate and House of Representatives, in General Assembly convened."

UNITED STATES SENATORS.

Oliver Ellsworth,	from	1789	to	1796.
William S. Johnson,	"	1789	"	1791.
Roger Sherman,	"	1791	"	1793.
S. M. Michell,	"	1793	"	1795.
Jonathan Trumbull,	"	1795	"	1796.
Uriah Tracey,	"	1796	"	1807.
J. Hillhouse,	"	1796	"	1810.
C. Goodrich,	"	1807	"	1813.
S. W. Dana,	"	1810	"	1821.
David Doggett,	"	1813	"	1819.
James Lanman,	"	1819	"	1825.
E. Boardman,	"	1821	"	1823.
H. W. Edwards,	"	1823	"	1827.
Calvin Willey,	"	1825	"	1831.
Samuel A. Foot,	"	1827	"	1833.
G. Tomlinson,	"	1831	"	1837.
Nathan Smith,	"	1833	"	1835.
John M. Niles,	"	1835	"	1839.
		1843	"	1849.
Perry Smith,	"	1837	"	1843.
Thaddeus Betts,	"	1839	"	1840.
J. W. Huntington,	"	1840	"	1847.
R. S. Baldwin,	"	1847	"	1851.
Truman Smith,	"	1849	"	1855.
Isaac Toucey,	"	1852	"	1857.
Francis Gillette,	"	1854	"	1856.
L. S. Foster,	"	1855	"	1867.
James Dixon,	"	1857	"	1869.
Orris Ferry,	"	1867	"	1873.

DELAWARE.

Delaware is one of the original thirteen States, and has an area of 2,120 square miles, equal to 1,356,800 acres. Population in 1860, 112,216.

It has one Representative in Congress; forms part of the third judicial circuit, (act of 1862), constitutes one judicial district; has one port of entry, Wilmington; and three ports of delivery, New Castle, Port Penn, and Delaware City.

The population of this State has never entitled it to more than one Member of Congress.

The capital is Dover. The elections are held in November. The Legislature meets on the first Tuesday in January, and meets only once in two years.

The enacting clause of the laws is: "Be it enacted by the Senate and House of Representatives of the State of Delaware, in General Assembly met."

UNITED STATES SENATORS.

George Read,	from	1789 to 1793.
R. Bassett,	"	1789 " 1793.
John Vining,	"	1793 " 1798.
Kensey Johns,	"	1794 " 1795.
Henry Latimer,	"	1795 " 1801.
Joshua Clayton,	"	1798 " 1799.
W. H. Wells,	"	{ 1799 " 1804. 1813 " 1817.
Samuel White,	"	1801 " 1810.
J. A. Bayard,	"	1804 " 1813.
O. Horsey,	"	1810 " 1821.
N. Van Dyke,	"	1817 " 1826.
C. A. Rodney,	"	1822 " 1823.
T. Clayton,	"	{ 1824 " 1827. 1837 " 1847.
D. Rodney,	"	1826 " 1827.
H. Ridgely,	"	1827 " 1829.
L. McLane,	"	1827 " 1829.
J. M. Clayton,	"	{ 1829 " 1837. 1845 " 1849.
A. Nordain,	"	1830 " 1836.
R. H. Bayard,	"	1836 " 1845.
P. Spruance,	"	1847 " 1853.
John Wales,	"	1849 " 1851.
J. A. Bayard,	"	1851 " 1864.
M. W. Bates,	"	1857 " 1859.
J. P. Comeygs,	"	1856 " 1857.
W. Saulsbury,	"	1859 " 1871.
G. R. Riddle,	"	1864 " 1869.
J. A. Bayard,	"	1864 " 1873.

FLORIDA.

Florida was admitted into the Union, March 3, 1845; making the twenty-seventh State. This State has an area of 59,268 square miles, equal to 37,931,520 acres. The population in 1860 amounted to 140,425, which gave her but one Representative in Congress.

Florida lies in the 5th judicial circuit, and forms two judicial districts; and has seven ports of entry—St. Augustine, Key West, Apalachicola, Pensacola, Magnolia, St. John's River, and Fernandina; and two ports of delivery—Palatka and Bay Port. This State was bought by the United States, of Spain in 1819.

The capital is Tallahasse. The State election is held the first Monday in October. The Legislature meets biennially on the first Monday in November.

The enacting clause of the laws is: "Be it enacted by the Senate and House of Representatives of the State of Florida, in General Assembly convened."

UNITED STATES SENATORS.

David L. Yulee,	from	1845 to 1861.
J. D. Wescott,	"	1845 " 1851.
Jackson Morton,	"	1849 " 1855.
S. R. Mallory,	"	1851 " 1861.

Florida seceded from the United States in 1861; and the remarks made at the end of the list of Senators from Alabama, are applicable to her.

GEORGIA.

Georgia is one of the thirteen original States, and has an area of 52,009 square miles, equal to 33,285,760 acres. She was named after George II.

The population in 1860, was 1,057,286, which entitled her to seven Representatives in Congress.

The State lies in the fifth judicial circuit, and has two judicial districts; also four ports of entry—Savannah, Brunswick, St. Mary's and Hardwicke; and two ports of delivery—Augusta and Sunbury.

The capital is Milledgeville. The State election is held on the first Wednesday of October. The Legislature meets on the first Thursday in November.

The enacting clause of her laws is: "Be it enacted by the Senate and House of Representatives of the State of Georgia in General Assembly met; and it is hereby enacted by the authority of the same."

UNITED STATES SENATORS.

William Few,	from	1789 to 1793.
James Gunn,	"	1789 " 1801.
James Jackson,	"	{ 1793 " 1795. 1801 " 1806.
George Walton,	"	1795 " 1796.
Josiah Tatnall,	"	1796 " 1799.
A. Baldwin,	"	{ 1796 " 1805. 1805 " 1807.
J. Melledge,	"	1806 " 1809.
George Jones,	"	1807 " 1807.
W. H. Crawford,	"	1807 " 1813.
Charles Tait,	"	{ 1809 " 1813. 1813 " 1819.
W. B. Bullock,	"	1813 " 1813.
Wm. W. Bibb,	"	1813 " 1816.
G. M. Troup,	"	{ 1815 " 1818. 1829 " 1833.
John Forsyth,	"	{ 1819 " 1819. 1829 " 1837.
F. Walker,	"	1819 " 1821.
John Elliot,	"	1819 " 1821.
Nicholas Ware,	"	1821 " 1823.
T. W. Cobb,	"	1824 " 1828.
O. H. Prince,	"	1828 " 1829.
John P. King,	"	1833 " 1837.
W. Lumpkin,	"	1837 " 1841.
J. M. Berrien,	"	{ 1825 " 1829. 1841 " 1851.

A. Cuthbert,	from	1837 to 1843.
W. T. Colquitt,	"	1843 " 1849.
H. V. Johnson,	"	1848 " 1849.
W. C. Dawson,	"	1849 " 1855.
Robert Toombs,	"	1853 " 1861.
R. M. Charleton,	"	1852 " 1853.
Alfred Iverson,	"	1855 " 1861.

Georgia was one of the seceding States, and the same remarks apply to her that have been made at the end of the list of Senators from Alabama.

ILLINOIS.

This State came into the Union on the third day of Dec., 1818, making the twenty-first State. It was carved out of what was then known as the Northwestern Territory. Illinois has an area of 55,405 square miles, equal to 35,459,200 acres; had a population in 1860 of 1,711,951; is entitled to fourteen Representatives in Congress, forms a part of the seventh judicial circuit. Forms two judicial districts,—Northern and

Southern—has one port of entry, viz.: Chicago; and four ports of delivery, viz.: Alton, Quincy, Cairo and Peoria.

The capital is at Springfield. The State election is held on the first Tuesday in November. The Legislature meets biennially on the second Monday in January.

The enacting clause of the laws is as follows: "Be it enacted by the people of the State of Illinois, represented in the General Assembly."

UNITED STATES SENATORS.

J. S. Thomas,	from	1818 to 1829.
N. Edwards,	"	1818 " 1824.
John McLean,	"	1824 " 1825. 1829 " 1830.
D. J. Baker,	"	1830 1 month.
E. K. Kane,	"	1825 " 1836.
J. M. Robinson,	"	1830 " 1841.
W. L. D. Ewing,	"	1835 " 1837.
R. M. Young,	"	1837 " 1843.
S. McRoberts,	"	1841 " 1843.
J. Semple,	"	1843 " 1847.
Sidney Breeze,	"	1843 " 1849.
S. A. Douglas,	"	1847 " 1861.
James Shields,	"	1849 " 1855.
L. Trumbull,	"	1855 " 1861.
O. H. Browning,	"	1861 " 1863.
W. A. Richardson,	"	1863 " 1865.
Richard Yates,	"	1865 " 1871.

INDIANA.

The State of Indiana was formed out of part of what was called the Northwestern Territory; was admitted as a State Dec. 11, 1816, making the nineteenth State. She has an area of 33,809 square miles, equal to 21,637,760 acres. Her population in 1860 was 1,350,428, which entitled her to eleven Representatives in Congress. Indiana is the seventh judicial circuit, and forms one judicial district. There is no port of entry in this State; but there are three ports of delivery, to-wit: Evansville, New Albany, and Madison; which are attached to the New Orleans collection district.

The capital is Indianapolis. The State election is held on the second Tuesday of October. The Legislature meets only once in two years, on the first Wednesday of January.

The enacting clause of her laws is in these words: "Be it enacted by the General Assembly of the State of Indiana."

UNITED STATES SENATORS.

James Noble,	from	1816 to 1831.
W. Taylor,	"	1816 " 1825.
W. Hendricks,	"	1825 " 1837.
R. Hanna,	"	1831 " 1831.
John Tipton,	"	1831 " 1839.
O. H. Smith,	"	1837 " 1843.
A. S. White,	"	1839 " 1845.
E. A. Hannegan,	"	1843 " 1849.
J. D. Bright,	"	1845 " 1862.
J. Whitcomb,	"	1849 " 1855.
C. W. Cathcart,	"	1852 " 1853.
John Pettit,	"	1853 " 1855.
G. N. Fitch,	"	1857 " 1861.
H. A. Lane,	"	1861 " 1867.
D. Turpee,	"	1863 " 1863.
J. A. Wright,	"	1862 " 1863.
T. A. Hendricks,	"	" 1869.
O. P. Morton,	"	1867 " 1873.

IOWA.

Iowa was admitted into the Union March 3, 1845,

making the twenty-eighth State. We have numbered this the twenty-eighth State, and Florida the twenty-ninth. Both, however, were admitted on the same day, and by one act. Iowa has an area of 55,045 square miles, equal to 35,228,800 acres. The population in 1860 was 674,913, which entitled her to six Representatives in Congress. This State lies in the eighth judicial circuit, and makes one judicial district. She has no port of entry, but has three ports of delivery, to wit: Burlington, Keokuk, and Dubuque; all of which are attached to the collection district of New Orleans, in the State of Louisiana.

Des Moines is the capital. The State election is held on the second Tuesday of October. The Legislature meets biennially on the second Wednesday in January.

The enacting clause of her laws is in these words: "Be it enacted by the General Assembly of the State of Iowa."

UNITED STATES SENATORS.

George W. Jones,	from	1848 to 1859.
Augustus C. Dodge,	"	1848 " 1855.
James Harlan,	"	{ 1856 " 1865. 1867 " 1873.
James W. Grimes,	"	1859 " 1871.
Samuel J. Kirkwood,	"	1866 " 1871.

KANSAS.

Kansas was admitted into the Union as a State, Jan. 29, 1861, making the thirty-fourth State. Kansas has an area of 78,418 square miles, equal to 50,187,520 acres. The population in 1860 was 107,206; entitling her to one Representative in Congress. This State is in the eighth judicial circuit, and forms one judicial district. It has no ports of entry or delivery.

Topeka is the capital. The State election is held on the first Tuesday in November. The Legislature meets on the second Thursday in January.

The enacting clause of the laws is as follows: "Be it enacted by the Legislature of the State of Kansas."

UNITED STATES SENATORS.

James Henry Lane,	from	1861	to 1866.
Samuel C. Pomeroy,	"	1861	" 1873.
E. G. Ross,	"	1866	" 1871.

KENTUCKY.

Kentucky was admitted into the Union on the first of June, 1792, and has an area of 37,680 square miles, equal to 24,115,200 acres.

The population in 1860 numbered 1,155,684. The State has now nine Representatives in Congress; is in the sixth judicial circuit, by an act of 1866; forms one judicial district; has one port of entry, Louisville; and two ports of delivery, Paducah and Columbus.

Before Kentucky was erected into a State, it formed a part of the State of Virginia.

It was the second State admitted, making the fifteenth State. Frankfort is the capital.

The State elections are held on the first Monday of August. The Legislature meets on the first Monday in December.

The enacting clause of the laws is in the following words: "Be it enacted by the General Assembly of the Commonwealth of Kentucky."

UNITED STATES SENATORS.

John Brown,	from	1792 to 1805.
John Edwards,	"	1792 " 1795.
Humphrey Marshall,	"	1795 " 1801.
John Breckenridge,	"	1801 " 1805.
Buckner Thurston,	"	1805 " 1810.
John Adair,	"	1805 " 1806.
Henry Clay,	"	1806 " 1807. 1810 " 1811. 1831 " 1842. 1849 " 1855.
John Pope,	"	1807 " 1813.
George M. Bibb	"	1811 " 1814. 1829 " 1835.
Jesse Bledsoe,	"	1813 " 1815.
George Walker,	"	1814 " 1814.
William T. Barry,	"	1814 " 1816.
Isham Talbot,	"	1815 " 1819. 1820 " 1825.
Martin D. Hardin	"	1816 " 1817.
John J. Crittenden,	"	1817 " 1819. 1835 " 1841. 1842 " 1849. 1855 " 1861.
Richard M. Johnson,	"	1819 " 1823. 1823 " 1829.
William Logan,	"	1819 " 1820.
John Rowan,	"	1826 " 1831.
James T. Moorehead,	"	1841 " 1847.
Jos'h R. Underwood,	"	1847 " 1853.
Thomas Metcalf,	"	1848 " 1849.
Archibald Dixon,	"	1852 " 1855.
David Meriwether,	"	1852 " 1852.
J. B. Thompson,	"	1853 " 1859.
Lazarus W. Powell,	"	1859 " 1865.
J. C. Breckinridge,	"	1861 " 1861.
Garrett Davis,	"	1861 " 1873.
James Guthrie,	"	1865 " 1871.
Thos. C. McCreery,	"	1868 " 1871.

LOUISIANA.

Louisiana was formed out of a part of the Louisiana purchase, made of France in 1803, and was admitted into the Union April 8th, 1812, making the eighteenth State.

She has an area of 46,431 square miles, equal to 29,715,840 acres. The population in 1860 numbered 708,002; entitling her to five Representatives in Congress.

Louisiana forms a part of the fifth judicial circuit, and constitutes two judicial districts, viz.: the eastern and western districts of Louisiana. This State has one collection district, denominated the district of New Orleans; which city is the only port of entry. The shores of the river Ohio, and all the rivers emptying into the Mississippi, are attached to the district of New Orleans, though most of them do not lie in the State. Several of the cities and towns on these rivers are made ports of delivery. Collection districts are not always confined to one State.

Baton Rouge is the capital. The Legislature meets on the third Monday in January, once in two years. The State election is held on the first Monday in November.

The enacting clause of her laws is as follows: "Be it enacted by the Senate and House of Representatives of the State of Louisiana, in General Assembly convened."

UNITED STATES SENATORS.

Thomas Posey,	October to December,		1812.
James Brown,	from	1812 "	1817.
		1819 "	1824.
Allan B. Macgruder,	"	1812 "	1813.
Eligius Fromentin,	"	1813 "	1819.
W. C. C. Claiborne,	"	1817 "	1818.
Henry Johnson,	"	1818 "	1824.
		1843 "	1849.
Wm. Kelly,	"	1822 "	1825.
Dominique Bouligny,	"	1824 "	1829.
Josiah S. Johnston,	"	1824 "	1833.
Edward Livingston,	"	1829 "	1831.
Geo. A. Waggaman,	"	1831 "	1835.
Alexander Porter	"	1833 "	1837.
Robert C. Nichols,	"	1833 "	1841.
Alexander Morton,	"	1838 "	1842.
Alexander Barrow,	"	1841 "	1847.
Charles M. Conrad,	"	1842 "	1843.
Pierre Soule,	"	1847 "	1847.
		1849 "	1855.
Solomon W. Downs,	"	1847 "	1853.
John Slidell,	"	1853 "	1861.
Judah P. Benjamin,	"	1853 "	1861.

Louisiana seceded with other Southern States in 1861, and the remarks made at the end of the list of Senators from Alabama, also apply to her.

MAINE.

Maine was admitted into the Union on the 15th day of March, 1820, making the twenty-third State. She has an area of 31,766 square miles, equal to 20,330,240 acres. In 1860 the population amounted to 628,279, in view of which she is now entitled to five Representatives in Congress. Maine forms a part of the first judicial circuit, and constitutes one judicial district. This State has thirteen ports of entry, and thirty-two ports of delivery. Until it was admitted into the Union, it formed a part of the State of Massachusetts.

Augusta is the capital. The State elections are held on the second Monday of September. The Legislature meets on the first Wednesday of January.

The enacting clause of the laws is as follows: "Be it enacted by the Senate and House of Representatives in Legislature assembled."

UNITED STATES SENATORS.

John Holmes,	from	1820 to 1833.
John Chandler,	"	1820 " 1829.
Albion P. Parris,	"	1827 " 1829.
Peleg Sprague,	"	1829 " 1835.
Ether Shepley,	"	1833 " 1836.
John Ruggles,	"	1835 " 1841.
Judah Dana,	"	1836 " 1837.
Reuel Williams,	"	1837 " 1843.
George Evans,	"	1841 " 1847.
John Fairfield,	"	1843 " 1847.
Wynan B. S. Moore,	"	1848 " 1848.
Jas. W. Bradbury,	"	1847 " 1853.
Hannibal Hamlin,	"	1848 " 1857. 1857 " 1861.
Amos Nourse,	"	1857 " 1857.
Wm. P. Fessenden,	"	1863 " 1864. 1865 " 1871.
Lot M. Morrill,	"	1861 " 1869.
Nathan A. Farwell,	"	1864 " 1865.

MARYLAND.

Maryland is one of the original thirteen States, and

has an area of 11,124 square miles, equal to 7,119,360 acres. The population in 1860 was 687,049, which gives her five Representatives in Congress. By an act of Congress, passed in 1866, this State was put in the fourth judicial circuit, which is composed of Maryland, Virginia, West Virginia, North and South Carolina. Maryland constitutes one judicial district; has ten ports of entry, viz.: Baltimore, Chester, Oxford, Vienna, Snow-Hill, Annapolis, Nottingham, St. Mary's, Georgetown, and Havre de Grace; and twelve ports of delivery.

Annapolis is the capital. The State election is held on the first Tuesday of November. The Legislature meets on the first Wednesday of January.

The enacting clause of the laws is as follows: "Be it enacted by the General Assembly of Maryland."

UNITED STATES SENATORS.

Charles Carroll, (of Carrollton)	from	1789 to 1793.
John Henry,	"	1789 " 1797.
Richard Potts,	"	1793 " 1796.
John E. Howard,	"	1796 " 1803.
James Lloyd,	"	1797 " 1800.
William Hindman,	"	1800 " 1801.
Robert Wright,	"	1801 " 1806.
Samuel Smith,	"	1803 " 1815. 1822 " 1833.
Philip Reed,	"	1806 " 1813.
R. H. Goldsborough,	"	1813 " 1819. 1835 " 1836.
Robert G. Harper,	"	1816 " 1816.
Alexander C. Hanson,	"	1816 " 1819.
William Pinkney,	"	1819 " 1822.

Edward Lloyd,	from	1819 to 1826.
Ezekiel F. Chambers,	"	1826 " 1835.
Joseph Kent,	"	1833 " 1838.
John S. Spence,	"	1836 " 1841.
William D. Merrick,	"	1838 " 1845.
John Leidsker,	"	1841 " 1843.
James A. Pearce,	"	1843 " 1862.
Reverdy Johnson,	"	{ 1845 " 1851. 1863 " 1868.
David Stuart,	"	1849 " 1850.
Thomas G. Pratt,	"	1850 " 1857.
Anthony Kennedy,	"	1857 " 1863.
Thomas H. Hicks,	"	1862 " 1864.
John A. J. Cresswell,	"	1865 " 1867.
Philip F. Thomas,	"	" 1867.
George Vickers,	"	1868 " 1871.

MASSACHUSETTS.

Massachusetts, the "Bay State," as she is commonly called, from the great bays indenting her eastern shore, is one of the original thirteen States, and has an area of 7,800 square miles, equal to 4,992,000 acres.

Her population in 1860 amounted to 1,231,066, which entitles her to ten Members of Congress.

Massachusetts lies in the first judicial circuit, which is composed of Massachusetts, Rhode Island, New Hampshire and Maine—and forms one judicial district.

There are now fourteen ports of entry in this State, and twenty-five ports of delivery. These have been so often changed, discontinued, or annexed to others, and will probably be hereafter, that we omit a list of them, and only remark that Boston is the principal one.

Boston is the capital. The Legislature meets on the first Wednesday of January. The State election is held on the first Tuesday in November.

The enacting clause of her laws is: "Be it enacted by the Senate and House of Representatives, in General Court assembled, and by the authority of the same, as follows."

UNITED STATES SENATORS.

Tristram Dalton,	from	1789	to	1791.
Caleb Strong,	"	1789	"	1796.
George Cabot,	"	1791	"	1796.
Theo. Sedgewick,	"	1796	"	1799.
Benj. Goodhue,	"	1796	"	1800.
Samuel Dexter,	"	1799	"	1800.
Dwight Foster,	"	1800	"	1803.
Jonathan Mason,	"	1800	"	1803.
John Q. Adams,	"	1803	"	1808.
Timothy Pickering,	"	1803	"	1811.
James Lloyd,	"	1808	"	1813.
		1822	"	1826.

Joseph B. Varnum,	from	1811 to 1817.
Christopher Gore,	"	1813 " 1816.
Eli P. Ashmun,	"	1816 " 1818.
Harrison Gray Otis,	"	1817 " 1822.
Prentiss Mellen,	"	1818 " 1820.
Elijah H. Mills,	"	1820 " 1827.
Nathaniel Silsbee,	"	1826 " 1835.
Daniel Webster,	"	1827 " 1841. 1845 " 1850.
Rufus Choate,	"	1841 " 1845.
John Davis,	"	1835 " 1841. 1845 " 1847. 1847 " 1853.
Isaac C. Bates,	"	1841 " 1845.
Robert C. Winthrop,	"	1850 " 1851.
Robert Rantoul,	"	1851 " 1851.
Charles Sumner,	"	1851 " 1869.
Edward Everett,	"	1853 " 1854.
Julius Rockwell,	"	1854 " 1855.
Henry Wilson,	"	1855 " 1871.

MICHIGAN.

The Territory of Michigan was changed into a State

on the 15th day of June, 1836, and as such was admitted to all the rights and privileges of the other States; making the twenty-fifth State, (Arkansas was admitted on the same day). Her area is 56,243 square miles equal to 35,995,520 acres. The population in 1860 was 749,113 which entitled her to six Representatives in Congress. By an act of 1866, Michigan was located in the sixth judicial circuit; and forms two judicial districts, and has four collection districts and four ports of entry, viz.: Detroit, Port Huron, Grand Haven, and Michilimackinac; also five ports of delivery, (if the President deem them necessary).

The capital is Lansing. The State election is held on the first Tuesday in November. The Legislature meets biennially on the first Wednesday of January.

The enacting clause of the laws is as follows: "The people of the State of Michigan enact."

UNITED STATES SENATORS.

Lucius Lyon,	from	1836	to	1839.
John Norvall,	"	1836	"	1841.
Augustus S. Porter,	"	1839	"	1845.
Wm. Woodbridge,	"	1841	"	1847.
Lewis Cass,	"	1845	"	1851.
Alpheus Fitch,	"	1847	"	1853.
Thomas Fitzgerald,	"	1848	"	1849.
Charles E. Stewart,	"	1853	"	1859.
Zachariah Chandler,	"	1857	"	1869.
Kingsley S. Bingham	"	1859	"	1861.
Jacob M. Howard,	"	1862	"	1871.

MINNESOTA.

This State was admitted into the Union on the 11th day of May, 1858, and made the thirty-second State. It has an area of 83,531 square miles, equal to 53,459,840 acres. The population in 1860 amounted to 172,123. In 1862, an act was passed increasing the number of Representatives in Congress from 233 to 241. This increase of eight members was given to the States of Pennsylvania, Ohio, Kentucky, Illinois, Iowa, Vermont, Rhode Island and Minnesota. By these means this State was allowed two Members of Congress.

It lies in the eighth judicial circuit, which is composed of Missouri, Iowa, Kansas, Arkansas and Minnesota. Minnesota forms one judicial district, and has no ports of entry or delivery.

St. Paul is the capital. The Legislature meets biennially on the first Tuesday in January. The State election is held on the first Tuesday in November.

UNITED STATES SENATORS.

Henry M. Rice,	from	1857	to	1863.
James Shields,	"	1857	"	1859.
Alex. Ramsey	"	1863	"	1869.
Daniel Norton,	"	1865	"	1871.
Mort. S. Wilkinson,	"	1859	"	1865.

MISSISSIPPI.

The Territory of Mississippi became a State in 1817; making the twentieth State. The area is 47,156 square miles, equal to 30,179,840 acres. The population in 1860 numbered 791,305; which entitled her to five Representatives in Congress. The State lies in the fifth judicial circuit, and is divided into two judicial districts, viz.: the Northern and Southern districts of Mississippi. She has three ports of entry, viz.: Natchez, Vicksburg, and one near the mouth of Pearl river, to be established whenever the President may direct;

also three ports of delivery, viz.: Grand Gulf, Ship Island and Columbus.

Jackson is the capital. The State election is held on the first Monday of October, and her Legislature meets biennally on the first Monday in January.

The enacting clause of the laws is in these words: "Be it enacted by the Senate and House of Representatives of the State of Mississippi in General Assembly convened."

UNITED STATES SENATORS.

Walter Leake,	from	1817 to 1820.
Thomas H. Williams,	"	1817 " 1829. 1838 " 1839.
David Holmes,	"	1820 " 1825.
Powhattan Ellis,	"	1825 " 1833.
Thomas B. Reed,	"	1826 " 1829.
Robert Adams,	"	1830 " 1830.
George Poindexter.	"	1830 " 1835.
John Black,	"	1832 " 1838.
R. J. Walker,	"	1835 " 1845.
James F. Trotter,	"	1838 " 1838.
John Henderson,	"	1839 " 1845.
Jesse Speight,	"	1845 " 1847.
Joseph W. Chambers,	"	1845 " 1847.
Jefferson Davis,	"	1847 " 1851. 1857 " 1861.
Henry S. Foote,	"	1847 " 1853.
John W. Rea,	"	1851 " 1851.
Walter Brooks,	"	1852 " 1853.
Albert G. Brown,	"	1854 " 1851.

Mississippi seceded from the Union in 1861, and is therefore in the same condition with Alabama, as stated at the end of the list of Senators from that State.

MISSOURI.

This State was formed out of a part of the Louisiana purchase, and was admitted in 1821; making the twenty-fourth State. Missouri is very large, and has an area of 67,380 square miles, equal to 43,123,200 acres. Her population in 1860 amounted to 1,182,012, which entitles her now to nine Representatives in Congress. This State is a part of the eighth judicial circuit, and formerly was one judicial district; but by act of 1857 was divided into two, the Eastern and Western. It has no port of entry, and but one port of delivery, Hannibal.

The capital is Jefferson City. The State election is held on the first Tuesday of November, and the Legislature meets on the last Monday of December.

The enacting clause of the laws is as follows: "Be it enacted by the General Assembly of the State of Missouri, as follows."

UNITED STATES SENATORS.

Thomas H. Benton,	from	1821 to 1851.
David Barton,	"	1821 " 1831.
Alexander Buckner,	"	1831 " 1833.
Lewis F. Linn,	"	1833 " 1843.
David R. Atchison,	"	1843 " 1849. 1849 " 1855.
Gratz B. Brown,	"	1863 " 1867.
Henry S. Geyer,	"	1851 " 1857.
Trusten Polk,	"	1857 " 1861.
James S. Green,	"	1856 " 1861.
Waldo P. Johnson,	"	1861 " 1862.
John B. Henderson,	"	1862 " 1869.
Charles D. Drake,	"	1867 " 1873.

NEBRASKA.

This State was admitted into the Union, February 9, 1867, making the thirty-seventh State. It has an area of 122,007 square miles, equal to 78,084,480 acres.

The population, when admitted, numbered over 12,000. It is entitled to one Member of Congress, is in the ninth judicial circuit, forms one judicial district, and has no ports of entry or delivery at this time.

UNITED STATES SENATORS.

John M. Thayer,	from	1867 to 1871.
Thomas W. Tipton,	"	1867 " 1869.

NEW HAMPSHIRE.

New Hampshire is one of the thirteen original States, and has an area of 9,280 square miles, which make 5,939,200 acres; also a population, in 1860, of 326,073, entitling her to three Members of Congress.

New Hampshire lies in the first judicial circuit, composed of this State, Massachusetts, Rhode Island and Maine. It constitutes one judicial district.

The whole State is embraced in one collection district—consequently there is but one port of entry in the State, at Portsmouth. There are also three ports of delivery, to-wit: New Castle, Dover and Exeter.

The capital is Concord. Here the Legislature assembles on the first Wednesday in June. The State election is held on the second Tuesday in March.

The enacting clause of the laws is as follows: "Be it enacted by the Senate and House of Representatives, in General Assembly convened."

UNITED STATES SENATORS.

Paine Wingate,	from	1789 to 1793.
John Langdon,	"	1789 " 1801.
Samuel Livermore,	"	1793 " 1801.
Simeon Olcott,	"	1801 " 1805.
James Sheafe,	"	1801 " 1802.
William Plummer,	"	1802 " 1807.
Nicholas Gilman,	"	1805 " 1814.
Nahum Parker,	"	1807 " 1810.
Charles Cutts,	"	1810 " 1813.
Jeremiah Mason,	"	1813 " 1817.
Thos. W. Thompson,	"	1814 " 1817.
David L. Morrill,	"	1817 " 1823.
Clement Storer,	"	1817 " 1819.
John F. Parrott,	"	1819 " 1825.
Samuel Bell,	"	1823 " 1835.
Levi Woodbury,	"	1825 " 1831. 1841 " 1845.
Isaac Hill,	"	1831 " 1835.
Henry Hubbard,	"	1835 " 1841.
John Page,	"	1836 " 1837.
Franklin Pierce,	"	1837 " 1842.
Leonard Wilcox,	"	1842 " 1842.
Charles G. Atherson,	"	1843 " 1849. 1852 " 1853.
Benning W. Jenness,	"	1845 " 1846.
Joseph Cilley,	"	1846 " 1847.

John P. Hale,	from	1847 to 1853. 1855 " 1865.
Moses Norris,	"	1849 " 1855.
Jared W. Williams,	"	1853 " 1854.
John S. Wells,	"	1855 " 1855.
James Bell,	"	1855 " 1857.
Daniel Clark,	"	1857 " 1866.
Aaron A. Cragin,	"	1867 " 1871.
James W. Paterson,	"	1867 " 1873.
George C. Fogg,	"	1866 " 1867.

NEW JERSEY.

New Jersey is one of the original thirteen States, and has an area of 8,320 square miles, equal to 5,324,800 acres. The population in 1860 numbered 672,035, which gives her now five Representatives in Congress. This State lies in the third judicial circuit, which is composed of this State and Pennsylvania, and forms one judicial district. There are six collection districts, and consequently six ports of entry in New Jersey, viz.:

Perth Amboy, Burlington, Bridgeton, Great Egg Harbor, Little Egg Harbor and Newark. There are also eight ports of delivery. A part of the eastern shore is attached to the port of New York.

The capital of New Jersey is Trenton. The State election is held on the first Tuesday in November, and the Legislature assembles on the second Tuesday of January.

The style of her laws, or the enacting clause thereof, is as follows: "Be it enacted by the Senate and General Assembly of the State of New Jersey."

UNITED STATES SENATORS.

Jonathan Elmer,	from	1789	to	1791.
William Patterson,	"	1789	"	1790.
Philemon Dickerson,	"	1790	"	1793.
John Rutherford,	"	1791	"	1798.
Fred'k Frelinghuysen,	"	1793	"	1796.
Richard Stockton,	"	1796	"	1799.
Franklin Davenport,	"	1798	"	1799.
James Schureman,	"	1799	"	1801.
Jonathan Dayton,	"	1799	"	1805.
Aaron Ogden,	"	1801	"	1803.
John Condit,	"	1803	"	1811.
Aaron Kitchell,	"	1805	"	1809.
John Lambert,	"	1809	"	1815.
Mahlon Dickerson,	"	1817	"	1833.
James J. Wilson,	"	1815	"	1821.
Samuel L. Southard,	"	1821	"	1823.
		1833	"	1841.
Joseph McIlvaine,	"	1823	"	1826.
Thos. Frelinghuysen,	"	1829	"	1835.
Ephriam Bateman,	"	1826	"	1829.
Garret D. Wall,	"	1835	"	1841.
Jacob Miller,	"	1841	"	1853.

William L. Dayton,	from	1842 to 1851.
John B. Thompson,	"	1853 " 1863.
William Pennington,	"	1858 " 1858.
William Wright,	"	1853 " 1859.
Robert F. Stockton,	"	1851 " 1853.
John C. Ten Eyck,	"	1859 " 1865.
Richard S. Field,	"	1862 " 1863.
James W. Wall,	"	1863 " 1863.
John P. Stockton,	"	1865 " 1866.
F. T. Frelinghuysen,	"	1867 " 1869.
Alexander G. Cattell,	"	1866 " 1871.

NEW YORK.

New York is one of the original thirteen States. Its area is 47,000 square miles, equal to 30,080,000 acres.

By the last census (1860) the population was ascertained to be 3,880,735—(4,000,000 in 1866)—which gives it thirty-one members of Congress.

It forms part of the second judicial circuit, which consists of New York, Vermont, Connecticut; and is divided into three judicial districts, the Northern, Southern and Eastern, (the Eastern was formed from the Southern, Feb. 26, 1865).

This State has a great length of sea, lake and river coast, and consequently has eleven ports of entry, viz.: New York, Sag Harbor, Hudson, Oswego, Niagara, Buffalo Creek, Oswegatchie, Dunkirk, Rouse's Point, Cape Vincent and Suspension Bridge; also fourteen ports of delivery; besides which the President is authorized to make eight or nine others if he deems it necessary to do so. The ports of delivery are at such places on the Hudson river, on the Long Island shores, and along the shores of the river St. Lawrence, lakes Ontario, Champlain and Erie, as the trade of these localities requires. Jersey City, in the State of New Jersey, is also attached to the collection district of New York.

The capital of New York is Albany. The State elections are held on the first Tuesday in November, and the Legislature meets on the first Tuesday in January.

The style of the laws, or the enacting clause, is as follows: "Be it enacted by the people of the State of New York represented in Senate and Assembly."

UNITED STATES SENATORS.

Philip Schuyler,	from	1789 to 1791.
Rufus King,	"	1789 " 1796. 1813 " 1825.
Aaron Burr,	"	1791 " 1797.

John Lawrence,	from	1796 to 1800.
John S. Hobart,	"	1798 " 1798.
William North,	"	1798 " 1798.
James Watson,	"	1798 Resigned.
Governeur Morris,	"	1800 " 1803.
John Armstrong,	"	1800 " 1802. 1803 " 1804.
DeWitt Clinton,	"	1802 " 1803.
Theodore Bailey,	"	1803 " 1804.
Samuel L. Mitchell,	"	1804 " 1809.
John Smith,	"	1804 " 1813.
Obadiah German,	"	1809 " 1815.
Nathan Sanford,	"	1815 " 1821. 1825 " 1831.
Martin Van Buren,	"	1821 " 1829.
Charles Dudley,	"	1829 " 1833.
William L. Marcy,	"	1831 " 1833.
Nath'l P. Tallmadge,	"	1833 " 1844.
Silas Wright,	"	1833 " 1844.
Daniel S. Dickinson,	"	1844 " 1851.
Henry A. Foster,	"	1844 " 1845.
John A. Dix,	"	1845 " 1849.
William H. Seward,	"	1849 " 1861.
Hamilton Fish,	"	1851 " 1857.
Preston King,	"	1857 " 1863.
Ira Harris,	"	1861 " 1867.
Edwin D. Morgan,	"	1863 " 1869.
Roscoe Conkling,	"	1867 " 1873.

NORTH CAROLINA.

This State is one of the original thirteen States, and has an area of 50,704 square miles, equal to 32,450,560 acres, with a population of 992,622, (one third colored,) which entitles her to seven members of Congress. North Carolina, by act of 1866, was located in the fourth judicial circuit, which is composed of Maryland, Virginia, West Virginia, North Carolina and South Carolina, and is divided into three judicial districts, called the districts of Albemarle, Pamlico, and Cape Fear. The collection districts, and the ports of entry and delivery in this State, have been so often modified and discontinued, that there is some uncertainty as to the number at this time. We can only make an approximate statement. There are, as near as we can determine, ten districts, ten ports of entry, and nine ports of delivery.

Raleigh is the capital. There the Legislature meets biennially on the third Monday of November. The

State election is held on the second Thursday in August.

The enacting clause of the laws is as follows: "Be it enacted by the General Assemblyof the State of North Carolina, and it is hereby enacted by the authority of the same."

UNITED STATES SENATORS.

Samuel Johnson,	from	1789 to 1793.
Benjamin Hawkins,	"	1789 " 1795.
Alexander Martin,	"	1793 " 1799.
Timothy Bloodworth,	"	1795 " 1801.
Jesse Franklin,	"	1799 " 1805. 1807 " 1813.
David Stone,	"	1801 " 1813.
James Turner,	"	1805 " 1816.
Nathaniel Macon,	"	1815 " 1828.
James Iredell,	"	1828 " 1831.
Montfort Stokes,	"	1816 " 1823.
John Branch,	"	1823 " 1829.
Bedford Brown,	"	1829 " 1840.
Willie P. Mangum,	"	1840 " 1853. 1831 " 1836.
Robert Strange,	"	1836 " 1840.
William A. Graham,	"	1840 " 1843.
William H. Haywood,	"	1843 " 1846.
George E. Badger,	"	1846 " 1855.
Asa Biggs,	"	1854 " 1858.
David S. Reed,	"	1855 " 1859.
Thomas L. Clingman,	"	1858 " 1861.
Thomas Bragg,	"	1859 " 1861.

NEVADA.

Nevada was admitted as a State, March 21st, 1864, making the thirty-sixth State in the Union.

It has an area of 63,473 square miles, or 40,622,720 acres. The population in 1860, while yet a Territory, was 6,857, but had greatly increased at the time of admission. In conformity with the Constitutional provision that every State shall have one Representative in Congress, Nevada has one. This State lies in the ninth judicial circuit, and forms one judicial district, called the district of Nevada.

Virginia City is the capital. The State election is held on the first Tuesday in November; and the Legislature meets on the first Monday in January.

The enacting clause of the laws is in the following words: "The people of the State of Nevada, represented in Senate and Assembly, do enact as follows."

UNITED STATES SENATORS.

James W. Nye, from 1865 to 1871.
William M. Stewart, " 1865 " 1869.

OHIO.

Ohio was admitted into the Union from what was then known as the Northwestern Territory, in 1802, and made the seventeenth State.

It has an area of 39,964 square miles, equal to 25,576,960 acres. The population in 1860 was 2,339,511, entitling it to nineteen Members of Congress.

It is in the sixth judicial circuit, and forms two judicial districts, viz.: the Northern and Southern districts of Ohio.

This State has three ports of entry, to wit: Cleveland, Toledo, and Portland; and four ports of delivery, to be located where the President directs.

The capital of this State is Columbus. The State election is now held on the second Tuesday of October. The Legislature meets on the first Monday of January, biennially.

The enacting clause of the laws is as follows: "Be it enacted by the General Assembly of the State of Ohio."

UNITED STATES SENATORS.

John Smith,	from	1803 to 1808.
Thos. Worthington,	"	1803 " 1807. 1810 " 1814.
Edward Tiffin,	"	1807 " 1809.
Return J. Meigs,	"	1808 " 1810.
Stanley Griswold,	"	1809 " 1809.
Alexander Campbell,	"	1809 " 1813.
Jeremiah Morrow,	"	1813 " 1819.
Joseph Kerr,	"	1814 " 1815.
Benjamin Ruggles,	"	1815 " 1833.
William A. Trimble,	"	1819 " 1821.
Ethan A. Brown,	"	1822 " 1825.
Wm. Henry Harrison,	"	1825 " 1828.
Jacob Burnett,	"	1828 " 1831.
Thomas Ewing,	"	1831 " 1837. 1850 " 1851.
Thomas Morris,	"	1833 " 1839.
William Allen,	"	1837 " 1849.
Benjamin Tappan,	"	1839 " 1845.
Thomas Corwin,	"	1845 " 1851.
Salmon P. Chase,	"	1849 " 1855.
Benjamin F. Wade,	"	1851 " 1869.
George Ellis Pugh,	"	1851 " 1861.
John Sherman,	"	1861 " 1873.

OREGON.

Oregon was admitted into the Union as a State on the 14th day of February, 1859, and made the thirty-third State. It has an area of 95,274 square miles, equal to 60,975,360 acres. The population amounted in 1860 to 52,465, which did not reach the number required to entitle it to a Member of Congress according to the fixed ratio. But every State is entitled to one member, whatever its population may be. By act of 1866, the States of Oregon, Nevada and California were constituted the ninth judicial circuit. Oregon forms one judicial district, and has one collection district, and one port of entry.

The capital is Salem, where her Legislature meets once in two years, on the second Tuesday of September. The State election is held on the 1st Monday in June.

UNITED STATES SENATOR.

Joseph Lane,	from	1859	to 1861.
Delazon Smith,	"	1859	" 1860.
Edward D. Baker,	"	1861	" 1861.
Benj. F. Harding,	"	1862	"
James W. Nesmith,	"	1861	" 1867.
Benjamin Stark,	"	1861	" 1862.
Geo. H. Williams,	"	1865	" 1871.
Henry W. Corbell,	"	1867	" 1873.

PENNSYLVANIA.

Pennsylvania is one of the original thirteen States, and is often figuratively called the Keystone State, from the central position she occupied in the original number of States.

Its area in square miles is 46,000, equal to 29,440,000 acres. The population in 1860 amounted to 2,906,115, which entitles her to twenty-four Members of Congress.

Pennsylvania lies in the third judicial circuit, which is composed of this State and New Jersey. It forms two judicial districts, viz.: the Eastern and Western districts of Pennsylvania.

There are two collection districts in Pennsylvania, and consequently two ports of entry, viz.: Philadelphia and Erie.

Harrisburgh is the capital. There the Legislature assembles on the first Tuesday in January; the State election is held on the second Tuesday in October.

The enacting clause of her laws is: "Be it enacted by the Senate and House of Representatives of the Commonwealth of Pennsylvania in General Assembly met; and it is hereby enacted by the authority of the same."

UNITED STATES SENATORS.

William Maclay,	from	1789	to	1791.
Robert Morris,	"	1789	"	1795.
Albert Gallatin,	"	1793	"	1794.
James Ross,	"	1794	"	1803.
William Bingham,	"	1795	"	1801.
Peter Muhlenburgh,	"	1801	"	1802.
Samuel Maclay,	"	1803	"	1808.
Michael Leib,	"	1808	"	1814.
Andrew Gregg,	"	1807	"	1813.
Abner Lacock,	"	1813	"	1819.
Jonathan Roberts,	"	1814	"	1821.
Walter Lawrie,	"	1819	"	1825.
William Findlay,	"	1821	"	1827.
William Marks,	"	1825	"	1831.
Isaac D. Barnard,	"	1827	"	1831.
George M. Dallas,	"	1831	"	1833.
William Wilkins,	"	1831	"	1834.
Samuel McKean,	"	1833	"	1839.

James Buchanan	from	1834 to 1845.
Daniel Sturgeon	"	1839 " 1851.
Simon Cameron,	"	1845 " 1849. 1857 " 1861. 1867 " 1873.
James Cooper,	"	1849 " 1855.
Charles R. Buckalew,	"	1850 " 1856. 1863 " 1869.
Richard Broadhead,	"	1851 " 1857.
Stephen Adams,	"	1852 " 1857.
William Bigler,	"	1855 " 1861.
Edgar Cowan,	"	1861 " 1867.
David Wilmot,	"	1861 " 1863.

RHODE ISLAND.

Rhode Island is one of the original thirteen States, but had no delegates in the Convention which formed the Constitution of the United States. She and Delaware are the two little States, Rhode Island being the smallest State in the Union, having an area of only

1,306 square miles, which make 835,840 acres. Her population in 1860 was 174,620, which entitled her to two Members of Congress. Rhode Island forms part of the first judicial circuit, which consists of the States of Rhode Island, Massachusetts, New Hampshire and Maine; constitutes one judicial district, called the district of Rhode Island, has three ports of entry, viz.: Newport, Providence and Bristol, and also seven ports of delivery.

Small as this State is, it has two capitals or places where the Legislature meets, viz.: Newport and Providence. The State election is held on the first Wednesday in April. The Legislature meets twice in a year, in May and January.

The style of her laws, or the enacting clause of them is as follows: "It is enacted by the General Assembly as follows."

UNITED STATES SENATORS.

Theodore Foster,	from	1790	to	1803.
Joseph Stanton,	"	1790	"	1793.
William Bradford,	"	1793	"	1797.
Ray Green,	"	1797	"	1801.
Charles Ellery,	"	1801	"	1805.
Samuel L. Potter,	"	1803	"	1804.
Benjamin Howland,	"	1804	"	1809.
James Fenner,	"	1805	"	1807.
Elisha Matthewson,	"	1807	"	1811.
Frances Malbone,	"	1809	"	1809.
C. G. Champlin,	"	1809	"	1811,
Jeremiah B. Howell,	"	1811	"	1817.
William Hunter,	"	1811	"	1831.
James Burrill,	"	1817	"	1821.
James D'Wolf,	"	1821	"	1825.

Nehemiah R. Knight,	from	1821	to	1841.
Asher Robbins,	"	1825	"	1839.
Nathan F. Dixon,	"	1839	"	1842.
James F. Simmons,	"	{ 1841	"	1847.
		1857	"	1862.
William Sprague,	"	1842	"	1844.
John B Francis,	"	1844	"	1845.
Albert C. Green,	"	1845	"	1851.
John H. Clarke,	"	1847	"	1853.
Charles T. James,	"	1851	"	1857.
Philip Allen,	"	1853	"	1859.
Henry B. Anthony,	"	{ 1859	"	1865.
		1865	"	1871.
William Sprague,	"	1862	"	1869.
Samuel G. Arnold,	"	1862	"	1863.

SOUTH CAROLINA.

South Carolina is one of the original thirteen States, and has an area of 29,385 square miles, which make 18,806,400 acres; with a population in 1860, of 703,-

708, (over half colored), which gives her four Members of Congress.

By an act of 1866, South Carolina was located in the fourth judicial circuit; it is divided into two judicial districts, called the Eastern and Western districts of South Carolina.

There are three collection districts in this State, and four ports of entry, to-wit: Georgetown, Charleston, Beaufort and Port Royal; but no ports of delivery.

The capital is Columbia. The State elections are held on the fourth Monday of November. The Legislature meets on the third Wednesday of October.

The enacting clause of the laws is as follows: "Be it enacted by the Honorable the Senate and House of Representatives, now met and sitting in General Assembly, and by authority of the same."

South Carolina made herself conspicuous by taking the lead in the recent rebellion against the United States government. She first seceded, and was the first to commence hostilities by firing on a government vessel in the harbor of Charleston, and then on Fort Sumter, one of the United States forts near the city.

UNITED STATES SENATORS.

Pierce Butler,	from	1790 to 1796. 1802 " 1804.
Ralph Izard,	"	1789 " 1795.
Jacob Read,	"	1795 " 1801.
John Hunter,	"	1796 " 1798.
Charles Pinckney,	"	1798 " 1801.
Thomas Sumpter,	"	1801 " 1810.
John E. Calhoun,	"	1801 " 1802.
John Gaillard,	"	1804 " 1802.

John Taylor,	from	1810 to 1816.
William Smith,	"	1816 " 1823. 1826 " 1831.
William Harper,	"	1826 " 1826.
Robert J. Hayne,	"	1823 " 1832.
Stephen D. Miller,	"	1831 " 1833.
John C. Calhoun,	"	1832 " 1842. 1845 " 1847.
William C. Preston,	"	1833 " 1842.
Daniel E. Huger,	"	1842 " 1845.
George McDuffie,	"	1842 " 1846.
Andrew P. Butler,	"	1846 " 1857.
Franklin H. Elmore,	"	1850 " 1850.
Robert W. Barnwell,	"	1850 " 1853.
William Desaussure,	"	1852 " 1853.
Josiah Evans,	"	1852 " 1858.
James H. Hammond,	"	1857 " 1860.
James Chestnut,	"	1858 " 1861.
Arthur P. Hayne,	"	1858.

South Carolina being one of the seceding States, has been, since 1861, in the same condition as Alabama.

TENNESSEE.

Tennessee was admitted into the Union, June 1st, 1796, and made the sixteenth State. Its area is 45,600 square miles, equal to 29,184,000 acres. The population in 1860 numbered 1,109,801. It has now eight Representatives in Congress, is in the sixth judicial circuit, forms three judicial districts, and has two ports of delivery, Memphis and Knoxville. Before Tennessee was admitted it formed a part of North Carolina.

Nashville is the capital. The State election is held on the first Thursday in August; and on the first Monday of October the Legislature meets, once in two years.

The enacting clause of the laws of this State is as follows: "Be it enacted by the General Assembly of the State of Tennessee."

UNITED STATES SENATORS.

William Blount,	from	1796 to 1797.
William Cocke,	"	1796 " 1797. 1799 " 1805.
Andrew Jackson,	"	1797 " 1798. 1823 " 1825.
Joseph Anderson,	"	1797 " 1815.
Daniel Smith,	"	1797 " 1809.
Jenkin Whiteside,	"	1809 " 1811.
Geo. W. Campbell,	"	1811 " 1818.
Jesse Wharton,	"	1814 " 1815.
John Williams,	"	1815 " 1823.
John H. Eaton,	"	1818 " 1829.
Hugh L. White,	"	1825 " 1840.
Felix Grundy,	"	1829 " 1840.
Ephraim H. Foster,	"	1838 " 1839. 1843 " 1845.
A. O. P. Nicholson,	"	1840 " 1843.
Alexander Anderson,	"	1840 " 1841.
Spencer Jarnagin,	"	1841 " 1847.
Hopkins L. Turney,	"	1845 " 1851.
John Bell,	"	1847 " 1853.
James C. Jones,	"	1851 " 1857.
Andrew Johnson	"	1857 " 1863.
David T. Patterson,	"	1865 " 1869.
J. S. Fowler,	"	1865 " 1871.

Tennessee was one of the seceding States in 1861, but came back in 1866. Between these two periods she was unrepresented in the United States Senate.

TEXAS.

The history of this State is unlike that of any other belonging to the Union. It is not one of the original States; neither was it first formed into a territory and afterwards changed into a State. Down to 1836, Texas was a part of Mexico; at that time the people of this Mexican province or colony revolted against the Mexican authority, and, after a short war with that power, gained their independence and established a government of their own. This they called the "Republic of Texas." But it was a small and feeble power, and could not sustain itself as an independent nation. In this helpless condition she applied to the United States government for permission to unite herself with it. The request was listened to and favorably received by the United States. The proposition was accepted, and in 1845 Texas was admitted—making the twenty-eighth State—and became a part of the

"Great Republic." Though larger than five such states as New York, she has continued to this day a single State, because her population has remained so small. But in the act of admission it was provided that Texas might be divided into four new States, besides that of Texas, making five in all. When this shall be done, all will be large States. The whole area of Texas is 237,504 square miles, which make 152,002,560 acres. The population in 1860—fifteen years after her admission—was only 604,215, which entitles her to four Members of Congress. Texas lies in the fifth judicial circuit, and makes two judicial districts, the eastern and western.

There are three collection districts in this State. The respective ports of entry for these districts are Galveston, Lasalle and Brazos Santiago. To these are attached nine ports of delivery.

The capital is Austin, where the Legislature meets biennially on the first Monday of November. The State election is held on the first Monday in August.

UNITED STATES SENATORS.

Thomas F. Rusk,	from	1846	to	1856.
Samuel Houston,	"	1846	"	1859.
Pinckney J. Henderson,	"	1857	"	1858.
Matthias Ward,	"	1858	"	1861.
John Hemphill,	"	1859	"	1861.
Lewis T. Wigfall,	"	1859	"	1861.

Texas was one of the seceding States; and therefore the remarks made at the end of the list of Senators from Alabama, apply to her.

VERMONT.

Vermont was admitted into the Union, March 4th, 1791, making the fourteenth State.

It has an area of 10,212 square miles, equal to 6,535,680 acres. The population in 1860 numbered 315,098. It now has three Representatives in Congress; forms part of the second judicial circuit; constitutes one judicial district; has one port of entry, located at such place as may be named by the President, who may also designate two places in the State as ports of delivery.

Vermont was the first new State admitted into the Union, and thus made the fourteenth State.

Montpelier is the capital. The State election is held on the first Tuesday in September, and the Legislature meets on the second Thursday in October.

The enacting clause of the laws is: "It is hereby enacted by the General Assembly of the State of Vermont."

UNITED STATES SENATORS.

Moses Robinson,	from	1791 to 1796.
Stephen R. Bradley,	"	1791 " 1795. 1801 " 1813.
Elijah Paine,	"	1795 " 1801.
Isaac Tichenor,	"	1796 " 1797. 1815 " 1821.
Nathaniel Chipman,	"	1797 " 1803.
Israel Smith,	"	1801 " 1802. 1803 " 1807.
Jonathan Robinson,	"	1807 " 1815.
Dudley Chase,	"	1813 " 1817. 1825 " 1831.
James Fisk,	"	1817 " 1817.
William A. Palmer,	"	1818 " 1825.
Horatio Seymour,	"	1821 " 1833.
Samuel Prentiss,	"	1831 " 1842.
Benjamin Swift,	"	1833 " 1839.
Samuel S. Phelps,	"	1839 " 1851.
Samuel C. Crafts,	"	1842 " 1843.
William Upham,	"	1843 " 1855.
Solomon Foote,	"	1851 " 1866.
Samuel S. Phelps,	"	1853 " 1854.
Brainard Lawrence,	"	1854 " 1855.
Jacob Collamer,	"	1854 " 1865.
Luke P. Poland,	"	1865 " 1867.
George F. Edmunds,	"	1866 " 1869.
Justin S. Morrill,	"	1867 " 1873.

VIRGINIA.

Virginia is also one of the original thirteen States, and had an area previous to the division in 1862, of 61,352 square miles, equal to 39,265,280 acres; but after West Virginia was set off as a separate State, there were but 38,352 square miles left of this once great State, equal to 24,545,280 acres.

The population in 1860 amounted to 1,596,318, which entitles the State to eleven Members of Congress. By the division the number of Representatives was cut down to eight; the new State receiving three out of the eleven.

Virginia lies in the fourth judicial circuit, which by the act of 1866 was composed of this State, Maryland, West Virginia, North Carolina and South Carolina. There were two judicial districts in this State, anterior to the division, the Eastern and the Western. There is now but one.

There were also twelve collection districts in this State, and twelve ports of entry, all of which remain the same as they were before West Virginia was cut off, for they were all located on the Atlantic coast, or on the bays and rivers running into the Atlantic Ocean; there are also ten ports of delivery.

Richmond is the capital. The State election is held on the fourth Thursday of May. The Legislature meets biennially on the second Monday of January.

The enacting clause of the laws of Virginia is: "Be it enacted by the General Assembly."

When the United States government was formed, Virginia was the largest, most populous and influential State in the Union. But after 1810 she fell behind New York in population; and in 1860, she had fallen to the fifth position in this respect. The division has reduced her much below that point.

This State is often called "the Old Dominion," because it was first settled by whites after the discovery of America, an English colony being planted here in 1607.

"The Mother of Presidents," is another appellation often given to her, because four of the Presidents were Virginians, viz.: Washington, Jefferson, Madison and Monroe. She was also the birthplace of several others, viz.: Jackson, Harrison and Tyler.

"The Old Dominion" is now divided into two States, Virginia and West Virginia. Her political power and influence have dwindled into insignificance.

UNITED STATES SENATORS.

William Grayson,	from	1789	to	1790.
Richard H. Lee,	"	1789	"	1792.
John Walker,	"	1790	"	1790.
James Monroe,	"	1790	"	1794.
John Taylor,	"	1792	"	1794.
		1803	"	1805.
		1822	"	1824.
Stephen T. Mason,	"	1794	"	1803.
John Tazewell,	"	1794	"	1799.
Wilson C. Nichols,	"	1799	"	1804.
Abraham B. Venable,	"	1803	"	1804.
William B. Giles,	"	1804	"	1815.
Andrew Moore,	"	1804	"	1809.
Richard Brent,	"	1809	"	1815.
James Barbour,	"	1815	"	1825.
Armistead T. Mason,	"	1816	"	1817.
John W. Eppes,	"	1817	"	1819.
James Pleasant,	"	1819	"	1822.
John Randolph,	"	1825	"	1827.
Littleton W. Tazewell,	"	1824	"	1832.
John Tyler,	"	1827	"	1836.
William C. Rives,	"	1832	"	1834.
		1836	"	1845.
Benjamin W. Leigh,	"	1834	"	1836.
Richard E. Parker,	"	1836	"	1837.
William H. Roane,	"	1837	"	1841.
William S. Archer,	"	1841	"	1847.
Isaac S. Pennybacker,	"	1845	"	1847.
James M. Mason,	"	1847	"	1861.
R. M. T. Hunter,	"	1847	"	1861.

Virginia was one of the seceding States in 1861.

WEST VIRGINIA.

There is a peculiarity in the description of this new State. It formed a part of one of the original thirteen States, but is yet a new State, and was admitted fully in 1863. Although the act of Congress making it a State was passed on the 31st of December, 1862, it was with the proviso that it should not take effect until 60 days after a proclamation issued by the President, giving notice to the world that West Virginia had been admitted as a sovereign State, and that it formed one of the United States of America. This proclamation was not issued until the year 1863, and in sixty days thereafter the law took effect, and West Virginia became a State, on an equal footing with all the other States. We have not the date of the proclamation, and cannot, therefore, name the day when the act went into full operation.

This is the only case in which a State has been divided. The Constitution contains a provision for making such division in case it should be desirable, and upon certain conditions, which were complied with in this case. As stated in another place, this event grew out of the late rebellion. Virginia seceded with others of the slave States; but that part of the State lying west of the Alleghany mountains, consisting of forty-eight counties, refused to go with the eastern part, seceded from it, and set up a separate State government, which was then recognized by Congress, and admitted into the Union. Thus West Virginia became a new State, made out of an old one. When admitted, it made the thirty-fifth State. It has an area of 23,000 square miles, equal to 14,720,000 acres.

The population, in 1860, was 349,628, which gives her three Members of Congress. West Virginia was subsequently put into the fourth judicial circuit, and constitutes one judicial district. Parkersburgh, also, was made a port of delivery.

Wheeling is the capital. The State election is held on the fourth Thursday in October. The Legislature meets on the third Tuesday in January.

UNITED STATES SENATORS.

Peter G. VanWinkle,	from	1863	to 1869.
Waitman T. Willey,	"	1863	" 1871.

WISCONSIN.

Wisconsin was admitted as a State on the 29th of May, 1848, and made the thirtieth State. It has an area of 52,924 square miles, equal to 34,511,360 acres. In 1860 the population amounted to 775,881, which gave her six Members of Congress. Wisconsin lies in the seventh judicial circuit, (which is composed of Wisconsin, Indiana and Illinois,) and forms one judicial district. It has one collection district, one port of entry, (Milwaukee,) and five ports of delivery, viz.: Southport, Racine, Sheboygan, Green Bay and Depere.

The capital of the State is Madison. The Legislature meets on the second Wednesday in January. The State election is on the first Tuesday in November.

The enacting clause of her laws is as follows: "The people of Wisconsin, represented in Senate and Assembly, do enact as follows."

UNITED STATES SENATORS.

Henry Dodge,	from	1848 to 1857.
Isaac P. Walker,	"	1848 " 1855.
Charles Durkee,	"	1855 " 1861.
James R. Doolittle,	"	1857 " 1869.
Timothy O. Howe,	"	1861 " 1867.

CHAPTER XCI.

Names and Mottoes of the States.

ALABAMA—So called from the Indian name of her principal river, meaning "here-we-rest." Has no familiar name.

ARKANSAS—Called after the Indian name of her principal river. Has the familiar name of "Bear State." Her motto, *Regnant Populi*, means "the people rule."

CALIFORNIA—Named from the great gulf on her coast, is called the "Golden State," and her Greek motto, *Eureka*, means "I have found it."

CONNECTICUT—The "Nutmeg State," is named from her principal river, which, in the Indian tongue, means "the long river." Her Latin motto means, "He who has transferred, sustains."

DELAWARE—Named in honor of Lord Delaware, is called the "Blue Hen."

FLORIDA—Named from the profusion of flowers found there.

GEORGIA—Was named in honor of George II, King of England.

ILLINOIS—The "Sucker" or "Prairie State," is named from her principal river.

INDIANA—Has the familiar name of "Hoosier State."

IOWA—Is the "Hawk-Eye State."

KANSAS—Means "Smoky Water," and her Latin motto means "to the stars through difficulties."

KENTUCKY—The "Blue-Grass State," bears the name of her principal river.

LOUISIANA—Called in honor of Louis XIV, of France, is known as the "Creole State."

MAINE—Named from a province in France, is called "the Pine Tree State."

MARYLAND—Was named in honor of the wife of Charles I, King of England. Her Latin motto means "increase and multiply."

MASSACHUSETTS—From the great bay on her coast, is called the "Bay State." Her Latin motto is translated, "With the sword he seeks placid rest in liberty."

MICHIGAN—Named from the great lake on her northern and western border, has for her familiar name "the Wolverine State."

Her Latin motto, *Tuebor*, means "I will defend." The other Latin words are translated, "If you seek a beautiful peninsula, look around you."

MINNESOTA—Means "Whitish Water." Her French motto means "North Star."

MISSISSIPPI—Is named after the river of that name, "the Father of Waters."

MISSOURI—Named from the river, which means "Muddy Water." Her Latin motto means "the highest law shall be the safety of the people."

NEBRASKA—Named from her principal river.

NEW HAMPSHIRE—Named after Hampshire in England, is called the "Granite State."

NEW JERSEY—Was named after the Island of Jersey.

NEW. YORK—Named in honor of the Duke of York, of England, is called the "Empire State." Her motto means "more excellent."

NORTH CAROLINA — The "Old North" or "Turpentine State," was named in honor of Charles IX, of France.

NEVADA—Was called after the range of mountains in the State. Her Latin motto means "willing and able."

OHIO—Called from the river of that name, is known as the "Buckeye State." Its motto means "An Empire in an Empire."

OREGON—Is called after its principal river.

PENNSYLVANIA—Was named after William Penn. Her familiar name is "the Keystone State."

RHODE ISLAND—"Little Rhody," has "Hope" for her motto.

SOUTH CAROLINA—Derived its name like North Carolina, and is known as "the Palmetto State."

TENNESSEE-was named after her river, and is known as "the Big Bend State."

TEXAS—Retains its Mexican name, and is known as "the Lone Star State."

VERMONT—Derives its name from two French words, *Verd Mont*, meaning Green Mountain—and that is her familiar name.

VIRGINIA—Named after the virgin Queen Elizabeth, of England, is called "the Old Dominion." Her motto means, "So, always, with tyrants," and is symbolized in her coat of arms.

WEST VIRGINIA—Was named from the old State. Her Latin motto means, "Mountaineers are always freemen."

WISCONSIN—Is named from her principal river, and is called "the Badger State."

CHAPTER XCII.

The Seceding States.

The secession of eleven of the Southern slave States at the end of the year 1860, and in the beginning of the year 1861, is too well known to require extended remarks in a work of this kind, and might be entirely omitted, were it not necessary to show their present status in the two houses of Congress. It is known that from the secession until 1866, the eleven seceding States were unrepresented in either house of Congress, neither did they take any part in the Presidential election of 1864. In 1866, Tennessee complied with the conditions prescribed by Congress, and returned into the Union of States. Her Representatives in Congress were then admitted, and the State again occupied her old position. Seven of the remaining States, viz.: Alabama, Arkansas, Georgia, Florida, North Carolina, South Carolina and Louisiana, subsequently also complied with the requirements of Congress, and were received back again to the privileges and favors they formerly possessed as members of the United States government. The Representatives of these seven States are now in Congress. Their Senators are as follows:

Alabama—Geo. E. Spencer,	term expires in	1873.
Millard Warner,	" "	1871.
Arkansas—Alex. McDonald,	" "	1871.
Benjamin F. Rice,	" "	1873.
Georgia—Joshua Miller,	" "	1871.
Virgil H. Miller,	" "	1873.

Florida—A. J. Welch,	term expires in		1871.
Thomas W. Osborn,	"	"	1873.
North Carolina—J. C. Abbott,	"	"	1871.
John Pool,	"	"	1873.
South Carolina—T. J. Robertson,	"	"	1871.
F. A. Sawyer,	"	"	1873.
Louisiana—John S. Harris,	"	"	1871.
William P. Kellogg,	"	"	1873.

The three remaining seceding States, (Virginia, Mississippi and Texas), are not at the present time (January, 1869,) represented in either house of Congress—they having, as yet, refused to comply with the conditions imposed by Congress. For this reason these three States took no part in the Presidential election of 1868.

CHAPTER XCIII.

Territories.

UNTIL a very recent date there has been, west of the States, a vast uninhabited stretch of country, extending to the Pacific ocean. This territory, however, was constantly becoming less as the people pushed out from the inhabited portions into these almost boundless and unoccupied regions. This process has been going on ever since order was established at the close of the Revolutionary war. But it was the discovery of rich mines of gold and silver in this western wilderness that gave emigration thither an unprecedented impulse. Within the past twenty years, heretofore unexplored, uninhabited, and almost unknown regions have become peopled. States have grown out of them, and the whole of this almost interminable waste has been explored and surveyed. Boundary lines have been fixed and Territorial governments established, so that no part now lies outside of an organized local government. Every spot of this heretofore trackless desert may now be localized and described as a part of some State or well-defined territory.

Having given a brief account of the States now in the Union, it remains for us to give a similar account of the Territories, which embrace all outside of the States, and, together with them, cover the whole area of the United States.

These Territories we give as they exist at the close of the year 1868. After a few years, several, if not all of them may become States. Besides, from their immense size, (as may be seen by looking at their areas, (shown below,) they will probably be divided into two or three parts, and these parts will receive new names, and finally come in as States. Each one of the most of them contains land enough to make three States, larger than the average size of those now in the Union. And in estimating the number there will be when all the existing Territories shall be formed into conveniently-sized States, we may safely say there will yet be added from twenty-five to thirty new ones, although we should not enlarge our boundaries by the acquisition of any new territory.

The following is a list of all the remaining Territories, placed in the order of the times when their Territorial governments were formed by acts of Congress:

	Organized as a Territory.	Square miles.	Acres.	Pop. in '60.
New Mexico,	Sept. 9, 1850.	243,063.	155,560,320.	93,516.
Utah,	Sept. 9, 1850.	128,835.	82,454,400.	40,273.
Washington,	Mar. 2, 1853.	175,141.	112,090,240.	11,594.
Dakota,	Mar. 2, 1861.	318,128.	203,601,920.	4,837.
Arizona,	Feb. 24, 1863.	Was cut off from New Mexico. Area and population unknown.		
Idaho,	Mar. 3, 1863.	Area and population unknown.		
Montana,	May 26, 1864.	Area and population unknown.		

In this brief statement we do not notice any of the laws made for their government, or the officers appointed to administer it. Suffice it to say that they have a Governor, Secretary and judges of their courts, who are appointed by the President, by and with the consent of the Senate. The laws organizing their Territorial governments are of course enacted by Congress; and so are all the general laws relating to their administration. But they are allowed to elect and organize a Territorial Legislature, and to regulate their own internal affairs. The laws of Congress, and all the provisions made by it, or by their Territorial legislation, and all the officers appointed to administer them, are of a temporary character, are made only for a temporary government, and all disappear as soon as the Territory is admitted as a State.

CHAPTER XCIV.

Indian Territory.

THIS part of the United States requires a special notice, because it differs widely from any other. While it is located within our own boundaries, it is in some respects like a foreign country, and its inhabitants like foreigners; yet it is not a foreign country, but a domestic dependency, and the various tribes inhabiting it are domestic dependent nations, if we dignify small tribes of savages by such a sounding title. The Indian Territory lies west of the Mississippi river, west of the State of Arkansas, and north of Texas, and is of large dimensions, containing no less than 71,127 square miles, or 45,521,280 acres. The United States government, finding that there were frequent collisions, broils and difficulties, and sometimes wars between the whites and Indians, while in close proximity to each other, in some instances persuaded the Indians, and in some cases compelled them to leave their homes and lands, and remove to this Territory, where they could live more apart from the whites, and enjoy their own laws and customs without molestation from white neighbors. This Territory has thus become the residence of a number of tribes, each having its own section of country within the Territory, or Indian country. Here the United States exercise no authority over them, excepting in certain crimes perpetrated by them against the whites. Of crimes committed by Indians against Indians, it takes no cognizance. For this purpose, the Indian Territory is annexed to the judicial district of the adjoining States, (viz.: to Arkansas and Missouri,) that they may be tried and punished by the United States circuit and district courts when sitting in these districts. They are allowed to live under their own laws, follow their own customs, and indulge in their own modes of life. The land has been ceded to the Indians, each tribe owning the portion allotted to it by the United States. It is quite probable that after the Indians have reached a higher grade of civilization, and become more assimilated to the customs and usages of the white people, that they will apply to Congress for admittance into the family of States, and become an integral part of the United States. But at present they occupy this semi-isolated condition, are under our protection, and partially under our criminal laws. The United States would protect them against foreign invasion or harm, in case interference should be attempted. The government protects them against our own people; for it will not allow them to trade with, nor even to go among them without permission. The provision made by the United States for the preservation and well-being of the Indians, by assigning them a location in the Indian Territory, does not, however, include all the Indian tribes; those now inhabiting this Territory are principally from the tribes east of the Mississippi river; many tribes west of that river still remain in their original homes, or have moved to certain localities which have been reserved for them, called Indian reservations, where they are protected by Indian agents appointed by the government for this purpose, and also to look after other Indian affairs.

The population of the Territory at the last census was 9,761; while the whole number of Indians in the United States amounts to about 300,000.

CHAPTER XCV.

The Wars of the United States.

1. So many acts of the government, and so many laws of Congress have had especial reference to the wars in which the country has been involved, that it will throw much light upon them to give a very brief historical sketch of the different wars in which the United States have been engaged.

2. The first in order of time, and in the results which followed, is the Revolutionary war, as it is called in our own country. This war was begun and consummated, however, before our government existed ; for it was fought for the express purpose of gaining the power to establish a government for ourselves. This the people could not do while they were under the power of the English government, which oppressed them with bad laws, and with corrupt and oppressive administration. Petitions for relief, and strong remonstrances against such oppression, proved utterly abortive. The people resorted to arms with a firm determination to redress their wrongs by force, as all other means had failed.

3. This statement gives the reasons for this war. It commenced on the 19th of April, 1775—or rather, on that day the first blood was spilt. Some preparations had been previously made, since it had been seen for some time that the stubborn acts of the English government, and the determination of the people to redress their greivances, would pretty certainly lead to a contest.

4. This war lasted seven years, and was attended with varied success. The colonies were poor, the population small, and to many it appeared preposterous to contend with the power of the mother country, which was rich in money and means to subdue the rebellion, as she termed this uprising of the people to vindicate their rights. There were other causes which protracted the struggle, and which caused more blood to be shed than the battles with the British armies would have cost, had all the people in the colonies been united, which was not the case. Numbers of them opposed the war, adhered to the old government, even took up arms on the side of England, and did all in their power to assist her in her efforts to put the colonies down. These men rendered material aid to the British during the whole period of the contest. They were then, and have ever since been called Tories; which meant enemies to their own country. They made themselves extremely odious to the people, and the name has been a term of reproach ever since.

5. But this was not all. Besides the power of England, against which the people had to contend, the English, by means of presents, induced the Indians, who were numerous at that time, to join them. This stratagem not only afforded much assistance to the English government, but added the horrors of savage barbarity to the war. The Indians not only went into battle with the English, but laid in ambush, watching and shooting the people wherever they could find them.

But all the power of Great Britain, aided by her partisans here, and by her savage allies, availed not. The bloody struggle went on till victory crowned the efforts of the colonies. Under the leadership of Washington, the Revolution was completed, a new nationality was created, and a new government took its place in the family of nations.

THE SECOND WAR.

6. Not more than ten years had elapsed since the close of the Revolutionary war with England, before a serious difficulty occurred between the United States and France, which had been our friend and ally during the struggle for independence. We say it was a serious difficulty, for it came very near involving the two countries in a destructive contest. But by the discreet and wise management of our government, nothing more than some hostile encounters at sea occurred, after which the two nations came to a good understanding, and no further hostile acts were perpetrated on either side. Before this the French government authorized the capture of American vessels. This was done in several instances; therefore Congress authorized American vessels to retaliate upon the French, and all treaties with France were declared void.

7. But why this hostility between those who recently were such firm friends? This may be explained; France was at war with England, and she wished to involve the United States in her controversy. She wanted us to assist her because she assisted us; quite a plausible reason; but President Washington, and many others of the wisest and best men in the country disapproved of commencing another war with England,

or of aiding her enemies so soon after we had concluded a peace with her. Besides, we were weak then; our resources almost exhausted, and we were deeply in debt. Washington's policy prevailed, and the nation escaped another war with our ancient enemy. France disliked this, and for a few years was quite hostile to us; but wiser counsels finally prevailed, and friendly relations were again established between the two nations.

THE THIRD WAR.

8. The third war, although hardly entitled to so sounding a name—for it was rather a fight with pirates—commenced in 1801, with Tripoli, one of the piratical Barbary powers of the north of Africa. She, with Morocco and Algiers, undertook a system of robbery upon all vessels trading up the Mediterranean sea, by demanding tribute for the privilege of navigating that sea. It was an assumption of power that could not be better explained than to call it piratical. They undertook to enforce these most unrighteous demands by capturing the ships, and imprisoning their crews, if they refused to comply. They tried the game on our vessels, captured several, and imprisoned their seamen. This was rather more than our government was disposed to endure; so it dispatched a squadron of ships under Commodore Preble, who had a fight with some of their vessels, knocked them to pieces, bombarded their town, and made them deliver up all the American prisoners. These energetic proceedings soon humbled the barbarians, and compelled them to relinquish their nefarious practice of demand-

ing tribute from American or any other vessels that traded up the Mediterranean sea.

THE FOURTH WAR.

9. This broke out in 1812, and in our histories and conversations is generally called the war of 1812, because it was commenced in that year. This was our second war with England, and lasted nearly three years. The reasons for it were very different from those which brought on the first; and may be given as follows: England claimed the right to board our ships, either national or private, wherever she found them, and to search them under pretense of searching for her seamen, who had deserted from their vessels, and were now employed on board of ours; and also for men who had once been subjects of the British government, but had subsequently emigrated to America, and became citizens of the United States. This right she claimed and actually enforced on many occasions, by carrying off every man of this description she found on board our ships, upon the assumption that if a man had ever been a subject of hers he must always remain so; and that he had no right to become a citizen of any other country: we did not subscribe to such a doctrine, but held that if any body wished to expatriate himself from his own country, and to become a citizen of ours, he had a perfect right to do so, and that when he did, it was as much the duty of our government to protect him as it was to protect a native citizen.

10. Such antagonistic principles, if carried into action as they were by the English, must necessarily end

in an appeal to arms. On the 19th of June, in conformity with an act of Congress, the President proclaimed war with England.

The contest, with varied success on both sides, was continued until the 8th of January, 1815, the day on which General Jackson defeated the British at New Orleans. Soon after, news reached the United States that the American and English commissioners, who had met at Ghent, had, on the 24th of December, 1814, concluded a treaty of peace. As soon as this was known, hostilities ceased on land. Several battles occurred at sea after this, for the news of peace did not reach the contestants until some time after it was known at home. By the treaty of Ghent, simply a treaty of peace was negotiated, seemingly because both parties had become tired of the war. The issue upon which the war broke out, was left unsettled by the commissioners, who ignored that question, but agreed to stop fighting. England has not since enforced her doctrine of the right to search our vessels, and to carry off our men, although they may have once been her subjects. The war was prosecuted principally on the seas, where a number of severe naval battles were fought, and many captures of ships made on both sides. Although England had a far more powerful navy than we had, yet in victories and captures the odds were on our side.

THE FIFTH WAR.

11. The fifth war was that with Mexico. It commenced on the 26th of April, 1846, and grew out of the annexation of Texas (early in 1845), to the United

States. Mexico had not yet entirely abandoned her claim to, and authority over Texas, which had so recently revolted against her government. She could not but look with great disapprobation and jealousy upon the action of the United States in taking her revolted province under their protection, and then annexing it to their own dominions. The people of Texas were afraid that Mexico would make an attempt to regain possession of the country, and called upon the United States government to protect them.

12. James K. Polk, of Tennessee, was then President, and had taken, before his election, a very prominent part in the annexation scheme. He was therefore quite ready and willing to defend this, our newly acquired territory, and promptly sent Gen. Taylor to the western part of Texas, under the pretense of guarding the frontiers against any invasion of the Mexicans. Gen. Taylor, in obedience to orders from the President, marched his army quite up to the Rio Grande, which Mr. Polk claimed as the western boundary of Texas. But this the Mexicans, (with good reason too,) disputed; declaring that the western boundary of Texas was far to the east of that river, and remonstrated strongly against the action of the United States, in sending a hostile army into her territory, and hence took measures to expel the invaders. As before stated, on the 26th of April, 1846, a small number of the hostile parties met, and a fight between them ensued.

Thus the war begun, and continued with almost unvaried success on the part of the United States army till the 2nd of February, 1848, when a treaty of peace was concluded.

During this short war of less than two years, we took all their strongholds of defence, including the city of Vera Cruz, together with their capital, the city of Mexico itself. Indeed the whole country was occupied, and might have been kept had we chosen to retain it. But in the treaty of peace we restored a part of their country, and retained all we desired of it, to-wit: California and New Mexico, and (in short) all the northern part of the country. But, to make the whole affair look less like robbery, we paid the Mexicans $10,000,000 for what we kept—which was nearly one-half of the whole country.

14. By this war we very much enlarged our territory, but gained very little military glory, and added nothing to our character for justice and magnanimity. We, a powerful nation, fell upon a weak one, crushed it, and took so much of its territory as we pleased; and that—to say the least of it—for a very trifling cause. A little wisdom, a little discreet diplomacy, would have averted this war, saved thousands of lives, millions of money, and preserved our character for justice and magnanimity.

THE SIXTH WAR.

15. This was by far the greatest, the most expensive, and most bloody war that was ever carried on upon this continent. In magnitude, in expense, in the lives it cost, and in the evil consequences which resulted from it, it surpassed all the preceding wars combined, and verified the old adage that "civil wars are the worst of all wars." This, as everybody knows, was a civil war; a war between the people of the same

country and government, having the same intrests and the same destiny.

16. Right here we might expand our remarks to an extent exceeding the whole contents of this volume, in tracing the causes, detailing the operations, and noticing the results of this most terrible and cruel war. Then we might dwell long upon the consequences which must inevitably follow in all coming time. But this would be foreign to our purpose. We have only undertaken to give the veriest outlines of our various wars, the time when they commenced, the time of their duration, and the results produced Just so much we will say of our civil war—between the North and the South. It was begun on the 12th of April, 1861, by the bombardment of Fort Sumpter in Charleston harbor. It was closed in April, 1865, by the surrender of Gen. Lee, the Southern commander-in-chief, with his army, to Gen. Grant, the commander-in-chief of the National forces, having lasted four years with varied success on both sides. All the details of this desperate struggle have been written and published by many able historians, to whose works I must refer the reader who wishes to peruse a complete history of this great event.

17. Here we will only add that it is impossible to say how many lives were lost in this devastating war; 500,000 on both sides is probably as correct an estimate as can be made. Eight or nine billions of dollars is probably as near an estimate of its cost as can be calculated. Other disasters and evils almost inconceivable followed in its train. It furnished the whole world with one of the most awful examples of the folly and the wickedness of war.

OUR INDIAN WARS.

18. In addition to, and in connection with the several wars mentioned in the preceding remarks, our numerous wars with the various Indian tribes should be briefly noticed. In both of our wars with England, the Indians were wheedled and enticed by presents to take sides with England and against us. This, together with their barbarous mode of warfare, and their savage cruelties, produced a strong antipathy in the minds of our people against them. This feeling was reciprocated by the Indians, and whenever any wrong was perpetrated by either party, it was an easy matter to make it a cause of war. The old animosities were there, and any offensive act from either side was almost certain to produce retaliatory acts from the other party. When the whites cheated the Indians, they in retaliation would steal from the whites. A pursuit and a massacre would follow, and then the government would be compelled to interfere.

19. From these and other causes we have had many wars with nearly all the tribes of Indians in the country. Some of these contests have been obstinate and bloody, costing many valuable lives, and a great deal of money. Any of the tribes—or all of them combined—could make but a feeble resistance to the power of the United States. Hence all our Indian wars have resulted in their final defeat, and sometimes in their almost utter destruction; at the present time (1869) a fierce and bloody war is raging between the government and the western Indians, who inhabit the country between the Mississippi river and the Rocky

mountains. Various tribes are combined to prevent the settlement of the whites upon their lands, and to prevent the construction of the Pacific railroad through their hunting grounds.

20. The Indians who remain do not exceed 300,000. They have been reduced to this small number by their frequent wars with the whites, but more especially by their almost perpetual war among themselves. Some of them have become partially civilized, and have turned their attention to agricultural pursuits, instead of wandering about on hunting excursions and warlike expeditions against each other. It is therefore to be hoped that our Indian wars will soon cease forever.

THE

DECLARATION OF INDEPENDENCE.

WHEN, in the course of human events, it becomes necessary for one people to dissolve the political bands which have connected them with another, and to assume among the powers of the earth, the separate and equal station to which the laws of nature and of nature's God entitle them, a decent respect to the opinions of mankind requires that they should declare the causes which impel them to the separation.

We hold these truths to be self-evident, that all men are created equal; that they are endowed by their Creator with certain unalienable rights; that among these are life, liberty and the pursuit of happiness. That to secure these rights, governments are instituted among men, deriving their just powers from the consent of the governed; that, whenever any form of government becomes destructive of these ends, it is the right of the people to alter or to abolish it, and to institute a new government, laying its foundation on such principles, and organizing its powers in such form, as to them shall seem most likely to effect their safety and happiness. Prudence, indeed, will dictate that governments long established should not be changed for light and transient causes; and, accordingly, all experience hath shown that mankind are more disposed to suffer, while evils are sufferable, than to right themselves by abolishing the forms to which they are accustomed. But when a long train of abuses and usurpations, pursuing invariably the same object, evinces a design to reduce them under absolute despotism, it is their right, it is their duty to throw off such government, and to provide new guards for their future security. Such has been the patient sufferance of these colonies, and such is now the necessity which constrains them to alter their former systems of government. The history of the present King of Great Britain is a history of repeated injuries and usurpations, all having in direct object the establishment of an absolute tyranny over these States. To prove this let facts be submitted to a candid world:

He has refused his assent to laws the most wholesome and necessary for the public good.

He has forbidden his Governors to pass laws of immediate and pressing importance, unless suspended in their operation till his assent should be obtained; and when so suspended, he has utterly neglected to attend to them.

He has refused to pass other laws for the accommodation of large districts of people, unless those people would relinquish the right of representation in the legislature; a right inestimable to them, and formidable to tyrants only.

He has called together legislative bodies at places unusual, uncomfortable, and distant from the depository of their public records, for the sole purpose of fatiguing them into compliance with his measures.

He has dissolved representative houses repeatedly for opposing, with manly firmness, his invasions on the rights of the people.

He has refused, for a long time after such dissolution, to cause others to be elected; whereby the legislative powers, incapable of annihilation, have returned to the people at large for their exercise; the State remaining, in the meantime, exposed to all the danger of invasion from without, and convulsions within.

He has endeavored to prevent the population of these States; for that purpose, obstructing the laws for naturalization of foreigners; refusing to pass others to encourage their migration hither, and raising the conditions of new appropriations of lands.

He has obstructed the administration of justice, by refusing his assent to laws for establishing judiciary powers.

He has made judges dependent on his will alone, for the tenure of their offices, and the amount and payment of their salaries.

He has erected a multitude of new offices, and sent hither swarms of officers to harass our people, and eat out their substance.

He has kept among us, in times of peace, standing armies, without the consent of our legislature.

He has affected to render the military independent of, and superior to, the civil power.

He has combined, with others, to subject us to a jurisdiction foreign to our constitution, and unacknowledged by our laws; giving his assent to their acts of pretended legislation.

For quartering large bodies of armed troops among us.

For protecting them, by a mock trial, from punishment, for any murders which they should commit on the inhabitants of these States.

For cutting off our trade with all parts of the world:

For imposing taxes on us without our consent:

For depriving us, in many cases, of the benefits of trial by jury:

For transporting us beyond seas to be tried for pretended offences:

For abolishing the free system of English laws in a neighboring province, establishing therein an arbitrary government, and enlarging its boundaries, so as to render it at once an example and fit instrument for introducing the same absolute rule into these colonies:

For taking away our charters, abolishing our most valuable laws, and altering fundamentally, the powers of our governments:

For suspending our own legislatures, and declaring themselves invested with power to legislate for us in all cases whatsoever.

He has abdicated government here, by declaring us out of his protection, and waging war against us,

He has plundered our seas, ravaged our coasts, burnt our towns, and destroyed the lives of our people.

He is, at this time, transporting large armies of foreign mercenaries to complete the work of death, desolation and tyranny, already begun, with circumstances of cruelty and perfidy scarcely paralleled in the most barbarous ages, and totally unworthy the head of a civilized nation.

He has constrained our fellow-citizens, taken captive on the high seas, to bear arms against their country, to become the executioners of their friends and brethren, or to fall themselves by their hands.

He has excited domestic insurrections amongst us, and has endeavored to bring on the inhabitants of our frontiers, the merciless Indian savages, whose known rule of warfare is an undistinguished destruction of all ages, sexes, and conditions.

In every stage of these oppressions, we have petitioned for redress, in the most humble terms; our repeated petitions have been answered only by repeated injury. A prince, whose character is thus marked by every act which may define a tyrant, is unfit to be the ruler of a free people.

Nor have we been wanting in attention to our British brethren. We have warned them from time to time, of attempts made by their legislature to extend an unwarrantable jurisdiction over us. We have reminded them of the circumstances of our emigration and settlement here. We have appealed to their native justice and magnanimity, and we have conjured them, by the ties of our common kindred, to disavow these usurpations, which would inevitably interrupt our connections and correspondence. They, too, have been deaf to the voice of justice and consanguinity. We must, therefore, acquiesce in the necessity, which denounces our separation, and hold them, as we hold the rest of mankind, enemies in war, in peace, friends.

We, therefore, the representatives of the UNITED STATES OF AMERICA, in GENERAL CONGRESS assembled, appealing to the Supreme Judge of the World for the rectitude of our intentions, do, in the name, and by the authority of the good people of these colonies, solomenly publish and declare, That these United Colonies are, and of right ought to be, FREE AND INDEPENDENT STATES; that they are absolved from all allegiance to the British crown, and that all political connexion between them and the State of Great Britian, is, and ought to be, totally dissolved; and that, as FREE AND INDEPENDENT STATES, they have full power to levy war, conclude peace, contract alliances, establish commerce, and to do all other acts and things which INDEPENDENT STATES may of right do. And, for the support of this declaration, and a firm reliance on the protection of DIVINE PROVIDENCE, we mutually pledge to each other, our lives, our fortunes, and our sacred honor.

The foregoing declaration was, by order of Congress, engrossed, and signed by the following members;

JOHN HANCOCK.

New Hampshire.

Josiah Bartlett,
William Whipple,
Matthew Thornton.

Rhode Island.

Stephen Hopkins,
William Ellery.

Connecticut.

Roger Sherman,
Samuel Huntington,
William Williams,
Oliver Wolcott.

New York.

William Floyd,
Philip Livingston,
Francis Lewis,
Lewis Morris.

New Jersey.

Richard Stockton,
John Witherspoon,
Francis Hopkinson,
John Hart,
Abraham Clark.

Pennsylvania.

Robert Morris,
Benjamin Rush,
Benjamin Franklin,
John Morton,
George Clymer,
James Smith,
George Taylor,
James Wilson,
George Ross.

Massachusetts Bay.

Samuel Adams,
John Adams,
Robert Treat Paine,
Elbridge Gerry.

Delaware.

Cæsar Rodney,
George Reed,
Thomas M'Kean.

Maryland.

Samuel Chase,
William Paca,
Thomas Stone,
Charles Carroll, of Carrollton.

Virginia.

George Wythe,
Richard Henry Lee,
Thomas Jefferson,
Benjamin Harrison,
Thomas Nelson, Jun.,
Francis Lightfoot Lee,
Carter Braxton.

North Carolina.

William Hooper,
Joseph Hewes,
John Penn.

South Carolina.

Edward Rutledge,
Thomas Heyward, Jun.,
Thomas Lynch, Jun.,
Arthur Middleton.

Georgia.

Button Gwinnett,
Lyman Hall,
George Walton.

Parmelee & Co. Philad^a.

THE DECLARATION OF INDEPENDENCE.

Engraved expressly for this work

CONSTITUTION

OF THE

UNITED STATES OF AMERICA.

WE, the People of the United States, in order to form a more perfect Union, establish justice, insure domestic tranquility, provide for the common defense, promote the general welfare, and secure the blessings of liberty to ourselves and our posterity, do ordain and establish this CONSTITUTION for the United States of America.

ARTICLE I.

SECTION 1. All legislative powers herein granted shall be vested in a Congress of the United States, which shall consist of a Senate and House of Representatives.

SECTION 2. The House of Representatives shall be composed of members chosen every second year by the people of the several States, and the electors in each State shall have the qualifications requisite for electors of the most numerous branch of the State Legislature.

No person shall be a Representative who shall not have attained to the age of twenty-five years, and been seven years a citizen of the United States, and who shall not, when elected, be an inhabitant of that State in which he shall be chosen.

Representatives and direct taxes shall be apportioned among the several States which may be included within this Union, according to their respective numbers, which shall be determined by adding to the whole number of free persons, including those bound to service for a term of years, and excluding Indians not taxed, three-fifths of all other persons. The actual enumeration shall be made within three years after the first meeting of the Congress of the United States, and within every subsequent term of ten years, in such manner as they shall by law direct. The number of Representatives shall not exceed one for every thirty thousand, but each State shall have at least one Representative; and until such enumeration shall be made, the State of New Hampshire shall be entitled to choose three, Massachusetts eight, Rhode Island and Providence Plantations one, Connecticut five, New York six, New Jersey four, Pennsylvania eight, Delaware one, Maryland six, Virginia ten, North Carolina five, and Georgia three.

When vacancies happen in the representation from any State, the Executive authority thereof shall issue writs of election to fill such vacancies.

The House of Representatives shall choose their Speaker and other officers, and shall have the sole power of impeachment.

SECTION 3. The Senate of the United States shall be composed of two Senators from each State, chosen by the Legislature thereof, for six years; and each Senator shall have one vote.

Immediately after they shall be assembled in consequence of the first election, they shall be divided as equally as may be into three classes. The seats of the Senators of the first class shall be vacated at the expiration of the second year, of the second class at the expiration of the fourth year, and of the third class at the expiration of the sixth year, so that one-third may be chosen every second year; and if vacancies happen by resignation, or otherwise, during the recess of the Legislature of any State, the Executive thereof may make temporary appointments until the next meeting of the Legislature, which shall then fill such vacancies.

No person shall be a Senator who shall not have attained to the age of thirty years, and been nine years a citizen of the United States, and who shall not, when elected, be an inhabitant of that State for which he shall be chosen.

The Vice President of the United States shall be President of the Senate, but shall have no vote unless they be equally divided.

The Senate shall choose their other officers, and also a President pro tempore, in the absence of the Vice President, or when he shall exercise the office of President of the United States.

The Senate shall have the sole power to try all impeachments. When sitting for that purpose they shall be on oath or affirmation. When the President of the United States is tried, the Chief Justice shall preside. And no person shall be convicted without the concurrence of two-thirds of the members present.

Judgment in cases of impeachment shall not extend further than to removal from office, and disqualification to hold and enjoy any office of honor, trust or profit under the United States: but the party convicted shall nevertheless be liable and subject to indictment, trial, judgment and punishment according to law.

SECTION 4. The times, places and manner of holding elections for Senators and Representatives, shall be prescribed in each State by the Legislature thereof; but the Congress may at any time by law make or alter such regulations, except as to the places of choosing Senators.

The Congress shall assemble at least once in every year, and such meeting shall be on the first Monday in December, unless they shall by law appoint a different day.

SECTION 5. Each house shall be the judge of the election, returns and qualifications of its own members, and a majority of each shall constitute a quorum to do business; but a smaller number may adjourn from day to day, and may be authorized to compel the attendance of absent members in such manner, and under such penalties as each house may provide.

Each house may determine the rules of its proceedings, punish its members for disorderly behaviour, and, with the concurrence of two-thirds, expel a member.

Each house shall keep a journal of its proceedings, and from time to time publish the same, excepting such parts as may in their judgment require secrecy; and the yeas and nays of the members of either house on any question shall, at the desire of one-fifth of those present, be entered on the journal.

Neither house, during the session of Congress, shall, without the consent of the other, adjourn for more than three days, nor to any other place than that in which the two houses shall be sitting.

SECTION 6. The Senators and Representatives shall receive a compensation for their services, to be ascertained by law, and paid out of the Treasury of the United States. They shall in all cases, except treason, felony and breach of the peace, be privileged from arrest during their attendance at the session of their respective houses, and in going to and returning from the same; and for any speech or debate in either house they shall not be questioned in any other place.

No Senator or Representative shall, during the time for which he was elected, be appointed to any civil office under the authority of the United States, which shall have been created, or the emoluments whereof shall have been increased during such time; and no person holding any office under the United States, shall be a member of either house during his continuance in office.

SECTION 7. All bills for raising revenue shall originate in the House of Representatives; but the Senate may propose or concur with amendments as on other bills.

Every bill which shall have passed the House of Representatives and the Senate, shall, before it becomes a law, be presented to the President of the United States; if he approve he shall sign it, but if not he shall return it with his objections to that house in which it shall have originated, who shall enter the objections at large on their journal, and proceed to reconsider it. If after such reconsideration two-thirds of that House shall agree to pass the bill, it shall be sent, together with the objections, to the other house, by which it shall likewise be reconsidered, and if approved by two-thirds of that House, it shall become a law. But in all such cases the votes of both houses shall be determined by yeas and nays, and the names of the persons voting for and against the bill shall be entered on the journal of each house respectively. If any bill shall not be returned by the President within ten days (Sundays excepted), after it shall have been presented to him, the same shall be a law, in like manner as if he had signed it, unless the Congress by their adjournment prevent its return, in which case it shall not be a law.

Every order, resolution or vote to which the concurrence of the Senate and House of Representatives may be necessary (except on a question of adjournment), shall be presented to the President of the United States; and before the same shall take effect, shall be approved by him, or being disapproved by him, shall be repassed by two-thirds of the Senate and House of Representatives, according to the rules and limitations prescribed in the case of a bill.

SECTION 8. The Congress shall have power—

To lay and collect taxes, duties, imposts and excises, to pay the debts and provide for the common defense and general welfare of the United States; but all duties, imposts and excises shall be uniform throughout the United States;

To borrow money on the credit of the United States;

To regulate commerce with foreign nations, and among the several States, and with the Indian tribes;

To establish a uniform rule of naturalization, and uniform laws on the subject of bankruptcies throughout the United States;

To coin money, regulate the value thereof, and of foreign coin, and fix the standard of weights and measures;

To provide for the punishment of counterfeiting the securities and current coin of the United States;

To establish post-offices and post-roads.

To promote the progress of science and useful arts, by securing for limited times to authors and inventors the exclusive right to their respective writings and discoveries;

To constitute tribunals inferior to the Supreme Court;

To define and punish piracies and felonies committed on the high seas, and offences against the law of nations;

To declare war, grant letters of marque and reprisal, and make rules concerning captures on land and water;

To raise and support armies, but no appropriation of money to that use shall be for a longer term than two years;

To provide and maintain a navy;

To make rules for the government and regulation of the land and naval forces;

To provide for calling forth the militia to execute the laws of the Union, suppress insurrections and repel invasions;

To provide for organizing, arming and disciplining the militia, and for governing such part of them as may be employed in the service of the United States, reserving to the States respectively the appointment of the officers, and the authority of training the militia according to the discipline prescribed by Congress.

To exercise legislation in all cases whatsoever, over such district (not exceeding ten miles square), as may, by cession of particular States and the acceptance of Congress, become the seat of the government of the United States, and to exercise like authority over all places purchased by the consent of the Legislature of the State in which the same shall be, for the erection of forts, magazines, arsenals, dock-yards and other needful buildings;—and

To make all laws which shall be necessary and proper for carrying into execution the foregoing powers, and all other powers vested by this Constitution in the government of the United States, or in any department or officer thereof.

SECTION 9. The migration or importation of such persons as any of the States now existing shall think proper to admit, shall not be prohibited by the Congress prior to the year one thousand eight hundred and eight, but a tax or duty may be imposed on such importation, not exceeding ten dollars for each person.

The privilege of the writ of habeas corpus shall not be suspended, unless when in cases of rebellion or invasion the public safety may require it.

No bill of attainder or ex post facto law shall be passed.

No capitation or other direct tax shall be laid unless in proportion to the census or enumeration herein before directed to be taken.

No tax or duty shall be laid on articles exported from any State.

No preference shall be given by any regulation of commerce or revenue to the ports of one State over those of another; nor shall vessels bound to, or from one State, be obliged to enter, clear, or pay duties in another.

No money shall be drawn from the Treasury, but in consequence of appropriations made by law; and a regular statement and accouut of the receipts and expenditures of all public money shall be published from time to time.

No title of nobility shall be granted by the United States; and no person holding any office of profit or trust under them, shall without the consent of the Congress, accept of any present, emolument, office, or title, of any kind whatever, from any king, prince or foreign State.

SECTION 10. No State shall enter into any treaty, alliance, or confederation; grant letters of marque and reprisal; coin money; emit bills of credit; make anything but gold and silver coin a tender in payment of debts; pass any bill of attainder, ex post facto law, or law impairing the obligation of contracts, or grant any title of nobility.

No State shall, without the consent of the Congress, lay any imposts or duties on imports or exports, except what may be absolutely necessary for executing its inspection laws, and the net produce of all duties and imposts laid by any State on imports or exports, shall be for the use of the Treasury of the United States; and all such laws shall be subject to the revision and control of the Congress.

No State shall, without the consent of Congress, lay any duty on tonnage, keep troops or ships of war in time of peace, enter into any agreement or compact with another State, or with a foreign power, or engage in war, unless actually invaded, or in such imminent danger as will not admit of delay.

ARTICLE II.

SECTION 1. The Executive power shall be vested in a President of the United States of America. He shall hold his office during the term of four years, and, together with the Vice President chosen for the same term, be elected as follows;

Each State shall appoint, in such manner as the Legislature thereof may direct, a number of electors, equal to the whole number of

Senators and Representatives to which the State may be entitled in the Congress; but no Senator or Representative, or person holding an office of trust or profit under the United States, shall be appointed an elector.

[*The electors shall meet in their respective States, and vote by ballot for two persons, of whom one at least shall not be an inhabitant of the same State with themselves. And they shall make a list of all the persons voted for, and of the number of votes for each; which list they shall sign and certify, and transmit sealed to the seat of the government of the United States, directed to the President of the Senate. The President of the Senate shall, in the presence of the Senate and House of Representatives, open all the certificates, and the votes shall then be counted. The person having the greatest number of votes shall be the President, if such number be a majority of the whole number of electors appointed; and if there be more than one who have such majority, and have an equal number of votes, then the House of Representatives shall immediately choose by ballot one of them for President; and if no person have a majority, then from the five highest on the list the said House shall in like manner choose the President. But in choosing the President, the votes shall be taken by States, the representation from each State having one vote; a quorum for this purpose shall consist of a member or members from two-thirds of the States, and a majority of all the States shall be necessary to a choice. In every case, after the choice of the President, the person having the greatest number of votes of the electors shall be the Vice President. But if there should remain two or more who have equal votes, the Senate shall choose from them by ballot the Vice President.]

The Congress may determine the time of choosing the electors, and the day on which they shall give their votes; which day shall be the same throughout the United States.

No person except a natural born citizen, or a citizen of the United States at the time of the adoption of this Constitution, shall be eligible to the office of President; neither shall any person be eligible to that office who shall not have attained the age of thirty-five years, and been fourteen years a resident within the United States.

In case of the removal of the President from office, or of his death, resignation, or inability to discharge the powers and duties of the said office, the same shall devolve on the Vice President, and the Congress may by law provide for the case of removal, death, resignation, or inability, both of the President and Vice President, declaring what officer shall then act as President, and such officer shall act accordingly, until the disability be removed, or a President shall be elected.

The President shall, at stated times, receive for his services a com-

---

*This clause within brackets has been superceded and annulled by the 12th amendment.

pensation which shall neither be increased nor diminished during the period for which he shall have been elected, and he shall not receive within that period any other emolument from the United States, or any of them.

Before he enter on the execution of his office, he shall take the following oath or affirmation:

"I do solemnly swear (or affirm) that I will faithfully execute the "office of President of the United States, and will, to the best of " my ability, preserve, protect and defend the Constitution of the " United States."

SECTION 2. The President shall be commander-in-chief of the army and navy of the United States, and of the militia of the several States, when called into the actual service of the United States; he may require the opinion, in writing, of the principal officer in each of the Executive departments, upon any subject relating to the duties of their respective offices, and he shall have power to grant reprieves and pardon for offences against the United States, except in cases of impeachment.

He shall have power, by and with the advice and consent of the Senate, to make treaties, provided two-thirds of the Senators present concur; and he shall nominate, and by and with the advice of the Senate, shall appoint ambassadors, other public ministers and consuls, judges of the Supreme Court, and all other officers of the United States whose appointments are not herein otherwise provided for, and which shall be established by law; but the Congress may by law vest the appointment of such inferior officers as they think proper in the President alone, in the courts of law, or in the heads of departments.

The President shall have power to fill up all vacancies that may happen during the recess of the Senate, by granting commissions which shall expire at the end of their next sessions.

SECTION 3. He shall from time to time give to the Congress information of the state of the Union, and recommend to their consideration such measures as he shall judge necessary and expedient; he may, on extraordinary occasions, convene both Houses, or either of them, and in case of disagreement between them, with respect to the time of adjournment, he may adjourn them to such time as he shall think proper; he shall receive ambassadors and other public ministers; he shall take care that the laws be faithfully executed, and shall commission all the officers of the United States.

SECTION 4. The President, Vice President and all civil officers of the United States, shall be removed from office on impeachment for, and conviction of treason, bribery, or other high crimes and misdemeanors.

ARTICLE III.

SECTION 1. The judicial power of the United States shall be vested in one Supreme Court, and such inferior courts as the Congress may from time to time ordain and establish. The judges, both of the Supreme and inferior courts, shall hold their offices during good behavior, and shall, at stated times, receive for their services a compensation, which shall not be diminished during their continuance in office.

SECTION 2. The judicial power shall extend to all cases, in law and equity, arising under this Constitution, the laws of the United States, and treaties made, or which shall be made, under their authority;—to all cases affecting ambassadors, other public ministers, and consuls;—to all cases of admiralty and maritime jurisdiction;—to controversies to which the United States shall be a party;—to controversies between two or more States;—between a State and citizens of another State;—between citizens of different States,—between citizens of the same State claiming lands under grants of different States, and between a State, or the citizens thereof, and foreign States, citizens or subjects.

In all cases affecting ambassadors, other public ministers and consuls, and those in which a State shall be a party, the Supreme Court shall have original jurisdiction.

In all the other cases before mentioned, the Supreme Court shall have appellate jurisdiction, both as to law and fact, with such exceptions, and under such regulations as the Congress shall make.

The trial of all crimes, except in cases of impeachment, shall be by jury; and such trial shall be held in the State where the said crimes shall have been committed; but when not committed within any State, the trial shall be at such place or places as the Congress may by law have directed.

SECTION 3. Treason against the United States shall consist only in levying war against them, or in adhering to their enemies, giving them aid and comfort. No person shall be convicted of treason unless on the testimony of two witnesses to the same overt act, or on confession in open court.

The Congress shall have power to declare the punishment of treason, but no attainder of treason shall work corruption of blood, or forfeiture except during the life of the person attainted.

ARTICLE IV.

SECTION 1. Full faith and credit shall be given in each State to the public acts, records, and judicial proceedings of every other State. And the Congress may by general laws prescribe the manner in which such acts, records and proceedings shall be proved, and the effect thereof.

SECTION 2. The citizens of each State shall be entitled to all privileges and immunities of citizens in the several States.

A person charged in any State with treason, felony or other crime, who shall flee from justice, and be found in another State, shall on demand of the Executive authority of the State from which he fled, be delivered up, to be removed to the State having jurisdiction of the crime.

No person held to service or labor in one State, under the laws thereof, escaping into another, shall, in consequence of any law or regulation therein, be discharged from such service or labor, but shall be delivered up on the claim of the party to whom such service or labor may be due.

SECTION 3. New States may be admitted by the Congress into this Union; but no new State shall be formed or erected within the jurisdiction of any other State: nor any State be formed by the junction of two or more States, or parts of States, without the consent of the Legislatures of the States concerned, as well as of the Congress.

The Congress shall have power to dispose of and make all needful rules and regulations respecting the territory or other property belonging to the United States; and nothing in this Constitution shall be so construed as to prejudice any claims of the United States, or of any particular State.

SECTION 4. The United States shall guarantee to every State in this Union a Republican form of government, and shall protect each of them against invasion, and on application of the Legislature, or of the Executive (when the Legislature cannot be convened) against domestic violence.

ARTICLE V.

The Congress, whenever two-thirds of both Houses shall deem it necessary, shall propose amendments to this Constitution, or, on the application of the Legislatures of two-thirds of the several States, shall call a convention for proposing amendments, which, in either case, shall be valid to all intents and purposes, as part of this Constitution, when ratified by the Legislatures of three-fourths of the several States, or by conventions in three-fourths thereof, as the one or the other mode of ratification may be proposed by the Congress. Provided that no amendment which may be made prior to the year one thousand eight hundred and eight shall in any manner affect the first and fourth clauses in the ninth section of the first article; and that no State, without its consent, shall be deprived of its equal suffrage in the Senate.

ARTICLE VI.

All debts contracted and engagements entered into, before the adoption of this Constitution, shall be as valid against the United States under this Constitution, as under the Confederation.

This Constitution, and the laws of the United States which shall be made in pursuance thereof, and all treaties made, or which shall be made, under the authority of the United States, shall be the supreme law of the land; and the judges in every State shall be bound thereby, anything in the Constitution or laws of any State to the contrary notwithstanding.

The Senators and Representatives before mentioned, and the members of the several State Legislatures, and all executive and judicial officers, both of the United States and of the several States, shall be bound by oath or affirmation, to support this Constitution; but no religious test shall ever be required as a qualification to any office or public trust under the United States.

ARTICLE VII.

The ratification of the Conventions of nine States shall be sufficient for the establishment of this Constitution between the States so ratifying the same.

DONE in Convention by the unanimous consent of the States present, the seventeenth day of September, in the year of our Lord one thousand seven hundred and eighty-seven, and of the Independence of the United States of America, the twelfth. IN WITNESS WHEREOF, We have hereunto subscribed our names

GEO. WASHINGTON,
President and Deputy from Virginia.

New Hampshire,

JOHN LANGDON,
NICHOLAS GILMAN.

Massachusetts.

NATHANIEL GORHAM,
RUFUS KING.

Connecticut.

WM. SAML. JOHNSON,
ROGER SHERMAN.

New York.

ALEXANDER HAMILTON.

New Jersey.

WIL. LIVINGSTON,
WM. PATERSON,
DAVID BREARLEY,
JONA. DAYTON.

Pennsylvania.

B. FRANKLIN,
ROBT. MORRIS,
THO. FITZSIMONS,
JAMES WILSON,
THOMAS MIFFLIN,
GEO. CLYMER,
JARED INGERSOLL,
GOUV. MORRIS.

Delaware.

GEO. READ,
JOHN DICKINSON,
JACO. BROOM,
GUNNING BEDFORD, JUN'R,
RICHARD BASSETT.

Maryland.

JAMES M'HENRY,
DANL. CARROLL,
DAN. OF ST. THOS. JENIFER.

Virginia.

JOHN BLAIR,
JAMES MADISON, JR.

North Carolina.

WM. BLOUNT,
HU. WILLIAMSON,
RICH'D DOBBS SPAIGHT.

South Carolina.

J. RUTLEDGE,
CHARLES PINCKNEY,
CHAS. COTESWORTH PINCKNEY,
PIERCE BUTLER.

Georgia.

WILLIAM FEW,
ABR. BALDWIN.

Attest: WILLIAM JACKSON, *Secretary.*

ARTICLES IN ADDITION TO, AND AMENDATORY OF, THE CONSTITUTION OF THE UNITED STATES OF AMERICA.

Proposed by Congress, and ratified by the Legislatures of the several States, pursuant to the fifth article of the original Constitution.

ARTICLE I.

Congress shall make no law respecting an establishment of religion, or prohibiting the free exercise thereof; or abrdging the freedom of speech, or of the press; or the right of the people peaceably to assemble, and to petition the government for a redress of grievances.

ARTICLE II.

A well regulated militia being necessary to the security of a free State, the right of the people to keep and bear arms shall not be infringed.

ARTICLE III.

No soldier shall in time of peace be quartered in any house without the consent of the owner, nor in time of war, but in a manner to be prescribed by law.

ARTICLE IV.

The right of the people to be secure in their persons, houses, papers, and effects, against unreasonable searches and seizures, shall not be violated, and no warrants shall issue but upon probable cause, supported by oath or affirmation, and particularly describing the place to be searched, and the persons or things to be seized.

ARTICLE V.

No person shall be held to answer for a capital or otherwise infamous crime, unless on a presentment or indictment of a Grand Jury, except in cases arising in the land or naval forces, or in the militia when in actual service in time of war or public danger; nor shall any person be subject for the same offense to be twice put in jeopardy of life or limb; nor shall be compelled in any criminal case to be a witness against himself, nor be deprived of life, liberty, or property, without due process of law; nor shall private property be taken for public use, without just compensation.

ARTICLE VI.

In all criminal prosecutions, the accused shall enjoy the right to a speedy and public trial, by an impartial jury of the State and district wherein the crime shall have been committed, which district shall have been previously ascertained by law, and to be informed of the nature and cause of the accusation; to be confronted with the witnesses against him; to have compulsory process for obtaining witnesses in his favor, and to have the assistance of counsel for his defense.

ARTICLE VII.

In suits at common law, where the value in controversy shall exceed twenty dollars, the right of trial by jury shall be preserved, and no fact tried by a jury shall be otherwise re-examined in any court of the United States, than according to the rules of the common law.

ARTICLE VIII.

Excessive bail shall not be required, nor excessive fines imposed, nor cruel and unusual punishments inflicted.

ARTICLE IX.

The enumeration in the Constitution, of certain rights, shall not be construed to deny or disparage others retained by the people.

ARTICLE X.

The powers not delegated to the United States by the Constitution, nor prohibited by it to the States, are reserved to the States respectively, or to the people.

ARTICLE XI.

The judicial power of the United States shall not be construed to extend to any suit in law or equity commenced or prosecuted against one of the United States by citizens of another State, or by citizens or subjects of any foreign State.

ARTICLE XII.

The electors shall meet in their respective States, and vote by ballot for President and Vice President, one of whom at least shall not be an inhabitant of the same State with themselves; they shall name in their ballots the person to be voted for as President, and in distinct ballots the person voted for as Vice President, and they shall make distinct lists of all persons voted for as President, and of all persons voted for as Vice President, and of the number of votes for each, which list they shall sign and certify, and transmit sealed to the seat of the government of the United States, directed to the President of the Senate. The President of the Senate shall, in presence of the Senate and House of Representatives, open all the certificates and the votes shall then be counted. The person having the greatest number of votes for President, shall be the President, if such number be a majority of the whole number of electors appointed; and if no person have such majority, then from the persons having the highest number not exceeding three on the list of those voted for as President, the House of Representatives shall choose immediately, by ballot, the President. But in choosing the President, the votes shall be taken by States, the representation from each State having one vote; a quorum for this purpose shall consist of a member or members from two-thirds of the States, and a majority of all the States shall be necessary to a choice. And if the House of Representatives shall not choose a President whenever the right of choice shall devolve upon them, before the fourth day of March next following, then the Vice President shall act as President, as in the case of the death or other Constitutional disability of the President. The person having the greatest number of votes as Vice President, shall be the Vice President, if such number be a majority of the whole number of electors appointed, and if no person have a majority, then from the two highest numbers on the list, the Senate shall choose the Vice President; a quorum for the purpose shall consist of two-thirds of the whole number of Senators, and a majority of the whole number shall be necessary to a choice. But no person Constitutionally ineligible to the office of President shall be eligible to that of Vice President of the United States.

ARTICLE. XIII.

SECTION 1. Neither slavery nor involuntary servitude, except as a punishment for crime, whereof the party shall have been duly convicted, shall exist within the United States, or any place subject to their jurisdiction.

SECTION 2. Congress shall have power to enforce this article by appropriate legislation.

ARTICLE. XIV.

SECTION. 1. All persons born or naturalized in the United States and subject to the jurisdiction thereof, are citizens of the United States, and of the State wherein they reside. No State shall make or enforce any law which shall abridge the privileges or immunities of citizens of the United States; nor shall any State deprive any person of life, liberty or property without due process of law, nor deny to any person within its jurisdiction the equal protection of the laws.

SEC. 2. Representatives shall be appointed among the several States according to their respective numbers, counting the whole number of persons in each State, excluding Indians not taxed; but when the right to vote at any election for the choice of electors for President and Vice President of the United States, Representatives in Congress, the executive and judicial officers of a State or the members of the Legislature thereof, is denied to any of the male inhabitants of such State, being twenty-one years of age and citizens of the United States, or in any way abridged except for participation in rebellion or other crimes, the basis of representation therein shall be reduced in the proportion which the number of such male citizens shall bear to the whole number of male citizens twenty-one years of age in such State.

SEC. 3. No person shall be a Senator or Representative in Congress or elector of President and Vice President, or hold any office civil or military, under the United States or under any State who, having previously taken an oath as a Member of Congress, or as an officer of the United States, or as a member of any State Legislature, or as an executive or judicial officer of any State, to support the Constitution of the United States, shall have engaged in insurrection or rebellion against the same, or given aid or comfort to the enemies thereof. But Congress may, by a vote of two-thirds of each house, remove such disability.

SEC. 4. The validity of the public debt of the United States authorized by law, including debts incurred for payment of pensions and bounties for services in suppressing insurrection or rebellion, shall not be questioned. But neither the United States nor any State shall assume or pay any debt or obligation incurred in the aid of insurrection or rebellion against the United States, or any loss or emancipation of any slave, but such debts, obligations and claims shall be held illegal and void.

SEC. 5. The Congress shall have the power to enforce, by appropriate legislation, the provisions of this article.

STANDING RULES AND ORDERS

FOR CONDUCTING BUSINESS IN THE

HOUSE OF REPRESENTATIVES OF THE UNITED STATES,

As Amended at the 1st Session of the 36th Congress.

TOUCHING THE DUTY OF THE SPEAKER.

1. He shall take the chair every day precisely at the hour to which the house shall have adjourned on the preceding day; shall immediately call the members to order; and, on the appearance of a quorum, shall cause the journal of the preceding day to be read.

2. He shall preserve order and decorum; may speak to points of order in preference to other members, rising from his seat for that purpose; and shall decide questions of order, subject to an appeal to the house by any two members—on which appeal no member shall speak more than once, unless by leave of the house.

3. He shall rise to put a question, but may state it sitting.

4. Questions shall be distinctly put in this form, to wit: "As many as are of opinion that (as the question may be) say *Aye;*" and after the affirmative voice is expressed, "As many as are of the contrary opinion, say *No.*" If the Speaker doubt, or a division be called for, the house shall divide; those in the affirmative of the question shall first rise from their seats, and afterwards those in the negative. If the Speaker still doubt, or a count be required by at least one-fifth of the quorum of the members, the Speaker shall name two members, one from each side, to tell the members in the affirmative and negative—which being reported, he shall rise and state the decision to the house.

5. The Speaker shall examine and correct the journal before it is read. He shall have a general direction of the hall, and the unappropriated rooms in that part of the capitol assigned to the house, shall be subject to his order and disposal until the further order of the house. He shall have a right to name any member to perform the duties of the chair, but such substitution shall not extend beyond an adjournment.

6. No person shall be permitted to perform divine service in the chamber occupied by the House of Representatives, unless with the consent of the Speaker.

7. In all cases of ballot by the house, the Speaker shall vote; in other cases he shall not be required to vote. unless the house be

equally divided, or unless his vote, if given to the minority, will make the division equal; and in case of such equal division, the question shall be lost.

8. All acts, addresses, and joint resolutions, shall be signed by the Speaker; and all writs, warrants and subpœnas, issued by order of the house, shall be under his hand and seal, attested by the clerk.

9. In case of any disturbance or disorderly conduct in the galleries or lobby, the Speaker (or chairman of the Committee of the Whole House,) shall have power to order the same to be cleared.

OF THE CLERK AND OTHER OFFICERS.

10. There shall be elected at the commencement of each Congress, to continue in office until their successors are appointed, a clerk, sergeant-at-arms, doorkeeper, and postmaster, each of whom shall take an oath for the true and faithful discharge of the duties of his office, to the best of his knowledge and abilities, and to keep the secrets of the House; and the appointees of the door-keeper and postmaster shall be subject to the approval of the Speaker; and, in all cases of election by the house of its officers, the vote shall be taken *viva voce.*

11. In all cases where other than members of the house may be eligible to an office by the election of the house, there shall be a previous nomination.

12. In all other cases of ballot than for committees, a majority of the votes given shall be necessary to an election; and where there shall not be such a majority on the first ballot, the ballots shall be repeated until a majority be obtained. And in all ballotings blanks shall be rejected, and not taken into the count in enumeration of the votes, or reported by the tellers.

13. It shall be the duty of the clerk to make and cause to be printed and delivered to each member at the commencement of every session of Congress, a list of the reports which it is the duty of any officer or department of the government to make to Congress; referring to the act or resolution and page of the volume of the laws or journal in which it may be contained, and placing under the name of each officer the list of reports required to be made, and the time when the report may be expected.

14. It shall be the duty of the clerk of the House at the end of each session, to send a printed copy of the journals thereof to the Executive, and to each branch of the Legislature of every State.

15. All questions of order shall be noted by the clerk, with the decision, and put together at the end of the journal of every session.

16. The clerk shall, within thirty days after the close of each session of Congress, cause to be completed the printing and primary distribution, to members and delegates, of the Journal of the House, together with an accurate index of the same.

17. There shall be retained in the library of the clerk's office, for the use of the members there, and not to be withdrawn therefrom,

two copies of all the books and printed documents deposited in the library.

18. The clerk shall have preserved for each member of the House, an extra copy, in good binding, of all the documents printed by order of either House at each future session of Congress.

19. The clerk shall make a weekly statement of the resolutions and bills (Senate bills inclusive) upon the Speaker's table, accompanied with a brief reference to the orders and proceedings of the house upon each, and the date of such order and proceedings; which statement shall be printed for the use of the members.

20. The clerk shall cause an index to be prepared to the acts passed at every session of Congress, and to be printed and bound with the acts.

21. All contracts, bargains, or agreements, relative to the furnishing any matter or thing or for the performance of any labor for the House of Representatives, shall be made with the clerk, or approved by him, before any allowance shall be made therefor by the Committee of Accounts.

22. It shall be the duty of the sergeant-at-arms to attend the house during its sittings; to aid in the enforcement of order, under the direction of the Speaker; to execute the commands of the house from time to time; together with all such process, issued by authority thereof, as shall be directed to him by the Speaker.

23. The symbol of his office (the mace) shall be borne by the sergeant-at-arms when in the execution of his office.

24. The fees of the sergeant-at-arms shall be for every arrest, the sum of two dollars; for each day's custody and releasement, one dollar; and for traveling expenses for himself or a special messenger, going and returning, one-tenth of a dollar for each mile necessarily and actually traveled by such officer or other person in the execution of such precept or summons.

25. It shall be the duty of the sergeant-at-arms to keep the accounts for the pay and mileage of members, to prepare checks, and, if required to do so, to draw the money on such checks for the members, (the same being previously signed by the Speaker, and endorsed by the member,) and pay over the same to the member entitled thereto.

26. The sergeant-at-arms shall give bond, with surety, to the United States, in a sum not less than five nor more than ten thousand dollars, at the discretion of the Speaker, and with such surety as the Speaker may approve, faithfully to account for the money coming into his hands for the pay of members.

27. The doorkeeper shall execute strictly the 134th and 135th rules, relative to the privilege of the hall. And he shall be required, at the commencement and close of each session of Congress, to take an inventory of all the furniture, books, and other public property in the several committee and other rooms under his charge, and shall report the same to the house; which report shall be referred to the Committee on Accounts, who shall determine the amount for which he shall be held liable for missing articles.

28. The postmaster shall superintend the post-office kept in the capitol for the accommodation of the members.

OF THE MEMBERS.

29. No member shall vote on any question in the event of which he is immediately and particularly interested, or in any case where he was not within the bar of the house when the question was put. And when any member shall ask leave to vote, the Speaker shall propound to him the question, "Were you within the bar before the last name on the roll was called?" and if he shall answer in the negative the Speaker shall not further entertain the request of such member to vote: Provided, however, that any member who was absent by leave of the house, may vote at any time before the result is announced.

30. Upon a division and count of the house on any question, no member without the bar shall be counted.

31. Every member who shall be in the house when the question is put, shall give his vote unless the house shall excuse him. All motions to excuse a member from voting, shall be made before the house divides, or before the call of the yeas and nays is commenced; and the question shall then be taken without debate.

32. The name of a member who presents a petition or memorial, or who offers a resolution for the consideration of the house, shall be inserted on the journals.

33. No member shall absent himself from the service of the house unless he have leave, or be sick and unable to attend.

OF CALLS OF THE HOUSE.

34. Any fifteen members (including the Speaker, if there be one), shall be authorized to compel the attendance of absent members.

35. Upon calls of the house, or in taking the yeas and nays on any question, the names of the members shall be called alphabetically.

36. Upon the call of the house, the names of the members shall be called over by the clerk, and the absentees noted; after which the names of the absentees shall again be called over; the doors shall then be shut, and those for whom no excuse or insufficient excuses are made may, by order of those present, if fifteen in number, be taken into custody as they appear, or may be sent for and taken into custody, wherever to be found, by special messengers to be appointed for that purpose.

37. When a member shall be discharged from custody, and admitted to his seat, the house shall determine whether such discharge shall be with or without paying fees; and in like manner whether a delinquent member, taken into custody by a special messenger, shall or shall not be liable to defray the expenses of such special messenger.

ON MOTIONS, THEIR PRECEDENCE, &C.

38. When a motion is made and seconded, it shall be stated by the Speaker; or, being in writing, it shall be handed to the chair and read aloud by the clerk, before debated.

39. Every motion shall be reduced to writing if the Speaker or any member desire it. Every written motion made to the house shall be inserted on the journals, with the name of the member making it, unless it be withdrawn on the same day on which it was submitted.

40. After a motion is stated by the Speaker, or read by the clerk, it shall be deemed to be in the possession of the house, but may be withdrawn at any time before a decision or amendment.

41. When any motion or proposition is made, the question, "Will the house now consider it?" shall not be put unless it is demanded by some member, or is deemed necessary by the Speaker.

42. When a question is under debate, no motion shall be received but to adjourn, to lie on the table, for the previous question, to postpone to a day certain, to commit or amend, to postpone indefinitely; which several motions shall have precedence in the order in which they are arranged; and no motion to postpone to a day certain, to commit, or to postpone indefinitely, being decided, shall be again allowed on the same day, and at the same stage of the bill or proposition.

43. When a resolution shall be offered, or a motion made, to refer any subject, and different committees shall be proposed, the question shall be taken in the following order:

The Committee of the Whole House on the state of the Union; the Committee of the Whole House; a Standing Committee; a Select Committee.

44. A motion to adjourn, and a motion to fix the day to which the house shall adjourn, shall be always in order; these motions and the motion to lie on the table, shall be decided without debate.

45. The hour at which every motion to adjourn is made shall be entered on the journal.

46. Any member may call for the division of a question, before or after the main question is ordered, which shall be divided if it comprehend propositions in substance so distinct that, one being taken away, a substantive proposition shall remain for the decision of the house. A motion to strike out and insert shall be deemed indivisible; but a motion to strike out being lost, shall preclude neither amendment nor a motion to strike out and insert.

47. Motions and reports may be committed at the pleasure of the house.

48. No motion or proposition on a subject different from that under consideration shall be admitted under color of amendment. No bill or resolution shall, at any time, be amended by annexing thereto, or incorporating therewith, any other bill or resolution pending before the house.

49. When a motion has been once made, and carried in the affirmative or negative, it shall be in order for any member of the majority to move for the reconsideration thereof, on the same or succeeding day; and such motion shall take precedence of all other questions, except a motion to adjourn, and shall not be withdrawn after the said succeeding day without the consent of the house; and thereafter any member may call it up for consideration.

50. In filling up blanks, the largest sum and longest time shall be first put.

ORDER OF BUSINESS OF THE DAY.

51. As soon as the journal is read, and the unfinished business in which the house was engaged at the last preceding adjournment has been disposed of, reports from committees shall be called for and disposed of; in doing which the Speaker shall call upon each standing committee in regular order, and then upon select committees; and if the Speaker shall not get through the call upon the committees before the house passes to other business, he shall resume the next call where he left off, giving preference to the report last under consideration: Provided, That whenever any committee shall have occupied the morning hour on two days, it shall not be in order for such committee to report further until the other committees shall have been called in their turn. On the call for reports from committees on each alternate Monday, which shall commence as soon as the journal is read, all bills reported during the first hour after the journal is read shall be committed, without debate, to the Committee of the Whole, and together with their accompanying reports, printed; and if during the hour all the committees are not called, then, on the next alternate Monday, the Speaker shall commence where such call was suspended: Provided, That no bill reported under the call on alternate Mondays, and committed, shall be again brought before the house by a motion to reconsider.

52. Reports from committees having been presented and disposed of, the Speaker shall call for resolutions from the members of each State and delegate from each Territory, beginning with Maine and the Territory last organized, alternately; and they shall not be debated on the very day of their being presented, nor on any day assigned by the house for the receipt of resolutions, unless where the house shall direct otherwise, but shall lie on the table, to be taken up in the order in which they are presented; and if on any day the whole of the States and Territories shall not be called, the Speaker shall begin on the next day where he left off the previous day: Provided, That no member shall offer more than one resolution, or one series of resolutions, all relating to the same subject, until all the States and Territories shall have been called.

53. A proposition requesting information from the President of the United States, or directing it to be furnished by the head of either of the Executive departments, or by the Postmaster General—shall lie on the table one day for consideration, unless otherwise ordered by the unanimous consent of the house, and all such propositions shall be taken up for consideration in the order they were presented, immediately after reports are called for from select committees, and when adopted, the clerk shall cause the same to be delivered.

54. After one hour shall have been devoted to reports from committees and resolutions, it shall be in order, pending the consideration or discussion thereof, to entertain a motion that the house do now proceed to dispose of the business on the Speaker's table, and to

the orders of the day—which being decided in the affirmative, the Speaker shall dispose of the business on his table in the following order, viz.:

1st. Messages and other Executive communications.

2d. Messages from the Senate, and amendments proposed by the Senate to bills of the house.

3d. Bills and resolutions from the Senate on their first and second reading, that they be referred to committees and put under way; but if, on being read a second time, no motion being made to commit, they are to be ordered to their third reading unless objection be made; in which case, if not otherwise ordered by a majority of the house, they are to be laid on the table in general file of bills on the Speaker's table, to be taken up in their turn.

4th. Engrossed bills and bills from the Senate on their third reading.

5th. Bills of the house and from the Senate, on the Speaker's table, on their engrossment, or on being ordered to a third reading, to be taken up and considered in the order of time in which they passed to a second reading.

The messages, communications, and bills on his table having been disposed of, the Speaker shall then proceed to call the orders of the day.

55. The business specified in the 54th and 130th rules shall be done at no other part of the day, except by permission of the house.

56. The consideration of the unfinished business in which the house may be engaged at an adjournment shall be resumed as soon as the journal of the next day is read, and at the same time each day thereafter until disposed of; and if, from any cause other business shall intervene, it shall be resumed as soon as such other business is disposed of. And the consideration of all other unfinished business shall be resumed whenever the class of business to which it belongs shall be in order under the rules.

OF DECORUM AND DEBATE.

57. When any member is about to speak in debate, or deliver any matter to the House, he shall rise from his seat and respectfully address himself to "Mr. Speaker"—and shall confine himself to the question under debate, and avoid personality.

58. Members may address the house or committee from the clerk's desk, or from a place near the Speaker's chair.

59. When two or more members happen to rise at once, the Speaker shall name the member who is first to speak.

60. No member shall occupy more than one hour in debate on any question in the house, or in committee; but a member reporting the measure under consideration from a committee may open and close the debate, provided that when debate is closed by order of the house, any member shall be allowed, in committee, five minutes to explain any amendment he may offer, after which any member who shall first obtain the floor shall be allowed to speak five minutes in opposition to it, and there shall be no further debate on the amend-

ment; but the same privilege of debate shall be allowed in favor of and against any amendment that may be offered to the amendment; and neither the amendment nor an amendment to the amendment shall be withdrawn by the mover thereof, unless by the unanimous consent of the committee. Provided further, that the house may, by the vote of a majority of the members present, at any time after the five minutes debate has taken place upon proposed amendments to any section or paragraph of a bill, close all debate upon such section or paragraph, or at their election upon the pending amendments only.

61. If any member in speaking or otherwise, transgress the rules of the house, the Speaker shall, or any member may call him to order; in which case the member so called to order shall immediately sit down, unless permitted to explain; and the house shall, if appealed to, decide on the case, but without debate; if there be no appeal the decision of the chair shall be submitted to. If the decision be in favor of the member called to order, he shall be at liberty to proceed; if otherwise, he shall not be permitted to proceed, in case any member object, without leave of the house; and if the case require it, he shall be liable to the censure of the house.

62. If a member be called to order for words spoken in debate, the person calling him to order shall repeat the words excepted to, and they shall be taken down in writing at the clerk's table; and no member shall be held to answer, or be subject to the censure of the house, for words spoken in debate, if any other member has spoken, or other business has intervened, after the words spoken, and before exception to them shall have been taken.

63. No member shall speak more than once to the same question without leave of the house, unless he be the mover, proposer or introducer of the matter pending; in which case he shall be permitted to speak in reply, but not until every member choosing to speak shall have spoken.

64. If a question depending be lost by adjournment of the House, and revived on the succeeding day, no member who shall have spoken on the preceding day shall be permitted again to speak without leave.

65. While the Speaker is putting any question, or addressing the house, none shall walk out of or across the house; nor in such case, or when a member is speaking, shall entertain private discourse; nor while a member is speaking, shall pass between him and the chair. Every member shall remain uncovered during the session of the house. No member or other person shall visit or remain by the clerk's table while the ayes and noes are calling, or ballots are counting.

66. All questions relating to the priority of business to be acted on shall be decided without debate.

OF COMMITTEES.

67. All committees shall be appointed by the Speaker, unless otherwise specially directed by the house, in which case they shall be ap-

pointed by ballot; and if upon such ballot the number required shall not be elected by a majority of the votes given, the house shall proceed to a second ballot, in which a plurality of votes shall prevail; and in case a greater number than is required to compose or complete a committee shall have an equal number of votes, the house shall proceed to a further ballot or ballots.

68. The first named member of any committee shall be the chairman; and in his absence, or being excused by the house, the next named member, and so on, as often as the case shall happen, unless the committee, by a majority of their number, elect a chairman.

69. Any member may excuse himself from serving on any committee at the time of his appointment, if he is then a member of two other committees.

70. It shall be the duty of a committee to meet on the call of any two of its members, if the chairman be absent, or decline to appoint such meeting.

71. The several standing committees of the house shall have leave to report by bill or otherwise.

72. No committee shall sit during the sitting of the house without special leave.

73. No committee shall be permitted to employ a clerk at the public expense, without first obtaining leave of the house for that purpose.

74. Thirty-one standing committees shall be appointed at the commencement of each Congress, viz.:

TO CONSIST OF NINE MEMBERS EACH—

A Committee of Elections.—Nov. 13, 1789.
A Committee of Ways and Means.—Jan. 7, 1802.
A Committee on Appropriations.—March 2, 1865.
A Committee on Banking and Currency.—March 2, 1865.
A Committee on the Pacific Railroad.—March 2, 1865.
A Committee on Claims.—Nov. 13, 1794.
A Committee on Commerce.—Dec. 14, 1795.
A Committee on Public Lands.—Dec. 17, 1805.
A Committee on the Post-Office and Post-Roads.—Nov. 9, 1808.
A Committee for the District of Columbia.—Jan. 27, 1808.
A Committee on the Judiciary.—June 3, 1813.
A Committee on Revolutionary Claims.—Dec. 22, 1813.
A Committee on Public Expenditures.—Feb. 26, 1814.
A Committee on Private Land Claims.—April 29, 1816.
A Committee on Manufactures.—Dec. 8, 1819.
A Committee on Agriculture.—May 3, 1820.
A Committee on Indian Affairs.—Dec. 18, 1821.
A Committee on Military Affairs.—March 13, 1822.
A Committee on Militia.—Dec. 10, 1835.
A Committee on Naval Affairs.—March 13, 1822.
A Committee on Foreign Affairs.—March 13, 1822.
A Committee on the Territories.—Dec. 13, 1825.
A Committee on Revolutionary Pensions.—Dec. 9, 1825.

A Committee on Invalid Pensions.—Jan. 10, 1831.
A Committee on Roads and Canals.—Dec. 15, 1831.
A Committee on Patents.—Sept. 15, 1837.

TO CONSIST OF FIVE MEMBERS EACH—

A Committee on Public Buildings and Grounds.—Sept. 15, 1837.
A Committee of Revisal and Unfinished Business.—Dec. 14. 1795.
A Committee on Accounts.—Nov. 7, 1804.
A Committee on Mileage.—Sept 15, 1837.
A Committee on Coinage, Weights and Measures.—Jan. 21, 1864.

75. It shall be the duty of the Committee of Elections to examine and report upon the certificates of election, or other credentials, of the members returned to serve in this house, and to take into their consideration all such petitions and other matters touching elections and returns as shall or may be presented or come into question, and be referred to them by the house.

76. It shall be the duty of the Committee on Appropriations to take into consideration all Executive communications and such other propositions in regard to carrying on the several departments of the government as may be presented and referred to them by the house.

In preparing bills of appropriations for other objects, the Committee on Appropriations shall not include appropriations for carrying into effect treaties made by the United States; and where an appropriation bill shall be referred to them for their consideration, which contains appropriations for carrying a treaty into effect, and for other objects, they shall propose such amendments as shall prevent appropriations for carrying a treaty into effect being included in the same bill with appropriations for other objects.

77. It shall also be the duty of the Committee on Appropriations, within thirty days after their appointment, at every session of Congress, commencing on the first Monday of December, to report the general appropriation bills for legislative, executive, and judicial expenses; for sundry civil expenses; for consular and diplomatic expenses; for the army; for the navy; for the expenses of the Indian Department; for the payment of invalid and other pensions; for the support of the Military Academy; for fortifications; for the service of the Post-office Department, and for mail transportation by ocean steamers; or, in failure thereof, the reasons of such failure. And said committee shall have leave to report said bills (for reference only) at any time.

78. It shall be the duty of the Committee of Claims to take into consideration all such petitions and matters or things touching claims and demands on the United States as shall be presented, or shall or may come in question, and be referred to them by the house; and to report their opinion thereupon, together with such propositions for relief therein as to them shall seem expedient.

79. It shall be the duty of the Committee on Commerce to take into consideration all such petitions and matters or things touching the commerce of the United States as shall be presented, or shall or

may come into question, and be referred to them by the house; and to report, from time to time, their opinion thereon.

80. It shall be the duty of the Committee on the Public Lands to take into consideration all such petitions and matters or things respecting the lands of the United States as shall be presented, or shall or may come in question, and be referred to them by the house; and to report their opinion thereon, together with such propositions for relief therein as to them shall seem expedient.

81. It shall be the duty of the Committee on the Post-Office and Post-Roads to take into consideration all such petitions and matters or things touching the post-office and post-roads as shall be presented, or shall come in question, and be referred to them by the house; and to report their opinion thereon, together with such propositions relative thereto as to them shall seem expedient.

82. It shall be the duty of the Committee for the District of Columbia to take into consideration all such petitions and matters or things touching the said District as shall be presented or shall come in question, and be referred to them by the house; and to report their opinion thereon, together with such propositions relative thereto as to them shall seem expedient.

83. It shall be the duty of the Committee on the Judiciary to take into consideration such petitions and matters or things touching judicial proceedings as shall be presented or may come in question, and be referred to them by the house, and to report their opinion thereon, together with such propositions relative thereto as to them shall seem expedient.

84. It shall be the duty of the Committee on Revolutionary Claims to take into consideration all such petitions and matters or things touching claims and demands originating in the Revolutionary war, or arising therefrom, as shall be presented, or shall or may come in question, and be referred to them by the house, and to report their opinion thereupon, together with such propositions for relief therein as to them shall seem expedient.

85. It shall be the duty of the Committee on Public Expenditures to examine into the state of the several public departments, and particularly into laws making appropriations of money, and to report whether the moneys have been disbursed conformably with such laws; and also to report from time to time such provisions and arrangements as may be necessary to add to the economy of the departments, and the accountability of their officers.

86. It shall be the duty of the Committee on Private Land Claims to take into consideration all claims to land which may be referred to them, or shall or may come in question; and to report their opinion thereupon, together with such propositions for relief therein as to them shall seem expedient.

87. It shall be the duty of the Committee on Military Affairs to take into consideration all subjects relating to the military establishment and public defense which may be referred to them by the house, and to report their opinion thereupon; and also to report,

from time to time, such measures as may contribute to economy and accountability in the said establishment.

88. It shall be the duty of the Committee on the Militia to take into consideration and report on all subjects connected with the organizing, arming and disciplining the militia of the United States.

89. It shall be the duty of the Committee on Naval Affairs to take into consideration all matters which concern the naval establishment, and which shall be referred to them by the house, and to report their opinion thereupon; and also to report, from time to time, such measures as may contribute to economy and accountability in the said establishment.

90. It shall be the duty of the Committee on Foreign Affairs to take into consideration all matters which concern the relations of the United States with foreign nations, and which shall be referred to them by the house, and to report their opinion on the same.

91. It shall be the duty of the Committee on the Territories to examine into the legislative, civil and criminal proceedings of the Territories, and to devise and report to the house such means as in their opinion may be necessary to secure the rights and privileges of residents and non-residents.

92. It shall be the duty of the Committee on Revolutionary Pensions to take into consideration all such matters respecting pensions for services in the Revolutionary war, other than invalid pensions, as shall be referred to them by the house.

93. It shall be the duty of the Committee on Invalid Pensions to take into consideration all such matters respecting invalid pensions as shall be referred to them by the house.

94. It shall be the duty of the Committee on Roads and Canals to take into consideration all such petitions and matters or things relating to roads and canals, and the improvement of the navigation of rivers, as shall be presented or may come in question, and be referred to them by the house, and to report thereupon, together with such propositions relative thereto as to them shall seem expedient.

95. It shall be the duty of the Committee on Patents to consider all subjects relating to patents which may be referred to them; and report their opinions thereon, together with such propositions relative thereto as may seem to them expedient.

96. It shall be the duty of the Committee on Public Buildings and Grounds to consider all subjects relating to the public edifices and grounds within the city of Washington which may be referred to them; and report their opinion thereon, together with such propositions relating thereto as may seem to them expedient.

97. It shall be the duty of the Committee of Revisal and Unfinished Business to examine and report what laws have expired, or are near expiring, and require to be revived or further continued; also to examine and report, from the journal of last session, all such matters as were then depending and undetermined.

98. It shall be the duty of the Committee of Accounts to superintend and control the expenditures of the contingent fund of the

House of Representatives; also to audit and settle all accounts which may be charged thereon.

99. It shall be the duty of the Committee on Mileage to ascertain and report the distance to the sergeant-at-arms for which each member shall receive pay.

100. There shall be referred by the clerk to the members of the Committee on Printing on the part of the house, all drawings, maps, charts, or other papers which may at any time come before the house for engraving, lithographing, or publishing in any way; which committee shall report to the house whether the same ought, in their opinion, to be published; and if the house order the publication of the same, that said committee shall direct the size and manner of execution of all such maps, charts, drawings, or other papers, and contract by agreement, in writing, for all such engraving, lithographing, printing, drawing, and coloring, as may be ordered by the house; which agreement, in writing, shall be furnished by said committee to the Committee of Accounts, to govern said committee in all allowances for such works, and it shall be in order for said committee to report at all times.

101. It shall be in order for the Committee on Enrolled Bills and the Committee on Printing to report at any time.

102. Seven additional standing committees shall be appointed at the commencement of the first session in each Congress, whose duties shall continue until the first session of the ensuing Congress.

COMMITTEES, TO CONSIST OF FIVE MEMBERS EACH—

1. A committee on so much of the public accounts and expenditures as relates to the Department of State;
2. A committee on so much of the public accounts and expenditures as relates to the Treasury Department;
3. A committee on so much of the public accounts and expenditures as relates to the Department of War;
4. A committee on so much of the public accounts and expenditures as relates to the Department of the Navy;
5. A committee on so much of the public accounts and expenditures as relates to the Post Office;
6. A committee on so much of the public accounts and expenditures as relates to the Public Buildings; and
7. A committee on so much of the public accounts and expenditures as relates to the Interior Department.

103. It shall be the duty of the said committees to examine into the state of the accounts and expenditures respectively submitted to them, and to inquire and to report particularly—

Whether the expenditures of the respective departments are justified by law;

Whether the claims from time to time satisfied and discharged by the respective departments are supported by sufficient vouchers, establishing their justness both as to their character and amount.

Whether such claims have been discharged out of funds appropriated therefor, and whether all moneys have been disbursed in conformity with appropriation laws; and

Whether any, and what, provisions are necessary to be adopted, to provide more perfectly for the proper application of the public moneys, and to secure the government from demands unjust in their character or extravagant in their amount.

And it shall be, moreover, the duty of the said committees to report, from time to time, whether any, and what, retrenchment can be made in the expenditures of the several departments, without detriment to the public service; whether any, and what, abuses at any time exist in the failure to enforce the payment of moneys which may be due to the United States from public defaulters or others; and to report, from time to time, such provisions and arrangements as may be necessary to add to the economy of the several departments and the accountability of their officers.

It shall be the duty of the several committees on public expenditures to inquire whether any officers belonging to the branches or departments, respectively, concerning whose expenditures it is their duty to inquire, have become useless or unnecessary; and to report from time to time, on the expediency of modifying or abolishing the same; also to examine into the pay and emoluments of all officers under the laws of the United States; and to report from time to time such a reduction or increase thereof as a just economy and the public service may require.

OF COMMITTEES OF THE WHOLE.

104. The House may at any time, by a vote of a majority of the members present, suspend the rules and orders for the purpose of going into the Committee of the Whole House on the State of the Union; and also for providing for the discharge of the Committee of the Whole House, and the Committee of the Whole House on the State of the Union, from the further consideration of any bill referred to it, after acting without debate on all amendments pending and that may be offered.

105. In forming a Committee of the Whole House, the Speaker shall leave his chair, and a chairman to preside in committee shall be appointed by the Speaker.

106. Whenever the Committee of the Whole on the State of the Union, or the Committee of the Whole House, finds itself without a quorum, the chairman shall cause the roll of the house to be called, and thereupon the committee shall rise, and the chairman shall report the names of the absentees to the house, which shall be entered on the journal.

107. Upon bills committed to a Committee of the Whole House, the bill shall be first read throughout by the clerk, and then again read and debated by clauses, leaving the preamble to be last considered; the body of the bill shall not be defaced or interlined; but all amendments, noting the page and line, shall be duly entered by the clerk on a separate paper, as the same shall be agreed to by the com-

mittee, and so reported to the house. After report, the bill shall again be subject to be debated and amended by clauses, before a question to engross it be taken.

108. All amendments made to an original motion in committee shall be incorporated with the motion, and so reported.

109. All amendments made to a report committed to a Committee of the Whole House shall be noted and reported, as in the case of bills.

110. No motion or proposition for a tax or charge upon the people shall be discussed the day on which it is made or offered, and every such proposition shall receive its first discussion in a Committee of the Whole House.

111. No sum or quantum of tax or duty, voted by a Committee of the Whole House, shall be increased in the House until the motion or proposition for such increase shall be first discussed and voted in a Committee of the Whole House; and so in respect to the time of its continuance.

112. All proceedings touching appropriations of money shall be first discussed in a Committee of the Whole House.

113. The rules of proceedings in the house shall be observed in a Committee of the Whole House, so far as they may be applicable, except the rule limiting the times of speaking; but no member shall speak twice to any question until every member choosing to speak shall have spoken.

114. In Committee of the Whole on the State of the Union, the bills shall be taken up and disposed of in their order on the calendar; but when objection is made to the consideration of a bill, a majority of the committee shall decide, without debate, whether it shall be taken up and disposed of, or laid aside; provided, that general appropriation bills, and, in time of war, bills for raising men or money, and bills concerning a treaty of peace, shall be preferred to all other bills at the discretion of the committee; and when demanded by any member, the question shall first be put in regard to them; and all debate on special orders shall be confined strictly to the measure under consideration.

OF BILLS.

115. Every bill shall be introduced on the report of a committee, or by motion for leave. In the latter case, at least one day's notice shall be given of the motion in the house, or by filing a memorandum thereof with the clerk, and having it entered on the journal; and the motion shall be made, and the bill introduced, if leave is given, when resolutions are called for; such motion, or the bill when intoduced, may be committed.

116. Every bill shall receive three several readings in the house previous to its passage; and the bills shall be dispatched in order as they were introduced, unless where the house shall direct otherwise; but no bill shall be twice read on the same day, without special order of the house.

117. The first reading of a bill shall be for information, and if opposition be made to it, the question shall be, "Shall this bill be rejected?" If no opposition be made, or if the question to reject be negatived, the bill shall go to its second reading without a question.

118. Upon the second reading of a bill, the Speaker shall state it as ready for commitment or engrossment; and if committed, then a question shall be, whether to a select or standing committee, or to a Committee of the Whole House; if to a Committee of the Whole House, the house shall determine on what day; if no motion be made to commit, the question shall be stated on its engrossment; and if it be not ordered to be engrossed on the day of its being reported, it shall be placed on the general file on the Speaker's table, to be taken up in order. But if the bill be ordered to be engrossed, the house shall appoint the day when it shall be read the third time.

119. General appropriation bills shall be in order in preference to any other bill of a public nature unless otherwise ordered by a majority of the house.

And the house may, at any time, by a vote of the majority of the members present, make any of the general appropriation bills a special order.

120. No appropriation shall be reported in such general appropriation bills, or be in order as an amendment thereto, for any expenditure not previously authorized by law, unless in continuation of appropriations for such public works and objects as are already in progress, and for the contingencies for carrying on the several departments of the government.

121. Upon the engrossment of any bill making appropriations of money for works of internal improvement of any kind or description, it shall be in the power of any member to call for a division of the question, so as to to take a separate vote of the house upon each item of improvement or appropriation contained in said bill, or upon such items separately, and others collectively, as the members making the call may specify; and if one-fifth of the members present second said call, it shall be the duty of the Speaker to make such divisions of the question, and put them to vote accordingly.

122. The bills from the Court of Claims shall, on being laid before the house, be read a first and second time, committed to a Committee of the Whole House, and, together with the accompanying reports, printed.

123. A motion to strike out the enacting words of a bill shall have precedence of a motion to amend; and, if carried, shall be considered equivalent to its rejection. Whenever a bill is reported from a Committee of the Whole, with a recommendation to strike out the enacting words, and such recommendation is disagreed to by the house, the bill shall stand recommitted to the said committee without further action by the house.

124. After commitment and report thereof to the house, or at any time before its passage, a bill may be recommitted; and should such

recommitment take place after its engrossment, and an amendment be reported and agreed to by the house, the question shall be again put on the engrossment of the bill.

125. All bills ordered to be engrossed shall be executed in a fair round hand.

126. No amendment by way of rider shall be received to any bill on its third reading.

127. When a bill shall pass, it shall be certified by the clerk, noting the day of its passage at the foot thereof.

LOCAL OR PRIVATE BUSINESS.

128. Friday and Saturday of every week shall be set apart for the consideration of private bills and private business, in preference to any other, unless otherwise determined by a majority of the house.

129. On the first and fourth Friday and Saturday of each month the calendar of private bills shall be called over, (the chairman of the Committee of the Whole House commencing the call where he left off the previous day,) and the bills to the passage of which no objection shall then be made shall be first considered and disposed of. But when a bill is again reached, after having been once objected to, the committee shall consider and dispose of the same, unless it shall again be objected to by at least five members

OF BILLS ON LEAVE AND RESOLUTIONS.

130. All the States and Territories shall be called for bills on leave and resolutions on each alternate Monday during each session of Congress; and, if necessary to secure the object on said days, all resolutions which shall give rise to debate shall lie over for discussion, under the rules of the House already established; and the whole of said days shall be appropriated to bills on leave and resolutions, until all the States and Territories are called through. And the Speaker shall first call the States and Territories for bills on leave; and all bills so introduced during the first hour after the journal is read shall be referred, without debate, to their appropriate committees; provided however, that a bill so introduced and referred shall not be brought back into the house upon a motion to reconsider.

OF PETITIONS AND MEMORIALS.

131. Members having petitions and memorials to present, may hand them to the clerk, indorsing the same with their names, and the reference or disposition to be made thereof; and such petitions and memorials shall be entered on the journal, subject to the control and direction of the Speaker; and if any petition or memorial be so handed in, which, in the judgment of the Speaker, is excluded by the rules, the same shall be returned to the member from whom it was received.

OF THE PREVIOUS QUESTION.

132. The previous question shall be in this form: "Shall the main question be now put?" It shall only be admitted when demanded by a majority of the members present; and its effects shall be to put an end to all debate, and to bring the house to a direct vote upon a motion to commit, if such motion shall have been made; and if this motion does not prevail, then upon amendments reported by a committee, if any; then upon pending amendments, and then upon the main question. But its only effect, if a motion to postpone is pending, shall be to bring the house to a vote upon such motion. Whenever the house shall refuse to order the main question, the consideration of the subject shall be resumed as though no motion for the previous question had been made. The house may also, at any time, on motion seconded by a majority of the members present, close all debate upon a pending amendment, or an amendment thereto, and cause the question to be put thereon; and this shall not preclude any further amendment or debate upon the bill. A call of the house shall not be in order after the previous question is seconded, unless it shall appear, upon an actual count by the Speaker, that no quorum is present.

133. On a previous question there shall be no debate. All incidental questions of order arising after a motion is made for the previous question and pending such motion, shall be decided, whether on appeal or otherwise, without debate.

OF ADMISSION ON THE FLOOR.

134. No person except members of the Senate, their secretary, heads of departments, the President's private secretary, foreign ministers, the Governor for the time being of any State, Senators and Representatives elect, and judges of the Supreme Court of the United States and of the Court of Claims, shall be admitted within the hall of the House of Representatives. Or any of the rooms upon the same floor or leading into the same.

OF REPORTERS.

135. Stenographers and reporters, other than the official reporters of the house, wishing to take down the debates, may be admitted by the Speaker to the reporters' gallery over the Speaker's chair, but not on the floor of the house; but no person shall be allowed the privilege of said gallery under the character of stenographer or reporter without a written permission of the Speaker, specifying the part of said gallery assigned to him; nor shall said stenographer or reporter be admitted to said gallery unless he shall state in writing for what paper or papers he is employed to report; nor shall he be so admitted, or, if admitted, be suffered to retain his seat, if he shall be or become an agent to prosecute any claim pending before Congress; and the Speaker shall give his written permissiom with this condition.

UNFINISHED BUSINESS OF THE SESSION.

136. After six days from the commencement of a second or subsequent session of any Congress, all bills, resolutions, and reports which originated in the house, and at the close of the next preceding session remained undetermined, shall be resumed and acted on in the same manner as if an adjournment had not taken place. And all business before committees of the house at the end of one session shall be resumed at the commencement of the next session of the same Congress as if no adjournment had taken place.

MISCELLANEOUS.

137. Whenever confidential communications are received from the President of the United States, the house shall be cleared of all persons, except the members, clerk, sergeant-at-arms, and doorkeeper, and so continue during the reading of such communications, and (unless otherwise directed by the house) during all debates and proceedings to be had thereon. And when the Speaker, or any other member, shall inform the house that he has communications to make which he conceives ought to be kept secret, the house shall, in like manner, be cleared till the communication be made; the house shall then determine whether the matter communicated requires secrecy or not, and take order accordingly

138. The rule for paying witnesses summoned to appear before this house, or either of its committees, shall be as follows: for each day a witness shall attend, the sum of two dollars; for each mile he shall travel in coming to or going from the place of examination, the sum of ten cents each way; but nothing shall be paid for traveling home when the witness has been summoned at the place of trial.

139. Maps accompanying documents shall not be printed, under the general order to print, without the special direction of the house.

140. No extra compensation shall be allowed to any officer or messenger, page, laborer, or other person in the service of the house, or engaged in or about the public grounds or buildings; and no person shall be an officer of the house, or continue in its employment, who shall be an agent for the prosecution of any claim against the government, or be interested in such claim otherwise than an original claimant; and it shall be the duty of the Committee of Accounts to inquire into and report to the house any violation of this rule.

141. When the reading of a paper is called for, and the same is objected to by any member, it shall be determined by a vote of the house.

142. When a question is postponed indefinitely, the same shall not be acted upon again during the session.

143. Every order, resolution, or vote, to which the concurrence of the Senate shall be necessary, shall be read to the house, and laid on the table, on a day preceding that in which the same shall be moved, unless the house shall otherwise expressly allow.

144. The rules of parliamentary practice, comprised in Jefferson's

Manual, shall govern the house in all cases to which they are applicable, and in which they are not inconsistent with the standing rules and orders of the house, and joint rules of the Senate and House of Representatives.

145. No standing rule or order of the house shall be rescinded or changed without one day's notice being given of the motion therefor; nor shall any rule be suspended, except by a vote of at least two-thirds of the members present; nor shall the order of business, as established by the rules, be postponed or changed, except by a vote of at least two-thirds of the members present; nor shall the Speaker entertain a motion to suspend the rules, except during the last ten days of the session, and on Monday of every week at the expiration of an hour after the journal is read, unless the call of the States and Territories for bills on leave and resolutions has been earlier concluded, when the Speaker may entertain a motion to suspend the rules.

146. All election of officers of the house, including the Speaker, shall be conducted in accordance with these rules, so far as the same are applicable; and pending the election of a Speaker, the clerk shall preserve order and decorum, and shall decide all questions of order that may arise, subject to appeal to the house.

147. These rules shall be the rules of the House of Representatives of the present and succeeding Congresses unless otherwise ordered.

148. An additional standing committee shall be appointed at the commencement of each Congress, whose duties shall continue until the first session of the ensuing Congress, to consist of five members, to be entitled a "Committee on a Uniform System of Coinage, Weights, and Measures;" and to this committee shall be referred all bills, resolutions, and communications to the house upon that subject.

149. The names of members not voting on any call of the ayes and noes shall be recorded in the journal immediately after those voting in the affirmative and negative, and the same record shall be made in the Congressional Globe.

150. It shall be the duty of the Committee on the Pacific Railroad to take into consideration all such petitions and matters or things relative to railroads or telegraph lines between the Mississippi valley and the Pacific coast, as shall be presented or shall come in question, and be referred to them by the house, and to report their opinion thereon, together with such propositions relative thereto as to them shall seem expedient.

151. It shall be the duty of the Committee of Ways and Means to take into consideration all reports of the Treasury Department, and such other propositions relative to raising revenue and providing ways and means for the support of the government as shall be presented or shall come in question, and be referred to them by the house, and to report their opinion thereon by bill or otherwise, as to them shall

seem expedient; and said committee shall have leave to report for commitment at any time.

152. It shall be the duty of the Committee on Banking and Bank Currency to take into consideration all propositions relative to banking and the currency as shall be presented or shall come in question, and be referred to them by the house, and to report thereon by bill or otherwise.

REMARKS UPON ARTICLE XIV.

Since the publication of the first edition of this work, (early in the year 1868,) the nation has been officially notified by the Hon. W. H. Seward, Secretary of State, under due instructions from Congress, that the Fourteenth Article of Amendment to the Constitution, submitted by Congress to the Legislatures of the several States, on or about the 16th day of June, 1866, and subsequently ratified by more than three-fourths of the said Legislatures, "has become valid to all intents and purposes as a part of the Constitution of the United States."

Thirty States have adopted this most important amendment, namely, the States of Connecticut, New Hampshire, Tennessee, New Jersey, Oregon, Vermont, New York, Ohio, Illinois, West Virginia, Kansas, Maine, Nevada, Missouri, Indiana, Minnesota, Rhode Island, Wisconsin, Pennsylvania, Michigan, Massachusetts, Nebraska, Iowa, Arkansas, Florida, North Carolina, Louisiana, South Carolina, Alabama and Georgia. Five States have rejected it, namely, Texas, Virginia, Kentucky, Delaware and Maryland. The remaining States, namely, California and Mississippi, do not appear to have taken final action thereon.

UNITED STATES CHRONOLOGY.

[In the following Chronological Table, we have inserted only such events and occurrences as relate to the government, to our wars, and to the distinguished men who have been conspicuous either as statesmen or commanders in our army or navy. To the events we have added numerous notes and comments, which make the following pages an epitome of the history of our country.]

1775.

April 19—Battle of Lexington, (10 m. N. W. of Boston,) the beginning of the Revolutionary war, when the first blood in that contest was spilt.

May 10—The Second Continental Congress met at Philadelphia, the First having met Sept. 5th, the year before, at the same place.

" 10—Colonels Allen and Arnold surprised and took Ticonderoga, New York, which surrendered without the loss of a man. The same day they took Crown Point (on the W. shore of Lake Champlain.)

" 10—Peyton Randolph, of Virginia, chosen President of the Continental Congress.

" 15—Congress resolved to issue paper money.

" 20—Articles of Union and Confederation agreed on by the thirteen colonies.

" 24—John Hancock chosen President of the Continental Congress.

" 25—The British Generals Howe, Clinton and Burgoyne arrive at Boston.

June 15—Congress unanimously elects George Washington commander-in-chief of the American army.

" 17—Battle of Bunker Hill (near Boston). British victorious, but not till twice repulsed with great slaughter. British forces, 3,000; American, 1,500; Br. killed and wounded 1,000; Am. about 400. Gen. Warren fell here. The English burnt Charlestown, near Boston, the same day.

" 22—Congress resolved to issue $2,000,000 in Bills of Credit.

August—Col. Arnold left Cambridge, Mass., with 1,000 men to invade Canada.

Oct. 18—Falmouth, in Mass., burnt by the British.

" 22—Peyton Randolph, the first President of the Continental Congress, died.

Nov. 13—Montreal surrendered to the Americans under Gen. Montgomery; St. John's had surrendered on the 3d.

Dec. 8—Battle at Norfolk, Va. Br. under Lord Dunmore, defeated.

" 13—Congress resolved to fit out a navy of 13 ships.

" 21—The English Parliament pass an act confiscating all American vessels found floating on the water, and for impressing their crews into the British navy, without distinction of persons.

" 31—Gen. Montgomery killed in an attempt, with Col. Arnold, to capture Quebec, and after a hard battle the Americans were compelled to surrender prisoners of war.

1776.

Jan. 1—Lord Dunmore, the Br. Governor of Virginia, burnt Norfolk and fled.

Mar. 3—The Americans, under Col. Bull, burn seven English ships, laden for Eng., near Savannah, Ga.

" 10—Boston plundered by British soldiers.

" 17—The Br. army evacuate Boston, and General Washington takes possession of it.

" 18—Sir Archibald Campbell, not knowing that the English had left Boston, entered the harbor with 1,700 men, all of whom were made prisoners of war by Washington.

" 18—Congress resolved to call in and burn all the Continental money issued prior to this date, and then issue $10,000,000 of new money.

May 3—Sir Peter Parker, with a Br. squadron of 20 sail, arrived at Cape Fear, with Lord Cornwallis on board.

" 5—Congress declared the authority of Great Britain abolished in the thirteen colonies.

" 25—Congress resolved to engage the Indians against the British.

June 8—The Americans made an unsuccessful attempt to capture some of the British forces at Trois Riveres, in Canada, but burnt St. Ann's on the St. Lawrence river.

" 11—Congress appoint Thos. Jefferson, Jno. Adams, Benj. Franklin and Robt. R. Livingston a committee to prepare a Declaration of Independence.

" 15—The British, under Sir H. Clinton, attacked Sullivan's Island, in Charleston harbor, and

" 28—They bombarded Fort Moultry, commanded by Col. Moultry, but were driven off.

July 4—Declaration of Independence of the United States declared and published at Philadelphia.

July 12—Lord Howe arrived from England with a fleet and 30,000 troops, principally Hessians.

" 12—The Algerines take 94 American prisoners from American ships.

Aug. 22—Br. troops to the number of 24,000, under Sir Wm. Howe, land on Long Island, N. Y.

" 27—Battle of Flatbush, on Long Island, near Brooklyn, when the Americans were surprised by the British and Hessians, and defeated with a loss of 500 killed and 1,100 taken prisoners.

Sept. 15—The English take possession of New York.

Oct. 28—Battle of White Plains, 25 miles from New York.

Nov. 1—Henry Laurens, of South Carolina, chosen President of the Continental Congress.

" 16—Fort Washington, on New York Island, taken by the British, but with a loss of nearly 1,000 men.

Dec. 6—The British take Rhode Island.

" 25—Washington took 1,000 Hessians near Trenton, N. J.

Dec. 26—Battle of Trenton N. J.

In the latter part of this year, Congress appointed Benj. Franklin, Silas Deane, and Thomas Jefferson Commissioners to France, to procure her aid.

1777.

Jan. 4—Battle of Princeton, N. J. Loss about 400 on each side, but Am. Gen. Mercer was killed.

Feb. 6—England granted Letters of Marque and Reprisal against American ships.

April 26—Danbury, Conn., burned by the British under General Tryon.

In the spring of this year Lafayette arrived in America from France, to aid us in our war with England.

April— —John Morton, of Pennsylvania, and

May 27—Button Gwinnet, of Georgia, signers of the Declaration of Independence, died.

May 24—Col. Meigs attacked the British shipping at Sag Harbor, N. Y., and destroyed 12 of their vessels.

June 22—The British evacuate New Brunswick, N. J.

July 7—After a fight, the U. S. frigate Hancock was captured by three British ships.

" 7—The Americans under Col. Livingston, were defeated by the Br. forces in a battle at Fort Ann, N. Y.

" 31—The Marquis Lafayette, by a vote of Congress, was made a Major General at the age of 21.

Aug. 3—Fort Schuyler, at the head of the Mohawk river, invested by the Br. Gen. Ganesvoort, however, held it.

" 6—Gen. Herkimer was ambushed by the British and Indians at Oriskany, and was defeated with a loss of 400 men.

" 16—Battle of Bennington, Vt. Americans, under Col. Stark, victorious.

" 19—Nichols Herkimer, a brave officer who was wounded at the battle of Oriskany, died.

Aug. 22—The siege of Fort Stanwix (on the Mohawk river) was raised by the British under St. Leger, who retreated with loss of artillery, tents and stores.

Sept. 11—Battle of Brandywine, Del. Americans, under Gen. Sullivan, defeated.

" 18—The Continental Congress, now in session at Philadelphia, adjourned to Lancaster on account of the approach of the British.

" 19—Battle of Stillwater, N. Y. Both parties claim the victory. Am., under Gen. Gates; Br., Gen. Burgoyne.

" 26—The English took possession of Philadelphia without opposition.

" 28—21?—Gen. Wayne, with 1,500 men surprised at Paoli, 20 miles from Phila., and 300 of his men killed.

Oct. 4—Battle of Germantown, near Phladelphia. Am., under Gen. Washington, defeated by the Br. under Gen Howe.

" 7—Second battle of Stillwater; Am. victorious.

" 13—Kingston, N. Y., burnt by the British.

" 17—Gen. Burgoyne surrendered his army to Gen. Gates, at Saratoga.

" 22—Battle of Red Bank, N. J. The Hessians, under Count Donop, defeated with a loss of 500 killed.

Nov. 15—Articles of Confederation adopted by the Continental Congress, which was the only Constitution during the war.

Dec. 11—Washington and his army go into winter quarters at Valley Forge, 20 miles from Philadelphia.

" 21—At this time great numbers of Am. officers and men were prisoners of war in New York, where they were confined in loathsome jails and sugar houses, and many of them starved to death.

1778.

Mar. 4—The American frigate Alfred, 20 guns, captured by the British ships Ariadne and Ceres.

" 11—Bills passed the English Parliament, in which everything the Colonies had asked was granted, and Commissioners were sent to America to offer terms of peace; but Congress now rejected them all. Soon after this, France acknowledged the Independence of the United States, and entered into a treaty of alliance and commerce with them, which Congress ratified.

" 21—The American ministers, Franklin, Deane and Lee publicly received at the French Court.

April 18—A French fleet, commanded by Count D'Estiang, sent to the United States to aid them against the English.

June 12—Philip Livingston, of N. Y., a signer of the Dec. of Independence, died.

" 18—The English evacuated Philadelphia.

June 28—Battle of Monmouth, N. J. Washington commanding the American, and Lord Cornwallis the British forces. Americans victorious.

July 4-5—Nearly 400 American troops, and the greater part of the inhabitants of the Valley of Wyoming, were msssacred by the Tories and Indians—known to this day as the "Wyoming Massacre."

Sept. 28—A regt. of American cavalry at Tappan, N. Y., surprised by the English, who rushed upon them with the bayonet, and killed, wounded or captured 67 of them.

Dec. 29—Savannah, Geo., taken by the English—100 Americans killed, and 453 taken prisoners.

1779.

May 2—Verplank's Point, on the Hudson river, with a garrison of 70 men, surrendered to the British, under Gen. Clinton.

" 10—Norfolk and Portsmouth, Va., taken by the British, who burnt many of the houses and vessels.

" Stony Point, on the Hudson, abandoned by the Americans, and then taken by the English, under Gen. Clinton.

June 6—Patrick Henry, a distinguished orator and statesman, of Va., died, aged 63.

July 5-7—N. Haven, Conn., plundered, and Fairfield, E. Haven and Norwalk, burnt by the British.

" 15—Gen. Wayne captured Stony Point from the English, who lost 600 men ; the Americans 100.

" 19—Battle of Paulus Hook, N. J.; when the Americans, under Gen. Lee, captured the English troops at that place.

Aug. 22—Gen. Williamson invaded the Indian country, and burnt 50,000 bushels of corn.

Aug. 29—"Battle of the Chemung," fought at Elmira, N. Y. Americans, under Gen. Sullivan, victorious.

Sept. 23—Great battle on the coast of Scotland, between a flotilla of American and French vessels, commanded by Paul Jones, and two Br. frigates. One Br. and one Am. ship sunk.

Oct. 9—The Americans made an assault on Savannah, Geo., to retake it from the English, but were repulsed. Count Pulaski and nearly 1,000 men were killed.

Joseph Hews, of North Carolina, Thomas Lynch, of South Carolina, and George Ross, of Pa., all signers of the Dec. of Independence, died this year.

1780.

May 6—Fort Moultry, at Charleston, S. C., surrendered to the English, who bombarded the city at the same time.

" 12—Charleston also surrendered. Gen. Lincoln and the troops under his command become prisoners of war, to the number of 2,500, with 400 cannon.

June 13—Maj. Gen. Gates ordered by Congress to take command of the Southern department.

" 23—Battle of Springfield, N. J. The British burnt the town.

July 10—A French fleet, with Count Rochambeau and 6,000 French soldiers on board, arrived at Rhode Island, for the purpose of assisting the Americans against England.

Aug. 6—Battle at Hanging Rock; 600 Americans, under Sumpter, almost entirely destroyed.

" 16—Battle at Sanders' Creek, near Camden, S. C. Lord Cornwallis commanding the English, and General Gates the Americans, who were defeated, and Baron DeKalb was mortally wounded.

Sept. —The traitor Benedict Arnold agrees to surrender West Point, N. Y., to the English; Major Andre, the British officer who negotiated with Arnold, was soon after captured and hung, and the plot failed.

John Hart, of N. J., a signer of the Declaration of Independence, died this year.

" 21—Major Andre, the British spy, landed in the night from the British ship Vulture, and proceeded to West Point to confer with Arnold for the surrender of that post.

" 23—Major Andre taken at Tarrytown, and hung Oct. 2d.

Oct. 7—Battle of King's Mountain, S. C. 300 British killed and wounded, 800 prisoners, and 1,500 stand of arms taken.

" 25—Gen. Marion, of S. C., attacked 200 British and Tories, under Col. Tyne, killed and took one-half of them.

1781.

Jan. 17—Battle of Cowpens, S. C.; Col. Morgan commanding the American, and Col. Tarleton the English forces. Americans victorious.

Feb. 23—Geo. Taylor, of Pa., and Feb. 28th, Richard Stockton, of N. J., signers of the Declaration of Independence, died.

March 15—Battle at Guilford Court House, N. C.; Gen. Green commanding the American, and Lord Cornwallis the English forces; the latter victorious. Loss of both about equal.

April 25—Battle of Camden, S. C.; Gen. Green commanding the American, and Lord Rawdon the English forces. The latter victorious.

May 21—The British fort Dreadnought succumbed to the Americans under General Lee.

" 28—The U. S. frigate Alliance, 32 guns, Capt. Barry, captured the British sloops Atalanta, 16 guns and Trespasser, 14 guns.

June 5—Fort Cornwallis, at Augusta, Geo. surrendered to the Americans, with 300 men.

" 20—Lord Cornwallis evacuated Richmond, Va., and

July 4—Williamsburgh, Va.

Sept. 6—Fort Griswold taken by the English, under the traitor Arnold, and the garrison put to the sword. Col. Ledyard, who commanded the fort, was run through with his own sword, after he had surrendered. The same day, New London, Conn., was burnt by the same infamous wretch.

" 8—Battle of Eutaw Springs, S. C.; General Green commanding the American, and Col. Stewart the English forces.

Oct. 19—Battle of Yorktown, Va., when after several days' fighting, Lord Cornwallis with 7000 troops surrendered to Gen. Washington.

" 25—Colonel Willett, of N. Y., defeated 600 English troops, under Major Ross.

Dec. 31—Henry Laurens, U. S. Minister to France, was liberated from prison, in London, and exchanged for the British Gen. Burgoyne.

1782.

March 4—Resolutions passed the English House of Commons in favor of peace between England and her American colonies, in consequence of which very few military operations were carried on this year.

April 19—The independence of the United States acknowledged by Holland.

July 11—The British evacuate Savannah, Geo., and Gen. Wayne took possession of it, who defeated a body of British troops near that city about the same time.

Sept. 30—Yorktown, Va., invested by the American and French armies, under Washington and Rochambeau.

Dec. 16—The British burnt Fort Arbuthnot, and a new fort on Sullivan's Island, S. C.

" 20—The U. S. frigate Charleston, of 40 guns, was (after 18 hours' chase), captured by the British ships Quebec and Diomede. The first American 74-gun ship was built this year at Portsmouth, N. H.

1783.

Jan. 20—Cessation of hostilities agreed upon between England and the United States.

Feb. 5—Independence of the U. States acknowledged by Sweden.

" 25—Independence of the United States acknowledged by Denmark.

March 24—Independence of the United States acknowledged by Spain.

July —Independence of the United States acknowledged by Russia.

April 19—Cessation of hostilities between England and the United States proclaimed just eight years from the day on which the Revolutionary war commenced. Estimated loss of men in this war, 70,000.

June 18—Washington announces to the Governors of the thirteen Colonies that he would soon resign the command of the army.

July 21—Three hundred of the Revolutionary soldiers, with fixed bayonets, surrounded the building in which Congress was assembled, and demanded relief from their sufferings.

Sept. 3—Treaty of peace between England and the United States signed, and the independence of the United States acknowledged by the former.

Oct. 18—Proclamation for disbanding the U. S. army issued.

Nov. 25—New York evacuated by the English troops, and in Dec. they evacuated Charleston, S. C.

Dec. 4—Washington took leave of the officers of the American army in New York.

" 24—Washington resigns his office as commander-in-chief of the army, and delivered up his commission to Congress at Annapolis, and while it was in session, Cæsar Rodney, of Delaware, one of the signers of the Declaration of Independence, died this year.

1784.

Feb. —First voyage from New York to China.

Oct. 22—Treaty between the United States and the six nations (of Indians) concluded at Fort Stanwix, now Rome, N. Y.

1785.

July 9—Treaty between the United States and Prussia.

" 13—Stephen Hopkins, of Rhode Island, a signer of the Declaration of Independence, died.

Nov. 28—William Whipple, of New Hampshire, a signer of the Declaration of Independence, died.

1786.

June 19—Gen Nathaniel Green, a distinguished officer of the Revolutionary war, died, aged 46. He was in the battles of Trenton, Princeton, Germantown, Monmouth, and Eutaw Springs, which closed the war at the South.

This year was distinguished by a rebellion which broke out in the State of Mass., also in New Hampshire, called Shay's rebellion, on account of the heavy taxes which those States imposed on the people, to sustain their credit.

1787.

Jan. 1—Arthur Middleton, of South Carolina, a signer of the Declaration of Independence, died.

In July a large extent of territory north of the Ohio river was formed into the Northwestern Territory.

Sept. 17—The Constitution of the United States agreed upon in convention at Philadelphia.
Oct. 5—Thomas Stone, of Maryland, one of the signers of the Declaration of Independence, died.

1788.

Previous to, and during this year, eleven of the States adopted the United States Constitution.

1789.

Jan. 4—Thomas Nelson, of Virginia, a signer of the Declaration of Independence, died.
Feb. 13—Ethan Allen, one of the most distinguished Revolutionary heroes, died.
April 30—Washington inaugurated the first President of the United States, and the government went into operation under the Constitution.
July 4—Congress passed the first act imposing duties on imported goods.
" 27—The Department and Secretary of "Foreign Affairs," created by act of Congress, but changed to Department and Secretary of State, in the following Sept.
Aug. 7—The Department and Secretary of War created by act of Congress.
" 23—Silas Deane, U. S. Minister to France in 1776, died in England in extreme poverty
Sept. 2—The Department and Secretary of the Treasury created by act of Congress.
Sept. 22—The Post-Office Department temporarily established, and the office of Postmaster General created by a law of Congress.
" 24—The act for the establishment of the Judicial system of the U. S. passed. By this act the U. S. Supreme Court, the Circuit and District Courts were created. Also the offices of the U. S. district attorneys and marshals.
In this month, Congress passed (two-thirds of both houses concurring) a resolution, proposing ten amendments to the Constitution, which were adopted by three-fourths of the States. These are the ten first amendments to that instrument.

1790.

March 1—Congress passed an act providing for taking the first Census this year.
" 24—First naturalization law passed.
April 15—First patent-right law passed.
" 30—Treason and piracy were defined by act of Congress, and death by hanging was made the penalty in both cases.

May 29—U. S. Constitution adopted by Rhode Island.
" 31—First act passed for securing copy-rights for the benefit of authors.
Gen. Israel Putnam, one of the most intrepid officers of the Revolution, died this month.
July 16—Seat of government, which was at this time at New York, was by act of Congress removed to Philadelphia, where it was to remain till A. D. 1800, when it was to be permanently fixed at Washington.
During this year, Virginia and Maryland ceded the District of Columbia to the United States as a location for the seat of government.
Benjamin Franklin, of Pa., William Hooper, of N. C., and Francis Hopkinson, of N. J., all signers of the Declaration of Independence, died this year.
Tennessee was formed into a Territorial government this year.

1791.

Feb. 25—First United States Bank chartered by Congress, with a capital not to exceed $10,000,000; charter to continue for twenty years.
March 4—Vermont admitted into the Union as a State, making the fourteenth State.
Nov. 4—General St. Clair attacked in camp by Indians, eighty miles north of Cincinnatti, O., and lost 600 out of 2,000 men. (See further.)
Dec. 20—The First United States Bank commenced business in Philadelphia.
This year, by act of Congress, a tax was laid on distilled spirits. This was the first attempt to raise revenue by internal taxes.
Benj. Harrison, of Va., one of the signers of the Declaration of Independence, died this year.
During this and the preceding year, the country was involved in a bloody war with the Indians north of the Ohio river

1792.

Feb. 16—Bounty to fishing vessels, first act for, passed.
" 20—An act permanently to establish post-offices and post-roads in the United States.
April 2—The act for establishing the U. S. Mint at Philadelphia, passed, directing what pieces of coin should be made.
" 14—First act apportioning the Representatives in Congress among the several States passed; this was based on the first census, taken in 1790
May 8—First act of Congress, providing for a uniform militia system throughout the United States.

June 1—Kentucky admitted into the Union. She was the second admission, making the fifteenth State.

Dec. 8—Henry Laurens, of South Carolina, first President of the Continental Congress, died.

In the autumn of this year, the second Presidential election occurred, when Washington was unanimously re-elected President, and John Adams Vice President.

1793.

Early in this year, Mr. Genet, Minister of the French Republic to the United States, arrived. But his conduct was so mischievous that President Washington requested the French government to recall him, which was done.

Feb. 12—First fugitive slave law passed.

" 18—The President's salary fixed by act of Congress at $25,000 per year, where it has remained ever since.

March 9—It was enacted by Congress that every male citizen, between the ages of 18 and 45, should be enrolled in the militia.

July 23—Roger Sherman, of Conn., one of the signers of the Declaration of Independence, died.

Oct. 8—John Hancock, of Mass., the first man who signed the Declaration of Independence, died.

Dec. 31—Thomas Jefferson resigned his office of Secretary of State.

1794.

March 22—The law passed prohibiting the slave trade, which made it a crime to bring slaves into or take them out of the country.

" 26—Congress laid an embargo on all vessels in United States ports for 30 days, which was extended to 60 days.

This year the eleventh amendment of the Constitution was recommended by resolution of Congress, which was adopted by the States.

June 4—The President was authorized by Congress to lay embargoes on all vessels in any of the ports of the United States, and to revoke the same whenever he deemed it necessary for the interests of the country.

" 19—Richard H. Lee, of Va.; Sept. — Abraham Clark, of N. H.; and Nov. 15, John Witherspoon, of N. J., three signers of the Declaration of Independence, died.

Aug. 19—Battle of Maumee in Ohio when Gen. Wayne, with a force of 3,000 men, met and routed the Indians, and laid their country waste.

In the autumnof this year, the whisky rebellion broke out in Pa. This was a resistance principally by the opponents of the administration to the law of Congress imposing a tax on the manufacture of whisky.

Nov. 28—Baron Steuben died at Steubenville, N. Y., aged 61.

1795.

Jan. 23—Gen. Sullivan, a gallant and heroic officer of the Revolution, died.

Jan. 29—Congress passed an act establishing a uniform rule of naturalization, which was more stringent than a former law on the same subject.

May 19—Josiah Bartlett, of N. H., one of the signers of the Declaration of Independence, died.

Nov. 28—A peace was concluded with Algiers, with whom a short naval war had been carried on by the United States this year.

1796.

Jan. 1—By act of Congress, Tennessee was admitted as a State, making the 18th State.

" 5—Samuel Huntington, of Conn., a signer of the Declaration of Independence, died.

June —Tennessee admitted as a State.

Sept. —Washington issued his farewell address to the people of the U. S., having determined to retire from public life at the end of his second Presidential term of office.

In the autumn of this year, the third Presidential election took place, which resulted in the choice of John Adams.

Dec. 14—Gen Wayne, commander-in-chief of the United States forces, died at Presque Isle, aged 51.

1797.

March 4—John Adams inaugurated the second President.

June 14—Congress enacted that no citizen of the United States should engage in privateering against any nation in amity with us.

Francis L. Lee, of Va., Carter Braxton, of Va., and Oliver Walcot, of Conn., all signers of the Declaration of Independence, died this year.

During this year the French Republic became exasperated at the United States because they refused to act with France against England, these two powers being then at war. France carried her spiteful feelings so far as to drive our minister, Mr. Pinckney, out of the country. She also authorized the capture and confiscation of American vessels. This state of things came near involving the two nations in a war; but fortunately it was soon afterwards settled.

1798.

April 3—The Navy Department created by act of Congress. Up to this time we had no Davy Nepartment.

" 7—Mississippi organized into a Territorial government.

April 25—An act of Congress authorized the President to order any alien to leave the country whom he had reasonable grounds to believe was here for treasonable purposes.

July 7 and 9—Congress authorize the capture of French vessels; and all treaties with France were declared void. But these difficulties were soon after settled by treaty.

" —Under an apprehension that there would be war with France, Gen. Washington was again appointed commander-in chief of the army.

During this and the ensuing year, the alien and sedition laws were passed. These laws rendered John Adams' administration very unpopular.

Lewis Morris, of N. Y., James Wilson, of Pa., and Geo. Read, of Del., all signers of the Declaration of Independence, died this year.

1799.

Feb. 9—Battle between the United States frigate Constitution, of 36 guns, Capt. Truxton, and the French frigate Insurgent, of 48 guns and 410 men. The Insurgent was captured.

By act of Congress, commercial intercourse with France was prohibited. Our ships were not allowed to enter French ports.

Dec. 19—Washington died in the 68th year of his age.

William Paca, of Maryland, one of the signers of the Declaration of Independence, died this year.

1800.

Jan. 23—Edward Rutledge, of S. C., one of the signers of the Declaration of Independence, died.

Feb. 1—Battle between the United States frigate Constitution, Capt. Truxton, and the French frigate La Vengeance. La Vengeance whipped.

April 4—An act establishing a uniform system of bankruptcy throughout the United States, passed by Congress.

May 7.—Congress pass an act to organize the Territory of Indiana.

In the summer of this year the seat of government was removed to Washington, and the Mississippi Territory was organized into a Territorial government.

Sept. 30—A treaty was concluded between the United States and France, now in the hands of Napoleon Bonaparte, and the long-standing difficulties between the two countries were amicably settled.

In the autumn of this year, the fourth Presidential election occurred, resulting in the choice of Thomas Jefferson.

1801.

March 4—Thomas Jefferson inaugurated the fourth President of the United States.

June 10—The Bashaw of Tripoli, one of the petty princes of the Barbary States in the north of Africa, declared war against the United States.

" 14—Benedict Arnold, the traitor, died in London.

1802.

Jan. 14—An act apportioning the Representatives in Congress among the States, based on the census of 1800, by which a member was allowed for every 33,000 population.

Ohio was admitted into the Union this year, making the 17th State.

April 14—Congress pass a new naturalization law, repealing all former laws on this subject.

May 3—The city of Washington incorporated by act of Congress.

In October, the Spanish Governor of Louisiana (which belonged to Spain at this time), closed the port of New Orleans against the United States.

1803.

Oct. 31—The United States frigate Philadelphia, Capt. Bainbridge, ran on a rock in the harbor of Tripoli, when the Tripolitans captured her. The Philadelphia was one of a number of U. S. ships sent into the Mediterranean sea to punish the Tripolitans for their piratical depredations upon our commerce.

Dec. 20—The United States took possession of Louisiana, which they had bought this year of France, for $15,000,000.

Matthew Thornton, of N. Y., Samuel Adams, of Mass., and Francis Lewis, of N. Y., all signers of the Dec. of Independence, died this year.

1804.

Feb. 2—George Walton of Georgia; and May 11, Robert Treat Paine, of Mass., signers of the Dec. of Independence died.

" 3—Lieut. Decatur of the U. S. navy, with a small schooner, in the night, ran into the harbor of Tripoli, and burnt the U. S. frigate Philadelphia, which had been captured by the Tripolitans.

July 12—Gen. Alexander Hamilton died of a wound received in a duel with Aaron Burr, the Vice-President of the U. S.

Aug. 3—Com. Preble, commanding the American squadron in the Mediterranean sea, had a severe action with several Tripolitan gun-boats, and captured a number of them; and then, in this, and the following months, he bombarded Tripoli several times.

Sept. 12—The American squadron in the Mediterranean sea captured, near Tripoli, two vessels loaded with wheat, for the city.

Nov. 18—Gen. Philip Schuyler died at Albany, N. Y.

In the fall of this year, the fifth Presidential election took place, at which Jefferson was re-elected for President, and George Clinton, of New York, Vice-President.

1805.

June 3—A treaty of peace was made with Tripoli, and the American prisoners liberated.

This year Michigan, which was a part of the great north-western territory, became distinct, Congress having established a Territorial government for it.

June 11—Mich. Territory organized into a Territorial government.

Sept. 27—William Moultry, a distinguished officer of the Revolution, who so bravely defended Sullivan's Island, in 1776, died.

1806.

April 10—Gen. Gates, a very distinguished General in the Revolutionary war, died in New York.

May 8—Robert Morris, of Pa.; June 8, George Wythe, of Va.; July 11, James Smith, of Pa., all signers of the Dec. of Independence, died.

Oct. 25—Henry Knox, a major-general in the Revolutionary war, and Secretary of War under Washington, died.

1807.

Feb. 10—The United States coast survey ordered by act of Congress.

Mar. 2—Congress enacted a law prohibiting the slave trade from Africa or any other country, after 1808.

June 22—The British ship Leopard attacked the American frigate Chesapeake, and took four men out of her, claiming them as British subjects: this, and other similar acts, led to the war of 1812 with England.

July 2—President Jefferson ordered all British ships of war, in any of the American waters, to leave.

During this year, Col. Aaron Burr was tried for treason, but the proof was insufficient to convict him.

Aug. 25—Com. Preble of the United States navy, who subdued Tripoli, died.

Nov. 26—Oliver Ellsworth, Chief Justice of the United States, died.

Dec. 17—The Milan decrees issued by Napoleon Bonaparte, denationalizing all vessels that submitted to the British order in council; this led to the capture of American vessels by French cruisers, and came near causing a war between the United States and France.

Dec. 22—Congress laid an embargo on all the shipping of the United States. This was done in retaliation towards England and France for their unfriendly acts toward us. But this annihilated all our foreign commerce; became unpopular, and was repealed in 1809.

1808.

Jan. 1—The act of Congress, passed in 1804, abolishing the slave trade, went into effect this day.

1809.

Feb. 3—Illinois organized into a Territorial government.
Mar. 1—Congress repealed the embargo it laid on all American vessels, Dec. 22, 1807.
" 4—James Madison inaugurated, the fourth President.
" 9—Thomas Haywood, of South Carolina, one of the signers of the Dec. of Independence, died. And on the 26th of Oct., John Penn, another of them, died.
Aug. 9—President Jefferson, on receipt of information that the late treaty with England was not ratified, suspended all intercourse with that country

1810.

Mar. 23—Napoleon Bonaparte, who, at this time, was at the head of the French government, issued a decree by which all American vessels and cargoes arriving in any French ports, were ordered to be seized and condemned; but in the following Nov., this and all other hostile decrees were revoked.

1811.

Feb. 26—Naval hospitals established by act of Congress.
May 16—Naval action between the U. States ship President and the English ship Little Bett, which was captured.
June 1—Gen. W. Eaton died, distinguished for his heroic conduct in the expedition against Tripoli.
June 19—Samuel Chase, a Judge of the Supreme Court, died; he was also one of the signers of the Dec. of Independence.
Aug. 2—Williams, of Conn., another of the signers, died.
Nov. 7—The frontier Indians at this time were very hostile to the United States; and on this day they attacked our troops commanded by Gen. Harrison, at Tippecanoe; a bloody battle ensued, and the Indians were defeated.
Dec. 2—The third apportionment of Representatives among the several States, based on the census of 1810, by which one Representative was allowed for every 35,000 people.

1812.

Mar. 4—The charter of the United States Bank expired by its own limitation.

April 4—Congress laid an embargo on all vessels in the ports of the United States. This was done in anticipation of a war with England.

" 8—Louisiana admitted into the Union, making the 18th State.

" 20—George Clinton, Vice-President of the U. States, died.

" 25—The General Land Office established at Washington.

" 29—The U. S. frigate Essex, Capt. Porter, captured two English ships in the Pacific ocean.

June 4—Missouri organized into a Territorial government.

" 18—The President, in conformity with an act of Congress passed a few days before, declared war with England.

July 12—Gen. Hull, with 2,000 troops, invades Canada.

Aug. 8—Gen. Hull, with his troops, evacuates Canada, and crosses over to Detroit.

" 9—Major VanHorn met a few British and Indians under the famous chief Tecumseh, and routed them with considerable loss.

" 15—The British Gen. Brock summoned the city of Detroit to surrender, which summons Gen. Hull, moved with cowardice or treason, basely obeyed.

" 15—Battle of Fort Chicago; which, after a bloody contest, surrendered to the Indians. The men and women were all murdered after the surrender.

" 19—The American frigate Constitution, of 44 guns, Capt. Hull, engaged the English frigate Guerrier, and in half an hour the Guerrier lost half her men and was a wreck.

Oct. 13—Queenstown, Upper Canada, captured by the U. S. troops under Gen. Solomon VanRenssalaer; but the English were reinforced and recaptured it. They were commanded by Gen. Brock, who was killed in this battle.

" 18—The U. S. sloop of war Wasp, Capt. Jones, captured the British brig Frolic, on the coast of North Carolina, after a bloody fight of three-fourths of an hour; but both were recaptured the same day by an English 74-gun ship.

" 25—The frigate United States, Capt. Decatur, engaged with the English frigate Macedonian, which struck her colors after an action of two hours. This occurred west of the Canary Islands.

Nov. 22—The British frigate Southampton captured the U. S. brig Vixen, after a severe action.

Dec. 29—The U. S. frigate Constitution, Com. Bainbridge, captured the British frigate Java, and burned her off the coast of Brazil.

During this year, our men-of-war and privateers captured nearly 300 English vessels—a year of blood and devastation! Horrid war!

1813.

Jan. 17—The English frigate Narcissus captured the U. S. brig Vixen, 12 guns.
" 18—A detachment of U. S. troops, under Cols. Lewis and Allen, attacked Frenchtown, (now Monroe,) in Mich., and routed the English troops there.
" 22—The British troops and Indians, under Gen. Proctor, attacked the Americans in the same place, who surrendered upon conditions, which were basely violated by the English.
" 23—Geo. Clymer, of Pa., one of the signers of the Declaration of Independence, died.
Feb. 8—The U. S. Govt. borrowed $16,000,000 to carry on the war.
" 24—Naval battle off the coast of Demarara, between the U. S. sloop of war Hornet, Capt. Lawrence, and the British brig Peacock, which was sunk in fifteen minutes.
Mar. 14—The Delaware river blockaded by several English ships.
April 19—Benj. Rush, of Pa., a celebrated physician and statesman, and one of the signers of the Dec. of Independence, died.
" 27—The Americans, under Gen. Pike, capture York, (now Toronto,) Canada, with a large quantity of public property.
May 1—The British Gen. Proctor attacked Fort Meigs, Ohio, commanded by Gen. Harrison.
" 5—Gen. Celay's troops attacked the besiegers and dispersed them; but,
" 8—while in pursuit, were themselves captured.
" 20—The U. S. frigate Congress, Capt. Smith, captured the English brig Jean; and on the 22d, the brig Diana, of 10 guns.
" 27—The English troops, under Sir George Prevost, attack Sacket's Harbor, N. Y., but were repulsed; and, on the same day, the Americans took Fort George on the Niagara river.
June 1—The U. S. frigate Chesapeake, Capt. Lawrence, was captured by the British frigate Shannon, after a terrible and bloody battle; Capt. Lawrence, and almost every officer on board, was killed.
" 20—The English made an attack on Oswego, N. Y., but were repulsed.
" 25—The British Admiral, Cockburn, ordered the village of Hampton, Va., to be pillaged.
July 31—Plattsburgh, N. Y., taken by the British.
" 31—Com. Chauncey took York, Upper Canada, and carried off the stores of the English army.
Aug. 2—The English attack our fort at Sandusky, Ohio, but were bravely repulsed by the Americans, under Major Crogan.
" 2—Congress laid a direct tax of $3,000,000, and apportioned it among the several States. This was done to support the war with England at this time.
" 12—Samuel Osgood, for a time Postmaster Gen., died, aged 65.

Aug. 13—The Br. ship Alert attacked the U. S. frigate Essex, but struck her colors in eight minutes.

" 14—The U. S. brig Argus was captured, after a severe battle with the British brig Pelican.

" 30—A party of Creek Indians capture Fort Mims, in Ala., and massacre nearly 300 men, women and children.

Sept. 5—The Br. ship Boxer, after a fight of forty minutes, surrendered to the American brig Enterprise, on the coast of Maine.

" 10—Battle on Lake Erie between the nine U. S. vessels commanded by Com. Perry, and a squadron of six English, commanded by Com. Barclay, all of which surrendered to Com. Perry.

" 27—Gen. Harrison took Malden, in Upper Canada, evacuated by the English, under Gen. Proctor.

Oct. 5—Battle of the Thames, (Upper Canada) eighty miles from Detroit. Here the great Indian chief Tecumseh, who was confederate with the English, was slain. Gen. Harrison commanded the U. States troops, and Gen Proctor the Br., who were nearly all killed or taken prisoners.

" 25—Battle between the U. S. frigate Congress, Capt. Smith, and the British ship Rose, which was destroyed.

Nov. 3—Col. Coffee attacked 200 of the Creek Indians, and killed every one of them in retaliation for what they had done at Fort Mims. A number of battles with the Creeks followed this, during this and the next year, and in Jan. 1814, in which nearly all their warriors were killed, and thus ended the Creek war.

" 11—Battle of Williamsburgh, Canada. American loss 300; English less than 200.

Dec. 13—Congress laid an embargo on all ships and vessels in all the ports of the United States. This was to cut off trade with England.

" 19—Fort Niagara captured by the British, with 250 men and 25 cannon; and, on the same day, Lewistown and Tuscarora villages, N. Y., were burnt by the Indians.

" 30—Buffalo and Black Rock, burnt by the British.

1814.

Mar. 24—Congress authorized the President to borrow $25,000,000, to cary on the war with England.

" 28—The U. S. frigate Essex, Capt, Porter, was captured in the harbor of Valparaiso by two British men-of-war.

April 24—The British took Washington, and burnt the public buildings.

" 29—Battle between the U. S. sloop-of-war Peacock, and the English man-of-war Empervier, which was captured with $118,000 in money.

May 6—The English, under Gen. Drummond, attacked Oswego, N. Y.; the Americans had to retreat.
June 9—The U. S. brig Rattlesnake, Lieut. Renshaw, captured the British ship John.
" 28—The sloop-of-war Wasp, Capt. Blakeley, captured the British sloop Reindeer, in nineteen minutes.
July 3—The Americans take Fort Erie from the English.
" 4—Battle of Chippewa, in Canada. U. S. troops, under Gen. Scott, victorious.
" 24—Battle of Bridgewater, (or Lundy's Lane) near Niagara Falls. Gen. Scott, commanding U. S. forces was victorious.
Aug. 3—The British crossed Niagara river to attack Buffalo, but were repulsed by 250 riflemen, under Morgan.
" 8—First meeting of U. S. and English commissioners at Ghent, (in Belgium) to treat for peace, and a treaty was concluded and signed on the 24 Dec. following.
" 9—10—11—Stonington, Conn., bombarded by the British.
" 15—The British attack Fort Erie, but were severely repulsed by Gen. Gaines, who commanded the U. S. troops, with a loss of nearly 1,000 men.
" 25—Washington evacuated by the British troops under command of Gen. Ross and Admiral Cockburn.
" 30—Alexandria, Va., capitulated to the British army, and delivered up the public property and shipping to save the city from being burnt.
Sept. 1—The U. S. sloop-of-war Wasp, Capt. Blakeley, fell in with ten British vessels, convoyed by a 74-gun ship—Capt. B. sunk one and burnt another.
" 6—11—Battle of Plattsburgh, or Lake Champlain—for it was on both land and water—Com. McDonough commanding the American fleet, and Com. Downie the English, whose loss was nearly 2,500 men.
" 12—13—14—Battles three days in succession, near Baltimore, one of which is called the battle of Baltimore, and the other the battle of Fort McHenry—Gen. Ross, the English commander, was killed the first day.
Nov. 7—Pensacola (Fla.) taken by Gen. Jackson.
" 23—Elbridge Gerry, of Mass., once Vice President, died.
In Dec., of this year, the celebrated Hartford convention met.

1815.

Jan. 8—Battle of New Orleans—Gen. Jackson commanding the U. States troops, 6,000 in number; Gen. Packenham the English, 12,000 in number. Packenham and 700 of his officers and men were slain, and 1,000 wounded; and, astonishing to say, only seven Americans were killed and six wounded. This closed the second war with England on the land; yet there were a number of naval battles after this, because the news of peace was not heard in time to prevent them.

Jan. 15—The U. S. frigate President, Com. Decatur, was captured by four English ships, after a chase of 18 hours.

Feb. 11—Fort Boyer, at Mobile, with a garrison of 375 men, surrendered to 5,000 English troops, under Lambert, with a fleet of thirteen ships.

" 18—Treaty of peace concluded at Ghent, Dec. 24, 1814, ratified by the U. S. Senate.

" 24—The Secretary of the Treasury was authorized by Congress to issue $25,000,000 in Treasury notes.

" 28—Battle between the U. S. frigate Constitution, Capt. Stewart, and the English frigate Cyane, and sloop Levant, and both of them were captured by the Constitution, off the island of Maderia.

Mar. 3—Congress declares war against Algiers, in Africa; and during this month the U. S. frigate Hornet captured the British brig Penguin, off the Coast of Brazil.

May 3—James McHenry, one of the signers of the Declaration of Independence, died at Baltimore.

June 17—Commodore Decatur, in the Mediterranean sea, captured an Algerian frigate of 46 guns. A treaty was thereupon negotiated between the United States and Algiers; after which, these piratical barbarians behaved themselves.

" 30—The U. S. vessel Peacock had a fight with the British ship Nautilus, which surrendered in fifteen or twenty minutes. This took place in the straits of Sunda.

1816.

In this year the second U. S. Bank was chartered, with a capital of $35,000,000, to continue twenty years.

Indiana, (a part of the great north-western territory,) was admitted as a State this year—making the 19th State.

Nov. 5—Gouverneur Morris, an eminent statesman, died at Morrissania, near New York.

1817.

Mar. 3—By a law passed this day, all American citizens were enjoined to observe our neutrality laws, and forbidden from rendering any aid to any nation which was at war with any other nation at peace with us.

" 4—James Monroe, the fifth President, inaugurated.

June 24—Thomas McKean, of Del., one of the signers of the Declaration of Independence, died.

December—The Mississippi Territory was divided, and the western part admitted as a State, making the twentieth; and the eastern part organized into a Territorial government, by the name of the Territory of Alabama.

In the latter part of this year, the Creek and Seminole Indians committed depredations in Georgia and Alabama, when Generals Gaines and Jackson were sent to subdue them.

1818.

May 24—Gen. Jackson took Pensacola, Fla., from the Spaniards, and sent the authorities to Havana. This was done during his campaign against the Seminole and Creek Indians.

" 25—Gen. Mitchell, of the Revolutionary war, died.

Dec. 3—Illinois admitted into the Union—making the twenty-first State.

" Dec. 10—Mississippi admitted as a State, by resolution of both houses of Congress.

1819.

Mar. 2—Arkansas formed into a Territorial government.

Dec. 14—Alabama admitted into the Union—making the twenty-second State.

1820.

Feb. 15—Wm. Ellery, of Rhode Island, a signer of the Declaration of Independence, died.

March 15—Maine admitted into the Union—making the twenty-third State.

Aug. 23—Com. Perry, the hero of the battle on Lake Erie, died of yellow fever at Trinidad, West Indies, on his birth-day.

October—Florida ceded by Spain to the United States for $5,000,000.

The question of the admission of Missouri as a free or slave State greatly agitated the country this year. The famous "Missouri Compromise" settled the question.

1821.

Mar. 4—James Monroe inaugurated upon his second term of the Presidency, and D. D. Tompkins upon his second term of the Vice Presidency.

Mar. 22—Com. Stephen Decatur died at Washington.

July 1—Gen. Jackson took possession of Florida.

Aug. 4—Wm. Floyd, of New York, a signer of the Declaration of Independence, died.

Missouri was admitted this year—making the twenty-fourth State.

1822.

March 7—Congress again apportions the Representatives in Congress among the several States, based on the census of 1820. By this act the ratio of representation was fixed at one Representative to 40,000 persons.

" 30—Florida was formed into a Territorial government.

May 5—Thomas Truxton, a distinguished naval officer, both in the Revolutionary war and in our short war with France, died.

" 8—Gen. Stark, a prominent officer of the Revolutionary war, died.

Oct. 27—William Lowndes, a distinguished statesman of South Carolina, died at sea.

During this year, gangs of pirates infested the West Indies, committing depredations upon our commerce, when the United States government sent a naval force to destroy them. It captured over twenty piratical vessels.

1823.

This year Com. Porter broke up and dispersed the remainder of the piratical gangs in the West India Islands, who had withstood the onslaught which our government had made upon them last year.

1824.

March 13—A convention at which the United States and England were represented, was held for the purpose of adopting measures to suppress the slave trade.

April—United States and Russian commissioners met to settle the north-western boundaries between the two countries.

Aug. 24—Lafayette arrived from France, and made a tour through the country.

Oct. 29—Charles Pinckney, of South Carolina, an eminent orator and statesman, and one of the framers of the Constitution, died.

The tenth Presidential election took place in the fall of this year; but there was no choice by the people, and the election went to the House of Representatives, when John Q. Adams was elected.

1825.

Mar. 3—An act to establish a navy yard on the coast of Fla. passed.

" 4—John Quincy Adams, the sixth President, inaugurated.

June 11—Daniel D. Tompkins, of N. Y., an ex-Vice-President, died.

Nov. 10—Com. McDonough, who commanded the U. S. fleet at the battle of Plattsburgh, on Lake Champlain, in 1814, died at Middletown, Conn.

1826.

July 4—John Adams, aged 91, and Thomas Jefferson, both of whom had been Presidents of the United States, and both signers of the Dec. of Independence, died.

1827.

We find nothing in the history of the United States worthy of particular notice during this year. We were at peace "with all the world and the rest of mankind;" there was very little political excitement, and the country was prosperous and happy under the good administration of good President John Quincy Adams.

1828.

Feb. 11—DeWitt Clinton died, while in the office of the Governor of New York.

A new protective tariff was enacted this year, with a view to encourage American manufactures.

The eleventh Presidential election took place in the autumn of this year, and resulted in the choice of Andrew Jackson.

1829.

Jan. 29—Timothy Pickering, Secretary of State under Washington and Adams, died.

Feb. 29—The Virginia House of Delegates passed a resolution denying the right of Congress to pass the tariff.

Mar. 4—Andrew Jackson, the seventh President, inaugurated, and John C. Calhoun entered upon his second term as V. Prest.

May 19—A treaty of peace, friendship, commerce and navigation, between the U. States and Brazil, ratified at Washington.

May 17—John Jay died at Bedford, N. Y. He was one of the Presidents of the Continental Congress, minister to Spain and to England, Governor of New York, and Chief Justice of the United States.

June 4—The U. S. frigate Fulton blown up at the navy yard, Brooklyn; 26 lives lost.

Aug. 12—Mr. McLane, minister to England, and Mr. Rives, minister to France, embark in the U. S. frigate Constitution, at New York.

Nov. 26—The Hon. Bushrod Washington, one of the Judges of the U. S. Supreme Court, died.

1830.

May 7—A treaty signed at Constantinople, between the United States and Turkey, by which the United States obtained the free navigation of the Black Sea.

May 29—The office of Solicitor of the Treasury created by act of Congress.

Aug. 4—Gen. Philip Stuart, an officer of the Revolution, died at Washington.

1831.

Jan. 10—The disputed northern boundary line, between the United States and England, settled by the king of the Netherlands, to whom the matter had been referred.

April 19—Dissolution of President Jackson's cabinet.

July 4—James Monroe, the fifth President of the United States, died at New York, aged 73.

Aug. 25—An eulogy on James Monroe delivered at Boston, by John Quincy Adams.

Sept. 26—The national anti-Masonic convention, at Baltimore, nominated William Wirt for President.

Oct. 1—A free-trade convention met at Philadelphia.

" 26—A tariff convention of over 500 delegates met at New York and adopted a memorial to Congress.

Nov. 5—Gen. Philip VanCourtlandt, an officer of the Revolutionary war, died at New York, aged 82.

Dec. 14—The national Republican party assembled at Baltimore, and nominated Henry Clay for President.

1832.

Jan. 25—The Senate, by the casting vote of the President, refused to confirm the nomination of Martin VanBuren as United States minister to England.

Mar. 3—The United States Supreme Court decided that the law of Georgia, by which several missionaries to the Indians in that State were imprisoned for four years in the penitentiary, was contrary to the laws and treaties of the United States, and therefore null and void.

April 1—A war broke out between the United States and the Winnebago Indians, called the Black Hawk war.

" 2—Treaty concluded with the Creek Indians, by which they sell all their lands east of the Mississippi river to the United States.

May 5—The treaty respecting commerce, navigation, and the boundary line between the United States and Mexico, ratified at Washington.

" 21—Com. Rogers died on board his ship off Buenos Ayres.

" 22—Martin Van Buren nominated by the Democrats, at Baltimore, for Vice President of the United States.

" 27—An act apportioning the Representatives in Congress, based on the fifth census, in which the ratio between Representatives and population was fixed at one Representative to 47,-700 people.

June 1—Gen. Thomas Sumpter, an officer in the Revolutionary war, died in South Carolina.

July 9—The office of Commissioner of Indian Affairs created by act of Congress.

" 10—An act to establish naval hospitals at Charlestown, Mass., Brooklyn, N. Y., and Pensacola, Fla., passed.

" " —President Jackson vetoed the bill re-chartering the United States Bank.

Aug. 27—Black Hawk, the celebrated Indian chief and warrior, captured.

Nov. 12—The anti-tariff convention meet at Milledgeville, Geo.

" 14—Charles Carroll, of Carrollton, Md., died. He was the last surviving signer of the Declaration of Independence.

" 19—A convention of delegates in South Carolina meet at Columbia, and pass an ordinance declaring the laws of Congress, in relation to the tariff, unconstitutional and void.

Dec. 10—President Jackson issues his proclamation, denouncing the proceedings of the South Carolina convention, and warning the people of that State of the consequences of following its dictates.

" 18—Treaty of commerce and navigation concluded between the United States and Russia, at St. Petersburgh.

" 20—Gov. Hayne, of South Carolina, issues a proclamation in answer to that of President Jackson.

" 28—John C. Calhoun, the Vice President, resigns his office.

The twelfth Presidential election occurred this fall, when Andrew Jackson was re-elected.

1833.

Mar. 1—The new tariff bill passed, called the compromise act.

" 4—Andrew Jackson inaugurated upon his second term.

" 10—Com. Samuel Tucker, of Maine, died.

" 31—The Treasury Department building burnt at Washington.

June 1—Oliver Wolcott, Secretary of the Treasury under Washington, died.

July 27—Com. Bainbridge died, aged 60.

Sept. 23—Wm. J. Duane, Secretary of the Treasury, was removed from his office by President Jackson, because he declined to remove the United States deposits from the U. S. Bank; and Roger B. Taney, of Md., was appointed in his place, who removed them on the first of October.

1834.

Mar. 28—The United States Senate passed a vote of censure of President Jackson, for removing the government deposits from the United States Bank.

Sept. 15—Wm. H. Crawford, of Georgia, died. He was an eminent statesman, and a candidate for the Presidency in 1824.

1835.

Jan. 1—Hugh L. White nominated for President of the United States by the Legislature of Alabama.

" 31—Daniel Webster nominated for the same office, by the Legislature of Massachusetts.

Mar. 3—By act of Congress three branch mints were established; one at New Orleans, one at Charlotte, N. C., and one at Dahlohnega, Ga.

May 14—A treaty concluded with the Cherokee Indians, in which they agreed to sell all their lands east of the Mississippi river for $5,262,251, and retire to the Indian Territory west of the Mississippi river.

" 20—A convention of the Democratic party met at Baltimore, and nominated Martin Van Buren for President.

July 6—Chief Justice John Marshall died, aged 80.

Aug. 30—Wm. T. Barry, Postmaster General under Gen. Jackson, died at Liverpool, on his way to Spain, as U. S. Minister.

Dec. 28—Battle of Tampa Bay, Fla., between a company of 110 U. S. troops under Major Dade, when all but three of his men were killed. About the same time another battle with the Indians was fought at Withlacoochie, Fla., and forty of them were slain. In this and the following year, the Seminole war raged in Florida. The Indians, under their chief Osceola, were finally driven out of their country, and across the Mississippi river. This war cost the United States $15,000,000—three times the money originally paid for Florida.

1836.

Jan. 20—A treaty of peace, friendship and navigation concluded between the United States and Venezuela, at Caraccas.

February—The U. S. Bank was chartered by the Legislature of Pennsylvania.

April 20—Wisconsin organized into a Territorial government.

May 23—Edward Livingston, Secretary of State under President Jackson, died.

June 15—Michigan admitted—making the 25th State.

" " —Arkansas admitted—making the 26th State.

" 23—State banks made the depositories of the United States moneys, instead of the U. S. Bank; and by the same act, the surplus funds of the government were loaned to the several States in proportion to their Representatives in Congress.

June 28—James Madison, ex-President of the United States, died, aged 86.

July 4—The office of Commissioner of Patents created.

Sept. 14—Aaron Burr, ex-Vice President of the United States, died, aged 81.

Dec. 15—The General Post Office, the Patent Office, and the Washington Post Office burnt—7,000 models, 163 large folio volumes of records, 9,000 valuable drawings, and 10,000 original descriptions destroyed.

During this year, in addition to the war with the Seminole Indians, the United States were at war with the Creek Indians, in Geo., but it was terminated this year.

The thirteenth Presidential election in the autumn of this year, and Martin Van Buren was elected.

1837.

Jan. 16—The United States Senate passed a resolution, 24 to 19, to expunge from its records (by drawing black lines around it,) the resolution passed March 28, 1834, viz.: that the President (Jackson) in the late Executive proceedings, in relation to the public revenue, had assumed authority not conferred by the Constitution or law, but derogatory to both.

Mar. 4—Martin Van Buren inaugurated the eighth President.

" 6—A treaty was signed by the Seminole Indians, agreeing to emigrate west of the Mississippi river, but through the influence of their chief, Osceola, they broke it; after which he was seized by Gen. Jessup, and confined in Fort Moultrie, where he died.

Sept. 29—By treaty between the United States and the Sioux Indians, they sold all their lands east of the Mississippi river (about 5,000,000 acres,) for $1,000,000.

Oct. 1—The Winnebago Indians did the same thing for $1,500,000, and agreed to move west of the Mississippi river.

" 12—Congress authorize the issue of $10,000,000 treasury notes.

" 25—A severe battle was fought with the Florida Indians, but the U. S. troops, under Gen. Taylor, defeated them.

All the banks in the United States suspended specie payment during this year, which greatly embarrassed the government; and the President called an extra session of Congress, which passed an act to issue $10,000,000 of Treasury notes, as a measure of relief.

1838.

Jan. 5.—President Van Buren issued a proclamation to the people of the United States, warning them not to violate our neutrality laws, by taking part in the rebellion of the Canadians against the English government, at this time.

June 12—Territorial government of Iowa organized.

Aug. 19—The United States exploring expedition sailed from Hampton Roads, Va., with six vessels, their officers, and a corps of scientific men, for the purpose of exploring the Arctic regions.

Near the close of this year the Cherokee Indians, of Georgia, completed their emigration from that State to the Indian Territory, west of the Mississippi river. This was in consequence of the hostile legislation of the State of Georgia against them. The Supreme Court of the United States had decided these laws to be unconstitutional; but this decision was disregarded, and the Indians were driven off. "Lo! the poor Indian!"

1839.

In the early part of this year, Gen. Macomb induced the Seminole Indians to make a treaty of peace with the United States, but they were treacherous, and many murders were still committed.

This year there was trouble between the United States and England, respecting our N. E. boundary line. For the settlement of this question, see July, 1842.

Dec. 2—Congress assembled, but it was three weeks before the house was organized.

" 4—A Whig convention, at Harrisburgh, Pa., nominate W. H. Harrison as their candidate for President.

1840.

May 5—A Democratic convention assembled at Baltimore, and nominated Martin Van Buren as their candidate for the office of President.

June 30—Congress passed the sub-treasury act, which had been defeated in 1837.

Dec. 19—Felix Grundy, U. S. Senator from Tennessee, a very prominent statesman, and zealous friend of President Jackson, died.

The fourteenth Presidential election arrives this fall, when the Whig candidate, Wm. H. Harrison, was elected. This was the most exciting election ever held in this country.

1841.

Jan. 14—Congress abolished imprisonment for debts due to the United States wherever it was abolished by State laws.

March 4—Wm. H. Harrison inaugurated the ninth President.

" 17—The President called (by proclamation) an extra session of Congress to meet on the 31st inst., to consider the subjects of revenue and finances of the country.

April 4—William H. Harrison President of the United States, died, and John Tyler, the Vice President, became acting President. This was the first time such an event had happened.

May 14—Acting President John Tyler had issued a proclamation recommending this day to be observed as a day of fasting and prayer, on account of President Harrison's death, which was so observed.

June 25—Alexander Macomb, chief in command of the United States army, died at Washington.

July 21—Congress authorized the President to borrow $12,000,000 for the support of government.

Aug. 9—The sub-treasury act repealed.

" 18—The United States bankrupt law went into operation; but it was repealed in 1843.

" 16—The President vetoed a bill to charter a U. S. Bank.

Sept. 9—He vetoed another bill for the same purpose. This made the fourteenth time the veto power had been used; Washington vetoed two bills, Madison four, Monroe one, Jackson five, Tyler two.

" 10—All the members of Tyler's cabinet, except Daniel Webster, resigned.

1842.

June 25—Congress again apportion the Representatives in Congress among the States, on the basis of the sixth census (1840), fixing the ratio of one Representative to 70,600 people.

July 23—The Bunker-Hill monument finished, which had been in progress seventeen years.

In July the Senate ratified the treaty which had just been negotiated by Daniel Webster for the United States, and Lord Ashburton, for England, in relation to the northeastern boundary between the United States and the British possessions in North America.

Aug. 14—It was officially announced that the war with the Indians in Florida had ceased.

" 26—By law the fiscal year of the United States government was made to commence on the 1st day of July of each year.

Oct. 2—The U. S. sloop of war Concord lost on the rocks in the Mozambique channel.

Nov. 26—Robert Smith, a member of the cabinet under Jefferson and Madison, died in Baltimore, aged 85.

1843.

March 3—Congress make an appropriation of $30,000 to enable S. F. B. Morse to erect an experimental telegraph between Washington and Baltimore. This was the first electric telegraph in the world.

March 3—Com. Porter, of the United States navy, but at this time American minister to Turkey, died at Constantinople.

April 1—John Armstrong, a prominent officer of the Revolutionary war, and Secretary of War under Madison, died at Red Hook, N. Y.

June —In this month the Dorr rebellion broke out in Rhode Island.

Aug. 26—The United States frigate Missouri, lying at anchor at Gibraltar, Spain, took fire and was consumed.

Dec. 18—Smith Thompson, a judge of the U. S. Supreme Court, died at Poughkeepsie, N. Y., aged 76.

1844.

Feb. 28—A very large wrought-iron gun burst on board the U. S. steamer Princeton, while firing a salute, and killed Abel P. Upsher, then Secretary of State, and a number of other distinguished gentlemen who were on board.

May 1—Henry Clay nominated for President, and Theodore Frelinghusen for Vice President, by a Whig convention assembled at Baltimore.

" 7—Morgan Lewis, a distinguished officer and statesman during the Revolution, died in New York.

" 27—James K. Polk nominated by the Democratic convention assembled at Baltimore, for President, and George M. Dallas for Vice President.

The fifteenth Presidential election occurred during the Fall, and resulted in the election of James K. Polk, of Tenn., over Henry Clay, of Ky.

1845.

Jan. 16—The treaty made by Mr. Cushing, United States minister to China, and the Chinese commissioners, unanimously ratified by the United States Senate.

" 23—Congress enact that hereafter all Presidential elections shall be held on the same day in all the States, viz.: on the first Tuesday after the first Monday in November in each year when such election is held.

" 25—A joint resolution to annex Texas to the United States passed the House, (it had previously passed the Senate,) by a vote of 120 to 98.

March 1—Texas annexed to the United States by resolution of both houses of Congress.

" 4—James K. Polk inaugurated the tenth regular President.

" 4—Florida admitted into the Union, making the twenty-seventh State.

June 18—Andrew Jackson died.

" 18—A joint resolution passed both houses of the Texan Congress, assenting to the annexation to the United States.

Sept. 10—Joseph Story, one of the judges of the United States Supreme Court, and one of the most able of American jurists, died, aged 66.

Dec. 15—A resolution offered by Mr. Cass, in the United States Senate, and a speech made by him, caused much excitement, as they portended a war with England about the boundary line between Oregon and the northwestern British possessions. It was this originated the Democratic saying, "54° 40′ or fight."

" 24—Texas admitted into the Union as a State, making the twenty-eighth.

" 28—Iowa, having complied with the conditions imposed upon her by an act of March 3, 1845, was now fully admitted into the Union, making the twenty-ninth State.

1846.

March 28—The American army, 3,500 strong, under Gen. Z. Taylor, post themselves on the Rio Grande, opposite Matamoras. The Mexicans regarded this as an invasion of their territory, and was the immediate cause of the Mexican war.

April 24—Hostilities commence between the U. S. and Mexico.

" 26—First battle, when the Mexicans made an attack on sixty-three United States dragoons, Capt. Thornton, who surrendered, with a loss of 16 men.

May 8—Battle of Palo Alto, with 6,000 Mexicans against 2,300 Americans under Gen. Taylor. Mexicans whipped, with a loss of 100 men killed. Americans, 4 killed and 40 wounded. Major Ringgold was killed at this battle.

" 9—Battle of Resaca de la Palma. The Mexicans again defeated, and their general (La Vega) taken prisoner. Gen. Taylor commanded the U. S. forces.

" 12—Congress passed an act declaring that war existed between the United States and Mexico, by the act of Mexico. Authorized the raising of 50,000 troops, and voted $10,000,000 to carry on the war.

" 13—President Polk issued a proclamation that war existed with Mexico.

July 6—Com. Sloat, of the United States navy, took Monterey, on the coast of California, and issued a proclamation that that country was annexed to the United States.

In the same month Com. Stockton took San Diego from the Mexicans.

" 9—Congress retrocede the county of Alexandria, in the District of Columbia, back to Virginia.

" 17—The treaty between the United States and England respecting the boundary line between Oregon and the English possessions in North America, was ratified in London.

" 22—Congress authorized the issue of $10,000,000 treasury notes. By this means the loan above mentioned was raised.

July 30—Congress pass a new tariff, reducing the duties on imported goods. This is known as the tariff of 1846.

Aug. 3—President Polk vetoed the river and harbor bill, on the ground that it was unconstitutional, and that the money was wanted to carry on the Mexican war.

" 8—He also vetoed the French spoliation bill, on the ground that it had not been sufficiently considered, and that the money could not be spared in time of war.

" 18—Gen. Kearney took peaceable possession of Santa Fe, in Mexico, and issued a proclamation absolving the Mexicans from their allegiance to the Mexican government.

" 19—Com. Stockton declared all the Mexican ports, south of San Diego, in a state of blockade.

" 22—The whole of California was at this time in the military possession of the United States.

Sept. 21, 22, 23, 24—Battle of Monterey between 4,700 United States troops, under Gen. Taylor, and 10,000 Mexicans, under Gen. Ampudia. On the 24th an armistice of eight weeks was agreed to, when the Mexicans surrendered the city.

Oct. 25—Tobasco was bombarded by the Gulf squadron, under Com. Perry, and all the Mexican vessels in the port were captured or destroyed.

Nov. 14—Com. Connor took peaceable possession of the Mexican seaport, Tampico.

Dec. 8—The United States brig Somers was capsized by a squall off Vera Cruz, and sank in ten minutes, with a loss of two officers and thirty-nine men.

" 25—Battle of Brazito, near El Passo, between 450 Americans, under Col. Doniphan, and a body of Mexican cavalry, who were defeated.

1847.

Jan. 8—The Mexican Congress voted to raise $15,000,000 for the war against the United States, by a mortgage upon or the sale of the property of the clergy.

Feb. 23—Battle of Buena Vista, with 4,759 United States troops, under Gen. Taylor, and from 17,000 to 22,000 Mexicans, under Gen. Santa Anna, who was defeated, with a loss of 1,500 men. United States loss, 756.

" 23—On this day, ex-President John Quincy Adams died at Washington.

March 1—Gen. Kearney, by proclamation, absolved the people of California from their allegiance to Mexico, and regarded them as citizens of the United States.

" 3—Wisconsin admitted into the Union by act of Congress, which took effect on the 29th May, 1848, making the thirtieth State.

" 9—Gen. Scott landed with 12,000 men at Vera Cruz. On the

22d, 23d, 24th, 25th and 26th, he bombarded the city, which finally surrendered.

April 18—Battle of Cerro Gordo; United States forces under Gen. Twiggs, Mexican under Gen. Santa Anna, who was defeated with a loss of 3,000 prisoners, 43 pieces of artillery, and 5,000 stand of arms.

Aug. 20—Cherubusco (near the city of Mexico) stormed and taken by Gen. Worth, with 9,000 troops, against a much superior force of Mexicans.

Sept. 8—Molino del Rey stormed and taken by Gen. Worth.

" 13—Chepultepec (near the city of Mexico) stormed and taken by the United States forces, under Gen. Scott; and on the 14th Sept. he took the city of Mexico. This ended the Mexican war.

" 17.—Gen. Scott imposed a contribution of $150.000 on the city of Mexico for the protection the United States army had given to the public property.

Dec. 31—The several Mexican States were assessed $3,000,000 for the support of the American army while it held the country.

1848.

Feb. 2—Treaty of peace agreed upon between the United States and Mexico at Guadaloupe Hidalgo, (a small city four miles from the city of Mexico.) By this treaty Mexico relinquished all claims to Texas, and ceded Upper California and New Mexico to the United States; in consideration of which the United States gave Mexico $15,000,000, and assumed Mexican debts owing to our citizens to the amount of $3,500,000. This treaty was subsequently ratified by the U. S. Senate, (March 10,) and by the Mexican government on the 20th May following.

March 31—Congress authorized a loan of $16,000,000, to pay Mexico.

June 7—Gen. Zachary Taylor nominated at Philadelphia by a Whig convention, for President, and Millard Fillmore for Vice President.

" 22–23—A convention of Democrats, dissatisfied with the nomination of Lewis Cass as the candidate of their party for President, met at Utica, N. Y., and nominated Martin Van Buren for that office. This was called the Free-Soil party, because they opposed the annexation of Texas.

Aug. 14—A Territorial government organized for Oregon.

Nov. 17—According to the provisions of an act of Congress previously passed, all the States vote on the same day for President and Vice President. This was the sixteenth Presidential election, and resulted in the choice of Gen. Taylor, the Whig candidate.

1849.

Jan. 26—The ratification of the postal treaty with England exchanged at London.

March 3—Congress ordered gold dollars and double eagles to be coined.

A Territorial government organized for Minnesota

" 4—Gen. Taylor, the eleventh President, inaugurated.

May 7—Gen. Worth, of the United States army, died.

Aug. 12—Albert Gallatin, a distinguished statesman, and Secretary of the Treasury under President Jefferson, died, aged 88.

Sept. —The people of California form a constitution, prohibiting slavery in the State, preparatory to admission into the Union.

Dec. 31—The House of Representatives on the sixty-third ballot elected Howell Cobb, of Georgia, Speaker. His competitor was R. C. Winthrop, of Mass.

1850.

Jan. 21—The chiefs of the Seminole Indians (of Florida) met Gen. Twiggs in council, and agreed to abandon the country and move to the west of the Mississippi river.

Feb. 22—The original manuscript of Washington's farewell address sold in Philadelphia for $2,300.

July 9—President Taylor died, and Vice President Fillmore became acting President.

Aug. 3—Jacob Jones, an eminent naval officer, died, aged 82.

Sept. 9—California admitted into the Union, making the thirty-first State.

" 9—Utah placed under a Territorial government.

" 12—The fugitive slave law passed. This, to the northern States, was probably the most offensive act ever passed by Congress.

" 20—The slave trade abolished in the District of Columbia by act of Congress.

The above last four acts nave ever since their passage been known as the "compromise measures of 1850."

Nov. 19—Richard M. Johnson, formerly Vice President, died.

1851.

March 3—By act of Congress, postage was reduced to three cents on all letters not weighing over half an ounce, and for all distances not exceeding 3,000 miles, if pre-paid; but to five cents if not pre-paid.

—John C. Calhoun, of S. Carolina, an eminent statesman, and once Vice President, died.

1852.

June 28—Henry Clay died.
July 3—A branch of the U. S. mint established at San Francisco, Cal., by act of Congress.
Oct. 24—Daniel Webster died.
Nov. —In this month the seventeenth Presidential election took place, which resulted in the choice of Franklin Pierce, the Democratic candidate, over General Scott, the Whig candidate.

1853.

March 2—Washington Territory cut off from the northern part of Oregon, and put under a Territorial government by act of Congress.
" 4—Franklin Pierce inaugurated the twelfth regular President.
Aug. 11—President Pierce issued a proclamation warning citizens of the U. S. against connecting themselves with Lopez against the island of Cuba.

1854.

March 23—A treaty of commerce with Japan, negotiated by Com. Perry, of the United States navy.
May 19—John Davis, a Senator from Mass., an eminent orator and statesman, known by the name of "Honest John Davis," died.
" 30—The Kansas and Nebraska bill passed in Congress. By this act these two Territories were organized under Territorial governments, and in the 14th section, the far-famed "Missouri compromise" act of 1820 was repealed, after it had been a law of the land for thirty-four years. This opened the old slavery discussion, and brought on the civil war in Kansas.

1855.

Feb. 24—The Court of Claims established in Washington, by act of Congress.

1856.

March 4—The free-State Legislature of Kansas, assembled at Topeka.
" 20—Com. Connor died.
May 18—John C. Spencer, Secretary of the Treasury under Pierce, died at Albany, N. Y.
" 31—John M. Niles, Postmaster General under Van Buren, died.
Nov. —In this month the eighteenth Presidential election took place, resulting in the choice of James Buchanan, the Democratic candidate, against John C. Fremont, the Republican, and Millard Fillmore the American candidates.

1857.

Feb. 2—Nathaniel Banks, of Mass., after 133 ballotings (which occupied the House of Representatives from the 3d of December of the last year to this time), was elected Speaker.

March 4—James Buchanan inaugurated the thirteenth regular President.

July —Wm. L. Marcy, Secretary of War under President Polk, and Secretary of State under President Pierce, died, aged 71.

1858.

May 11—Minnesota admitted into the Union, making the thirty-second State.

1859.

Feb. 14—Oregon admitted into the Union, which made the thirty-third State.

1860.

Nov. 6—The nineteenth Presidential election occurred, and Abraham Lincoln, the Republican candidate, was elected, against Stephen A. Douglas, John C. Breckenridge and John Bell.

Dec. 10—Howell Cobb, U. S. Secretary of the Treasury, resigned, and President Buchanan appointed P. F. Thomas, of Maryland, in his place.

" 14—Lewis Cass, United States Secretary of State, resigned, when the President nominated Jeremiah S. Black, of Pa., in his place.

" 20—South Carolina seceded from the government of the United States. This was the first act of secession; but ten more of the slave States soon followed her example in the early part of 1861.

" 28—The United States arsenal, post office and custom house at Charleston, S. C., were seized by the authorities of that State.

" —John B. Floyd, Secretary of War, resigned, and Joseph Holt, of Ky., was appointed in his place the next day.

1861.

Now we have come to the period when the great rebellion of the southern States was fairly inaugurated. A number of events had occurred in the month of December, in 1860, which foreshadowed the coming storm, such as the resignation of the southern members of Mr. Buchanan's cabinet, and of southern Senators and Members of Congress, with the seizure of property belonging to the United States in Charleston, &c. Yet, hopes were still entertained of a pacification, as the spirit of rebellion had not showed itself in much strength outside of South Carolina; but this "smoking flax" burst into a consuming flame with the opening of this year. To chronicle all the events of this most terrible war, during the four following years, would require a volume of the size of this to contain them; we must therefore only notice the most important of them, and many of these we shall so condense as to preserve the facts, without recording, in every case, the day of the month on which they occurred.

January—During this month, Fort Macon, at Beaufort, the United States works at Wilmington, and the U. S. arsenal at Taylorsville, forts Caswell and Johnson, in North Carolina, the forts Pulaski and Jackson, and the arsenal at Savannah Geo., fort Morgan and the U. S. arsenal at Mobile, Ala., forts St. Philip and Jackson, fort Pike and the U. S. arsenal at Baton Rouge, in Louisiana, fort Barancas and the U. S. navy-yard, Fla., the U. S. arsenal at Augusta, Geo., the U. S. custom-house and mint in New Orleans, were all seized by the southerners in the States where they stood.

And in this month Florida, Georgia, Louisiana and Mississippi, five States, all passed ordinances of secession, and the Members of Congress from Georgia, Alabama and Mississippi withdrew during this month.

" 29—Kansas admitted into the Union—making the thirty-fourth State.

Feb. 1—Texas seceded from the Union.

" 4—A peace convention, with delegates from eighteen States, assemble at Washington; and on the same day a convention from the seceded States assembled at Montgomery Ala., to organize a confederate government.

" 5—John Slidell and Judah P. Benjamin, U. S. Senators from Louisiana, withdrew from the Senate.

" 9—Jeff. Davis and Alex. Stephens chosen President and Vice President of the Confederate States for one year.

Feb. 25—About this time Gen. Twiggs, in command of the U. S. troops in Texas, delivered up his men to the southerners as prisoners of war.

" 28—Colorado organized into a Territorial government.

March 2—Dakota and Nevada organized into Territorial governments.

" 4—Abraham Lincoln inaugurated the fourteenth regular President of the United States.

" 5—Gen. Beauregard takes command of the southern forces at Charleston.

" 6—The Senate of the confederate States confirm Jeff Davis' nominations of the members of his cabinet, viz.: for Secretary of State, R. Toombs, of Geo.; for Secretary of Treasury, C. S. Meminger, of South Carolina; for Secretary of War, L. P. Walker, of Ala.; for Secretary of Navy, S. R. Mallory, of Fla.; for Postmaster, J. H. Reagan, of Texas; for Attorney General, J. P. Benjamin, of La.

" 11—The Constitution of the confederate States adopted in convention at Montgomery, Ala., which was ratified afterwards by the several confederate States.

April 11—Gen. Beauregard demands of Major Anderson the surrender of Fort Sumter, which was refused.

" 12—Bombardment of Fort Sumter. This was the real commencement of the great civil war between the North and South.

April 14—Major Anderson and his men leave fort Sumter.

" 15—President Lincoln calls for 75,000 men to defend Washington.

" 17—Virginia secedes, and the Governor recognizes the act by proclamation.

" 18—The U. S. arsenal at Harper's Ferry destroyed, to prevent its falling into the hands of the south.

" 19—A mob, in Baltimore, attacked the Massachusetts troops who were going to Washington, in obedience to the President's call; and the mayor of Baltimore notified the President that no more troops should pass through that city.

" 19—The President, by proclamation, declares the ports of the seceded States blockaded.

" 20—The U. S. mint at Charlotte, N. C., seized, and on the same day the railroads in Maryland were destroyed and bridges burnt. On the same day the U. S. navy yard at Gosport, Va., was destroyed by the men having it in charge, to prevent its falling into the hands of the south. Property lost worth $25,000,000.

" 26—Gov. Brown, of Georgia, forbids the citizens of that State from paying their debts due to the people of the north.

May 3—President Lincoln calls for 82,714 additional troops.

" 6—Virginia admitted as one of the confederate States, and the State of Tennessee passed an ordinance of secession.

May 10—Gen. R. E. Lee took command of the southern troops in Va.
" 15—The Legislature of Massachusetts offer to loan the U. S. government $7,000,000 to carry on the war.
" 21—North Carolina secedes from the United States.
" 21—The southerners blockade the Mississippi river at Memphis.
" 24—Col. Ellsworth shot.
" 27—100 slaves took refuge in fortress Monroe, and Gen. Butler declared them "contraband" of war.
" 27—Mobile blockaded; Savannah ditto, on the next day, by the U. S. blockading squadron.
" 31—A fight of two hours between the Union gunboats at Acquia Creek and the batteries at that place.
June 2—Battle of Phillippa, Va. Union troops victorious.
" 3—U. S. Senator Douglas, of Illinois, died.
" 10—Battle of Big Bethel, Va. Union troops repulsed.
" 14—The southern forces evacuate and burn Harper's Ferry, when the Union forces occupy the place.
" 17—A convention of Union men vote the independence of West Virginia—in other words, that part of Virginia seceded from old Virginia.
" 18—Battle of Booneville, Mo. Gen. Price routed by the Unionists under Gen. Lyon.
" 23—Forty-eight locomotives of the Baltimore and Ohio R. R. destroyed by the southern forces.
" 26—President Lincoln recognizes the Wheeling government as the government of Virginia.
July 2—Battle near Martinsburgh, Va. Patterson, Union, defeated by Gen. Jackson.
" 5—Congress assembled, and the President called for 400,000 men, and $400,000,000 to put down the rebellion.
" 5—Battle at Carthage, Mo. Gen. Siegel commanded the Union and Gen. Jackson the southern forces.
" 11—Battle at Rich Mountain, Va. Union Gen. Rosecrans defeated Gen. Pegram.
" 11—U. S. Senate expelled nine Senators from the southern States for treason.
" 13—Battle of Carrickford, Va. Union Gen. Morris opposing Garnett, who was killed.
" 21—Battle of Bull Run. Union Gen. McDowell against Beauregard. Union troops defeated after ten hours' fighting, yet the south lost the most men.
" 25—Gen. Geo. B. McClellan took command of the army of the Potomac.
Aug. 2—Congress passed an act for raising 500,000 men, and $500,000,000 by tax and tariff.
" 7—The village of Hampton, Va., burnt, to prevent its falling into the hands of the Unionists.
" 10—Battle of Wilson's Creek. Union Gen. Lyon killed; 263 troops killed, and 421 of the enemy. Battle lasted six hours.

Aug. 15—Jeff. Davis ordered all northern men to quit the confederate States in forty days.

" 16—President Lincoln, by proclamation, declared all commercial intercourse with the rebel States at an end.

" 23—The Cherokee Indians join the south.

" 28—Bombardment and capture of forts Hatteras and Clark, N. C., by the combined action of the army, under Gen. Butler, and the navy, under Com. Stringham.

" 31—Gen. Fremont issued a proclamation confiscating the property of disloyalists in Missouri, and also freeing the slaves. This was countermanded by the President.

Sept. 1—the village of Boom Court House, Va., burnt.

" 12—Col. John A. Washington, of the Southern army, killed while reconnoitering.

" 12—Battle of Cheat Mountain, Va. Unionists victorious.

" 18—Some of the members of the Legislature of Maryland arrested and imprisoned for talking treason.

Oct. 3—Battle of Greenbrier, Va. Unionists victorious.

" 16—The U. S. troops re-capture Lexington, Mo.

" 16—Battle of Pilot Knob, Mo. Unionists victorious.

" 21—Battle of Ball's Bluff—which was a severe fight—the Unionists defeated; Col. Baker killed, with 918 men killed or wounded.

" 29—The great naval and military force, consisting of 75 vessels, (of all sorts,) and 27,000 men, sailed from Hampton Roads, Va., and bound south, under command of Com. DuPont, and Gen. T. W. Sherman.

Nov. 1—Gen. Scott retired from the command of the army, with full pay; and Gen. McClellan took his place.

" 1—Confederate Gen. Floyd tried to capture Gen. Rosecrans and his army at Gauley, Va., but failed.

" 4—Houston, Mo., taken by the Union troops, who captured a large amount of property.

" 4—A part of the great naval expedition arrived at Port Royal, South Carolina.

" 7—A great naval battle at Hilton Head, S. C., when forts Beauregard and Walker were captured.

" 8—Battle of Belmont, Mo. Great slaughter on both sides.

" 8—Mason & Slidell, commissioners to Europe, were taken from the British steamer Trent by the U. S. ship San Jacinto, but on the demand of the English government they were given up to her.

" 10—The village of Guyandotte, Va., burnt by Union soldiers, because some of them had been murdered by the inhabitants.

" 20—Thirty old whale ships, loaded with stone, sailed from New London and New Bedford, to be sunk in the channels of some of the southern sea ports. This was accomplished.

Dec. 3-4—Congressmen Bennett, of Ky., Reed, of Mo., and John C. Breckenridge, U. S. Senator from Ky., were expelled from Congress for treason.

" 5—At this time there were, as shown by the reports of the Secretaries of War and of the Navy, nearly 700,000 men in the army and navy of the U. States.

" 16—Platte City, Mo., burnt by the southern forces.

" 17—More than twenty stone vessels sunk in the channels to the harbors of Charleston and Savannah.

" 31—At the close of this year there were 246 vessels (of all kinds) in the United States navy, carrying 22,000 men and nearly 2,000 guns.

1862.

Jan. 2—Battle on Port Royal Island, S. C. The southern forces driven from the island.

" 10—A fight near Prestonburgh, Ky., between Union Gen. Garfield, and Gen. Humphrey Marshall's forces. Marshall defeated.

" 10—Senators Johnson and Polk, of Mo., expelled from the U. S. Senate as traitors.

" 12—125 vessels, with 15,000 troops, left Fortress Monroe for the south, under Com. Goldsborough and Gen. Burnside.

" 13—Simon Cameron, Secretary of War, resigned, and Edwin M. Stanton, of Pa., appointed in his place.

" 18—John Tyler, of Va., and once acting President, died.

" 19—Battle of Mill Spring, Ky. Union forces under Gen. Thomas completely victorious over Gens. Crittenden and Zollicoffer—the latter was killed. Unionists make a great haul of provisions and arms.

" 27—Bishop Ames, of the Methodist Church, and Gov. Fish, of New York, appointed to visit prisoners at Richmond and other places, but the southern authorities would not allow them to enter their lines.

Feb. 4—Congress enact that the names of every person who had taken up arms against the United States should be struck from the pension rolls.

" 5—Jesse D. Bright, of Indiana, expelled from the U. S. Senate for his secession sentiments.

" 6—The western gun-boats capture Fort Henry, on the Tennessee river, under Com. Foote. The southern Gen. Tilghman taken prisoner.

" 8—Great battle on Roanoke Island, which, with all its fortifications and guns, were captured, together with over 2,500 prisoners. Gen. Burnside commanded the Union forces.

" 10—Naval battle between gun-boats, off Elizabeth City, N. C. All but one of the enemy's boats captured.

" 12—Gen. Grant, with 40,000 trooops, invests Fort Donnelson, on the Cumberland river, where there were 18,000 troops under Genls. Floyd, Pillow and Buckner. The fighting continued during the 13th, 14th, 15th and 16th, when the fort surrendered to the Union forces, with 13,300 prisoners of war, 3,000 horses, 48 guns, and 20,000 small arms.

Feb. 13—Congress authorize the construction of twenty iron clad gunboats.

" 18—The southern Congress assembled at Richmond, Va.

" 19—Jeff Davis and Alexander H. Stephens were unanimously elected President and Vice President of the Confederate States for six years.

" 23—Nashville occupied by Union forces.

" 25—Congress authorize the Secretary of the Treasury to issue $150,000,000 of United States notes, (greenbacks) and make them a legal tender.

Mar. 2—A battle between the Union gunboats and the batteries at Pittsburgh Landing, Tenn. The southern forces repulsed with great slaughter.

" 3—Gen. Beauregard took command of the southern army in Mississippi.

" 4—Congress fix the number of Representatives in Congress at 241—based on the census of 1860.

" 6-8—Battle of Pea Ridge. Union Gen. Curtis, with 22,000 men, against Benj. McCullough with 35,000 men—McC. was killed. This battle lasted three days.

" 8-9—The Southern steamer Merrimac, or Virginia, with four gunboats, attack the U. States ships lying at Hampton Roads, and burnt and sunk several of them, when the U. S. Monitor came into the fight and very soon disabled the Merrimac. This was the first trial of iron clads.

" 14—Battle of Newbern, N. C.; where the Unionists found an immense amount of stores and ammunition.

" 23—Battle of Winchester, Va. The southern forces defeated with great loss.

April 6-7—Battle of Pittsburgh Landing or Shiloh, on the Tennessee river; the Unionists victorious—Southern Gen. A. S. Johnson, killed, and 3,000 of his men. This was one of the most terrible battles during the rebellion, and would have been lost but for the aid of the gunboats. Gen. Grant commanded the Union forces, and Gen. Beauregard the enemy. 100,000 men were in the battle, and 20,000 were killed, wounded or missing.

" 11—Fort Pulaski bombarded thirty-six hours, and taken by Gen. Hunter.

" 16—Slavery in the District of Columbia abolished by act of Congress.

" 18—The Union fleet of 51 vessels, under Com. Farragut and Porter, ascend the Mississippi river and bombard forts

Jackson and St. Philip six days, and ran past them on their way to New Orleans, where they arrived on the 25th, when Com. Farragut demanded the surrender of the city, which was done.

April 21—A branch mint established at Denver, in Colorado, by act of Congress.

May 1—251 Union cavalry captured at Pulaski, Tenn.

" 4—Yorktown, Va., evacuated by the enemy, and occupied by the Union forces.

" 5—Battle of Williamsburgh, Va. lasting all day. Unionists victorious.

" 10—Norfolk, Va., surrendered to the Union troops.

" 11—The southerners burn their ship Merrimac.

" 11—The southern forces evacuate Pensacola, Fla, and burn the public buildings and navy yard.

May 15—The Agricultural Department created by act of Congress.

" 24—Battle at Bottom's Bridge, over the Chickahominy river, a Union victory.

" 30—The Union forces occupy Corinth, Miss., and 2,000 prisoners taken.

" 31—Battle of Fair Oaks, Va. After long and hard fighting the Union troops retreated.

June 1—Battle of Fair Oaks re-commenced—the Southerners driven back. Union loss 4,739 killed, wounded and prisoners; the enemy nearly 6,000.

" 6—Gun-boat fight at Memphis, on the Mississippi river. Memphis surrendered, and nearly all the enemy's boats were destroyed or captured.

" 8—Battle of Cross Keys, Va. Union loss 581 killed and wounded—southern, about 1,000.

" 14—Battle on James Island, S. C., near Charleston—Unionists defeated.

" 17—125 Union men killed and wounded by the explosion of the gun-boat Mound City, on the White River, Ark., while in a fight.

" 19—Congress pass an act prohibiting slavery in any of the Territories of the United States.

" 25—Battle of Fair Oaks. Southerners repulsed.

" 26—Battle near Mechanicsville, Va. The southern forces 60,000 strong, under Jackson. Union troops driven back to Gaines' Mill, where the loss was heavy on both sides. This battle was renewed the next day, and lasted all day.

" 27—Bombardment of Vicksburgh by Union gun-boats.

" 30—Battles of White Oak Swamp, and Charles City Cross Roads, Va. Loss heavy on both sides.

July 1—The internal revenue bill passed.

" 1—Congress pass an act prohibiting polygamy in any part of the United States—(a hit at the Mormons.)

" 1—The Union Pacific Railroad chartered by Congress.

July 1—Battle of Malvern Hill, Va. Union victory. With this battle ended the seven days' fighting near Richmond, which cost the Union army over 15,000 men in killed, wounded and missing.

" 1—President Lincoln called for 600,000 volunteers to put down the rebellion.

" 2—Congress pass an act in which a new oath of office is prescribed, much more comprehensive than any former oath, which has been called "the Iron-clad oath."

" 7—Gen. Curtis' army encountered 1,500 southern troops at Bayou de Cache, Ark., when a severe fight ensued of two hours' length—the enemy routed, leaving over 100 dead on the field.

" 11—Gen. H. W. Halleck made commander-in-chief of the army of the United States.

" 12—The southern forces, with 4,000 cavalry, capture Murfreesborough, Tenn., after a severe fight, with about an equal loss on both sides.

Aug. 4—The President ordered a draft of 300,000 men to serve in the army nine months.

" 5—Battle of Baton Rouge, where Gen. Breckenridge, with 6,000 troops, attacked the Unionists under Gen. Williams, who, after a bloody fight, forced the enemy to retreat.

" 5—The United States gunboat Essex attacked the steamer Arkansas, a little below Baton Rouge; fired red hot shot into her, and blew her up.

" 5—Gen. Robert McCook assassinated while sick.

" 9—Battle of Cedar Mountain, Va. Union troops under Gen. Banks; enemy under Gen. Jackson. After a three hours' fight, both parties retired.

" 16—Gen. McClellan leaves Harrison's Landing on the James river.

" 21—Gen. Siegel opened his masked batteries on five regiments of southern troops, who had just crossed the Rappahannock river, slaughtered 700 of them, and took 2,000 prisoners.

" 26—A Union naval expedition went up the Yazoo river, Miss., capturing everything in its way.

" 28—Battle at Centreville, Va., under Union Gens. Siegel and McDowell; Gen. Jackson was defeated.

" 29—Battle of Groveton, near Bull Run, Va. Unionists under Gen. Pope. The battle lasted all day, when the enemy retreated. Col. Fletcher Webster was killed here. The fight was renewed the next day, and with great loss, when Pope retreated.

" 30—Battle near Richmond, Ky. Unionists, under Gen. Nelson, defeated with great loss.

" 31—Battle of Weldon, Va. The southerners badly beaten.

Sept. 1—On this day three battles were fought. 1. At Chantilly, two miles from Fairfax Court House, Va., in which two Union generals were killed, to wit: Kearney and I. J. Stevens; their loss in men was also large. 2. At Britton's Lane, Tenn., lasting four hours—enemy fled. 3. At Jackson, Tenn., where the southerners left 110 dead on the field.

" 5—The southern army ford the Potomac river and cross into Maryland, and on the 6th they occupy Frederick City, in that State.

" 6—1,200 troops attack the Union garrison at Washington, N. C., but were repulsed.

" 8—Gen. Lee issued a proclamation to the people of Maryland.

" 9—On this day these three events happened—1. Col. Grierson attacked the southerners at Coldwater, Miss., and drove them back. 2. They attack the Union forces at Williamsburgh, Va., where they were repulsed. 3. Fredericksburgh, Va., was evacuated by the southern forces.

" 10—Gov. Curtin, of Pa., (expecting an invasion of the State,) called on all the able bodied men to organize for defence.

" 10—In Cincinnati, O., so great were the fears of an attack, that 3,000 laborers were put into the trenches to fortify the city.

" 11—The Union forces at Ganby, Va., burn all the government property and abandon the place. On the same day, Mayville, Ky., and Bloomfield, Mo., were taken by the southern forces.

" 12—Fight on Elk river, Va., near Gauley, which lasted all day. On the same day Charleston was bombarded and burnt.

" 13—The southerners opened fire on Harper's Ferry, when an artillery duel was fought all day.

" 14—Battle of South Mountain, Md. Unionists, under McClellan, attack; the battle lasted all day, when the enemy fled in the night. Here Gen. Reno was killed, with about 350 men.

" 15—Harper's Ferry surrendered to the southern forces, who took 11,500 prisoners and sixty cannon.

" 16-17—Battle of Antietam, Md.—100,000 men on each side. This was one of the bloodiest battles of the war. Union Generals Hooker, Porter, Burnside and McClellan, opposed Generals Lee, Hill, Jackson and Longstreet. Union loss over 12,000, enemy about 25,000.

" 20—Battle of Iuka, Miss. Enemy defeated with a loss of over 14,000. Union loss over 700.

" 22—President Lincoln's proclamation, declaring all the slaves free in the rebel States, in case they continued the war 100 days longer.

" 23—About this time the Sioux Indians in Minnesota became very troublesome, and many of them were killed.

Sept. 27—The Union garrison at Augusta, Ky., surrendered to 600 cavalry, after 90 of them were killed.

Oct. 4—Battle of Corinth, Miss. Union loss in killed, wounded and missing, 2,300—enemy over 9,000, including prisoners.

" 8-9—Battle of Perryville, Ky. Gen. Rousseau commanded the Union forces—Bragg, Buckner and Cheatham the enemy, who were routed with a loss of 600 killed—Union 468.

" 10-11—Southern cavalry reach Chambersburgh, Pa., capture 500 horses, a quantity of government stores, and fled back to Virginia.

" 14—A donation of $100,000 was sent from San Francisco for the Sanitary Commission.

" 15—A hard battle was fought near Richmond, Ky., between 45,000 southern troops, and 18,000 Union forces, who lost 2,900 men—southern loss 3,300.

" 22—Battle of Maysville, Ark. 5,000 southern troops routed.

" 24—The English steamer Scotia, loaded with arms and powder for the enemy, captured on the coast of South Carolina.

" 30—Gen. Mitchell, (the astronomer), in command of the southern division of the U. S. army, died at Beaufort, S. C.

Nov. 5—The southern troops attacked Nashville, Tenn., but were repulsed.

" 25—Southern troops attacked Newbern, North Carolina, but left soon.

" 28—Battle of Cane Hill, Ark., when 5,000 Union soldiers, under Gen. Blunt, drove the southern troops, under Gen. Marmaduke, twelve miles, in a running fight.

Dec. 5—Battle of Coffeeville, Miss., of two hours duration. Southern loss heavy—Union, light.

" 7—Battle of Prairie Grove, Ark. Union loss 1,000 in killed and wounded.

" 8—Steamer Lake City destroyed by the southerners.

" 9—Concordia, on the Mississippi river, burnt by the Unionists.

" 10—Port Royal was bombarded by the Unionists.

" 11—Fredericksburgh shelled.

" 13—Battle of Fredericksburgh, Va., where Generals Taylor, Bayard, and Jackson, of the Union army, and Gregg and Cobb, of the southern, were killed.

" 14—Battle of Kingston, N. C., where the Union men killed and wounded several hundred, and took 400 prisoners and a quantity of arms.

" 16—Fredericksburgh evacuated by the Union army—which was equal to a defeat at the battle there on the 13th.

" 17—Baton Rouge, the capital of Louisiana, captured by General Banks' troops.

" 19—The southern forces re-took Holly Springs, Miss.; 200 Unionists killed and wounded, and half a million of dollars in property destroyed, with 4,000 bales of cotton.

Dec. 26—Thirty-eight Indians hung in Minnesota, for murdering the whites.

" 27—Vicksburg, Miss., attacked by the Union troops on land, and by the gunboats on the river, but on the 29th had to fall back.

" 31—The famous iron Monitor, which whipped the Merrimac, was sunk at sea in a storm.

" 31—A severe fight at Murfreesboro', Tenn.; Unionists driven back. This battle was renewed the next morning, and continued four days, when the enemy retreated. Union loss in killed, wounded and prisoners, over 11,000; the enemy's much less.

1863.

Jan. 1—Battle of Galveston between United States blockading squadron and the batteries. Here the U. S. steamer Harriet Lane was captured, and the steamer Westfield was blown up by her commander, and all hands on board were lost.

" 1—Gen. Sullivan, with 60,000 men, attacked the southern forces under Gen. Forrest, near Lexington, Tenn. This battle lasted all day, with great loss on both sides. Enemy defeated.

" 1—President Lincoln issued his proclamation liberating the slaves in all the rebel States.

" 1—Battle of Stone River, for ten hours without any result.

" 9—Twenty thousand prisoners exchanged.

" 11—On this and the day previous there was hard fighting at forts Hindman and Arkansas Post. Union loss about 1,000. Southern prisoners nearly 8,000.

" 11—Union gunboat Hatteras sunk by the steamer Alabama.

" 13—The southern steamer Oreto, afterwards called Florida, escapes from Mobile.

" 17—By joint resolution of Congress, $100,000,000 U. S. notes were issued to pay off the soldiers.

" 21—Engagement on the coast of Texas, when two U. S. vessels were captured.

" 22—Gen. Fitz John Porter dismissed from the U. S. service.

" 25—First regiment of negro soldiers organized at Port Royal, S. C.

" 26—Gen. Hooker succeeds Gen. Burnside in the command of the army of the Potomac.

" 26—The barque Golden Rule burnt, and the ship Washington captured by the southern steamer Alabama.

Feb. 3–5—The southern forces attack Fort Donelson on both these days, but were repulsed.

" 5—The Union ram Queen of the West, destroys three transports loaded with supplies, on the Red River.

" 9—Gen. Hunter (in S. C.) conscripts all able-bodied negroes in his department.

Feb. 12—The ship Jacob Bell captured and burned by the Florida. Her cargo was worth $1,000,000.

" 21—Ships Golden Eagle and Olive Jane, burnt by the Alabama, on the coast of Africa.

" 24—Territorial government for Arizona created by act of Congress.

" 24—Union gunboat Indianola taken by four steamers.

" 25—Cavalry fight at Strasburgh, Va. Union loss 200 in killed and prisoners.

" 25—An act to prevent correspondence with the rebels, under a penalty of $10,000, passed and approved.

" 25—The bureau of currency created in the Treasury Department, the head of which is the comptroller of the currency, who is appointed for five years by the President, upon the nomination of the Sec. of the Treasury. This act also provides for a national currency, secured by a pledge of U. S. stocks. Under this act our present national banks were organized.

" 26—The Cherokee council repeal their act of secession, and abolish slavery.

" 28—The iron clad Nashville, which laid in the Ogeechee river, Geo., destroyed by the Union gunboat Montauk.

March 1—The third fruitless attack upon fort McAllister, Geo., by the Union gunboats.

" 2—By act of Congress the number of generals in the service of the United States (of all grades) were increased from 253 to 358.

" 3—Act of Congress approved authorizing the Secretary of the Treasury to borrow $900,000,000 on the credit of the United States, and to issue $50,000,000 in fractional currency. This loan was issued in what is called 10.40 bonds, because they had from ten to forty years to run.

" 3—Congress authorize the President to suspend the privilege of the writ of habeas corpus during the rebellion.

" 3—The office of Assistant Treasurer created by act of Congress.

" 3—An act to establish a branch mint at Carson City, Nevada, approved.

" 3—An act forming a Territorial government for Idaho, approved.

" 3—The gunboat Indianola destroyed by the enemy, and the gunboat Geo. Washington was blown up in Broad river.

" 3—The President authorized to issue letters of marque and reprisal to privateers for three years.

" 5—Gen. Van Dorn attacks the Union troops at Springfield, Tenn., routed them, and captured many prisoners.

" 6—Franklin, Tenn., taken by the southern forces, who killed 300 and took 1,000 prisoners.

" 10—Jacksonville, Fla., taken by U. S. negro troops.

Mch. 13—Battle at the mouth of the Tallahatchie river between the gunboat Chillicothe and fort Pemberton, which was silenced.

" 14—The U. S. fleet bombarded fort Hudson, La. In the attempt to pass the batteries, the flag ship Mississippi was disabled, and burnt by order of Com. Farragut.

" 17—Averill's cavalry (Union) reached Kelly's Ford, where they attacked the enemy, under Stuart and Fitzhugh Lee. The battle lasted five hours, when the enemy fell back. This battle was one of the most gallant cavalry fights of the whole war.

" 19—The English steamer Georgiana, with arms for the south, destroyed off Charleston, S. C.

" 25—Two Union rams destroyed in attempting to pass the batteries at Vicksburgh.

April 1—Admiral Farragut's fleet pass all the batteries at Grand Gulf.

" 6—To show the effects of the war on the south, we quote the prices of several articles at Richmond, Va. At this date, butter $3 per lb. ; hams $1.45 per lb. ; brandy $24 per gal. ; corn $7.50 per bushel; candles $3 per lb.; coffee $4.50 per lb.

" 7—A number of ironclads attack fort Sumter, in Charleston harbor, but they were badly punished, and left. Here the Union monitor Keokuk sunk two days after, from damages received.

" The ship Morning Star captured by the steamer Alabama.

" 8—Two Union steamboats on the Cumberland river captured and burnt.

" 8—Admiral Farragut captures the steamer J. D. Clark.

" 12—Battle at Teche, La., Unionist under Gen Banks. Another fight occurred on the 14th, between the same parties, when the enemy ran and lost three of their gunboats.

" 16—Porter's fleet of six gunboats and a number of transports, ran by all the batteries at Vicksburgh.

" 20—President Lincoln issued a proclamation that West Virginia had complied with the act of Congress, imposing a certain condition of admission as a separate State ; gave notice that in sixty days from this date she would come into the Union.

" 23—Gen. Hunter gives Jeff. Davis notice that he will retaliate for the killing of our negro soldiers and their officers.

" 24—On this day the Union forces were defeated in a fight at Beverly, Va., and were victorious at Weber Falls, Ark., and also on the Iron Mountain railroad, near St. Louis, Mo.

" 26—Three hundred and fifty thousand bushels of corn destroyed on Deer Creek, Miss., by a party of Union raiders.

" 27—Texas Legion captured at Franklin, Tenn.

" 28—Cavalry fight at Sand Mountain, Geo. Southern troops flee, leaving 200 dead and wounded.

During this month no less than eighty-five battles, skirmishes or attacks took place on land and upon the water, (the latter principally by gunboats.)

May 1—Battle of Port Gibson; 11,000 southern troops defeated. They also suffer another defeat at Monticello, Ky., and another at South Quay, Va. The Unionists suffer a defeat also in a skirmish at Lagrange, Ark. The battle of Chancellorsville, Va., also commenced this day.

" 2—Battle of Chancellorsville, Va. This was the second day of fight. The Union forces under Gen. Hooker; opposed by Gen. Lee. On the third day loss heavy on both sides.

" 2—Col. Grierson's raiders reach Baton Rouge, La., after 15 days' ride through Mississippi, in which time they had several fights, took prisoners, destroyed railroads, burnt bridges, and did much damage.

" 3—Col. Streight's Union raiding force of 1,600 men captured near Gadsden, Ala.

" 3—Gen. Sedgwick captured Fredericksburgh, Va., but it was retaken the next day.

" 3—Capture of Grand Gulf, Miss., by Admiral Porter's fleet.

" 5—Vallandigham arrested in Ohio for treason.

" 10—Stonewall Jackson died.

" 12—Battle of Farnden's Creek, Miss. Between Gen. Gregg and the Unionists under Gen. Logan—each about 5,000 men. Union victory.

" 13—Yazoo City captured by the Union gunboats, with two millions of property.

" 16—Battle at Baker's Creek, Miss.; Gen. Grant, Union, against Gen. Pemberton, who was defeated, with a loss of 4,000 men. This victory was followed up by another battle the next day, when 2,000 more prisoners were taken.

" 18—Vicksburgh invested by the forces of Gens. Grant, Sherman, McPherson and McClernand, and the terrible battle began, while Admiral Porter aided them with his fleet of gunboats. (See 4th of July next.)

" 21—The southern troops offer terms of capitulation, being completely surrounded in their fortifications at Vicksburgh; but Gen. Grant refused any other terms than unconditional surrender.

" 26—Gen. Breckenridge defeated in Tennessee.

" 27—Gen. Banks repulsed in his second attack on Port Hudson, La. He also failed in two or three subsequent attacks on the same place.

June 7—Battle at Milliken's Bend. The Union force in the main action were negroes, who drove back the enemy.

" 9—Two cavalry fights take place this day on the Rappahannock river, the latter at Brandy station.

" 11—Col. Montgomery starts from Hilton Head, S. C., with a regiment of colored troops, for a raid in Georgia.

" 11—The Clarence captures six vessels off the Chesapeake bay.

June 15—President Lincoln calls for 100,000 men to repel Gen. Lee's army, now marching north.

" 16—The governors of Pennsylvania and New Jersey call for volunteers to defend Pennsylvania from invasion.

" 17—The steamer Nashville captured.

" 18—The southern troops, under Milroy, arrive at Bedford, Pa., and within a few days after several other large bodies of their troops enter the State at Chambersburg, Carlisle, Shippensburg, Gettysburg, and York, amounting in all to more than 100,000 men.

" 20—The new State of West Virginia organized.

July —Missouri abolishes slavery in that State.

" 1-2-3—Successive fighting for three days at Gettysburg, Pa., which ended in a Union victory. This was one of the greatest battles of our civil war: 6,000 men were buried on the field, and about 200,000 were in the fight; Union loss 23,000 in killed, wounded and missing. General Lee, in the night, crossed the Potomac river into Virginia.

" 4—Vicksburg, Miss., surrendered to Gen. Grant, after holding out against our bombarding and shelling since the 18th of May last. Gen. Pemberton not only surrendered the place, but his whole army of 31,000 men, 220 guns, and 70,000 small arms. The battle of Gettysburg and the surrender of Vicksburg may be considered as the turning point of the war.

" 4—Gen. Lee fled. President Lincoln announces the victory of Gettysburg, and Gen. Meade issues a congratulatory address to his army on their victory.

" 8—Surrender of Port Hudson, on the Mississippi river, to Gen. Banks, with 7,000 prisoners, and a great number of cannon and small arms. This opened the Mississippi to trade.

" 13—Great riot in New York. It became necessary for the government to send troops to that city to put down the riot. The colored orphan asylum was burnt, negroes hung in the streets, houses robbed and burnt.

" 15—The riot in New York continues. The United States troops had arrived; they fire upon the rioters, and kill and wound several hundred of them.

" 15—President Lincoln issues a proclamation appointing the 6th of August as a day for thanksgiving for the recent great victories by our armies.

" 23—Battle of Manassas Gap, Va.; southern loss about 400 killed and wounded.

" 26—Morgan, the guerilla, who had been scouring Indiana and Ohio, burning, killing and robbing, was captured with 400 of his men in Ohio.

" 26—John J. Crittenden, long in the Senate of the United States from Kentucky, died at Frankfort in that State.

Aug. 1—Two battles between cavalry took place this day in Virginia; one at Kelly's Ford, on the Rappahannock, and one at Culpepper.

Aug. 4—The steamboat Ruth accidentally burnt on the Mississippi river, with $250,000 of government money on board. About this time, the Indians in Minnesota were hostile, and Gen. Sibley had three battles with them, and drove them off.

" 12 to 20—Gen. Gilmore bombards Fort Sumter, and on the 21st, 22d, 23d, and 25th, threw shells into Charleston, S. C., at a range of nearly six miles.

" 27—John B. Floyd, Secretary of War under Buchanan, died.

" 31—A squadron of United States war vessels attack fort Moultrie, in Charleston harbor.

During this month, Mississippi and Tennessee swarmed with guerillas.

Sept. 1—Knoxville, Tenn., captured by Gen. Burnside's troops. An artillery fight at Port Royal, Va.

" 2—Kingston, Tenn., captured by Gen. Burnside.

" 5—Forts Wagner and Gregg, near Charleston, bombarded by Gen. Gilmore, and on the 6th the enemy evacuated them.

" 8—Cumberland Gap, with 2,000 prisoners, surrendered to Gen. Burnside.

" 10—Little Rock, Ark., evacuated and occupied by the Union troops.

" 19—Battle of Chickamauga, Geo. This battle raged for two days, and ended in a great defeat for the Union army, and a loss of over 15,000 men in killed, wounded and missing. Gen. Rosecrans commanded the Union, and Gen. Bragg the southern troops.

" 22—A heavy battle at Madison Court House, Va. Unionists victorious.

" 28—The enemy attacked Gen. Burnside, at Knoxville, Tenn., but were repulsed.

Oct. 3—Union troops threw Greek fire into Charleston.

" 5—The enemy attacked Murfreesboro, Tenn., but were repulsed. Chattanooga, Tenn., bombarded by Gen. Bragg.

' 5—The "New Ironsides," in Charleston harbor, attacked by a gunboat and torpedo, but they failed in the attempt, and the assailants were captured.

" 14—Battle of Bristoe Station, Va. Result, 450 Southern prisoners.

" 16—Henry Ward Beecher lectures in England in relation to our civil war.

" 16—Gen. Grant takes command of the departments of Tennessee, Cumberland and Ohio.

" 17—The President calls for 300,000 more troops.

" 21—Three fights occur this day—1. At Tuscumbia, Ala. 2. At Philadelphia, Tenn. 3. At Corinth, Miss.

" 26—Charleston again bombarded from forts Wagner, Gregg and the Union gunboats.

Oct. 27—Battle of Brown's Ferry, on the Tennessee river, near Chattanooga Southern troops repulsed with loss.

" 28—Lookout mountain taken by Gen. Hooker's forces.

" 31—Battle of Shell Mound, Tenn. Union troops under Gen. Hooker gain another victory.

Nov. 2—Gen. Banks lands his army in Texas, and two days after takes peaceable possession of Brownsville.

" 5—Chattanooga bombarded for several days about this time.

" 5—Gen. Averill defeats the enemy at Lewisburg, Va., capturing a large amount of arms, wagons and other property.

" 6—About this time the north was horrified at the starvation of Union prisoners in the prisons at Richmond, Va.

" 7—Gen. Meade drives the enemy across the Rappahannock river, and captures 2,000 prisoners.

" 11—The British minister (Lord Lyons) informed our government that the enemy intended to invade the United States from Canada.

" 15—Gen. Banks captured Corpus Christi Pass, Texas.

" 15—Gen. Longstreet drove Gen. Burnside from Holston, Tenn., to Bull's Station.

" 16—Gen. Sherman and Gen. Thomas' forces unite at Chattanooga, Tenn.

" 17—Gen. Longstreet besieges the city of Knoxville, Tenn., at this time in Gen. Burnside's possession.

" 17—Charleston again shelled, as it had been on the 10th and 11th inst.

" 19—Union National Cemetery consecrated at Gettysburg for the soldiers who fell at the great battle at that place in July.

" 20—Mosby, having his men disguised by Union uniforms, attacks our troops at Bealton Station. This was discovered and frustrated.

" 23—Battles of Chattanooga and Lookout Mountain. The fight was continued three days. Gen. Hooker drove the enemy from the mountain. This fight was above the clouds. Gens. Hooker, Thomas and Sherman commanded the Union troops, and Gen. Bragg the enemy.

" 26—The Union troops pursued them to Chickamauga. But they had fled, after destroying their stores.

" 26—Cavalry fight near the Rapidan river.

" 26—Gen. Grant reported that Gen. Bragg's rout was complete, with a loss of sixty guns.

" 28—Gen. John Morgan escaped from prison at Columbus, Ohio.

" 28—The southern forces attacked Knoxville, Tenn., and were repulsed the next day with great slaughter.

Dec. 4—Gen. Longstreet abandoned Knoxville, and two days after, Gen. Sherman's troops arrived there to relieve Gen. Burnside.

" 7—President Lincoln, by proclamation, recommended a day of thanksgiving, to be observed by all loyal people, on account of the recent great victories.

Dec. 8—The President issued another proclamation, offering pardon (with few exceptions) to all who had taken part in the rebellion, upon consideration of their taking an oath hereafter to support the Constitution, the union of all the States, and the laws of Congress.

" 12—Gen. Butler gave notice that the authorities at Richmond refused to receive any more supplies for the Union prisoners.

" 16—Gen. Averill's cavalry destroyed the Virginia and Tennessee railroad, and a depot containing 4,000 barrels of flour and meat, 160,000 bushels of grain, and other military supplies.

" 17—The steamer Chesapeake, which had been captured by passengers on the 6th inst., retaken by a United States gunboat near Halifax, N. S.

" 24—The bombardment of Charleston still continued.

1864.

Jan. 7—Two blockade runners were captured this day: 1. The Dare, a British steamer, was run ashore at Wilmington, N. C., and destroyed. 2. The John Scott at Mobile Bay.

" 11—Two more blockade runners beached and burned on the coast of North Carolina. These made 22 which had been captured or burnt in the last six months.

" 19—The office of Assistant Secretary of War created by act of Congress.

" 25—Cornelius Vanderbilt received a vote of thanks from Congress for his gift to the government of the steamer Vanderbilt, worth $800,000. This ship had just returned from a year's cruise.

Feb. 1—The President ordered a draft of 500,000 men for three years or during the war.

" 5—The United States gunboat Cambridge destroyed the English steamer Dee; and the gunboat De Soto captured the British steamer Cumberland, with a cargo of arms, off Mobile.

" 9—Over 1,000 bales of cotton burnt at Wilmington, N. C., valued at $700,000.

" 20—Battle of Olustee, Fla. Union troops, under Gen. Seymour, were defeated with great loss. Two negro regiments covered his retreat and saved his army.

" 23—Admiral Farragut began his six days' bombardment of fort Powell, below Mobile.

" 25—Grierson and Smith's cavalry return to Memphis. During their expedition they took 1,500 negroes, and 300 horses; destroyed 3,000,000 bushels of corn, 4,000 bales of cotton, 2,000 hides and 40 miles of railroad.

" 27—Gen. Sherman's expedition returns to Vicksburgh, having destroyed 150 miles of railroad, 20 locomotives, 10,000 bales of cotton, 2,000,000 bushels of corn, and freed 10,000 negroes.

During this month, in addition to the two raids above mentioned, several others of less importance took place. The amount of property destroyed was immense, besides which, eighteen vessels (blockade runners and others) were captured or destroyed.

March 1—Gen. Ulysses S. Grant nominated for Lieutenant General, and confirmed by the Senate the next day.

" 12—He was appointed commander-in-chief of the United States army.

" 15—The President calls for 200,000 more men.

" 25—Gen. Forrest, with 6,500 men, attacks Paducah, Ky., but was repulsed, by aid of Union gunboats, with heavy loss.

" 28—Battle of Cane river, La., when 8,000 Union troops, under Mower and Dudley, defeat 12,000 under Gen. Taylor.

April 4—Gen. Steele defeats Gen. Marmaduke's cavalry, 4,000 strong, on the little Missouri river, Ark.

" 6—Gen. Sheridan put in command of the cavalry of the army of the Potomac.

" 8—Gen. Banks' troops defeated, with a loss of 2,000 men and 24 guns, at Mansfield, La., by Kirby Smith.

" 8—Gen. Banks' forces again attacked by the enemy, who were repulsed. Banks now gives up his Red river expedition, having lost about 4,000 men and 300 wagons.

" 12—Gen. Forrest storms fort Pillow, and after its surrender, of the garrison, consisting of 250 whites and 350 negroes, not 200 escaped.

" 21—North Carolina salt works, near Wilmington, destroyed by a party from our gunboats. These works were worth $100,000. Before this, the Union commanders had made it their business to destroy all the salt works in the southern States which could be found, and millions of dollars worth were thus destroyed.

May 2—400 Union prisoners reach Annapolis, almost dead from starvation.

" 4—Grant's army, consisting of about 80,000 men, cross the Rapidan and encamp at Chancellorsville and the Wilderness.

" 5—The great battle of the Wilderness, Va., begins—Grant commanding the Union army. Nothing decisive this day, but loss heavy on both sides.

" 6—Second days' fighting commenced early in the morning. Here Gen. Wadsworth (U.) was mortally wounded, and about 30,000 men, on both sides, were killed or wounded. Neither party could claim victory.

" 6—At this date Sherman's army, posted on the borders of Tennessee and Georgia, (not far from Chattanooga,) amounted to nearly 100,000 men and 250 guns; while the forces under Joe Johnson, in the vicinity, were not over 60,000 strong.

May 7—Lee retreats to-day from the battle-ground of the Wilderness for Spottsylvania Court House—the Union army starts for the same place—several fights occur on the way.

" 7—From official reports it appeared that from the commencement of the war to this date, there had been over 150,000 officers and men taken prisoners by the Unionists.

" 8—Hard battle to-day at Spottsylvania Court House, between Grant and Lee's forces—Gen. Sedgwick was killed, but no decisive result, except that Gen. Sheridan captured immense supplies at Beaver Dam station.

" 10—The same battle still continued, but nothing decisive, with a loss on each side of probably 10,000.

" 12—Another hard fight to-day, but still undecisive.

" 16—Gen. Butler's besieging forces at fort Darling, on the James river, were attacked and defeated by a loss of 3,500 men in killed, wounded and prisoners.

" 26—The Territory of Montana organized into a Territorial government, by act of Congress.

June 1—Battle of Cold Harbor, Va. This continued three days, but was undecisive.

" 7—A. Lincoln nominated by a Republican convention at Baltimore for a second Presidential term.

" 14—General (and Bishop) Polk killed by a cannon shot.

" 15—Gen. W. F. Smith attacks Petersburg, Va., with 15,000 men, principally colored, for three successive days. Attacks were continued but without success. These various assaults cost the Unionists nearly 10,000 men.

" 19—The steamer "Alabama," commanded by R. Semmes, was sunk on the coast of France by the U. S. gunboat "Kearsarge," Capt. Winslow, after a two hours' fight.

" 28—The fugitive slave law of 1850, repealed.

" 30—Salmon P. Chase, Secretary of the Treasury, resigns his office, and Senator Fessenden was appointed in his place.

July 1—The public debt of the United States, at this date, was $1,740,690,489.49.

" 1—Gen. Sherman takes 3,000 prisoners this day.

" 4—An act passed by Congress to establish a branch mint at Dalles City, Oregon.

" 8—The "Florida" burns several vessels off the coast of Maryland.

" 9—Battle of Monocacy—Gen. Early victorious.

" 18—President Lincoln calls for 500,000 more troops.

" 20—Fight at Winchester, Va., between Gen. Early, and Gen. Averill—southerners retreated with loss.

" 20-22—Two severe battles in Georgia. Gen. Hood attacks Gen. Sherman's army with a loss of 20,000 men in killed, wounded and prisoners. Union Gen. McPherson killed on the 22d.

July 25—The mine under the fort before Petersburgh completed, and charged with four tons of powder.

" 28—Battle of Four Mile Creek, north of the James river, Va. The gain nothing.

" 30—The great mine under the fort before Petersburgh exploded —blowing up the fort, with the regiment which garrisoned it, but from bad management, it proved a disastrous affair. Union loss 4,000, the enemy, only 1,050.

" 30—Gen. McCausland entered Chambersburgh, Pa., and burnt it. Loss, $1,000,000.

" 30—Gen. Stoneman's troops attacked by a great force at Macon, Geo.; and, after some hours' fighting, surrendered.

During this month Petersburgh Va., was cannonaded nearly every day.

Aug. 2—Gen. Banks puts all the negroes, between the ages of 18 and 40, (in the department of the Grand Gulf,) into his army,

" 3—Gen. Hood attacks Gen. Logan's lines at Atlanta, Geo., and drove them back, but in the evening Logan regained his position.

" 5—Admiral Farragut enters Mobile bay with 32 vessels, silencing the forts as he passed them. Inside, he attacks the iron-clad ram Tennessee, which surrendered with her admiral, Buchanan, and her crew. At this engagement the monitor Tecumseh was blown up and sunk, by a torpedo.

" 6—Fort Powell, on Mobile bay, abandoned, when it fell into the hands of Gen. Granger, with 18 guns.

" 7—Gen. Averill defeats the force at Moorfield, W. Va., taking all their guns, 420 prisoners, and 400 horses—when they fled to the mountains.

" 7—English steamer Prince Albert sunk in Charleston harbor by our fleet.

" 7—The shelling of Petersburgh continues.

" 8—Fort Gaines, at Mobile bay, surrenders to Farragut and Granger—56 officers, 818 men, and 26 guns.

" 9—Atlanta, Ga., bombarded from all parts of Sherman's lines.

" 11—The pirate Tallahassee, off Fire Island, burns five merchant vessels, and during this month she burnt and sank as many more.

" 13—Mosby, the guerilla leader, attacks and captures a Union supply train of 75 wagons, 500 horses, 200 cattle, and 200 prisoners, near Berryville, Va.

" 19—The enemy attack the Union lines at Ream's Station, Va., and took 3,000 prisoners.

" 21—The enemy attempt to drive Gen. Warren from the Weldon railroad and lost 600 men killed, and 1,100 prisoners—among their killed were Gens. Saunders and Lamar.

" 23—Fort Morgan (in Mobile bay,) surrenders to Admiral Farragut and Gen. Granger; 600 men and 60 guns were taken.

" 25—Battle of Ream's Station, Va., in which the enemy drove our troops out, killed and wounded 1,000 of them, and make prisoners of 2,000 more.

At the close of August, we may say summarily that during this month Gen. Grant was operating before Richmond, Va.; Gen. Thomas at Atlanta, Ga., and Admiral Farragut in Mobile bay.

Sept. 2—Gen. Hood, the commander at Atlanta, Ga., evacuates the place after destroying 80 carloads of ammunition and a vast quantity of military stores; and the Union troops under Gen. Slocum, take possession, while Gen. Thomas pursues Hood.

" 8—Petersburgh, Va., still cannonaded and shelled,

" 12—Gen. Sherman sends all the inhabitants of Atlanta out of the place.

" 13—Gen. Sheridan operating generally in the Shenandoah valley, Va.

" 16—A strong cavalry force, under Hampton, at Caggin's Point, on the James river, Va., drove off 2,500 beeves, intended for the Union army there.

" 19—Battle of Oquequan, Va. Here Sheridan defeated Gen. Early, who lost over 8,000 men in killed, wounded and prisoners, besides 6,000 small arms.

" 20—A shotted salute over Sheridan's victory, fired into Petersbugh, which caused an artillery duel all along our lines.

" 22—Battle of Fisher's Hill, when Gen. Sheridan again defeats Early, who lost 1,500 killed and wounded, besides 2,400 prisoners, 21 cannon, and a great quantity of small arms.

" 30—Our blockading force captured and destroyed about fifty blockade runners this month.

Oct. 7—Gen. Sheridan returns from his raid up the valley of the Shenandoah, where he has destroyed 2,000 barns and their contents, with 70 mills. He also took 4,000 cattle, 3,000 sheep and a great number of horses.

" 7—Commander Collins of the ship Wachussett, ran down the Florida, at Bahia, Brazil, and brought her home

" 10—The English blockade running steamer Bat, captured off Wilmington, N. C., on her first trip; she and her cargo were of great value.

" 11—Maryland votes for a new Constitution, with a section in it abolishing slavery.

" 19—Great battle at Cedar Creek, Va., in which Gen. Sheridan defeats Early. This victory was gained after Sheridan's troops had fled from the battle field. Sheridan stopped the retreat, turned his men about and whipped the enemy; who, flying, left everything behind them. The enemy's loss 2,000 men, with 1,300 prisoners, 48 cannon, 398 horses, 65 ambulances, 50 wagons, and an immense amount of arms and ammunition.

" 19—A number of refugees, who were harbored in Canada, enter St. Albans, Vt., and robbed three banks, stole what they wanted, and returned to Canada.

Oct. 27—Gen. Grant's army makes a reconnoisance on both sides of the James river, but it resulted in nothing but the loss of 1,500 men in killed, wounded and prisoners.

" 28—Gen. Price, with his army, driven out of Missouri into Arkansas. This was the end of Price's invasion of that State. He left it with about one-third of his men.

Nov. 3—The battle of Franklin, Tenn., to-day, resulted in a decided Union victory—Gen Hood commanding the enemy, and Gen. Stanley the Unionists. Union loss 2,500 to 3,000.

" 8—Abraham Lincoln re-elected President of the United States, and Andrew Johnson, Vice President.

" 8—Gen. George B. McClellan resigns his commission as commander-in-chief of the United States army.

" 9—Gen. Sherman issues orders for his army to march from Atlanta, Georgia, to Savannah.

" 11—The gunboat Tulip bursts her boiler on the Potomac river, killing nearly all on board.

" 13—Gen. Breckenridge attacks Gen. Gillem, near Bull's Gap, Tenn., in the night, and routed his army.

" 14—Gen Sherman leaves Atlanta, Ga., after blowing up and burning the public buildings and factories. His army moves in two columns towards the sea—one under Gen. Howard, and the other under Gen. Slocum.

" 15—Atlanta burning all day.

" 19—At the approach of Sherman, Gov. Brown and his Legislature, of Georgia, ran away from Milledgeville, the capital of the State.

" 22—Sherman's army enter Milledgeville; and on the

" 23—Some of his soldiers hold a mock session of the Legislature, and pass highly loyal resolutions.

" 24—Thanksgiving was observed by the army of the Potomac, with 59,000 lbs. of turkeys sent them from the north; and 36,000 lbs. were sent to Sheridan's army.

" 25—An attempt was made to-night to fire New York city by southern desperadoes, who set fire in their rooms in fifteen hotels in the city, and also in several other places; but the plot failed of success.

Dec. 1—Including those now in course of construction, we have 671 vessels in our navy, carrying over 4,600 guns and 51,000 men. These have captured 324 vessels during the past year, and 1,379 since the war began—267 of which were steamers.

" 5—Up to this date 65 blockade runners (steamers) have been either taken or destroyed before Wilmington, N. C. Ships and cargoes worth $12,000,000.

" 6—Ex-Secretary (of the Treasury) Chase appointed Chief Justice of the United States Supreme Court, in place of Roger B. Taney, deceased.

Dec. 12—Sherman's army reach Savannah, where Gen. Hardee is found, with 15,000 troops. In his march from Atlanta to this place his army destroyed 15,000 bales of cotton, captured 6,000 beeves and 1,800 horses and mules, and 15,000 negroes came into our lines.

" 13—Gen. Hazen's division, under Sherman, storm fort McAlister, near Savannah, Georgia, and take it, with 200 prisoners and all its stores.

" 14—Gen. Dix issues an order to follow any invaders from Canada on to Canadian soil, if necessary to seize them; but the President disapproved the order.

" 15—Battle of Nashville, Tenn., in which Gen. Thomas (Union) gained a victory over Gen. Hood. This battle lasted two days, on both of which the Unionists were victorious.

" 15—Battle of Murfreesborough, Tenn., in which Union Gen. Rousseau defeats Gen. Forrest, who lost 1,500 men.

" 19—President Lincoln issues a call for 300,000 volunteers.

" 20—Gen. Stoneman attacks three forts at Saltville, drove out the southern forces, and destroyed their salt works and lead mines, with 50 railroad bridges.

" 20—Gen. Sherman demands the surrender of Savannah. Gen. Hardee refuses, but fled during the night.

" 21—Gen. Sherman enters the city without opposition; captures 800 prisoners, 33,000 bales of cotton, 150 cannon, 13 locomotives, 190 cars, 3 steamers, with much ammunition and stores; makes Gen. Geary military Governor. The people submit gracefully to their new masters.

" 21—Admiral Farragut made vice admiral, as a reward for his great services.

1865.

Jan. 1—Since July 3, 1861, 66,390 pension certificates had been granted.

" 11—The Missouri State convention passed an ordinance emancipating the slaves in that State.

" 14—One vessel starts from Boston and another from New York, with charitable supplies for the people of Savannah, Ga.; and on the 16th instant another vessel left New York with further supplies, worth in all $100,000.

" 15—Gen. Terry, with a force of 9,000 men, aided by the fleet at that place, captures fort Fisher, on the coast of North Carolina, after three days fighting. Gen. Whiting and Col. Lamb commanded the fort. We took 1,800 prisoners; killed and wounded 400 more; our loss was over 1,000 killed and wounded. This was a terrible blow to the enemy; it left them without a single port.

Jan. 15—Edward Everett, a most distinguished scholar, statesman and orator, died at Boston, aged 71.

" 16—The magazine at fort Fisher exploded, and killed and wounded 300 of our troops.

" 17—The monitor Patapsco blown up and sunk by a torpedo in Charleston harbor; 7 officers and 65 men went down with her.

" 23—The southern Gen. Hood formally takes leave of the southern army, having been succeeded by Gen. Taylor.

" 28—Gen. Breckenridge succeeds Mr. Seddon, as southern Secretary of War.

" 29—A. H. Stephens, R. M. T. Hunter, and A. J. Campbell, obtain permission of Gen. Grant, at City Point, Va., to go to Fortress Monroe, to try and negotiate a peace.

" 31—The House of Representatives passes the Senate joint resolution to amend the Constitution, so as to abolish slavery in the United States, by 119 to 56.

Feb. 1—Secretary Seward goes to fortress Monroe to meet the three southern commissioners.

" 1—The legislature of Illinois ratifies the emancipation amendment, just passed both houses of Congress. This was the first State to do so.

" 2—President Lincoln goes to fortress Monroe to meet the southern peace commissioners—but nothing was agreed on.

" 2-3—Rhode Island, Massachusetts, New York, Pennsylvania, Maryland and West Virginia all ratify the Constitutional amendment, and on the 7th, Maine and Missouri do the same: and, on the 8th, Ohio also.

" 17—Columbia, S. C., burnt accidentally.

A paper dollar was worth but two cents in specie, in Richmond, Va.

" 18—The Union troops enter Charleston this day, and take 450 good cannon and the blockade runners Cyrene and Deer.

" 18—Gen. Lee writes a letter in favor of arming the slaves, saying the whites could not carry on the war alone.

" 25—Eight hundred southern soldiers came into our lines, all of whom had deserted during the last week.

Mar. 1—The Legislature of New Jersey rejects the Constitutional amendment (the 14th).

" 2—Gen. Sheridan attacks Gen. Early between Staunton and Waynesborough, Va., and completely routed him, capturing nearly 1,700 of his troops.

" 4—President Lincoln is inaugurated on his second term.

" 9—Vermont ratified the fourteenth amendment of the U S. Constitution.

" 14—Gen. Sherman destroys the great arsenal, with much machinery, at Fayetteville, N. C.

" 15—At this date it was estimated that more than 60,000 Union soldiers had been starved to death in southern prisons.

Mar. 16—The battle of Averysborough, between a portion of Sherman's army, and confederate Gen. Hardee. Our loss was nearly 1,000 men. At night Hardee's troops ran away.

" 18—The confederate Congress adjourns *sine die*—never to meet again. One of its last acts was the passage of a law raising a negro force.

" 19—Battle at Bentonsville, west of Goldsboro', N. C., between Gen. Johnston's infantry of 30,000 men, and Gen. Slocum's wing of Gen. Sherman's army. This battle lasted all day, but Slocum held the field.

" 25—The southern forces under Gen. Gordon attack and take fort Steadman, near Petersburgh, Va.; but we soon retook it, capturing over 1,700 rebels, and defeated their whole force.

" 28—Gen. Grant's lines before Richmond extended 39 miles, and well fortified all the way.

At the close of this month we may make this general remark: Gen. Grant had lain with his army before Richmond for a long time, and now Gen. Sherman's army from the south had arrived, or was near at hand, and so had Gen. Sheridan's from the Shenandoah valley. Gen. Lee was hemmed in, and it was clearly seen that secession and rebellion must fail.

April 1—Gen. Sheridan's forces capture 6,000 men and fifteen guns to-day.

" 2—The southern forces in the night at Richmond blow up their forts and rams, preparatory to evacuating the city.

" 2—Gen. Lee evacuates Richmond and Petersburgh, in consequence of an attack all along Gen. Grant's line. Lee retreated westward, with his army demoralized. The power of the southern confederacy was gone, and our great civil war virtually finished. Jeff. Davis, his family, and some of his late cabinet, fled from Richmond.

The same day Gen. Wilson attacks Gen. Forrest, who held the defenses at Selma, Ala., with 7,000 troops; they were routed after one hour's fight. Wilson took the town, with 2,000 prisoners, 100 guns, stores, &c.

" 3—The Union troops, under Gen. Weitzel, enter and take possession of Richmond. On the same day the Union troops enter Petersburgh. When the enemy left Richmond, they set fire to it, and burnt a large portion of the city. The Richmond "Whig" quotes flour at $900 to $1,000 per barrel, corn at $100 per bushel, and butter at $20 per ℔. in confederate money.

" 4—Gen. Grant pursues Gen. Lee. Lee lost 50,000 men in killed, wounded, deserters, &c.

" 4—Gen. Weitzel reports that he took in Richmond 28 locomotives, 150 cars, 500 cannon, 5,000 stand of arms, with 1,000 well, and 5,000 sick prisoners.

April 4—Jeff. Davis issues a proclamation, from Danville, N. C., asserting that the cause was not hopeless, and urges further resistance!

" 8—A correspondence between Gens. Grant and Lee respecting the surrender of the southern army, is carried on to-day.

" 8—Gen. Canby's troops capture Spanish Fort, near Mobile, by assault, securing 25 officers, over 500 men, and 25 guns.

" 8—Gen. Lee surrenders his army to Gen. Grant.

" 10—Gen. Lee issues his farewell address to his army, congratulating them upon having faithfully discharged their duty to their country.

" 10—The southern forces evacuate Mobile.

" 11—The parolling of Lee's troops begins to-day.

" 12—Gen. Stoneman defeats the force defending Salisbury, N. C., and occupies the place, capturing and destroying 7,000 bales of cotton, with a million rounds of ammunition, and an arsenal.

" 12—Gen. Canby's troops enter Mobile without resistance.

" 13—The official report of Lee's surrender in men and property was stated at 26,115 men, 15,918 small arms, 159 cannon, 1,100 wagons, and 4,000 horses.

" 14—President Lincoln assassinated by J. Wilkes Booth in Ford's Theatre.

" 14—One of Booth's confederates, by the name of Powell, gets into Mr. Seward's room, and stabs him while in bed.

" 14—Gen. Anderson, who, four years ago, was obliged to surrender fort Sumter, to-day hoists the United States flag in the same place from which it had been lowered when it surrendered in 1851.

" 15—President Lincoln died at twenty-two minutes past seven this morning.

" 15—Andrew Johnson, the Vice President, sworn in as President.

" 15—The United States 7.30 bonds were yesterday and to-day subscribed for to the amount of over $9,000,000, such was the confidence in our government, notwithstanding the President's death.

" 16—The whole country was in mourning for Lincoln's death, by every demonstration of sorrow which could be shown.

" 18—Paine, or Powell, who attempted to assassinate Secretary Seward, was arrested at Mrs. Surratt's house in Washington. Mrs. S. was also arrested.

" 18—Gen. Sherman agrees to a basis of peace with Gen. Johnson, which was approved of by Jeff. Davis and Breckenridge.

" 19—Funeral ceremonies of President Lincoln are performed at Washington.

" 21—Lincoln's body lies in state in Baltimore.

" 21—Gen. Sherman's terms made with Johnson for peace were

disapproved by the cabinet, and he was ordered to resume hostilities.

April 23—The body of President Lincoln lies in state at Philadelphia, and was visited by an immense concourse of people.

" 24—It arrives in New York.

' 24—Gen. Grant arrives at Gen. Sherman's headquarters, when word was sent to Gen. Johnson that no civil matters could be treated of with him.

" 25—Great military and civic procession in New York on the removal of Lincoln's remains westward. Some say there were 700,000 people upon the streets.

" 25—Booth, the assassin of Lincoln, and Harold, his confederate, captured in a barn three miles from Port Royal, Va. Harold surrendered, but Booth refused to come out of the barn in which he was secreted, when sergeant Corbett (in violation of the orders of his superior officer) shot Booth in the neck, and he died four hours afterwards. Thus, by the over-zeal of a soldier, the gallows was cheated of its lawful due—for no assassin, in all history, had so little justification for murder as Booth had.

" 26—Gen. Johnson surrenders to Gen. Grant all the southern troops from Virginia to the Chattahoochee river, on the same terms granted to Gen. Lee.

" 28—The steamboat Sultana, with over 2,000 persons on board, mostly U. S. soldiers, blew up on the Mississippi river, near Memphis—not more than 700 of all these were saved.

" 29—The arms and military stores of Gen. Johnson's army are delivered up to the United States at Greensboro.

May 2—Reward offered for the arrest of Jeff. Davis, and others who were supposed to have been parties to the assassination of President Lincoln.

" 3—President Lincoln's remains arrived at his home, Springfield, Ill.

" 4—The southern Gen. Dick Taylor surrendered to Gen. Canby all the southern forces yet remaining west of the Mississippi river.

" 9—The southern Gen. Forrest disbanded his troops and advises them to go home peaceably.

" 10—The trial of President Lincoln's assassins commenced.

" 10—Jeff. Davis captured, dressed in woman's clothes, in Georgia, by Col Pritchard, of the fourth Michigan cavalry.

" 13—Over $30,000,000 of the seven-thirty loan taken this day.

" 21—Hon. Jeremiah Clemens, ex-United States Senator from Alabama, died.

" 30—The great northwest sanitary fair opened at Chicago.

June 1—This day was observed as a day of national humiliation, on account of President Lincoln's death.

' 4—Robert Toombs, of Georgia, committed suicide to avoid arrest.

July 4—The corner stone of the Gettysburg monument was laid to-day, amid appropriate ceremonies, and in presence of many distinguished persons.
" 5—The assassins of President Lincoln found guilty. Four of them were hanged the next day, or on the 7th inst.
" 11—Gen. Robt. E. Lee elected president of the Washington College, Va.
Sept. 20—Capt. James N. Moore reports having marked over 12,000 graves of our prisoners, who died at Andersonville, Ga.
Sept. 29—Osage Indians cede 1,000,000 acres of their lands for $300,-000.
Oct. 20—Champ Ferguson, one of the very worst of the guerillas during the war, was this day hanged at Nashville.
Nov. 10—Henry Wirz, keeper of the Andersonville prison, in Georgia, was executed to-day at Washington.
Dec. 18—Secretary Seward formally announced the final extinction of slavery in the United States. This was of course the case, as soon as three-fourths of the States had adopted the fourteenth amendment of the Constitution, which had been done; and Sec. Seward now notifies the world of the fact.

1866.

Jan. 1—Emancipation celebration at Nashville.
" 2—Hon. Henry Winter Davis' funeral at Baltimore.
" 12—Henry Clay's homestead sold to the Kentucky University.
" 17-23—Slavery Constitutional amendment passed by the Legislature of New Jersey. Nearly all the other States had done this before now. But,
" 25—Kentucky rejected it.
" 31—Commissary and quartermaster's warehouses burnt at fort Riley, Kansas. Loss $1,000,000.
Feb. 2—Civil rights bill passed the Senate.
" 11—The U. S. Sanitary Commission held its last anniversary, at Washington.
" 12—Memorial services in honor of President Lincoln held in the capitol; address by Hon. Geo. Bancroft.
" 19—Acting President Johnson vetoed the freedman's bureau bill.
" 22—The 134th anniversary of Washington's birth day celebrated at Washington.
" 26—Richmond meeting held to ratify President Johnson's policy.
March 5—Democratic convention in Pennsylvania nominated Heister Clymer for Governor.
" 10—North Carolina passed a negro rights bill, and two days after the negro testimony bill.
" 12—Texas State convention declared their secession ordinance null and void.
" 13—The civil rights bill passed the house, as amended.

March 14—It passed the Senate.
" 19—The reciprocity treaty with Canada expired this day.
" 20—Gen. Burnside nominated for Union Governor of Rhode Island.
" 27—The civil rights bill vetoed by President Johnson.
This and the two preceding months were distinguished by great fires, and the destruction of both public and private property, amounting to many millions.
April 2—Gen. Hawley elected Republican Governor of Connecticut.
" 4—Gen. Burnside elected Governor of Rhode Island.
" 6—Civil rights bill passed the Senate, over the veto, and, April 9, passed the house in the same way.
" 30—Two churches of colored people burnt in Petersburg, Va., by incendiaries.
May 15—The President vetoes the bill admitting Colorado as a State.
" 29—Lieut. Gen. Scott died at West Point.
June 3—Gen. Meade sent to Buffalo to prevent the Fenians from crossing into Canada.
" 6—The President issued a proclamation against the invasion of Canada.
" 8—The 14th amendment of the U. S. Constitution passed the Senate, and, June 13, it passed the house.
July 4—Tremendous fire at Portland, Me.; $15,000,000 burnt. We notice this great fire because the U. S. government was a great loser by it.
" 16—The freedman's bureau bill vetoed by acting President Johnson.
" 23—Tennessee re-admitted by joint resolution of both houses of Congress. She was the first State re-admitted after the rebellion.
" 25—Lieut. Gen. Grant nominated general, and Vice Admiral Farragut to be admiral.
" 27—Hon. Mr. Harlan, Secretary of the Interior, resigns, and the President nominated O. H. Browning as his successor.
" 28—The Great Eastern arrives at Heart's Content with the Atlantic cable. Great rejoicings.
" 30—Great riot at New Orleans on the re-assembling of the State convention. Many negroes and whites were killed.
Aug. 1—Gen. Sherman commissioned as Lieutenant General.
" 8—Emma, dowager Queen of the Sandwich Islands, arrives at New York as a national guest.
" 12—Complete telegraphic communication between New York and Europe by the Atlantic cable.
" 31—American and English naval commanders destroy 22 Chinese piratical junks, besides killing and capturing many of the pirates.
Sept. 6—The monument to the memory of Stephen A. Douglas, at Chicago, inaugurated. It was the President's journey to attend this inauguration that was called his "swinging the circle"—a figure borrowed from one of his own speeches.

Oct. 9—Gen. Geary elected Governor of Pennsylvania.

" 23—Dedication of the Stonewall Jackson cemetery at Winchester, Va.

Nov. 6—State elections to-day in New Jersey, Delaware, Maryland, Massachusetts, Michigan, Missouri, Minnesota, Illinois, Wisconsin, Kansas, Nevada and New York.

" 20—The Grand Army of the Republic hold a convention at Indianapolis, Ind.

" 22—Raphael Semmes, of the Alabama, appointed professor of moral philosophy in the Louisiana State Seminary.

Dec. 7—The Louisiana Legislature rejects the fourteenth Constitutional amendment, as a number of the southern States had before done.

" 13—The Legislature of the Territory of Colorado organized.

" 16—The U. S. frigate New Ironsides burned at League Island.

" 22—Three officers and 90 soldiers massacred by Indians near fort Kearney.

" 24—U. S. minister John A. Dix presented to the Emperor Napoleon.

1867.

Jan. 7—District of Columbia suffrage bill vetoed by the President, and passed by the Senate over the veto.

" 8—The fourteenth Constitutional amendment ratified by Missouri, and on the 9th, rejected by Virginia—ratified by New York on the 10th.

" 10—The Territorial franchise bill passed, and "pocketed" by the President.

" 28—The Nebraska bill vetoed by the President, but subsequently passed over his veto.

During this month the greater number of the northern States ratified the Constitutional amendment, while most of the southern States rejected it.

Feb'y 20—Military government bill passed by both houses.

March 1—Nebraska proclaimed a State by the President.

" 2—The President vetoes the military government bill; also the civil tenure of office bill. Both, however, were re-passed over his vetoes.

" 4—The 39th Congress closed, and the 40th organized.

" 11—Military generals assigned to their various districts in the south.

" 30—The President announces the treaty with Russia by which the United States bought all her North American possessions for $7,200,000.

April 3—Gen. Burnside re-elected Governor of Rhode Island.

May 13—Jeff. Davis admitted to bail in $100,000; Horace Greeley and others becoming his bondsmen.

June 19—The Arch-duke Maximillian shot by order of the Mexican government. We notice this to show how the French movement, which was inimical to the United States, ended.

July 13—The steam ram Dunderberg, having been bought by France, sailed for Cherbourg.

August 1—Gov. Brownlow re-elected Governor of Tennessee.

" 5—The President requests Sec. Stanton to resign his office, but Sec. Stanton would not do it, when the President suspended him, and appointed Gen. Grant Secretary of War *ad interim.*

" 23—Grand ovation to Admiral Farragut by Russian officers at Cronstadt.

Sept. 17—The Antietam National Cemetery dedicated, with imposing ceremonies.

Dec. 7—The resolution to impeach President Johnson, voted down by 108 to 57, in the House; that is, 108 were for impeachment, and 57 against it. A two-thirds' vote was required to carry it, which would be 110.

1868.

Jan. 1—Fourth emancipation anniversary celebrated in Richmond and Charleston.

" 6—Censure of the President by Congress for removing General Sheridan from his command of the 5th military district.

Feb. 7—The resignation of U. S. minister Adams announced in London.

" 19—U. S. Senate refused to admit P. F. Thomas, of Maryland, to a seat on account of his disloyalty.

" 20—The New Jersey House concurs with the Senate in withdrawing its approval of the fourteenth amendment of the U. S. Constitution.

The Legislatures of New Jersey, Ohio and Oregon each distinguished themselves by this same act.

" 21—The President discharges Secretary Stanton, and appoints Gen. Lorenzo Thomas in his place. The Senate thereupon deny his power to do so.

" 22—Thaddeus Stephens reports resolutions to impeach the President.

" 24—The House resolve (126 to 57) that the President be impeached.

March 2—New articles of impeachment adopted by the House.

" 5—The U. S. Senate organizes itself into a court of impeachment, with Chief Justice Chase at its head, for the trial of President Johnson.

April 24—Gen. Schofield nominated for Secretary of War by the President.

May 16—The President acquitted on the vote in the Senate for his impeachment—35 votes for, to 19 against it.

" 20—The Republican convention at Chicago nominated General U. S. Grant for President.

May 22—The Chinese embassy arrive at New York.
" 29—Gen. Schofield confirmed by the Senate as Secretary of War.
June 1—Grant and Colfax accept their nominations for President and Vice President.
" 4—John W. Forney resigned as secretary of the Senate.
" 5—Hon. Anson Burlingame and the Chinese embassy presented to the President.
" 6—The Arkansas admission bill passes Congress.
" 9—Admission bills for the States of North Carolina, South Carolina, Georgia, Louisiana, Alabama and Florida, pass the Senate.
" 12—Senator Reverdy Johnson confirmed as minister to England.
" 20—The Arkansas admission bill vetoed by the President, and passed over his veto.
" 24—The President also vetoed the southern States admission bill, which was disposed of in the same way.
July 4—Horatio Seymour, of New York, nominated for President by the Democratic convention held in Tammany Hall, N. Y. city, and Francis P. Blair, of Mo., for Vice President.
" 4—General political amnesty proclamation issued by President Johnson.
" 11—Ratification of the fourteenth amendment by North Carolina and Florida, proclaimed by the President.
" 16—Admiral Farragut and officers entertained by the Queen of England.
" 20—Bill to exclude the electoral votes of the non-organized States, vetoed by the President, and re-passed by Congress.
" 21—Congress declares the fourteenth amendment ratified.
" 28—Naturalization treaty with Hesse concluded.
" 28—Proclamation by the Secretary of State that the fourteenth amendment of the Constitution of the United States had been ratified by three-fourths of the States.
" 28—Military government ceases in Arkansas, North Carolina, South Carolina, Louisiana, Georgia, Florida and Alabama.
Aug. 6—Jeff. Davis arrives at Liverpool.
" 13—The U. S. steamers Wateree and Fredonia lost by the terrible earthquake in Peru. By this earthquake 40,000 lives are supposed to have been lost.
Sept. 1—Vermont State election. Gov. Page (Rep.) re-elected.
" 2—Negro members of the Georgia Legislature expelled on account of color.
" 14—Maine State election. Gov. Chamberlain (Rep.) re-elected.
" 48—Battle with Indians near Republican river. Lieut. Beecher and Dr. Moore killed.
" 19—Serious political riots at Camilla, Geo., and many colored persons killed and wounded.
" 21—Congress met and adjourned to Oct. 16.

Sept. 29—Gen. Reynolds issues an order prohibiting the election on the 3d of Nov. in Texas, for President and Vice President.

Oct. 13—State elections in Pennsylvania, Ohio, Indiana and Nebraska. Republicans victorious in all these States.

" 17—The Oregon Legislature withdraws its assent to the fourteenth Constitutional amendment.

Nov. 3—Gen. Ulysses S. Grant and Schuyler Colfax elected for President and Vice President of the United States by 309,722 majority of the popular vote.

The whole popular vote for President in 1868, was 5,722,984, but the vote of Nevada is only estimated, while Virginia, Mississippi and Texas did not vote at all. Florida chose her Presidential electors by her Legislature. The electoral vote was: For Grant and Colfax, 214; Seymour and Blair, 80.

" 27—Black Kettle's band of Indians defeated by Gen. Custer on Washita river. The chief and over 100 of his warriors killed.

Dec. 1—Fort LaFayette, in New York, destroyed by fire.

" 3—Political murders continue in the State of Arkansas.

" 7—The third session of the 40th Congress commences.

" 15—A re-union, at Chicago, of all the Union armies of the late war.

" 25—General proclamatiou of amnesty issued by the President. This might be called a kind of "winding up" of the great rebellion, and the result would indicate that treason, as a crime, is not to be punished in this country.

READ THIS! READ THIS!

Publication Office of PARMELEE & CO.,
Philadelphia, Pa.

Every one who reads this attentively will find something to his or her advantage. If you have not time or inclination to do this, please do not look further, but hand it to some one else, and thus incur the risk of doing some good.

—o—

A STARTLING OFFER!

We will give every person who applies to us, PERMANENT EMPLOYMENT in a good, honorable and paying business, and GUARANTEE to all who will WORK, better pay for their services than can be obtained in any other equally respectable calling. LADIES are especially qualified for this pursuit which we have in view, and it is nearly or quite the only one in which they are paid the same as men for the same services performed.

THE BUSINESS

Is soliciting subscribers for our publications, or, in other words, ***Selling Goods by Sample.*** A very large portion of the business of this country is done through solicitors, who obtain orders for goods. This convenient system is being extended every year, and as its advantages are perceived, it is carried into every branch of industry. Instead of striving to secure patronage in an indirect and often under-handed way, the energetic business man sends a trusty messenger to solicit the custom. ***We want to engage such a Solicitor in every Town.***

THE PAY

Will be such as may be agreed upon between us, the amount depending entirely upon your capacity, ranging from $40 to $120 a month, and upwards. ☞ There is NO MISTAKE ABOUT THE FIGURES.☜ Call and see us if you can, but if at a distance, write to us for full particulars, and for any information you may desire. We will cheerfully respond.

A REQUEST.

You may not be interested in the foregoing, but we respectfully request you to send us a list of the names and post-office address of persons of your acquaintance who may be interested, and who may desire light and profitable employment. Please send us such a list, embracing the names of Ministers, School Teachers, Farmers, &c.

PAY FOR YOUR TROUBLE.

We will send you a copy of any work of our publication, through any agent whom we may secure from the list sent us, when the agent orders the first 25 copies of such book.

Of course, if you send us the names of experienced Agents, you will receive your reward the sooner.

THE CHARACTER OF OUR PUBLICATIONS

Is such that they commend themselves to the people. They are first class, standard, useful, popular works. We have had great success for this reason, and are conscious of doing good while making money, which is the object of all business. ☞ We have not fortunes to give away, but we have the means of enabling any one to earn a COMPETENCY BY WORK.

OTHER BOOKS,

Of any Publication, whether published by Subscription or otherwise, we can furnish to order, at the Publisher's lowest prices. We respectfully solicit orders in this department. Come and see us, or write us.

Yours Respectfully,

PARMELEE & CO.

A NEW DICTIONARY OF THE BIBLE,

Comprising its Antiquities, Biography, Geography, & Natural History.

BY WILLIAM SMITH, L.L.D.

Classical Examiner in the University of London, and Editor of the Dictionaries of "Greek and Roman Antiquities," "Biography and Mythology," and "Geography."

Dr. William Smith, of the University of London, and the most eminent Lexicographer in the world, associated with himself over seventy distinguished Divines and Authors of both Europe and this country, in the great task of preparing a comprehensive Dictionary of the Bible, and supplying the want that had been long felt by the religious public. The result of these labors has at last appeared in three *large* and very *costly* volumes, and is a wonderful monument of learning. An abridgement for popular use made by Dr. Smith *himself*, is offered in this volume. It is a condensation of thousands of volumes of essays, histories, travels, and commentaries for the elucidation and illustration of the Bible.

The present work contains every name in the Bible respecting which anything can be said. It embraces the results of Historic Research, Antiquarian Investigation, the study of Languages and Dialects, and the discoveries of the modern travelers and explorers in the Holy Land—Robinson, Rawlinson, Ferguson, Layard, Offert and Stanley. It gives a more complete list of the proper names of the Bible than is contaimed even in Cruden's great Concordance.

The Publishers are confident that in this work they offer to the American public a volume that possesses many excellencies, which commend it to the patronage of the American public.

This work has the high commendation of Christian scholars, and is needed in every household, and by every student of the Bible.

The book is printed from new Electrotype Plates, on good paper, and appropriately illustrated with over Two Hundred Engravings, including Scenes in the Holy Land, characteristic Figures, a series of authentic maps, etc., etc.

It contains over 1,000 closely printed, double columned pages, and is furnished to Subscribers in a neat and substantial binding, at the following prices, payable on delivery:

Extra Fine Eng. Cloth, Sprinkled Edge, per copy, $4.50
Leather, Library Style, " " " 5.00

This is the most useful and valuable book ever issued from tha press, as an aid to Families, Teachers, Sunday School Superintendents, and Bible readers and Bible Students generally, in studying and understanding the Scriptures. It describes every animal, bird, insect and reptile, every plant and every mineral, every implement and domestic utensil mentioned or alluded to in the Bible. "The simple explanations of this work, unlike the expositions of a commentary, admit of no denominational or sectarian coloring, and it is, therefore, equally valuable to Bible readers of every diversity of belief.

PARMELEE & CO., Philadelphia, Pa.

AGENTS WANTED.—Address PUBLISHERS. 6

www.ingramcontent.com/pod-product-compliance
Lightning Source LLC
LaVergne TN
LVHW021313110826
845150LV00003B/555

* 9 7 8 1 4 2 5 5 5 8 1 3 0 *